I have personally had the jo
Ann Goll for more than fort
City for over a decade in var .... demonstrating a
lavish love for Jesus. I commend to you these vintage writings. The
Golls are among those who long to see Jesus receive the rewards for His
suffering. I give a hearty *amen* to the lineage and legacy of Michal Ann's
ministry and to the teachings found in this book.

—MIKE BICKLE, IHOP-KC director and author
of *Passion for Jesus* and many other titles

When seeking the Lord for a prophetic leader to move to our city to
help in equipping the church, I searched the United States. The Lord
highlighted James Goll to me. But in choosing him we got two for one:
Michal Ann too! This couple exemplified godly living with a prophetic
edge, prayerful actions, and an unusual partnering that still resounds
across the globe yet to this day. The Holy Spirit chose well when he
pointed them out to me. Now it is your turn to be impacted by their life
and ministry.

—DR. DON FINTO, pastor emeritus, Belmont Church,
Nashville, TN, and founder of the Caleb Company

I have personally known the Golls for years, and I had the honor of
commissioning them as apostolic prophets within our HIM global network. Sue and I cherish our years with them as a couple and cheer James
on as he continues to carry the kingdom message of Jesus around the
world. Together they birthed a fresh movement, now stewarded by others, called Women on the Frontlines. I applaud their work together and
the distinct lineage and legacy of Michal Ann's life message as expressed
in this book.

—DR. CHE AHN, HRock Church and
Harvest International Ministries founder

With a balanced presentation, Michal Ann and James challenge women
and men both to fulfill their potential in God without compromise. I
have known this family well for years and had the pleasure of serving

on their board of directors. They have lived their message well. In the Women on the Frontlines series, this "Female Hall of Fame" of courage, intimacy, and compassion will especially inspire our younger sisters, who have so few heroes and heroines to look up to as examples.

—ELIZABETH ALVES, Increase International found and
author of *Mighty Prayer Warrior* and other books

Michal Ann herself was a woman on the front lines as she became more and more courageous with each fresh revelation from her Lord. In my opinion, she stands alongside the nine "ordinary women" of this book as one who knows an extraordinary God, becoming strong, standing firm, and doing exploits for Him. May the Holy Spirit use this book to open each reader's eyes to see her awesome potential in Him.

—MARY AUDREY RAYCROFT, pastor of Equipping Ministries
and Women in Ministry, Catch the Fire Toronto,
and author of *Releasers of Life*

This book is intelligent, wise, inspiring, and warm because it flows from the life of the late Michal Ann Goll and her husband, James. Clearly, this remarkable woman was chosen to tenderly lead the women of this generation into their destined wholeness and kingdom impact. Michal Ann is one of the women I would tell my daughter in her formative years of growing up to follow as Michal Ann followed Jesus. I can give no higher praise.

—STEPHEN L. MANSFIELD, author and
founder of the Mansfield Group

While reading the Women on the Frontlines series, my spirit was stirred, motivated, and encouraged to never settle for less than God's purpose and call for my life. This first book will take the reader from feeling unimportant and ordinary to realizing that she is God's chosen vessel with a powerful purpose. I believe the Holy Spirit intends us to experience more than mere enjoyment and inspiration from this book's pages; He desires us to receive the invaluable impartation of Michal Ann's zeal and heart to fulfill all of God's mandate.

—SHIRLEY SUSTAR, copastor of Heartland Worship Center
and author of *Women of Royalty*

This is a book about a journey to which all of us have been called. It will no doubt help men and women alike, as Michal Ann and James have brought wonderful insights, moving personal testimonies, and stories about our heroes of the faith who embraced the same journey. This priceless couple has once again brought us a gem that will help us come into the fullness of Christ.

—BILL JOHNSON, author of *When Heaven Invades Earth* and other books

The Women on the Frontlines series is full of encouragement, exhortation, and compassion for women who are struggling to become the women of destiny God has created them to be. Michal Ann poured out her heart in a vulnerable, even tender way to her fellow sisters in Christ. It is almost as if she is God's cheerleader for the reader even to this day, exhorting them, "Go on, Sister, you can do it!" It is my honor, along with my husband, Mike, to continue to walk with James now that Michal Ann has graduated to her heavenly reward. So, come on now, pick up the baton! Let love take action in your life and make a difference for Jesus Christ's sake!

—CINDY JACOBS, Generals International

We loved our years ministering together with Michal Ann and James Goll. Their writings have impacted the global body of Christ. Beautifully, they have called us to take courage, dwell in the secret place, and to let compassionate love take action. These many anecdotes and examples from both the past and the present from those who made a difference in this life call us to follow in their footsteps. Michal Ann used to exhort us to have our own Hall of Heroes. As you read these Women on the Frontlines books, I am sure she will be added to yours. Now it is our turn to answer the call of the Holy Spirit and volunteer freely in the day of His power. Above all, like Michal Ann, let love have the final say.

—WESLEY AND STACEY CAMPBELL, Be a Hero Ministries, Kelowna, British Columbia, Canada

I believe the message of this book is both timely and prophetic for the days we are living in. It is in the place of intimacy with the Lord where we are changed into His likeness. It is in the place of intimacy that His power and anointing begin to flow through us in the most wonderful ways. I encourage you to live out the message of this book and watch your life be radically transformed.

—CAROL ARNOTT, Catch the Fire,
Toronto, Ontario, Canada

Before we can release God's love to the world, we must first let God's love touch us. That is what being a "laid-down lover" is all about. James and Michal Ann Goll have been a rare breed of a husband-wife team, showing us how to dwell in the secret place of the Most High God. Sweet Michal Ann now basks in unfeigned worship directly before the throne while James continues His pilgrimage on this side. But together they touched the lives of many and most importantly, touched the very heart of God Himself.

—HEIDI BAKER, Iris Ministries International,
Pemba, Mozambique

This book brings you directly into God's presence as you come to know the women "saints" Michal Ann selected to write about. Some lived several hundred years ago; others are contemporary women who have responded to God's call to the secret place. As you read, follow your own desire to enter God's quiet sanctuary. You will yearn to open yourself more to His voice, His direction, His love. Abandon yourself to His call.

—QUIN SHERRER, author of many books about prayer

Few people have touched my life like Michal Ann Goll. Her life, her love for God, her ministry, and her writings have left our lovely Savior's impact upon me. For years, James and Michal Ann have been friends of Life Center in Harrisburg, Pennsylvania, and of my husband, Charles, and me. Though Michal Ann has graduated to heaven, I continue to read this Women on the Frontlines book over and over. You will want to also.

—ANNE STOCK, Life Center, Harrisburg, Pennsylvania

WOMEN ON THE FRONTLINES

HEROINES OF

FAITH

WOMEN OF COURAGE, COMPASSION, AND THE SECRET PLACE

JAMES AND MICHAL ANN GOLL

Cover design by Steve Fryer at SteveFryer.com
Interior by Katherine Lloyd at theDESKonline.com

Printed in the United States of America
21 22 23 24 25 5 4 3 2 1

CONTENTS

A Call to Courage
Overcoming Fear and Becoming Strong in Faith

FOREWORD *by Cindy Jacobs* 5

INTRODUCTION *by James W. Goll* 6

Chapter 1
NO MORE FEAR.. 10

Chapter 2
I'M IN THE ARMY NOW 23

Chapter 3
Joan of Arc: THE COST OF COURAGE 36

Chapter 4
Vibia Perpetua: FAITHFUL UNTO DEATH 49

Chapter 5
Sojourner Truth: "AIN'T I A WOMAN?" 56

Chapter 6
Harriet Tubman: GO DOWN, MOSES 66

Chapter 7
Aimee Semple McPherson: YESTERDAY, TODAY, AND FOREVER....... 73

Chapter 8
Lydia Christensen Prince: THE PEACE OF JERUSALEM................ 83

Chapter 9
Bertha Smith: WALKING IN THE SPIRIT............................ 92

Chapter 10
Corrie ten Boom: NO PIT SO DEEP 101

Chapter 11
Jackie Pullinger: LIGHTING THE DARKNESS 111

Chapter 12
YOU ARE CHOSEN 122

ACKNOWLEDGMENTS 135

A Call to Courage NOTES.. 136

A Call to Compassion
Taking God's Unfailing Love to Your World

FOREWORD *by Patricia King*. 145

INTRODUCTION *by Michal Ann Goll* 148

Chapter 1
GOD'S HEART OF COMPASSION. 153

Chapter 2
THE COMPASSIONATE POWER OF TEARS 163

Chapter 3
Catherine Booth: THE MOTHER OF THE SALVATION ARMY 176

Chapter 4
Nancy Ward: BELOVED WOMAN OF THE CHEROKEE 189

Chapter 5
Florence Nightingale: THE LADY WITH THE LAMP 200

Chapter 6
Gladys Aylward: REJECTED BY MAN, APPROVED BY GOD 211

Chapter 7
Mother Teresa: THE HUMBLE ROAD 228

Chapter 8
LITTLE WOMEN—BIG GOD. 239

Chapter 9
Heidi Baker: BLESSED ARE THE POOR. 255

Chapter 10
IT'S GOT TO BE PERSONAL 270

Chapter 11
COMPASSION ACTS 281

AFTERWORD 293

ACKNOWLEDGMENTS 296

A Call to Compassion NOTES 297

A Call to the Secret Place
Pursuing the Prize of God's Presence

FOREWORD *by Elizabeth (Beth) Alves* 304

INTRODUCTION *by James W. Goll.* 306

Chapter 1
WHEN I'M CALLING YOU. 308

Chapter 2
THE DEPTHS OF GOD. 319

Chapter 3
Jeanne Guyon (1648–1717): CALLED DEEPER STILL 330

Chapter 4
Teresa of Avila (1515–1582): POSSESSED BY GOD'S LOVE 346

Chapter 5
Fanny Crosby (1820-1915): SONGS FROM THE SECRET PLACE 356

Chapter 6
Susanna Wesley (1669–1742): THE MOTHER OF REVIVAL 368

Chapter 7
Basilea Schlink (1904–2001): GOD SENT ME TO THE CROSS 380

Chapter 8
Gwen Shaw (1924–2013): A PASSION FOR NATIONS 390

Chapter 9
Elizabeth Alves: THE GRANDMA OF THE PRAYER SHIELD 399

Chapter 10
SHELTER FOR THE SWALLOW. 408

ACKNOWLEDGMENTS 415

A Call to the Secret Place NOTES 416

ABOUT THE AUTHORS 419

WOMEN ON THE FRONTLINES

A Call to Courage

Overcoming Fear and Becoming Strong in Faith

James & Michal Ann Goll

DEDICATION

We would like to dedicate this first book in the Women on the Front-lines series—*A Call to Courage*—to two groups of people: the pioneers and those who carry on the modern-day and future legacy of Women on the Frontlines.

First of all, we desire to dedicate this book to all the dear women from the past—countless numbers of known but mostly unknown courageous saints who have paid the price of service and true devotion to our Lord. Thank you for passing along to us the baton of faith, hope, and love. Thank you for watching us and cheering us on as we fight our daily battles to "win for the Lord the rewards of Christ's suffering."

Second, we wish to dedicate this book to all those dear ones who have their future still ahead of them, who are ready and waiting to serve and love the Lord wholeheartedly. May you press forward and be courageous champions for God. Always give Him everything, for He gave everything for you.

Michal Ann, who has joined the "great cloud of witnesses," has simply shifted positions from cheering on this side to cheering from the grandstands of heaven.

FOREWORD

Cindy Jacobs

I knew Michal Ann well, and my husband and I continue to walk alongside her prophetic husband, James, to this day. Michal Ann was a woman of great courage. We are family. So from years of perspective I share the following with you from my heart.

As I read over the chapters of this wonderful book, my thoughts went back to another woman who struggled with the same issues discussed in these pages—a woman who couldn't even pray aloud in a group of ten or twenty; a woman who would rehearse words to prayers that she was never able to pray openly. That woman was me, Cindy Jacobs. To this day I marvel as I climb platforms in nations around the world and look into the faces of crowds that sometimes number 30,000 or even more from nation to nation.

A Call to Courage is full of compassion, exhortation, and encouragement for women who are struggling to become the women of destiny that God has created them to be. It is almost as if Michal Ann is God's cheerleader for the reader: *Go on, Sister, you can do it!* and, *Fear and intimidation don't need to control you!*

God is speaking in a clear voice to His women today, saying, *Women, daughters, handmaidens—it's your time. Rise up, free of the bondages that hold you back from your destiny. Don't be content with second best. You are a treasure!*

Women and men of God, please read this book. It will change your life.

—Cindy Jacobs
Cofounder of Generals International
Author of *Possessing the Gates of the Enemy,*
Women of Destiny, and many other books

INTRODUCTION

James W. Goll

I remember the night so well. In about the fifth week of visitations from God in our home in the fall of 1992, Michal Ann and I had a pivotal conversation. With the fear of God on me, I stated, "I don't know who you are or who you are becoming."

She responded with equal intensity, "I don't know who I am or who I am becoming either." I know this may be hard to comprehend, but we both sighed with relief, because at least we were still in agreement, were still very much in the Lord's hands, and could continue on this revolutionary journey of "becoming all that He has intended us to be."

What does this have to do with this book, you say? Everything. My wife's life changed. Our lives continued to be challenged and changed. Now I want to see this same God of change come and rock _your_ boat, delivering you from the shackles of fear and intimidation, and infusing you with this same spirit of courage and might that so powerfully impacted my wife in those days. That's what this book is all about—the contagious change, through the empowering work of the Holy Spirit, that is called courage.

If that is what you hunger and thirst for, then know that this book was penned with you in mind. Let me give you a brief overview of what to expect.

Part One, "Down With Intimidation," tells of my late wife's personal journey in her walk with the Lord. This first part is filled with true-to-life stories from an authentic, normal, everyday woman of God who was my beloved wife.

Part Two, "Women of Courage," takes a journey through church history up to today and showcases examples of women used by God on the front lines. The first chapter in Part Two is Michal Ann's look at the life of Joan of Arc, whose story dramatically inspired her in the final years of her life. Then we move on to these women: Perpetua, a martyr for her faith in the early Church; Sojourner Truth, a black woman leader in the antislavery movement; and Harriet Tubman, another dedicated black pioneer of the Underground Railroad to freedom in the time before the Civil War. We consider the inspiration from the lives of Aimee Semple McPherson, a woman healing evangelist at the turn of the twentieth century; Lydia Christensen Prince, forerunner for the cause of orphans and the purposes of God among the Jewish people; and Bertha Smith, a Baptist woman missionary and revival leader in Shantung, China.

We also take a look at the courageous life of Corrie ten Boom, who suffered for the cause of Christ and the Jewish people during the Holocaust of World War II, and lastly, we shine a light on a courageous woman of this generation: Jackie Pullinger, a British evangelist and missionary in the Walled City of Hong Kong.

The third and last part of *A Call to Courage*, "Seize the Day," takes us back to some inspiring lessons of courage from my dear late wife's life and teaching. But please note—this is more than a women's testimonial book. The truths in this book apply to each one of us, whether we are men or women, old or young. These lessons about the power of the Holy Spirit learned in the trenches of authentic Christianity enable each one of us to be more than conquerors through Christ Jesus, our Master and Lord.

I strongly recommend this book to you, and not just because I loved and believed in the lady who wrote it. I recommend it because it shows the true grit of ordinary women who were changed by God into vessels of honor and courage. May the impact of this first book in the Women on the Frontlines series, *A Call to Courage*, be as mighty as those weeks of visitation were to us in the fall of 1992.

Go, Holy Spirit—overwhelm these readers and make them into radical, courageous, God-fearing Christians for the honor of Your great name.

Part One

Down with Intimidation

Chapter 1

NO MORE FEAR

D on't let your fears stand in the way of your dreams."
Does that statement speak to you? It sure spoke to me the first time I read it. I had always been by nature a very quiet and reserved person. But until then I had also been bound by fear and intimidation, and I hated it. There was so much in me that wanted to come out, but I felt tied down inside. I was like a runner who longed to run but couldn't because heavy chains and weights hung on her ankles, holding her back.

Sometimes I wanted to just reach out to someone who was hurting and give her a hug or an encouraging word—simple things—but I couldn't. I just wasn't able to step out beyond myself. For years I cried out, "Lord, I want to be totally sold out to You. I want to be so consumed with You that my fear is completely annihilated."

Eventually, God answered my prayer, granting me the grace to walk in places where I had never walked before.

It all started when my husband, James, and I were leading a retreat in Nashville, Tennessee. While there I found myself particularly preoccupied with this whole issue of fear and intimidation. In my heart I wanted so badly to be free. It weighed heavily on my mind, eating away at me on the inside.

On the Sunday morning of the retreat, I was feeling a strong intercessory burden from the Lord for the people there and was crying out to Him on their behalf. Many of them were in situations that allowed no real opportunity for service or ministry. They felt bottled up, as if they were all crowding together trying to get a whiff of the tiny amount of oxygen that was coming through the narrow neck of a bottle. In the middle of this intercession, two ladies, dear friends of mine, came up to me and asked if they could pray for me. We went into a little side room, and immediately they began spiritual warfare over me, coming against the spirit of intimidation. As soon as they started praying, I let out a loud scream.

Not long after that, someone came to the door and said that we were too noisy. The group in the other room had gotten very quiet because they were taking communion. I wanted to be sensitive to what was going on in there, but I also was afraid that if I held back at that point, I would never get free. It was as though the Lord was challenging me: *How badly do you want to be delivered from this thing?*

My friends kept praying and I kept yelling until all of a sudden it was as though something literally lifted right out of the top of my head, leaving an empty space. The best way I can describe it is that this thing felt like a railroad spike—six inches long and about two inches in diameter at the top, tapering to a point at the bottom. It was the strangest sensation. I've never felt anything like it either before or since. I knew something had happened in me, but at first I didn't really know what it was.

The retreat ended and the people went home, but Jim, as I always called him, and I stayed an extra night. We had decided to remain at the retreat center overnight so we could have some time alone. Later that day we went for a walk. With the meetings over, Jim was in a relaxed, silly mood while I was still in a contemplative frame of mind, trying to figure out what God had done with me and what I was supposed to do now.

As we walked along, Jim was playfully clapping his hands and hitting me on the shoulder. I didn't really want that right then. He was invading my personal space. So I said as nicely as I could, "Jim, please don't do that."

"Don't do what?"

"Please don't hit me."

"Hey, I'm not hitting you," he teased as he kept whapping my shoulder.

After I appealed to him again, he turned to me, rolled up his sleeve, and said, "Okay, you hit me."

I looked at his arm and, seeing what a good target it was, doubled up my fist and popped him good. I didn't hit him very hard, but the fact that I did it at all shocked both of us. I had never hit anyone in my life! The expression on Jim's face said, *I can't believe you did that!* My jaw dropped too: "I can't believe I did that!" Then we both started laughing. We realized at that moment that what my friends had prayed for had happened. God had truly delivered me from intimidation.

To intimidate means to make someone timid or fearful; it is to frighten them with threats. At one time the enemy's threats had made me timid; I lacked courage, self-confidence, boldness, and determination. He had filled my mind with fearful thoughts: *If you try this, you are going to fail. You're going to fall flat on your face. You will be misunderstood and all alone.*

Sometimes panic welled up inside as I found myself saying, *I can't do this! I'm not smart enough, not spiritual enough. I know I'm going to fail!* For a long time I lacked the courage and boldness I needed to press on through.

No More Fear

Once God delivered me, however, it was as though He had attached jumper cables to my spiritual battery. The life and energy of the blood of Jesus flooded my being and set me free. The fear of man was gone— that anxious dread and concern about what other people would think or say about me. Now I could enter into a fuller dimension of the fear of the Lord.

The fear of man had filled me with shame and panic; the fear of the Lord filled me with profound reverence and awe toward God. "The fear of the Lord is clean, enduring forever" (Ps. 19:9, AMP). It brings my sins into the light, not to shame or embarrass me, but to cleanse me, forgive me, and justify me, just as if I had never sinned.

I still struggled with intimidation on occasion. Although it was no longer in me, it tried to come against me from time to time, and I had to be alert and ready to deal with it. Intimidation can be a demonic stronghold or spirit, and many Christians, both men and women, are bound by it.

God wants us all to be free, not just for the sake of freedom, but so we can truly commune with Him face-to-face. He wants to take us to a place where we can walk with Him, full of the fear of the Lord, where the fear of man is completely gone. He wants to deliver us from intimidation and its companion spirits of comparison, shame, guilt, and the fear of man. He wants us to be able to fulfill our destiny, to complete our calling in Him, to do those things that each of us is uniquely qualified and designed to accomplish.

Fearless and Free

God seeks and desires a personal relationship with each and every one of us, and He is protective about that relationship. He is fighting on our behalf to set us free from the cloaks of fear, intimidation, and comparison that the enemy uses to try to smother the life breath out of us.

I was raised in a devout Methodist family, and I cherish that rich heritage from which I received a deep deposit of the Word of God. However, I did not understand the ways of the Spirit.

For a long time after I married Jim, I tried to hang on to his coattails; I simply followed what he was doing. Unknowingly, I was comparing my walk with God to his walk, thinking that his was better than mine. God did not see it that way, and He told me so. One day the Lord said to me, *Ann, you can't hold on to Jim's coattails. Hold on to Mine. I am your God. I created you, and I am jealous over you. I won't settle for a relationship through your husband. I want a relationship with you.*

He desires the same for each of us. We cannot relate to Him through anyone else—our spouse, pastor, parents, friends, or anyone. Our God is a personal God.

We are His beloved and we are beautiful in His eyes. He sees us through the precious blood of Jesus, His Son. He doesn't see our faults; rather, He sees only Jesus' righteousness covering us. Instead of sin, He sees the beauty of a forgiven soul. We are beautiful to Him whether we're sweating, lying on the floor in deep travail, or crying with a runny nose because God is touching our hurting heart. We are beautiful to Him whether we're shaking, trembling, or jumping. We are beautiful to Him when we are alone with our hearts breaking and we think no one knows or cares.

God looks for the beauty of the heart. I believe that anytime we bring life into the world, or into some needy soul, is a time of unparalleled beauty in God's eyes. God loves life. Consider for a moment the appearance and condition of a woman in childbirth: vulnerable, in pain, travailing. (Most of us who have been through it don't want to be reminded of our appearance!) The important thing, though, is that a new life is coming forth; that's what God values.

Our approval from God doesn't depend on whether or not our fingernails are polished, our hair is combed, or our house is neat and tidy with everything in order. God looks at the heart. He created each of us as a unique individual with a fragrance all our own, and He waits in longing to smell that fragrance rising to Him.

No More Fear

God loves us and fashioned us to be creative according to how He has gifted us. Let Him release you to be who He made you to be: a creative individual free from intimidation and the fear of man.

Have you ever found yourself at a buffet and, as you pick up your plate to go through the line, you check to see how much food everyone else is taking, then take the same amount? You don't want to take "too much." After all, you have to be careful how you present yourself, right? That's intimidation speaking.

I have good news for you: God has a buffet all laid out, and He wants you to take the biggest plate you can find and load it up. He wants you to pull your chair right up to the table and dig in because the table is spread for you. There are all kinds of breads, pastries, salads and vegetables, luscious fruits, scrumptious desserts, and more. He is a God of abundance and you don't have to hesitate to receive from Him.

Exposing the Enemy

Let's cast the light of God's Word into the darkness surrounding this issue; let's expose the enemy.

The Lord wants all His children to be free. He has given His Spirit to His children to help us obtain this freedom. Paul wrote to the Corinthians, "Now the Lord is the Spirit, and where the Spirit of the Lord is, there is liberty [emancipation from bondage, true freedom]" (2 Cor. 3:17, AMP).

The Holy Spirit in us does not produce fear, but power: "For God did not give us a spirit of timidity or cowardice or fear, but [He has given us a spirit] of power and of love and of sound judgment and personal discipline [abilities that result in a calm, well-balanced mind and self-control]" (2 Tim. 1:7, AMP). His goal is to produce in us a full and perfect love that eliminates and replaces fear.

> There is no fear in love [dread does not exist]. But perfect (complete, full-grown) love drives out fear, because fear involves [the expectation of divine] punishment, so the one who is afraid [of God's judgment] is not perfected in love [has not grown into a sufficient understanding of God's love]. (1 John 4:18, AMP)

Favored and Forgiven

According to Esther 2:9, the young Jewish maiden Esther, who was destined to be the queen of King Xerxes, found favor in the eyes of Hegai. Now Hegai was the eunuch in charge of the king's harem. He gave Esther seven personal maidservants and moved all of them into the most favored place in the harem. That is favor!

In the same way, God has given us, His daughters, the most favored place. Unfortunately, many of us as women struggle with thoughts or feelings of unworthiness and low self-esteem. Some have trouble trusting men because men have stepped on them and held them back. God wants to heal all that. He wants to reprogram our thinking. He wants to remove the intimidation as well as the spirit of comparison that makes us think that we can't do anything until we first become like somebody else.

I believe God is saying to us, *Be yourself. I created you, and I love you just the way you are.* What about the past? All of us have painful memories of sins or mistakes that we have made. One of Satan's most powerful weapons is to bring those past things before us and beat us over the head with them. Too many times we help him out by listening to his accusations and agreeing with him. As a result, guilt, shame, fear, and intimidation rise up and tie us down, holding us back from all that God wants to do in us.

Don't be bound by the mistakes of the past. Don't allow them to keep rising up, or they will keep you from stepping out for fear of failure. There is complete freedom and release in God's forgiveness. John, the beloved apostle, wrote:

> If we [freely] admit that we have sinned *and* confess our sins, He is faithful and just [true to His own nature and promises], and will forgive our sins and cleanse us *continually* from all unrighteousness [our wrongdoing, everything not in conformity with His will and purpose]. (1 John 1:9, AMP)

Whatever God forgives, He forgets. He says in Isaiah, "I, even I, am he who blots out your transgressions, for my own sake, and remembers your sins no more" (Isa. 43:25). King David reminds us, "As far as the east is from the west, So far has He removed our transgressions from us" (Ps. 103:12, AMP).

When we confess our sins, God forgives them and then forgets them. He remembers our sins no more, and we stand clean and pure before Him. He wants to woo us, to draw us into His holy presence. When we come into that place, all fear simply drops away. We walk unashamed with our heads lifted high, our eyes meeting His eyes, like a bride approaching her bridegroom. No shame, no embarrassment, no fear, no intimidation—all are cast out by the power of His captivating and all-consuming love.

The sound of His voice delights us as we hear Him say, *Oh, how I've waited for you to come! How I've longed to embrace you, to be with you, to be in union with you.* His love goes far beyond what we can possibly ask, think, or imagine (see Eph. 3:20).

Visitations in the Night

There was a time after we had started our family, when I got quite jealous of my husband. Jim (James to some of you) would travel in ministry to different conferences and meetings and such, and I would be at home with the children. He would come back all pumped up and excited over what the Lord had done, while I had spent the weekend with dirty diapers and a house that showed all the evidences of four small children.

In addition, I was attempting to homeschool our oldest child and our family was in the midst of a major move. Jim was getting all these neat blessings from God and I was missing out. I simply had no time for anything. One day, out of despair and frustration, I leaned against the wall and said, "Lord, I want so much to be with You, but I am so busy. I just don't have the time to sit and soak in Your presence. From the time I get up in the morning until I go to bed at night, my time is not my own. Even at night my kids wake up, and I have to be there."

The Lord answered me so sweetly and gently. He said, *Ann, I know all that. I am the God of the impossible, and what you think is impossible is possible with Me. I will come to you. I will visit you in the night.*

Shortly after that, He began speaking to me in dreams, which totally rearranged my perception of both myself and Him. He showed me how He could use me as I gave Him complete control of my life. He showed me how much He loved me and longed for fellowship with me.

For example, I had one dream in which God was represented by an older gentleman whom I could sense loved me deeply. He loved the fragrance of my hair and yearned for me to reach out and hug Him. He could hardly wait for me to embrace Him so that He could smell my hair. I had never, ever imagined that anyone could love me that way, but that's the way God loves us!

During this time of visitation, the Lord gave me a dream that dealt with this whole issue of intimidation—how strong of a force it can be and how it can tempt us to do things that we would not otherwise do. In this dream, my oldest son, Justin, and I were in China running food, clothing, and other items to needy people. We had to be very careful, moving quickly from place to place so that the enemy would not catch us.

As I was preparing to leave one house, the authorities broke in and grabbed me. Justin had already left, so he escaped. I, however, was taken into the yard to face the enemy leader. He wanted to punish me by torture—hanging me by the neck, not until I died but long enough to choke me and leave rope marks on my neck. There were several other prisoners in the yard who had already been punished this way. It was a very intimidating situation.

I almost consented to the punishment when all of a sudden a light went on inside me. *How foolish of me to entrust my life into the enemy's hands!* Once the noose was around my neck, I would be completely at his mercy. How could I trust the word of the enemy?

In the dream, rather than giving in to the intimidation and agreeing to the punishment, I began preaching the gospel to the enemy leader. He was intrigued and let me continue, leading me and the other prisoners into his court chamber, where there were approximately fifty chairs around a huge oval-shaped table.

There was another table and a row of chairs on an elevated platform at one end of the room. Both the room and the furniture were dark. As I continued preaching the Word to this enemy leader, I felt like Paul preaching to King Agrippa. I pulled from my pocket an uncut, unpolished purple gem, like an amethyst. As I spoke, the gem grew larger and larger and became brighter and brighter. The enemy leader reached out to take the stone in his hand. It continued to grow as I continued to preach the Word. He was holding a miracle, a wonder of God in his own hand, and with his own eyes watched it grow and glow.

It seems to me that the gem in this dream symbolizes the Word coming forth from within. When we are on the verge of a breakthrough, the enemy will come and try to intimidate us and make us settle for something less than we should. If we press through and confront the enemy of intimidation, though, allowing the boldness of the Holy Spirit to come on us, we become like the stone, growing and glowing with the truth and power of God's Word.

We must stir up the gifting and the calling that are within us. If we allow intimidation to take over, it will choke us. We cannot speak with nooses around our necks. When we let the boldness of the Lord come out, however, those uncut gems in us glow and grow—a visible miracle to the world.

The time has come for us to do business with God and with the enemy. It's time to decide to not let intimidation and fear strangle us any longer; to not give our lives to the enemy, trusting him to hurt us only a little. God has set the day of deliverance! It's time for us to take the nooses off, bring the gems out of our pockets, and witness the miracle that God wants to do in us.

Building Bridges

Do you find it easier to believe that God will do something for someone else than to believe that He will do something for you? Do you find it difficult to accept the possibility that God could really use you, that He can take you out of your shell and remove all fear from your heart? God does not have favorites, and if He did it for me, He will do it for you.

Once I was on a plane, settling into my seat to read a book during the flight. As it happened, it was a book about how to deal with intimidation, and I was on my way to a conference to speak on that very subject. I was in an aisle seat. Soon I became uncomfortably aware of a man in the aisle seat across from me staring at me. I found myself thinking, *Am I going to have to walk through this issue of intimidation right now?*

So I sat there with this man staring at me the whole time, and I was telling myself over and over, *I will not be intimidated...I will not be intimidated...I will not be intimidated...*while I sat there trying to read my book and my Bible. This continued for the entire flight, a little over an hour.

Finally, as we were preparing to land, he leaned over and asked, "What synagogue do you go to?"

At first I did not understand what he meant. Then I realized that he had seen the Star of David I was wearing (a symbol of my love and burden for the Jews and for the nation of Israel). I said to him, "Oh, I'm a Christian, but I love the Jews."

I think I totally confused him. He did not know what to do. Here he had sat on the plane for over an hour trying to figure out how to ask me that question; and when he finally did, my answer baffled him.

I mention this incident because as we learn to deal with fear and intimidation, we will find that God will bring circumstances across our paths that may intimidate us or make us fearful, when actually God just wants to use us. We have to get out of our comfort zone and open our heart and mouth for His sake.

As God uses us to draw people to Him, people will begin looking at us and talking with us. We have to learn to not be fearful when that happens. Instead, we need to recognize both the hand of God as He moves in that other person's life and the part we are to play in what He is doing.

We need to change our "stinking thinking." Up with the positive, down with the negative. It's time for divine appointments. God wants to do so much through us, but we have to get rid of our fear. For example, He wants to release in us new ways of evangelism that we have not even dreamed of. We have become so bound up in our minds by traditional ideas of what evangelism looks like and how it should be done that God has trouble getting through to us. He is saying, *I have all kinds of creative ways and ideas that I want to release, but you've got to get rid of your fear.*

I've heard it said that the word F-E-A-R stands for "False Evidence Appearing Real." The devil is a liar and a thief; he will steal us blind if we let him. God speaks the truth. It is vital to our life in Him that we reject all the lies the devil has fed us and step out in faith into what God says. We must get into the Bible, studying it and reading for ourselves God's promises toward us. It is only by knowing the goodness and faithfulness of God and by applying the power of the name of Jesus in our lives that we can cut down Satan's plans.

We have to be free to see, but we can't see if we're bound up in fear. Have you ever been introduced to someone and not caught his or her name because you were so concerned about what you were going to say in response? That's intimidation. Once you are free of it, you can look at someone and think about that person rather than worrying about yourself. In that way you can be God's hands and God's voice to people and build bridges of love, not fear.

Getting rid of fear and intimidation means getting out of yourself and into Christ; moving from concern over how you look or what you are going to say, to asking, *Lord, what do You have for this person?* It is when you get out of yourself that you become truly free. Learning to be free is a lifelong process; but in Christ you have everything you need, and it is never too late to begin.

Dare to Dream

Several years ago I was scheduled to speak at a women's conference in Kansas City on the theme "Overcoming Intimidation." At that time I had not spoken at many conferences and still felt insecure about doing it. I knew that I had to conquer the intimidation that was coming against me, and thought I needed a lot of prayer time in order to prepare. But the only "quiet" times I had came in fifteen-minute segments while I drove back and forth between home and the school. On the Friday that the conference began, just a few hours before the first meeting, my final desperate prayer was, "God, let me do this with no fear!"

As soon as I uttered the words, I saw a picture in my mind of me wearing a T-shirt with the words "No Fear" across the front. I said to God, "All right, as I speak on Saturday morning, I will envision 'No Fear' written across my heart, guarding me. In faith I will believe that You will accomplish this."

When I told Jim about it later that evening, he insisted that I had to get a "No Fear" T-shirt and wear it. I had no time for shopping, though, so he did it for me while I was at the Friday night meeting. I returned home to find laid out on the kitchen counter two T-shirts and two hats with "No Fear" on the front. One set was for me; the other was for Jim. In addition, inside the rim of my hat were the words that opened this chapter: "Don't let your fears stand in the way of your dreams."

Here was yet another testimony to God's faithfulness and to the personal, individual care He gives to each of us. After years of trying to deal with my fears and after many, many dreams through which God had given me hope, the time had come for me to apply what I had been learning. God was saying to me, *Gird your mind with the dreams I have placed in you and go, girl!*

I want to issue this challenge to you: *Dare to dream.* Open your heart in a fresh way and ask God to put a dream there. Ask Him to dust off the promise book with your name on it and make those promises real and fresh to you.

Don't let your fears stand in the way of your dreams. Take out the spike of intimidation and, like the Israelite woman Jael did to the Philistine Sisera in Judges 4, drive it into the enemy's head and kill the plans and schemes he has devised against you. We must be ruthless with the devil; he surely has no mercy on us!

There is no fear in love. But perfect love drives out fear, because fear has to do with punishment. The one who fears is not made perfect in love. (1 John 4:18)

Father, in the name of Jesus I declare that Your perfect love working in me displaces old vestiges of fear that have bound me. I shall know the truth and the truth shall set me free. So I declare that intimidation is not my friend, and that I am a new creation in Christ Jesus. Old things have passed away and behold all things are new. Praise the Lord! Amen.

Chapter 2

I'M IN THE ARMY NOW

Any army that hopes to achieve victory in battle must have disciplined and well-trained soldiers, dependable supply lines, and a clear strategy. If any of these elements are weak or lacking, the chance of success decreases drastically. In the same way, before we as soldiers of the Lord can successfully engage in battle with an enemy as ruthless and merciless as the devil, we must become well-trained, well-equipped disciples committed to carrying out our Commander's plan of action.

We are individual soldiers joined together in a great army called the church, and we are commissioned to do battle "against the powers, against the world forces of this [present] darkness, against the spiritual forces of wickedness in the heavenly (supernatural) places" (Eph. 6:12b, AMP). Victory depends on all of us working together in obedience to our Lord and not trying to move out on our own. None of us by ourselves is a match for the enemy. In fact, any believer who tries to take on the devil alone is embarking on a suicide mission.

When Jesus established His church, He promised that the gates of hell would not prevail against it (see Matt. 16:18). His promise is for the *church*—individual believers working together in unity and harmony to fulfill Jesus' commission to make disciples of all the nations. Just as soldiers are trained to do specific jobs in conjunction with others to achieve the overall mission, so each of us must find our place and operate in our gifts in conjunction with each other in order to accomplish our mission as Christ's army, the church.

Annie, Get Your Gun

Years ago God spoke to me in a dream about the importance of being thoroughly prepared to do battle with the enemy. The images were so vivid and intense that they have remained with me ever since. In my dream I was inside the comfortable old farmhouse of my childhood. Normally full of warmth, charm, family love, and belonging, the house was now a place of fear and panic. I was alone and in an upstairs bedroom, and an intruder had entered the house.

Spread out on the bed before me were several handguns of different styles and calibers, along with bullets for each of them. The intruder began coming up the stairs. My mind screamed, *Which one? Which one?* as I fumbled with the weapons, trying frantically to figure out which bullets went with which gun so I could load one of them and use it to defend myself. Before I could do so, the bedroom door burst open and the intruder entered, pointing a gun at me. Rushing over to the bed, he quickly overpowered me and dragged me to the floor. Then he was on top of me, and I was fighting desperately to get him off.

My dream ended at that point, leaving me with a terrible fear in my heart. I realized that I did not know the weapons of my warfare. Oh, I knew that I had some, but I wasn't familiar enough with them to use them effectively. I didn't even know how to load them, and I did not have any of the guns loaded and ready. How could I possibly be prepared for attacks from the enemy? I couldn't very well say to him, *Wait a minute! You can't come after me yet. I have to load my gun!*

This started me on a major quest of asking the Lord, "Please, God, show me what my spiritual weapons are and how to use them. Help me to be ready to use them against the enemy whenever he comes against me."

I needed to be a trick shooter like Annie Oakley, as skilled with my weapons as she was with hers. Courage on the front lines of faith requires a thorough knowledge of the spiritual weapons and other resources we have, as well as supreme devotion to and confidence in the One for whom we fight and who fights for us, taking our battles upon Himself. We can be encouraged in the assurance that God's banner is over us, His blessings are upon us, and His boldness is in us.

God's Banner Over Us

It is written in the Song of Solomon, "He has brought me to his banqueting place, And his banner over me is love [waving overhead to protect and comfort me]" (Song 2:4, AMP). God has stretched this great protective banner of His love over our heads. As we look up, we can see written on it the words "God is faithful, God is true." Yet the words are hard to make out because we who are believers have covered them with a film of unbelief that clouds them. Whenever anything negative comes along, the enemy infiltrates our thoughts and eats away at our confidence in God's love and care and protection. Here and there, we begin to see holes in the banner and the film across the words makes them harder to see.

All of us go through bad experiences from time to time; and if we are not careful, Satan uses them to eat away at our faith. Maybe you tried to do something that you believed God wanted you to do. You stepped out like Peter when he climbed out of the boat to walk to Jesus on the water, but something went wrong and you sank. All of a sudden the banner over your head that says "God is faithful" has a chunk out of it. You are left thinking, *Well, God is faithful, but maybe He's not as faithful with me as He is with someone else.* The seeds of doubt begin to grow.

Perhaps you are praying faithfully and fervently for someone's healing and don't understand when that person dies and goes to be with the Lord. Another hole appears in the banner and you think, *Well, if God is faithful, why does He heal sometimes but not at others?* Such questions enter our minds, are written on our hearts, and block us from fully believing that God truly is faithful and that He really will do everything that He says He will do.

This process can reach the point where we believe that God will move in somebody else's life but not in ours. He will work in their church but not in ours. He will come through for them but not for us. There are just enough negative experiences for us to wonder about God. Is God faithful? Can we trust Him to be true to His Word?

King David wrote, "Your love, Lord, reaches to the heavens, your faithfulness to the skies" (Ps. 36:5). Psalm 100 affirms, "For the Lord is good and his love endures forever; his faithfulness continues through all generations" (Ps. 100:5). The prophet Isaiah proclaimed, "O Lord, You are my God; I will exalt You, I will praise and give thanks to Your name; For You have done miraculous things, Plans formed long, long ago, [fulfilled] with perfect faithfulness" (Isa. 25:1, AMP). The book of

Lamentations says, "Because of the Lord's great love we are not consumed, for his compassions never fail. They are new every morning; great is your faithfulness" (Lam. 3:22–23).

Yes, God *is* faithful! Yes, you can trust Him to be true to His Word. The Lord wants to really shine down on you. He wants for you simply to believe Him. It's time for you to settle this issue once and for all. It's time to remove the questions from your mind and the doubts from your heart and to acknowledge to God: "Lord, I have fallen for the enemy's lies. He has come in and chipped away little pieces out of me and out of my faith in You. Forgive me, Lord. Please restore to me all those things that he has taken. Give me the faith and courage to step out and remove the dark film from the banner, to boldly reclaim Your promise that says, 'God is faithful.'"

The Heavens Declare God's Faithfulness

In fact, like Solomon's banner, God's faithfulness is written in the skies above us (see Ps. 89:2). When our oldest son, Justin, was in the sixth grade, all the students in his grade gave a presentation on the constellations for all the parents and teachers. Each student took one constellation, made a large replica of it, and identified by name the different stars that made up the constellation. These are ancient names; some of them go back 5,000 years. Each student also researched the meanings of these ancient names.

When I heard the word *constellation,* I tended to think of astrology and the zodiac, so I was a little uneasy about the assignment. Then I realized that Satan had taken what the Lord placed in the heavens as signs of His faithfulness, and twisted and distorted them until we will barely see God's handiwork in them.

The presentation was wonderful. It was incredible to see all the pictures and hear about the meanings behind the stars' and constellations' names. As it turned out, all of it was a reminder of God's lovingkindness and mercy, which is displayed in the heavens. Some of the children showed pictures of sheep coming into the sheepfold, and of Jesus the great Shepherd guarding the sheepfold and protecting them. One was about Jesus, the strong and mighty warrior, with His boots on, crushing the head of the serpent underneath His feet.

Later, I told Justin's teacher how impressed I was with the whole thing. It was wonderful to hear about how God's lovingkindness is displayed in the heavens day after day, year after year. Those stars are millions and billions of miles away. Some are closer to us than others, yet God has arranged them in such a way that from our perspective we see shapes in the night sky, sometimes almost as clearly as if they were pictures hanging on a wall. The constellations are a constant reminder to us of God's faithfulness. Like a heavenly banner, He set the stars in place to remind us, generation after generation after generation, of His faithfulness.

God wants to restore His banner of love and faithfulness not only over each of us individually, but also over everyone. He wants us to stretch it out over our families, our churches, and our communities so that we are no longer saying only God is faithful to me but also, God is faithful to my family, my church, and my city.

As we proclaim God's faithfulness and as everybody takes their own banner, eventually the banners interlace together as one large, sheltering canopy. That releases the Lord to do more, because everyone together is affirming His loving faithfulness. God has said that His banner over us is love and that He is faithful, and God is always true to His Word.

God's Blessings Upon Us

Courage for faithful service on the front lines also comes in the knowledge that the Lord does not send us out on our own. His presence is always with us, and His blessings are upon us to especially equip us for the work He has called us to do. In Psalm 103, King David provides a wonderfully encouraging list of blessings that God has given to His children. Appropriately, David begins the psalm with praise: "Bless the Lord, O my soul: and all that is within me, bless his holy name. Bless the Lord, O my soul, and forget not all his benefits" (Ps. 103:1–2, KJV).

David calls the blessings of God "His benefits." That makes me think of an insurance salesman sitting down at the table and saying, *Okay, now let me show you all the benefits you will receive if you sign up for our policy.* God provides many benefits.

"Who forgives all your sins…" (Ps. 103:3a). God forgives it all: our mistakes, our stubbornness, our pride. He forgives our attempts to control Him and others. Whatever our sin, if we confess it to Him, He forgives it. Whatever God forgives, He forgets. It is as if we were to hand God a piece of paper with all our sins written on it (it would be a long piece of paper!) and say, *Lord, here are my sins. Please forgive me.* He would return the paper to us not with the sins checked or even scratched out, but with them completely gone! The paper would be perfectly white without wrinkle or mark; it would be fresh, clean, and new. God's forgiveness makes it as though we had never sinned. His forgiveness removes sin guilt as a weapon for Satan to use against us. God is faithful.

"Who heals all your diseases" (Ps. 103:3b, AMP). God is our healer; He heals all our diseases. Now I don't understand why some people don't get healed, but I do know that God is faithful and that He has great compassion for His children. My mother died of cancer in 1982. Before she died, I really expected God to heal her. When He didn't, I had some questions at first about His faithfulness. Mom was a Christian, so I knew that she was with Jesus. After she died, I had many dreams of her in heaven, happy and at peace, a new creation with her health restored, and I knew that she was much better off being with the Lord. My questions subsided. Once again, God had proven His faithfulness.

There have been times, I confess, when I have felt cheated at not having my mom. She and I were just becoming really good friends and were growing very close at the time of her death. She also never got to meet any of her grandchildren, although she had the feeling that some-one in the family was pregnant. As it turned out, I was carrying our first child, Justin, but didn't find out until after Mom died. Justin's birth was a great balm to my soul, coming as it did so soon after Mom's death and after eight years of barrenness. In the midst of it all, God showed once more that He is faithful.

"Who redeems your life from the pit, Who crowns you [lavishly] with lovingkindness and tender mercy" (Ps. 103:4, AMP). Isn't that beautiful? Think of the transformation: Jesus lifts us from the slime, dirt, mud, and refuse of the world. He cleans us up, giving us new clothes and a crown engraved with the words "lovingkindness and ten-der mercy." He elevates us to reign with Him.

"Who satisfies your desires with good things so that your youth is renewed like the eagle's. The Lord works righteousness and justice for all the oppressed" (Ps. 103:5–6). God knows just how to meet our needs, whatever our age or situation. His presence and provision always renew our strength so that we can fly. Whenever we are oppressed by our employer or a fellow worker, or under pressure anywhere else, we can trust that God is faithful to see our need and respond in righteousness and justice.

"The Lord is compassionate and gracious, slow to anger, abounding in love. He will not always accuse, nor will he harbor his anger forever" (Ps. 103:8–9). How many times have you tried and failed repeatedly at something until you felt that the Lord would be really mad at you if you failed again? Repeated failure can bring discouragement. Maybe you remember a time when you really messed things up and your mistake affected the lives of a lot of people. Doesn't the Lord remember too and hold it against you? No way! He is merciful, gracious, slow to anger, and never holds a grudge. Those negative thoughts are attacks from the enemy. Shoot them down with the weapons of God's faithfulness, mercy, and lovingkindness.

The depth of God's love, mercy, and blessings toward us is brought out in the next several verses of the psalm:

> He has not dealt with us according to our sins [as we deserve], Nor rewarded us [with punishment] according to our wickedness. For as the heavens are high above the earth, So great is His lovingkindness toward those who fear and worship Him [with awe-filled respect and deepest reverence]. As far as the east is from the west, So far has He removed our transgressions from us. Just as a father loves his children, So the Lord loves those who fear and worship Him [with awe-filled respect and deepest reverence]. (Ps. 103:10–13, AMP)

Isn't it wonderful that God hasn't given us the judgment that our sins deserve, but has instead poured out His mercy on us? What confidence we can have in Christ when we know that our sins have been removed from us "as far as the east is from the west"! God blesses us and supports us because He knows how weak we are and how much in need we are; He knows that we cannot last on our own. Both the confidence that our sins are forgiven and the presence of the Holy Spirit in us give us a holy boldness as we serve on the front lines of faith.

After hearing a report from Peter and John regarding the threats they had received from the chief priests for preaching the gospel, the church in Jerusalem came together and prayed for boldness in the face of opposition. Acts 4:31 says that after their prayer, the place where they were meeting was shaken. They were all filled with the Holy Spirit and proclaimed Christ with courage and boldness. It was because of this divine boldness and power that the early church was so effective in spreading the gospel throughout the world of its day. Today, God provides us that same boldness and courage to spread the gospel throughout our world.

God's Courage

Unfortunately, many believers have the wrong concept of courage. The enemy has fed us a lie that says courage means being without fear, completely fearless, and that if we struggle with fear, then we must not be courageous enough. That is absolutely not true. All of us, even the most courageous among us, have to deal with fears.

Courage does not mean having no fear. On the contrary, courage means acknowledging fear, turning it over to God, and pressing ahead in spite of it. Courage means regarding the dream as more powerful and worthwhile than the fear that would keep us from it. Courage arises out of the security of knowing who God is and our identity in relation to Him. We can take courage in the Lord, not because of who we are or what we have, but because of His indwelling presence with us through the Holy Spirit.

By ourselves we are weak and can do nothing. But because He dwells in us, we have *His* power, wisdom, and courage. As we walk with Him, we understand more and more how much He loves us, and He begins to reveal His heart to us. We can take courage from these things.

Courage arises from confidence in the vision the Lord has given to us; it comes from the quiet place of contemplation before the Lord where He visits us and speaks to us. Courage comes out of glorying in our own weakness and resting in His strength.

Courage also means taking one step at a time without demanding to know the complete journey up front. We tend to want to have everything mapped out in advance so we can know what we're getting into before we start. God rarely works that way. He says, *I'm not going to tell you what it looks like at the end. I'm giving you insight for right now. Trust Me and follow Me.*

There is a reason He does this: walking one step at a time builds faith. God knows that our puny little brains can't handle the whole picture all at once. Sometimes God speaks things to us that seem so overwhelming that we can't see how in the world He will ever do it. Yet He pours out His grace and leads us one step at a time. We take that step and then watch for the next one. The Lord will open a doorway of grace to enable us to take the next step and the next and the next. As we walk this way, our faith grows and so does our courage.

Our Testimony

In the book of Revelation, John, the beloved apostle, presents a powerful picture of the victory that lies ahead for the bold and courageous church:

> And there was war in heaven: Michael and his angels fought against the dragon; and the dragon fought and his angels, And prevailed not; neither was their place found any more in heaven. And the great dragon was cast out, that old serpent, called the Devil, and Satan, which deceiveth the whole world: he was cast out into the earth, and his angels were cast out with him. And I heard a loud voice saying in heaven, Now is come salvation, and strength, and the kingdom of our God, and the power of his Christ: for the accuser of our brethren is cast down, which accused them before our God day and night. And they overcame him by the blood of the Lamb, and by the word of their testimony; and they loved not their lives unto the death. (Rev. 12:7–11, KJV)

Satan and his angels were defeated and cast out of heaven; never again could he accuse the brethren. It is the brethren—all believers—who have overcome Satan. How did this happen? They overcame by means of "the blood of the Lamb and by the word of their testimony."

Sometimes when believers get together, the pastor or leader will ask if anyone has a testimony to give. A testimony is simply a telling of what God has done or is doing in your life. Your testimony may seem small and insignificant in your mind compared to others that you hear, but it is still important. There may be someone who needs to hear just exactly the word from the Lord that your testimony would give them.

There is great power in our testimonies—power to defeat and overcome the enemy. The power lies in what Christ accomplished for us on the cross. Satan and his legions cannot stand against that kind of power. That is why it is important for us to share our testimonies, to tell of God's faithfulness and of His showing Himself strong on our behalf. It doesn't matter if the event is big or little; if God does it, we should tell it. The more we tell it, the more we take the chains off ourselves and off those who hear us, and put those chains where they belong: on the enemy.

When you step out with His banner of love and faithfulness over you, with the blessings of His grace, mercy, forgiveness, and healing upon you, and with the boldness and authority of His Word on your lips, you can face the world and the enemy with confidence and courage. No weapon that the enemy can fashion against you will stand because the power and purpose of God cannot be defeated. You have an unbeatable combination in the Word of God: *This is what the Lord says...* And along with that, the word of your testimony: *Let me tell you what the Lord has done for me...*

Satan will try to intimidate you with all sorts of things to keep your mouth shut. He'll try to convince you that it isn't important or that no one will be interested or that you were mistaken in thinking it was God who did it. Shoot down all those attacks with the weapons that God has given. Instead of being intimidated, claim the divine boldness that is yours by right as a child of God. You need to have the courage and faith to open your mouth and speak your testimony. God will do the rest. He hasn't called you to be successful—only faithful. When you are faithful, He will bring about success through you.

The chapters that follow profile nine ordinary Christian women who displayed extraordinary courage in following the call of God on their lives. Because they were faithful, God used them to accomplish amazing things. We can take courage from their examples. If God could use them, He can use you and me.

Put on the full armor of God, so that you will be able to stand firm against the schemes of the devil. For our struggle is not against flesh and blood, but against the rulers, against the powers, against the world forces of this darkness, against the spiritual *forces* of wickedness in the heavenly *places*. Therefore, take up the full armor of God, so that you will be able to resist in the evil day, and having done everything, to stand firm. (Eph. 6:11–13, NASB)

Papa God, in Jesus' name I volunteer freely to be a part of Your strong and yet humble army in the day of Your power. I choose to put on the full armor of God, by which I will be able to put out the flaming arrows of the Evil One. I purpose to arise above the attacks of the enemy and, together with likeminded others, declare, "Greater is He who is with us than he who is in the world," for the glory of Your name throughout the earth. Amen.

Part Two

Women
of Courage

Chapter 3

≝

Joan of Arc

THE COST OF COURAGE

S ome of you may think that you are the most unlikely candidate for God to use to do anything significant. Most of us think of ourselves in that way. The world teaches us that it is the rich, the powerful, or the beautiful who are important and make a difference in the world. That's not what God teaches. He doesn't think or work the way the world does. The prophet Isaiah recorded, "'For My thoughts are not your thoughts, nor are your ways My ways,' declares the Lord. 'For *as* the heavens are higher than the earth, so are My ways higher than your ways and My thoughts than your thoughts'" (Isa. 55:8–9, NASB).

I like the way Randy Clark puts it: "God can use little ole me!" Yes, God can use anyone or anything He desires to accomplish His purpose. In fact, He prefers to use people and means considered insignificant by the world. The apostle Paul told the Corinthians:

> God has selected [for His purpose] the weak things of the world to shame the things which are strong [revealing their frailty]. God has selected [for His purpose] the insignificant (base) things of the world, and the things that are despised and treated with contempt, [even] the things that are nothing, so that He might reduce to nothing the things that are. (1 Cor. 1:27–28, AMP)

If, even after reading these words, you still wonder whether or not God can or will use you, take courage, as I have, from the story of a young woman who was, humanly speaking, one of the most unlikely heroes in history: Joan of Arc. Her life has been a tremendous tool of inspiration to me.

A Time for Leadership

The fourteenth and fifteenth centuries were filled with great political and national turmoil for France. From 1337 to 1453, France and England fought a series of battles that became known as the Hundred Years' War. At stake was the territory of Aquitane, a rich land in southwestern France that had been under English control since the twelfth century. France wanted it back; England was determined to keep it.[1]

In addition, in 1338 King Edward III of England, through his mother a direct descendant of King Philip IV of France, claimed title to the French throne, thus setting off conflict between the two nations over royal succession in France.

By 1380, when King Charles V of France died, the situation had stabilized somewhat and a lasting peace seemed possible. The king's son, Charles VI, was only twelve years old when his father died. He was put under the guardianship of a ducal council until 1388, when he began ruling in his own right. He married Isabella of Bavaria and ruled well until 1392, when he had his first bout with the insanity that plagued the remainder of his reign.

During these times, Isabella served as his regent, and in effect she ruled in her husband's place. Charles' insanity and the resulting internal power struggle weakened the kingdom. The English eventually took advantage of the turmoil and invaded France. In 1415, King Henry V of England inflicted a devastating defeat on the French at Agincourt, leaving the country divided into three parts. In 1420, Isabella, serving as regent for her mad husband, signed the Treaty of Troyes. This treaty, among other things, secured for Henry V accession to the French throne upon the death of Charles VI. At the same time, courting Henry's favor, Isabella disowned her own son, the dauphin, Charles VII, and gave her daughter Catherine to Henry in marriage. All this strengthened Henry's claim to the French throne.

Thus Charles VII, the otherwise legitimate heir to the throne of France, was cut off. Around 1400 an ancient French prophecy was revived that said the kingdom would be brought to ruin by a woman and restored by a daughter of the people. Many came to believe that Isabella had fulfilled the first part of the prophecy when she signed the Treaty of Troyes, giving the French throne to the English king.[2] But who would be the "daughter of the people" who would arise to restore the kingdom?

The situation in France was made worse in 1422 when both Charles VI and Henry V died and Henry's infant son (Henry VI) was proclaimed king of both England and France. The people of France were in a desperate state; children died of hunger in the streets by the thousands. It is said that wolves even came into Paris at night to feed on the bodies of the unburied dead in the city streets. There was great lawlessness and immorality, and many people lived little better than beasts.[3] The disinherited Charles, from his base in central and southwestern France, attempted to assert his authority and claim to the throne, but with little success. The French people as a whole would not recognize him as the legitimate king unless he was formally coronated in the traditional place, the cathedral in the now English-controlled city of Rheims.[4] If ever there was a time for a strong and courageous leader to arise, it was now.

An Unlikely Champion

In the midst of this political unrest and social upheaval, Joan appeared. Born in 1412 in the village of Domremy, in the Champagne district of northeastern France, Joan was the youngest in a family of five. Although skilled in sewing and spinning, she never learned to read or write. From a very early age she displayed an unusually deep devotion to God. She spent hours absorbed in prayer and was known to have a tender heart for the poor and needy.[5]

From her childhood on, Joan simply loved God. She never received any theological training and knew very little about the formal structures and official doctrines of the Roman Catholic Church, the only church in France at that time. All Joan knew was that when she went to mass, God met her there. Joan knew God, loved to spend time with Him, and would do anything for Him.

In the summer of 1425, when she was thirteen, Joan experienced her first heavenly visitation: a blaze of bright light accompanied by a voice. She received numerous such visitations during the months that followed and gradually discerned the identities of those who spoke to her. Joan identified one of them as Michael the archangel. St. Catherine of Alexandria and St. Margaret of Antioch, both early Christian martyrs, were the others.[6]

Although to modern minds these may seem to be strange messengers, remember that, in the case of Michael, angelic visitations have biblical precedent. As for the other two, it is natural that Joan would have understood and interpreted her visitors in a manner consistent with the religious environment of her day. From the historical records of her life, her trial and execution, and the later rehabilitation of her reputation, in my understanding there is little doubt today of the divine nature of her visitations.

At first Joan's "voices" told her such things as "Be a good girl and obey your parents." However, over the course of three years the messages began to change. She had dreams of horses running in battle and of herself being led away with an army of men. During this time she gradually became aware of the call of God on her life. He seemed to be telling her that she was to go to the aid of the disinherited Charles, the true king of France; drive the English away from Orleans and out of the country; and lead the procession to see Charles enthroned. At first she resisted: *I'm just a girl. I have no education, no training in military skills. Who's going to listen to me?* Her voices continued, however, and became more and more insistent.

By May 1428, Joan was convinced beyond a shadow of a doubt that God was leading her to go to Charles' aid. Her life of fellowship and communion with the Lord had been such that once she was convinced of her call, the vision so convicted and consumed her that she let nothing stand in her way. She had such a concrete understanding of who her Father was and loved Him so much that she would go anywhere and do anything to fulfill His desire. Nothing was too great a task for Him to ask of her. She believed that God was true and that He would back her up in everything that He called her to do.

A Divine Mission

A month later, under the insistent direction of her "voices," Joan presented herself and her mission to Robert Baudricourt, the commander of Charles' forces in the neighboring town of Vaucouleurs. Baudricourt showed little but contempt for Joan and her ideas, telling the cousin who had accompanied her to "take her home to her father and give her a good whipping."[7]

Joan returned to Domremy, apparently defeated. In the meantime, Charles' situation worsened as the English besieged the city of Orleans on October 12, 1428. By the end of the year, total defeat for the French seemed near at hand. Joan's visitations continued, her "voices" becoming increasingly urgent. When she tried to resist, they told her, "It is God who commands it." Finally, in January 1429, Joan returned to Vaucouleurs for another try.[8]

This time, she stayed in the town and gradually made an impression on Baudricourt. According to one account, he waved a sword in her face, saying, "What do your 'voices' say to this?" In response, Joan grabbed a short dagger-like sword from a nearby attendant and brought its blade down against the blade of Baudricourt's sword, severing it as if it were paper. Baudricourt then arranged for her to see Charles and sent Joan with a three-man escort to Chinon, where Charles was staying. Joan traveled in men's clothing, probably for modesty and practicality.

Charles, not knowing what to make of this teenage girl who was coming to see him, decided to test Joan by disguising himself and surrounding himself with attendants. However, when Joan was brought in, she somehow immediately recognized him and addressed him as the king. Despite this, Charles was still skeptical.

Joan offered to prove that she had been sent by God by answering for Charles three questions that were known only to him and to God: whether or not he was the true heir to the French throne, that if France's troubles were because of his sins that he alone be punished and the nation spared, and that if the war was due to the sins of the people that they be forgiven and the troubles lifted.[9]

Joan's divinely inspired insight convinced Charles, at least halfheartedly, to believe in her mission. Before she was entrusted with military operations, however, Joan was sent to the city of Poitiers, where she was examined by a large committee of highly educated bishops and doctors. This illiterate young woman held her own against the searching and deep questions put to her. In the end, her faith, simplicity, and honesty made a very positive impression on these learned theologians, who found nothing heretical in her claims of supernatural guidance.[10]

Returning to Chinon, Joan began preparing for her campaign. It was at this early stage that two significant events appeared to confirm even more the divine nature of her mission. Joan needed a sword, and she knew where to find one. She wrote to the priests at the chapel of Saint Catherine of Fierbois, informing them that her sword was buried behind the altar. Indeed, a sword was found at that exact spot.[11]

The second event involved a letter, which still exists, written on April 22, 1429, and delivered and duly registered before any of the events referred to in the letter took place. The writer of the letter reported that Joan had said that she would deliver the city of Orleans, she would compel the English to raise the siege, she herself would be wounded but would survive, and Charles would be crowned king before the end of the summer.[12]

As it turned out, all of these things were fulfilled just as Joan predicted.

An Army of the Lord

Joan had such an incredible presence of the Lord on her that she drew people to her everywhere she turned. By the time she arrived on the field, Charles' army was at a very low point; they were exhausted, defeated, discouraged, and disillusioned. Many of the soldiers had begun to desert. Then Joan appeared, proclaiming, "I have a vision from God. He has called me to raise an army for our nation and for Him."

As Joan's presence became known, soldiers began to rush to her side by the thousands. The call was given and they came gladly. Rough, vulgar, immoral, and intemperate though many of them were, the men found her innocence, spiritual piety, and patriotic fervor irresistible. Her presence filled them with new vigor and courage. She held up for them a standard of righteousness, purity, and devotion to the Lord, and they rallied around her. Even though she was a young woman in the midst of an army of men, Joan had a holy quality about her that blocked their tendencies to regard her in a sexual manner.

Joan made clear what the requirements were for being a part of her "army of the Lord." First, she told the soldiers that the camp prostitutes had to go. Second, the soldiers had to attend mass every day. Third, there was to be no more cursing or swearing. Amazingly, Joan's influence was so great that her army embraced these standards enthusiastically. As miraculous as it seems, they agreed as one body to come into holy living and purity.

Joan had absolutely no training in military operations or strategy, but God gave her battle plans on the field. Some of the generals were still not completely convinced, however, and tried to trick her by following other strategies. God revealed to Joan what was going on, and she challenged the generals: "In God's Name, the advice of Our Lord is wiser and more certain than yours. You thought to deceive me, but it is you who are deceived, for I bring you the best help that ever came to any soldier or to any city."[13]

The conviction from her words pierced their hearts. After the English rejected a demand from Joan that they leave French soil, Joan and her army moved rapidly and entered the city of Orléans on April 30, 1429. Within a week they had captured all the English forts surrounding the city. Although Joan was wounded in the breast by an arrow on the last day of battle, she was insistent on pressing forward with the campaign. One reason for this was her warlike instinct. The other was that her "voices" had already told her that she had only one year. She knew time was important.[14]

Joan's insistence prevailed against the reluctance of the king and his advisers. A short campaign along the Loire River led to a great victory on June 18 at Patay, where English reinforcements sent from Paris were completely defeated. Joan pressed on, still laboring to overcome the reluctance of the commanders. Nevertheless, they captured the city of Troyes, opening the way to Rheims where, on July 17, 1429, Charles VII was solemnly crowned king with Joan standing by as a witness.[15]

Reversal and Betrayal

Although the principal purpose of her mission had been accomplished, Joan remained with the army throughout the rest of the summer. An attempt to retake Paris from the English failed, and in a later battle Joan was wounded again, this time in the thigh. The king signed a truce with the Duke of Burgundy, who was allied with the English, and there was no further fighting until the following year.

Joan spent a miserable winter among the worldly and jealous members of the king's court. On December 29, 1429, Charles raised Joan and her entire family to the rank of nobility, perhaps partly in an attempt to console her. She was probably more than ready when she took to the battlefield the following April when the truce ended.[16]

Her "voices" continued to speak to her, telling her that she would be taken prisoner before midsummer. This happened on the evening of May 24, 1430, while Joan and troops under her command were defending the city of Compiègne against Burgundian attack. The commander of the city accidentally raised the drawbridge while Joan and many of her soldiers were still outside. She was pulled from her horse and made a prisoner of war.[17]

Although they had several important English prisoners whom they could have traded for Joan, Charles VII and his advisors did nothing to try to rescue her. The English, on the other hand, were desperate to get their hands on her. They both feared and hated her because of the defeat and embarrassment they had suffered at her hands and were determined to somehow take her life. The English struck a deal with Joan's Burgundian captors, who sold her for a sum of money that today would equal hundreds of thousands of dollars.[18]

Trial and Martyrdom

The English knew that they could not legitimately execute Joan simply because she had defeated them in battle. Instead, their strategy was to have her condemned to death as a witch and a heretic. To this end, they claimed that Joan's "voices" were satanic in nature and that the only way she could have defeated them in battle was with the help of the powers of darkness. Joan's practice of wearing male dress was also used against her as evidence of her heresy.

The trial of Joan of Arc is one of the most thoroughly documented events of that period of history. After months of imprisonment in disgraceful conditions, she was questioned intensively by the most learned theologians of the day. There is a complete record both of the questions she was asked and of her answers. Throughout the entire proceeding, Joan's faith, integrity, and spiritual insight shone brightly.

Despite being a young woman not yet out of her teens, unable to read or write and without any formal religious training of any kind, being examined and questioned about fine points of religion, faith, and theology by men who were determined to find something with which to condemn her, Joan stood firm. God held her up.

He gave her the wisdom and the words to answer every question. The record of her trial leaves little room to doubt either her absolute devotion to God or the courage with which she stood for Him. At this time when the institutional church held almost absolute authority over the people, here is how Joan responded to questions regarding her spiritual allegiance:

Q: If the Church Militant tells you that your revelations are illusions, or diabolical things, will you defer to the Church?

A: I will defer to God, Whose Commandment I always do.... In case the Church should prescribe the contrary, I should not refer to anyone in the world, but to God alone, Whose Commandment I always follow.

Q: Do you not then believe you are subject to the Church of God which is on earth, that is to say to our Lord the Pope, to the Cardinals, the Archbishops, Bishops, and other prelates of the Church?

A: Yes, I believe myself to be subject to them, but God must be served first.

Q: Have you then command from your voices not to submit yourself to the Church Militant, which is on earth, not to its decision?

A: I answer nothing from my own head, what I answer is by command of my voices, they do not order me to disobey the Church, but God must be served first.[19]

In the end Joan was condemned to death for heresy. She signed a retraction that she probably did not fully understand, and her sentence was changed to imprisonment for life. A few days later, however, she resumed wearing male dress in the prison, which gave her enemies the excuse to condemn her again as a "relapsed heretic." Joan was turned over for execution by burning at the stake. Sadly, that execution was carried out on May 30, 1431.

Joan's behavior when facing death was admirable, moving even her bitter enemies to tears. The normal practice when someone was burned at the stake was for the wood to be laid at the front and, after the flames and smoke had risen up, for the executioner to strangle the victim from behind. It was a merciful gesture intended to spare the victim the agony of the burning.

This practice was not followed in Joan's case. She faced the flames fully conscious. As the flames rose, Joan called out for the cross. When it was held up before her, she called repeatedly on the name of Jesus, forgiving those who had wronged her and pouring out words of love and devotion to Him.

Apparently everyone who watched was deeply moved by her witness. Many were deeply convicted by what they had done, recognizing that Joan certainly could not have been a heretic. In fact, some were so convicted that they were moved to repentance on the spot. According to some accounts, some people claimed to have seen the name of Jesus written in the flames, while others said they saw a white dove fly out of the flames.[20]

The executioner himself is reported to have said that Joan's heart would not burn.[21]

Twenty-five years after her death, Joan's case was reopened and the facts reexamined. As a result, Joan was declared to be completely innocent of all crimes, being neither a witch nor a heretic but a victim of jealousy, hatred, and political intrigue. For centuries she has been considered a French national heroine, and in 1920 the Catholic Church canonized her.[22]

Joan's Legacy

What does the life of this fifteenth-century teenaged girl have to say to us today?

First, I believe that we can take courage from the simple fact that Joan was so ordinary. There was nothing obvious that made her stand out. By normal human standards she had no qualifications for the mission she undertook. She had no education, no religious training, no leadership experience. She was not ordained to the ministry. In fact, she lived during a time when women's freedom in both church and society was greatly restricted.

What made the difference? Joan possessed the only qualification that mattered: she loved God with all her heart, soul, mind, and strength. She was completely sold out to Him. God chose her and used her because she made herself available to Him. Her executioner claimed that her heart would not burn. If this was so, perhaps it was because her heart had already been burned by her passion for God.

She was so consumed by Him that nothing else could touch her. We can all take courage from the fact that the only thing God requires of us in order for Him to use us is that we know Him, love Him, and make ourselves available to Him. God's army is an army of *volunteers*.

The standards Joan laid down for her army show us that the Lord has called His army (us) to a life of purity, holiness, and complete devotion to Him. If we are to be effective and fully usable, we must put away all filth and uncleanness, all sin and evil thinking, and be clean vessels before the Lord. God has raised His standard of righteousness for us to rally under and has told us, "YOU SHALL BE HOLY, FOR I AM HOLY" (1 Pet. 1:16b, NASB).

The apostle Paul expressed it well when he wrote:

Therefore, I urge you, brothers and sisters, in view of God's mercy, to offer your bodies as a living sacrifice, holy and pleasing to God—this is your true and proper worship. (Rom. 12:1)

We must be blameless in our behavior, wholesome in our speech, and consistent in our walk. Regardless of what the world tries to do to us, we can walk blamelessly, undefiled before God. The purity and holiness that He places in us can come out as an extension of us, and we can then pass them on to other people. We don't have to be tainted by the world. On the contrary, we can influence the world for Christ. It isn't easy, and it costs everything, but with God's help it can be done. And He receives the glory!

Joan's example encourages us to dare to believe that we can do whatever God calls us to do. It assures us that He will back us up in our call and bring it to pass as we obey and follow Him. It is inconceivable that Joan could have done what she did without the hand of God on her life.

One thing that the Lord told Joan again and again was, *Go on! Go on, daughter of God! Go on; I will be with you and I will be your help.* He says the same thing to us today: *Go on into your destiny, into your calling, into your place before the Lord. Go on! Push through! Endure! Let Me show Myself strong on your behalf.*

God is looking for men and women who will be sold out to Him; He wants people who will let their hearts and minds be so consumed with Him that nothing else matters. All that mattered to Joan was reaching Rheims and seeing her king crowned according to God's will. Doing so required pressing through the heart of the English army, moving through the hardest and greatest difficulties to reach the place of victory. It is the same for us. We need to go to the place that is the most difficult for us, where the enemy seems to have the greatest stronghold, and enthrone Jesus there. We need to raise His banner and make a way for Him to come and receive the honor due His name.

The cost to Joan for courage was her life, but her reward was the company and presence of God and the fulfillment of His purpose in and through her. To have courage will cost us everything as well: our whole lives given completely to the Lord in sacrifice and devotion. What is our reward? Life! We want to proclaim life, not death; blessing, not cursing; and light, not darkness. However, it is only in losing our life that we find it. And what we find is His life, not ours.

Courage is not something we can drum up from within ourselves; it comes from knowing God and trusting Him completely. As we learn to depend on Him rather than on ourselves, He releases His power in and through us—and that power can change our families, our friends, our communities, our nation, and even the whole world. God is not a respecter of persons. If He used someone as ordinary as Joan of Arc, He will use you too. Dare to believe!

> Your people will volunteer freely in the day of Your power; in holy array, from the womb of the dawn, Your youth are to You *as* the dew. (Psalm 110:3, NASB)

By the grace of God, I choose to take up my cross, deny myself, and follow Christ Jesus wherever He may lead. I declare I am being clothed with the supernatural authority of the Holy Spirit to enable me to do mighty exploits for His holy name's sake. Counting the cost, I also ask that I be filled with the very courage of God. What You did before, Lord, You shall do again! Amen.

Chapter 4

🌿

Vibia Perpetua

FAITHFUL UNTO DEATH

I saw a golden ladder which reached from earth to the heavens; but so narrow, that only one could mount it at a time. To the two sides were fastened all sorts of iron instruments, as swords, lances, hooks, and knives; so that if any one went up carelessly he was in great danger of having his flesh torn by those weapons. At the foot of the ladder lay a dragon of an enormous size, who kept guard to turn back and terrify those that endeavored to mount it. The first that went up was Saturus, who was not apprehended with us, but voluntarily surrendered himself afterwards on our account: when he was got to the top of the ladder, he turned towards me and said: "Perpetua, I wait for you; but take care lest the dragon bite you." I answered: "In the name of our Lord Jesus Christ, he shall not hurt me." Then the dragon, as if afraid of me, gently lifted his head from under the ladder, and I, having got upon the first step, set my foot upon his head. Thus I mounted to the top, and there I saw a garden of an immense space, and in the middle of it a tall man sitting down dressed like a shepherd, having white hair. He was milking his sheep, surrounded with many thousands of persons clad in white. He called me by my name, bid me welcome, and gave me some curds made of the milk which he had drawn: I put my hands together and took and ate them; and all that were present said aloud, Amen. The noise awaked me, chewing something very sweet. As soon as I had related to my brother this vision, we both concluded that we should suffer death.[1]

With these words Vibia Perpetua, a young noblewoman of Carthage in northern Africa, recorded a vision that she received from God in response to her prayer asking whether or not she faced martyrdom. Her question was quite relevant, for at the time of her vision Perpetua and five others were in prison; they had been charged with defying Emperor Septimus Severus' prohibition against conversions to Christianity.

The year was A.D. 203, and a general persecution that had begun a few years earlier in the European part of the Roman Empire had finally reached Africa. Perpetua's companions in prison were a slave named Revocatus; Revocatus' fellow slave, Felicitas, who was seven months pregnant; and two free men, Saturninus and Secundulus. All five were catechumens (new believers who were being instructed in doctrine and discipline before being admitted to baptism and church membership). As it happened, they all received baptism while in prison. They were joined in prison by their instructor in the faith, Saturus (the one mentioned in Perpetua's vision), who, although not present when the others were arrested, had given himself up voluntarily in order to be with them during their ordeal.

An Allegiance Higher Than Family

Vibia Perpetua, twenty-two years old, came from a good family and had married a man of quality in Carthage, although he is strangely absent in the existing accounts of her imprisonment and martyrdom. It is possible that Perpetua was a widow; she released her infant son, who was brought to her regularly for nursing, into the care of her mother, since apparently her death would make the child an orphan. Perpetua's two surviving brothers (a third had died as a child) were believers, as was her mother, but her father was a pagan. He loved Perpetua more than all his other children and made several attempts to persuade her to recant or deny her Christian faith in order to spare her life.

One day shortly after her imprisonment began, Perpetua's father visited her, appealing to her, for the sake of her life and for that of her nursing baby, to renounce her faith. Pointing to a waterpot or some other container, Perpetua asked her father, "Can that vessel, which you see, change its name?" When he answered that it could not, Perpetua said to him, "Nor can I call myself any other than I am, that is to say, a Christian."[2]

On another occasion, as Perpetua's trial before the Roman procurator approached, her father tried again. In Perpetua's own words:

> My father came over from the city worn out with exhaustion, and he went up to me in order to deflect me, saying: "My daughter, have pity on my white hairs! Show some compassion to your father, if I deserve to be called father by you….do not bring me into disgrace in all men's eyes! Look at your brothers, look at your mother and your aunt—look at your son, who won't be able to live if you die. Don't flaunt your insistence, or you'll destroy us all: for if anything happens to you, none of us will ever be able to speak freely and openly again." This is what my father said, out of devotion to me, kissing my hands and flinging himself at my feet; and amid his tears he called me not "daughter" but "domina" [my lady]. And I grieved for my father's condition—for he alone of all my family would not gain joy from my ordeal. And I comforted him, saying: "At the tribunal things will go as God wills: for you must know that we are no longer in our own hands, but in God's." And he left me griefstricken.[3]

A short time later, as Perpetua stood before Hilarian, the procurator of the province, her father made a final attempt. Apparently Perpetua was the last of the prisoners to be examined, because she records that all those who were questioned ahead of her boldly confessed Jesus Christ. When it was her turn, her father suddenly appeared, carrying her infant son. He appealed to her motherly instinct, begging her to consider the misery that she would bring on her son if she persisted. Even the judge Hilarian joined in, saying, "What! Will neither the gray hairs of a father you are going to make miserable, nor the tender innocence of a child, which your death will leave an orphan, move you? Sacrifice for the prosperity of the emperor."

Perpetua replied, "I will not do it."

Hilarian asked her directly, "Are you then a Christian?"

"Yes, I am." After this reply the judge sentenced Perpetua and all her companions to be exposed to wild beasts at the emperor's festival games.[4]

A Vision of Victory

Secundulus apparently died in prison, but Perpetua and the others faced their impending deaths with anticipation. In the spirit of the apostles of the New Testament, they rejoiced that they were considered worthy to suffer for their Lord (see Acts 5:41). During the final days before the games, the Lord encouraged each of them through dreams and visions that assured them of victory and of His presence with them throughout. In Perpetua's vision, a deacon named Pomponius led her to the center of the amphitheater, encouraging her to not be afraid. Then, according to Perpetua:

> I saw much people watching closely. And because I knew that I was condemned to the beasts I marveled that beasts were not sent out against me. And there came out against me a certain ill-favored Egyptian with his helpers to fight me. Also there came to me comely young men, my helpers and aiders. And I was stripped naked and I became a man. And my helpers began to rub me with oil as their custom is for a contest; and over against me saw that Egyptian wallowing in the dust. And there came forth a man of very great stature, so that he overpassed the very top of the amphitheater...bearing a rod like a master of gladiators, and a green branch whereon were golden apples. And he besought silence and said: The Egyptian, if he shall conquer this woman, shall slay her with the sword; and if she shall conquer him, she shall receive this branch....[The Egyptian] tried to trip up my feet, but I with my heels smote upon his face. And I rose up into the air and began so to smite him as though I trod not the earth....And I caught his head, and he fell upon his face; and I trod upon his head. And the people began to shout, and my helpers began to sing. And I went up to the master of gladiators and received the branch. And he kissed me

and said to me: Daughter, peace be with you. And I began to go with glory to the gate called the Gate of Life. And I awoke; and I understood that I should fight, not with beasts but against the devil; but I knew that mine was the victory.[5]

Courage and Faithfulness

By all accounts, Perpetua and her companions remained steadfast in faith and witness throughout the days of their imprisonment and on the day they met their deaths in the arena. In fact, the keeper of the prison, a man named Pudens, was himself converted to Christ by the faithful testimony of his prisoners. During the customary final meal, which was eaten in public, the Christians did their best to turn the affair into an agape meal or love feast, talking freely with the crowd watching them, testifying to Christ, threatening the judgments of God, and rejoicing in their own sufferings. Their steadfast faith and courage so impressed the onlookers that several of them were converted.

On the day of the games, the condemned marched from the prison to the amphitheater, joy in their eyes and characterizing their every word and gesture. The two women, Perpetua and Felicitas, walked together. An eyewitness wrote that "Perpetua walked with a composed countenance and easy pace, as a woman cherished by Jesus Christ, with her eyes modestly cast down."[6]

Felicitas was especially joyful to be with her friends because it had appeared for a while that her pregnancy would prevent her from dying with them. (Roman law forbade the execution of pregnant women.) But through her prayers and the prayers of her friends, she had safely delivered a daughter while in prison. The baby was taken into the home of a Christian woman who raised the child as her own.

As they reached the gate of the arena, they were given the customary robes that had been consecrated to the Roman gods, to wear. The condemned Christians refused to wear the idolatrous clothing, however. Perpetua forcefully stood her ground, telling the Roman tribune that they had agreed to come of their own accord on the promise that they would not be forced to do anything contrary to their religion. The tribune allowed them to proceed in their own clothes.

Revocatus and Saturninus were dispatched rather quickly after being attacked first by a leopard and then by a bear. Saturus' death took a little longer. He was exposed first to a wild boar, which promptly turned on and fatally wounded its keeper. Then it did nothing more than drag Saturus. Next he was exposed to a bear, which refused to come out of its den. Finally, Saturus died from a single bite of a leopard.

Perpetua and Felicitas were exposed to a wild cow that, when it attacked, tossed first Perpetua and then Felicitas. Perpetua landed on her back, then sat up and gathered her torn clothes about her to preserve her modesty. She stood up, tied up her hair, which had fallen loose, and helped the badly mauled Felicitas to her feet. They stood together, expecting another assault from the cow when the crowd cried out that it was enough. Perpetua and Felicitas were then taken to the Gate of Life, which is where victims who survived the beasts were put to death by gladiators. The two women exchanged a final kiss of peace. The gladiator assigned to execute Perpetua was a novice, young and very nervous. He was shaking so much that he was able to inflict only a few painful but not deadly wounds. Perpetua herself then calmly guided his hand and sword to her own neck where he then finished the job.

Perpetua's Legacy

There are several remarkable things about Perpetua and her martyrdom that can encourage us. First, the existing account of her imprisonment, trial, and death is regarded as reliably historical (as compared to some other martyr accounts that contain much legend) and is one of the earliest historical accounts of Christianity after the close of the New Testament. The fact that much of the story was written by Perpetua herself makes it one of the earliest pieces of writing by a Christian woman.

The story was so highly regarded that it was read widely in African churches for the next several centuries and was treated as almost equivalent to Scripture. Perpetua faced her martyrdom with a confidence and courage that did not come strictly from within herself, but was given to her by the Lord whom she so faithfully gave witness to. Her experience is full of evidence of how Christ sustained her and the others throughout their ordeal. He never abandoned them, but remained close to them. They drew constant strength from His presence.

Jesus is the same yesterday, today, and forever (see Heb. 13:8), and what He did for them He will do for us. He has promised never to leave us or forsake us (see Heb. 13:5).

Perpetua's courage inspires us even more when we remember that she and all the others, with the possible exception of Saturus, were *new* believers; it was only after they were in prison that they received baptism. They were in the early stages of learning the doctrines and disciplines of the faith. This shows us that what counts ultimately is our commitment to Christ, not knowledge. Knowledge of our faith is very important, but knowledge alone does not give us the courage to stand firm. That comes only through the Person and presence of Jesus Christ in our lives.

Essentially, Perpetua was no different from any of us. She was an ordinary woman who trusted Christ completely and was given the courage and confidence to be faithful unto death. As we learn to trust Christ, we will find that He gives us the courage and confidence to meet whatever challenges come our way as well. Although not all of us are called to be a martyr for our faith, each of us is called to die to ourselves, and it takes courage to do that. May we learn how to gain strength for the journey from the example of Perpetua, who was faithful unto death.

Jesus, You are my Lord, and you died for me on the cross. Now You show me not only how to live but how to take up my own cross daily, living and dying for you at the same time. I cannot manufacture the willpower to follow you, and I often lack faith-filled courage. Come to my aid, Holy Spirit, today and every day. I trust you wholeheartedly. Amen.

Chapter 5

✿

Sojourner Truth

"AIN'T I A WOMAN?"

On November 28, 1883, a crowd of nearly a thousand people gathered before a modest house in Battle Creek, Michigan, to pay their final respects to one of the most remarkable American women of the nineteenth century. Silently, on foot and in carriages, they fell into line behind the hearse bearing the body of Sojourner Truth: ex-slave, mother, evangelist, abolitionist, author, women's rights advocate, temperance activist, and proponent of land grant benefits for ex-slaves. Her coffin borne by white residents of Battle Creek, the eighty-six-year-old African American was laid to rest in the Oakhill Cemetery. Many of her friends from the women's rights and abolitionist movements spoke of her "rare qualities of head and heart" and remembered her as a "dynamic woman with strength, integrity, poise, and wit."[1]

Sojourner was a powerful public speaker, captivating her mostly white audiences wherever she went. No one who met her or heard her speak ever forgot her. Nearly six feet tall with a deep, powerful voice, Sojourner Truth was an imposing presence. Never one to back down from a challenge, she was one of the first black women in the United States to win a court case, which she did not once but three times. Her influence brought her into contact with many important leaders of the day, both religious and political. She even had private meetings with three US presidents.

What makes the accomplishments of this formidable woman even more amazing is that throughout her long life she was illiterate. Even though she published an autobiography and knew large portions of the

Bible by heart, Sojourner Truth, like Joan of Arc centuries before her, never learned how to read or write.

From Slavery to Freedom

Named Isabella by her parents but called "Belle," Sojourner Truth was born to a slave couple on a farm in upstate New York around 1797. From the beginning, her parents instilled in her the importance and value of hard work. Belle's mother also taught her to pray to God during times of trouble. Belle learned both lessons well even though she didn't think about God very much while she was growing up and, as a slave, had little opportunity to learn about Him. By the time she was in her midtwenties, Belle had belonged to five different masters. She had married another slave named Tom and had given birth to five children.

In 1824 Belle heard the news that the New York state legislature had passed a law abolishing slavery in the state. Under the terms of the law, she and Tom would become free on July 4, 1827. In 1825 John Dumont, Belle's owner of fifteen years, was impressed with her hard work and offered her a deal: if she worked extra hard for the next year, he would free her and Tom a year early. Belle accepted eagerly and did her part. At the end of the year, however, a poor harvest caused Dumont to feel he could not afford to free them as he had promised. Feeling betrayed, Belle determined to run away, even though by law she would be free in another year.

Belle wondered when to make her attempt. Running away during the day would be foolish, and she was afraid of the dark. As her mother had taught her, Belle prayed to God, and He showed her what to do: leave around dawn, while everyone else was still asleep but there was enough light to see. Taking her youngest child, Sophia, Belle fled to the home of a Quaker couple a few miles away who gave them shelter. When Dumont found them there the next day, Belle refused to return. The Quaker couple bought her and Sophia from Dumont for twenty-five dollars, then promptly set them free.

Belle looked forward to the day when all her family would be free. But before that day arrived, Dumont sold her only son, Peter, to a doctor who found the boy unsuitable to his needs. The doctor turned Peter over to his brother, who sold Peter to an Alabama planter. Belle was furious because Alabama was a "slave-for-life" state. She was deter-mined, whatever the cost, to get her son back. Encouraged by her Quaker friends, Belle sought legal action to have Peter returned. An attorney assured her that Peter's out-of-state sale was illegal and began to work on her behalf. Things looked promising but were then delayed because court was not in session. Her lawyer asked her to be patient with the court system, but Belle could not.

While walking home that day, Belle cried out to Jesus, asking Him to intercede for her before the throne of God. Her prayer was answered when, on the road, she met a perfect stranger who asked her if her son had been returned yet. When she said no, the stranger pointed to a nearby house and told her that an attorney who could help her lived there. Belle went to see him, and within twenty-four hours the court had returned Peter to her. For the rest of her life, Belle testified that she was certain that the stranger she had met on the road was sent from God to help her.[2]

"This is Jesus!"

Under the provisions of the New York emancipation law, slaves born after July 4, 1799, were freed when they reached a particular age: twen-ty-eight for men and twenty-five for women. For this reason Belle's other three daughters remained on the Dumont farm, where she could visit them regularly. After a while Belle settled her differences with the Dumonts and sent Sophia there to live with her sisters while Belle and Peter lived with the Quaker couple who had originally helped her.

Years before her freedom, when Belle had prayed to God for help in becoming free, she had promised Him that if it happened, she would try to be good and remember to pray. Once she was free, however, and things began to settle down, she forgot about God. Then, on a festi-val day, John Dumont brought a wagon and invited Belle to visit her family on his farm. What happened next was a pivotal event in Belle's life. Years later, Sojourner Truth described the event to Harriet Beecher Stowe, the author of *Uncle Tom's Cabin*, who wrote it down:

> Well, jest as I was goin' out to git into the wagon, *I met God*! an' says I, "O God, I didn't know as you was so great!" An' I turned

right round an' come into the house, an' set down in my room; for 'twas God all around me. I could feel it burnin', burnin', burnin' all around me, an' goin' through me; an' I saw I was so wicked, it seemed as ef it would burn me up. An' I said, "O somebody, somebody, stand between God an' me! for it burns me!" Then, honey, when I said so, I felt as it were somethin' like an *amberill* [umbrella] that came between me an' the light, an' I felt it was *somebody*,—somebody that stood between me an' God; an' it felt cool, like a shade; an' says I, "Who's this that stands between me an' God?"...I begun to feel 'twas somebody that loved me; an' I tried to know him....An' finally somethin' spoke out in me an' said, *This is Jesus*! An' I spoke out with all my might, an' says I, "*This is Jesus*! Glory be to God!" An' then the whole world grew bright, an' the trees they waved an' waved in glory, an' every little bit o' stone on the ground shone like glass; an' I shouted an' said, "Praise, praise, praise to the Lord!" An' I begun to feel such a love in my soul as I never felt before,—love to all creatures. An' then, all of a sudden, it stopped, an' I said, "Dar's de white folks that have abused you an' beat you an' abused your people,—think o' them!" But then there came another rush of love through my soul, an' I cried out loud,—"Lord, Lord, I can love *even de white folks*!"...I jes' walked round an' round in a dream. Jesus loved me! I knowed it,—I felt it. Jesus was my Jesus.[3]

Belle's conversion to Christ made a profound impact on her. Almost immediately she began preaching and talking about Jesus every chance she got. She took her children to church regularly and became very involved in the African Methodist Episcopal (AME) church. In fact, one member of the Dumont family described Belle during this time as a "roaring Methodist."[4]

Taking her son Peter with her, Belle moved to New York City in 1829, where she worked as a housekeeper until Peter was old enough to take care of himself. After many years in New York City, Belle felt God leading her to become an itinerant evangelist, going wherever He led her and depending on His providence to care for her needs. She already had a reputation as a powerful, forceful, and convincing preacher in her church; now God wanted her to step out and preach to others.

Belle felt that the name given her as a slave was inappropriate for a person setting out on a new life as God's pilgrim, so she asked God to give her a new name. She recalled a verse from Psalm 39: "Hear my prayer, O Lord, and give ear unto my cry...for I am a stranger with Thee, and a sojourner, as all my fathers were" (Ps. 39:12, KJV). She felt that "Sojourner" was a good name for someone who wandered up and down the land, showing the people their sins.[5]

She also wanted a new last name. Again remembering Scripture, she was inspired by Jesus' words, "And ye shall know the truth, and the truth shall make you free" (John 8:32, KJV). Since Sojourner now had only one master, God, and His name was Truth, she became Sojourner Truth.[6]

Years later, she explained her name change to Harriet Beecher Stowe:

> When I left the house of bondage, I left everything behind. I wa'nt goin' to keep nothin' of Egypt on me, an' so I went to the Lord an' asked Him to give me a new name. And the Lord gave me Sojourner, because I was to travel up an' down the land, showin' the people their sins, an' bein' a sign unto them. Afterwards I told the Lord I wanted another name, 'cause everybody else had two names; and the Lord gave me Truth, because I was to declare the truth to the people.[7]

Rise of an Activist

Following God's instruction to "go east," Sojourner headed across Long Island, preaching on the farms and in villages along the way. She had no trouble gathering a crowd because a black woman itinerant preacher was an oddity. Those who came to hear Sojourner were moved by the hymns she sang and by the persuasive power of her message and personality. Before long, her reputation spread until she was so popular that whenever she showed up at a religious gathering in a town or village, people flocked to hear her. Her message focused on the love and mercy of God and on the evils of slavery, which quickly became the central focus of her ministry.

Sojourner's travels eventually brought her to Northampton, Massachusetts, where she stayed for a while at a cooperative community, the Northampton Association of Education and Industry. The community, which operated a silkworm farm and made silk, was run by Samuel L. Hill, an ex-Quaker, and George Benson. Both men were ardent supporters of the abolition of slavery, and Benson was the brother-in-law of William Lloyd Garrison, who was considered by many to be the leader of the antislavery movement.[8]

Sojourner's stay at Northampton brought her into contact with many of the prominent abolitionist leaders of the day: Garrison, Wendell Phillips, Park Pillsbury, David Ruggles, and Frederick Douglass. Because of the forcefulness of her personality and her captivating hold on audiences, Sojourner was recruited by the abolitionists and began to travel with some of them, lecturing in many towns and villages. Also during her stay at Northampton, Sojourner heard lecturers advocating equal political and legal rights for women. This call for women's freedom struck a responsive chord in Sojourner's heart, and she became an active supporter and lecturer for women's rights. These were natural responses for her because she was black and a woman in a society that placed severe restrictions on both blacks and females.[9]

Where did Sojourner Truth get the courage to be so bold as a black woman in such a repressive society? She was absolutely convinced that God would protect her as she tried to follow His instructions and do His will. Once, before a meeting, trouble was anticipated. Her friends encouraged her to carry a pistol, but Sojourner responded, "I carry no weapon; the Lord will preserve me without weapons. I feel safe even in the midst of my enemies; for the truth is powerful and will prevail."[10]

God honored her faith. Even though she suffered much ridicule and abuse, at times being shouted down, spat upon, and even stoned, she never gave up, never lost faith, never wavered in courage, and never was seriously injured. The focus of Sojourner's abolitionist message was different from that of others. Whereas most abolitionists stressed the plight of the slaves, Sojourner stressed the plight of the slave owners, who, she warned, would end up in hell if they did not change. This was not speech tinged with hatred but rather Christlike concern.

At a meeting in Syracuse, New York, in 1850, she shared the podium with a popular abolitionist speaker named George Thompson. Some of the audience who had come to hear Thompson were angry when Sojourner rose to speak first. She demonstrated her remarkable ability to calm a crowd and speak right to their hearts when she said to them, "I'll tell you what Thompson is going to say to you. He is going to argue that the poor Negroes ought to be out of slavery and in the heavenly state of freedom. But, children, I'm against slavery because I want to keep the white folks who hold slaves from getting sent to hell."[11]

On another occasion, when the radical abolitionist Henry C. Wright bitterly attacked churches that cooperated with slavery, calling them "so-called churches," Sojourner disagreed. She said, "We ought to be like Christ. He said, 'Father, forgive them, they know not what they do.' If we want to lead the people, we must not be out of their sight."[12]

Advocate for Women

Sojourner Truth is remembered most for an extemporaneous speech she gave at a convention on women's rights held in Akron, Ohio, in 1851. Her attendance at the convention was unexpected. She had been lecturing in another Ohio town when she heard of the meeting in Akron. When she arrived, the church hosting the convention was already full.

Amid whispers and murmurs, Sojourner walked proudly to the front and sat down on one of the steps leading to the pulpit. No other seats were available. The others attending the conference had mixed reactions to Sojourner's presence. Some were eager to hear her speak, while others, fearing that her involvement with the abolitionist movement would lead to negative publicity for the Akron conference, appealed to Mrs. Frances Gage, the convener of the conference, to not let Sojourner speak.

During the first day of the conference, Sojourner made no attempt to speak. She simply sat quietly, listening to the different speakers. Both sides of the issue were debated. Most of those in attendance favored equal rights for women, but a number of people did not. Many of these were members of the clergy who sought to attack the movement on biblical grounds.

On the second day of the conference, Sojourner listened as a succession of ministers spoke. One claimed that men deserved greater rights and privileges than women because men were more intelligent than women. Another claimed that men should rule over women because Christ was a man. A third said that women had a lower status because Eve had committed the original sin. Still another minister said that women were inferior to men because they were weaker and had to be helped into carriages and over mud puddles and the like.

After this verbal barrage the room was silent. In those days there were few women who dared to speak up in a public meeting, particularly in the face of a strong male presence. Sojourner, however, had no such timidity. She stood up and moved to the podium, looking at Mrs. Gage for permission to speak. There were hisses and murmurs from those in the audience who did not want to hear her. Mrs. Gage hesitated for a few moments, then introduced the speaker by saying simply, "Sojourner Truth."

Sojourner calmed her audience by slowly and deliberately removing her bonnet and waiting for a few moments before beginning. She addressed point by point the arguments presented by the ministers who had preceded her:

> Dat man ober dar say dat womin needs to be helped into carriages, and lifted ober ditches, and to hab de best place everywhar. Nobody eber helps me into carriages, or ober mud-puddles, or gibs me any best place! And ain't I a woman? Look at me! Look at my arm! I have ploughed, and planted, and gathered into barns, and no man could head me! And ain't I a woman? I could work as much and eat as much as a man—when I could get it—and bear de lash as well! And ain't I a woman? I have borne...chilern, and seen 'em mos' all sold off to slavery, and when I cried out with my mother's grief, none but Jesus heard me! And ain't I a woman?[13]

Regarding the claim that men are more intelligent than women, Sojourner said, "What's intellect got to do wid womin's rights or black folks' rights? If my cup won't hold but a pint, and yours holds a quart, wouldn't you be mean not to let me have my little half-measure full?"[14]

To the minister who claimed women's inferiority because Christ was a man, Sojourner gave this rebuke: "Whar did your Christ come from? From God and a woman! Man had nothin' to do wid Him."[15]

Concerning Eve's position as the first sinner and thus relegating women to a lower position than men, Sojourner said, "If de fust woman God ever made was strong enough to turn de world upside down all alone, dese women togedder ought to be able to turn it back, and get it right side up again! And now dey is askin' to do it, de men better let 'em. Bleeged to ye for hearin' on me, and now ole Sojourner han't got nothin' more to say."[16]

Loud cheers and long applause followed Sojourner's spontaneous speech. It was the turning point of the conference, winning the day for the supporters of women's rights.

Sojourner's Legacy

Sojourner Truth approached life with dignity, courage, and deep commitment to the God who had shown His love to her in such a profound way. She remained a staunch advocate for women's rights and the abolition of slavery. Like many others she rejoiced at President Lincoln's signing of the Emancipation Proclamation in 1863. After the Civil War she worked tirelessly for the betterment and advancement of her race. We can take courage from the life of Sojourner Truth because, by God's help and direction, she overcame obstacles and met challenges greater than any that most of us will ever face.

She was black, female, and illiterate; yet she captivated and moved countless numbers of white, educated, and highly refined people. She conquered hatred and bitterness in her own heart and returned love and compassion to everyone, even to those who hated her and abused her. Sojourner's motivation for everything that she did was her love for God and His love shed abroad in her heart. She was endowed with a supernatural courage from beyond herself that made her fearless in the face of opposition. When she gave herself to the Lord, she gave herself completely, and He used her accordingly. Sojourner Truth spent more than fifty years on the front lines, and God sustained her and guided her steps.

God never changes in nature, purpose, or character. As He guided and sustained Sojourner Truth, so He will guide and sustain you and me as we trust and follow Him. The same courage He gave to her, He will give to us. We can believe Him and claim His promise.

Lord, I see that each one of us is a sojourner for Your truth, going through our lives in complete reliance on You. Help me to respond to your distinct call on my own life, and to obey you with all my strength. Give me the courage to face fear after fear, year after year. Whether or not my name ever becomes famous to other people, may I come know Your joy in me. Glory to Your holy name. Amen.

Chapter 6

🌿

Harriet Tubman

GO DOWN, MOSES

One day in April 1860, a fugitive slave named Charles Nalle was captured in Troy, New York. According to the Fugitive Slave Law of 1850, it was legal to capture runaway slaves found in the North and return them to their owners in the South. Nalle had escaped from a Virginia plantation in 1858 and joined his wife and children, who had been set free earlier, in Pennsylvania. They later moved to Troy, where Charles had found work. Charles and his wife were "octoroons"—one-eighth black and seven-eighths white—and therefore looked white. Nevertheless, a man in Troy suspected Charles of being a runaway and had him arrested.

Charles was held in the city courthouse, which was soon surrounded by angry protesters from the strongly antislavery town. The officials were hesitant to bring Nalle down through the crowd to a waiting wagon. Then an old black woman walked into the courthouse. Seeing a young boy nearby, she told him to run outside and yell, "Fire, fire!" as loudly as he could. In the ensuing chaos on the streets, the officials saw their chance and brought Charles downstairs. The old woman yelled through a window to the crowd, "Don't let them take him! Don't let them take him!" Then she attacked the nearest officer holding Nalle, knocking him down. Grabbing Nalle by the arm, she pulled him out of the courthouse and into the midst of the crowd.[1]

Nalle was transported by the crowd down to the river where a rowboat took him across. His mysterious rescuer followed in a ferryboat. On the other side a policeman saw Nalle's handcuffs and detained him.

He was taken to a nearby house. The old black woman and other rescuers promptly stormed the house. Two of them were wounded by police gunfire, but the woman and the others succeeded in rescuing Nalle once again. By chance, a man was passing by in a wagon. Upon finding out what was happening, he immediately relinquished his wagon. Nalle was put aboard with a few of his supporters, and they escaped to Schenectady, New York, and subsequently to Canada.[2]

The "old" black woman who so boldly secured Charles Nalle's rescue was in fact forty-year-old Harriet Tubman, herself a runaway slave with a heavy price on her head. Since her own escape from a Maryland plantation eleven years earlier, Harriet had repeatedly put her life on the line by returning to the South to lead many fellow slaves to freedom. On that day in Troy, Harriet was visiting a cousin and had heard about Nalle's capture. Although the broad daylight and public nature of the rescue were not typical of Harriet's methods, the bold action and unshakable courage were certainly characteristic of her.

Liberty or Death

Harriet's commitment to freedom—for herself as well as for others—was forged by two major influences in her life. The first of these was slavery itself. As a young child of six years, Harriet had been hired out by her owner to work for a succession of different people, many of whom abused her terribly. Very early she learned to endure the lash of the whip on her back and was often beaten severely for minor offenses—sometimes for no reason at all. As Harriet grew older, the conviction grew in her heart that everyone deserved to be free. Slavery was unjust. Freedom was worth any price.

The second influence in the development of Harriet's character was her faith. Along with many other slaves, Harriet and her family found strength and comfort in the community they shared together. Sundays afforded them the opportunity to gather for informal worship services. They listened to Bible stories, sang songs inspired by those stories, and prayed. The slaves found hope and encouragement in the experiences of biblical characters such as Job, Joseph, Noah, Paul, Abraham, and Moses. Jesus was especially dear to them because He had suffered the way they suffered.[3]

By the time Harriet reached adulthood, her hatred of slavery had made her determined to be free at any cost, while her faith in God had instilled in her a confidence in her success and a fearlessness regarding her own personal safety. Those who saw Harriet in action during her years of personally leading slaves to freedom were impressed by the fact that she displayed absolutely no fear for herself while taking every care to protect the runaways she was responsible for. She believed implicitly that God was directing her steps and protecting her, and that she would be taken only when and if God willed it. As Harriet herself expressed it to friends years later, "There are two things I have a right to, liberty or death. If I can't have one, I will have the other. For no man will take me alive. I will fight for my liberty as long as my strength lasts, and when the time comes for me to go, the Lord will let them take me."[4]

When she was twenty-five, Harriet married John Tubman, a free black man. John had been born free and therefore had never known what slavery was like. He had a difficult time understanding Harriet's burning desire to be free. When Harriet made the decision to run away, she could not persuade John to come north with her, so she determined to go alone.

Five years after her marriage, Harriet knew that the time had come to make her escape. She was prompted to act by the rumor and fear that she was about to be "sold south"—sold to another master in the deep South where escape was much less likely and conditions for slaves much worse than in Maryland. Harriet knew it was now or never. Carrying a slip of paper bearing the name of someone who would help her, Harriet took off through the woods one night. The paper had been given to her by a Quaker woman who had also given Harriet directions for finding the house where this person lived.

Harriet found the house and was welcomed and sheltered during the day hours. Then in the night she was taken to the edge of town and given directions for finding the next place of shelter. Harriet was now a "passenger" on the "Underground Railroad" that she had heard about since her childhood. Gradually over many days, traveling at night and taking shelter by day, Harriet covered more than ninety miles, finally reaching Wilmington, Delaware. She took shelter with a Quaker named Thomas Garrett, who ran a shoe store. He allowed Harriet to rest for a day and gave her new shoes to replace her worn-out ones. That night he took her to the road north and told her to watch for the wooden sign that would mark the state line between Delaware and Pennsylvania.

The moment she walked across the state line into Pennsylvania, which was a free state, Harriet was overwhelmed with joy. For the first time in her life she was free. Years later she described the feeling: "I looked at my hands to see if I was the same person now I was free. Dere was such a glory trou de trees and ober de fields, and I felt like I was in heaven."[5]

The "Moses" of Her People

Harriet made her way to Philadelphia, where she found work as a cook and maid at a hotel. She also found an inexpensive place to rent and began enjoying life as a free woman. Her heart was burdened, however, at the thought of her family—her brothers and sisters and her aging parents—still in bondage. She resolved within herself that with the Lord's help she would see all of them to freedom. Before long she became involved with the Philadelphia Vigilance Committee, a branch of the Underground Railroad. The Committee helped runaway slaves in every way possible—from organizing escapes to helping escapees adjust to freedom.

In 1850 the Committee learned that Harriet's sister Mary Ann and her family wanted to escape. They were in danger of being "sold south." The Committee made arrangements to get them as far as Baltimore, but they needed someone to bring them the rest of the way. Without a moment's hesitation Harriet said she would go.

Some of Harriet's friends were worried that she might be caught if she went back into Maryland, but Harriet herself had no such fear. She traveled to Baltimore, where she waited until her sister, brother-in-law, and their children arrived. Harriet hid them for several days and then successfully brought them to Philadelphia. This was the first of a total of nineteen trips into Maryland that Harriet made in the decade before the Civil War. She is credited with personally leading more than three hundred slaves to freedom, including, as she had promised, her parents and all her brothers and sisters and their families.

What is even more remarkable is that she never lost a single one.

Every slave who followed Harriet was delivered safely to freedom in the North. Harriet was bold, fearless, creative, cunning, and, when necessary, severe. Most of the runaways who followed her trusted her absolutely. Occasionally one or two would give in to fear and want to turn back. Whenever this happened, Harriet would pull a pistol from beneath her skirt and promise to shoot anyone who turned back. (Any runaways who returned home would be tortured into revealing information about the Underground Railroad, possibly endangering many lives. There was too much at stake.)

Time after time Harriet ventured into Maryland on her missions of freedom. Her reputation spread far and wide among the slaves, who called her the "Moses" of her people, as well as among the slaveholders, who put a $40,000 price on her head. Despite this, she labored on fearlessly, working hard and giving God the credit: "Jes' so long as he wanted to use me, he would take keer of me, an' when he didn't want me no longer, I was ready to go; I always tole him, 'I'm gwine to hole steady onto you, an' you've got to see me trou.'"[6]

Harriet talked to God constantly, and, in answer to her prayers, He spoke to her through dreams and visions. As a child of thirteen, Harriet had been severely injured when a plantation overseer, trying to stop a fleeing slave, had thrown an iron weight at him. Instead of hitting the man, the weight hit Harriet squarely on the forehead, crushing in the front of her skull. For weeks she had lingered at the point of death, in and out of consciousness. It took her months to recover. After this, she began to have vivid, even prophetic, dreams.

For the rest of her life, Harriet also suffered periodic attacks of narcolepsy—she would suddenly fall asleep in the middle of whatever she was saying or doing, sleep for a few minutes, then wake up, picking up where she had left off as though nothing had happened.

In 1851 Harriet made a trip into Maryland to lead James, her oldest brother, to freedom. James and two friends left with Harriet in the middle of the night. Unfortunately, their escape was discovered very early and they were quickly pursued by bloodhounds and men on horseback. It seemed that only a miracle could save them.

As they ran through the woods, Harriet heard a voice inside warning her of danger ahead. She turned to the left and the men followed, only to find their way blocked by a river. Harriet's voice told her to cross the river. Without hesitation she plunged in and began wading to the other side. The water rose to her waist, then to her shoulders, then to her chin. Then it got shallower again until she reached the other side. The three men with her hesitated at first, then plunged in after her with their pursuers close behind them in the woods. The four of them soon came to a cabin where a family of free blacks lived. There they received shelter and food. Later, Harriet learned that just ahead of them, before they had turned to cross the river, posters had been placed advertising rewards for their capture and officers had been waiting for them.[7]

Had Harriet not listened to the voice inside her, she and her charges would surely have been captured. This is just one example of the divine guidance and providence that sustained Harriet and helped her succeed against incredible odds. Harriet and those with her made it safely to the Wilmington, Delaware, home of Thomas Garrett, the Quaker who had originally helped Harriet during her own escape.

Garrett was quite impressed with Harriet, and particularly by her confidence in and dependence upon God. He said of her:

> For in truth I never met with any person, of any color, who had more confidence in the voice of God, as spoken direct to her soul....She talked with God, and he talked with her every day of her life....She felt no more fear of being arrested by her former master, or any other person, when in his immediate neighbor-hood, than she did in the State of New York, or Canada, for she said she never ventured [except] where God sent her, and her faith in the Supreme Power was great.[8]

Harriet's Legacy

Harriet settled with her parents in Auburn, New York, in 1857 and made her last trip into Maryland in November 1860, just a few months before the Civil War began. During the war she was recruited as a spy and a scout for the Union, and successfully carried out several infor-mation-gathering missions behind Confederate lines. She also served as a nurse, gaining quite a reputation as a healer. Harriet had learned from her father many native remedies from herbs and tree roots, and the medicines she made from these often worked better than the more modern kinds that the doctors used.

After the war she returned to Auburn, married Nelson Davis, a black soldier she had met during the war, and became involved in the women's suffrage movement. (Her first husband, who had stayed in Maryland, had also remarried.) She always opened her home to any who were in need—particularly blacks—and was so generous with her resources that she struggled all her life to have enough money for her own needs.

In her later years she established on her property a home for aged and impoverished blacks. Eventually, Harriet deeded the property and the home to the AME Zion Church, in which she was actively involved during her years in Auburn. Harriet Tubman died in Auburn on March 10, 1913, greatly admired and respected for her courage, service, and high Christian and moral character. She was given a military funeral.

Harriet Tubman's life is a testimony to what a person can do when he or she learns to listen to God's voice and obey without question. Because she trusted not in herself but in Him, she found His courage, strength, wisdom, insight, and protection available to her. Those same resources are ours as well if we will trust God and not depend on ourselves.

Heavenly Father, I offer myself to You once again, asking You to show me more clearly how to fulfill my destiny. I know that, like Harriet Tubman's call, mine will involve leading people out of slavery and bondage—of many kinds—into the glorious freedom of the kingdom of God. Although I may never speak on a public platform or see my name published, I want to serve You with a steady and courageous heart. Yes and amen!

Chapter 7

Aimee Semple McPherson

YESTERDAY, TODAY, AND FOREVER

It was a sight no one in Mount Forest, Ontario, had ever seen before: a slim, attractive young woman standing on a chair in the middle of the small town's main intersection. With her eyes closed and her arms raised, she said nothing and did not move. The crowd that quickly gathered around her was curious, amused, puzzled. Murmured questions were passed from one to another, receiving shrugged shoulders in reply. There were a few snickers. For several minutes the young woman stood silent and motionless as the ever-growing crowd stared at her.

Suddenly, she jumped off the chair, picked it up, and ran down the street, calling back to the crowd, "Follow me!" They did, and she led them into a small mission church building where, after the doors were closed behind them, she preached Christ to them. It was August 1915. The audience-gathering technique was a Salvation Army tactic known as a "Hallelujah run"; the meeting place was a tiny, struggling Pentecostal church named Victory Mission; and the energetic woman preacher was a twenty-four-year-old evangelist named Aimee Semple McPherson. This day was a significant one for Aimee; until her death nearly thirty years later, she never again had to work at gathering a crowd.[1]

One source of Aimee's tremendous appeal to the millions who flocked to her meetings over the years was that she never forgot who she was, a simple Canadian country farm girl. In fact, her story of how

God called her from her simple origins to do the work of His kingdom became a major theme in her preaching.

Another source of her popularity was her flair for the dramatic. Her style was different from that of anyone else. Early on, she developed the use of "illustrated sermons"—staged messages that eventually reached a complexity and quality equal to those of Hollywood films and professional theater. The primary reason for her lasting appeal, however, was the sincerity and simplicity of her message. Aimee Semple McPherson was genuinely concerned about the spiritual condition of the people who came to hear her, and it showed in her actions.

She preached a simple gospel centered on Hebrews 13:8: "Jesus Christ the same yesterday, and to day, and for ever" (KJV). How did a simple Canadian farm girl rise up to become one of the most popular, prominent, and influential Christian evangelists of the twentieth century, even being referred to by many as "the female Billy Sunday"?

Humble Beginnings

Aimee Elizabeth Kennedy was born October 9, 1890, in Salford, Ontario, Canada, to James and Minnie Kennedy. Minnie was James' second wife and was thirty-five years his junior—younger than any of his children by his deceased first wife. Minnie was originally brought into the Kennedy home to care for James' first wife as she struggled with her terminal illness. After her death, James decided to marry his wife's nurse. It was a marriage of convenience: James needed a woman on the farm, and Minnie, an orphan who had been traveling with some Salvation Army officers, needed a home.[2]

Aimee's early life revolved around the slow seasonal cycles of the farm, the Methodist church of her father, and the Salvation Army of her mother. All these factors helped shape Aimee's personality and character. Both Methodism and Salvationism were major influences in the later development of her spiritual attitudes and approach to ministry. From an early age Aimee displayed a talent for public speaking; during her school years she won several medals. She was a bright student, and by her teen years was in demand locally for parties, concerts, plays, and other types of entertainment. Popular, energetic, and fun loving, Aimee brightened up whatever corner she was in.

One day on the way to a drama rehearsal in nearby Ingersoll, Aimee stopped in at a small Pentecostal mission. She had heard a little about the "Pentecostals," was curious, and wanted to observe for a few minutes. In spite of herself she was captivated by the handsome young visiting evangelist who spoke with a melodic Irish brogue. His name was Robert Semple. After only a few minutes, Aimee was hooked, not only by Robert, but by his message as well. Realizing her need to repent of her sins and come to Jesus, Aimee agonized for three days over the cost of following God, then threw herself heart and soul into her new-found faith.[3]

For Aimee, once she had made her decision, there was no turning back, no halfway measures. It was all or nothing.

A Rocky Start

Before long, romance blossomed between Aimee and Robert, and they married at Aimee's home in August 1908. The newlyweds embarked on evangelistic work together, spending about a year ministering alongside William Durham, a former Baptist and early Pentecostal leader in Chicago. Answering the call for world evangelization that so many Pentecostals felt at the time, Robert and Aimee left Chicago in January 1910 to go to China as missionaries. They arrived in Hong Kong on June 1, 1910, and joined several other Pentecostal missionaries who were already there.

Their excitement was short lived, however. In August, after barely two months in China, both Robert and Aimee contracted severe cases of malaria. Aimee, eight months pregnant, recovered slowly, but Robert did not. On August 19, 1910, one week after their second anniversary, Robert died.

Sad, lonely, and confused, Aimee returned to the United States with her infant daughter, Roberta, and moved in with her mother, who was now living in New York City. (Minnie had answered the call of Salvation Army work in New York, leaving her aged husband James on the farm in Salford.) Aimee did some Salvation Army work for a few weeks but was increasingly restless. She took Roberta and went to Chicago to renew relationships with friends whom she and Robert had known there. A brief visit to her father in Salford followed. Aimee then went back to Chicago, hoping to settle and get involved in Pentecostal work there. Roberta's poor health intervened, however, and Aimee returned to New York City.

Early in 1911 Aimee met Harold McPherson. After several months of dating, he proposed marriage and she accepted. Minnie disapproved, however, so Harold and Aimee eloped to Chicago, where they were married in a civil ceremony. A church wedding followed a few weeks later. With this marriage to an American, Aimee became an American citizen.[4]

Unfortunately, the marriage was troubled from the start. Harold wanted Aimee to focus on him and their relationship, but Aimee quickly became heavily involved once more with her Pentecostal friends and the activities and ministries she and Robert had worked in a couple of years before.

During this time Aimee struggled with guilt over the feeling that she had abandoned the call of God that had once seemed so clear. She began to feel that she was being forced to make a decision between Harold and God. Even the birth of a son, Rolf, in March 1913, did not settle the domestic situation for Aimee and Harold. It took a severe health crisis for Aimee to decide her direction in life.

Late in 1913 Aimee fell ill and required surgery. She did not recover adequately and needed additional surgery. She resisted, apparently in the hope that God would heal her. An attack of appendicitis made her condition critical. Even after surgery she was not expected to live. While lying in a room set apart for the dying, Aimee heard a voice she believed to be God's saying, *"Now will you go?"* Recognizing that she had a choice of either entering eternity or entering the ministry, she yielded. Instantly her pain went away and she could breathe more easily. Within two weeks she was up and about.[5]

Harold did not understand Aimee's renewed commitment to God's call to full-time ministry. Aimee believed that God had spared her only because she had vowed to obey His call. She felt she had to follow God whether Harold did or not. In late June 1915, while Harold was out of town, Aimee took her children and went to Salford. Leaving them with her father and her mother, who was visiting from New York, Aimee attended a camp meeting in a nearby town where she ministered powerfully, speaking in tongues and praying for people to receive the baptism of the Holy Spirit. Her career as an evangelist was off and running.[6]

Immediately after leaving with their children, Aimee had sent a telegram to Harold: "I have tried to walk your way and have failed. Won't you come now and walk my way? I am sure we will be happy."[7]

After failing to persuade her to return through numerous letters and telegrams, Harold did show up for the meetings in Mount Forest, Ontario, where one night he received the baptism of the Holy Spirit. Following this, Aimee and Harold embarked together on a full-time evangelistic ministry, traveling up and down the eastern United States and holding meetings wherever they could. Harold was not really cut out for this kind of life, however, and they began to drift apart. Early in 1918, he and Aimee separated. They divorced in 1921.

San Diego, California, 1921

The end of her marriage to Harold was difficult personally for Aimee, but it enabled her to give single-minded devotion to her ministry. Once she began in earnest in 1915, her fame spread and her popularity grew. This remained true even later, despite the stigma of her divorce. Everywhere she went she experienced overflow crowds and the apparent presence and power of God in her meetings and messages.

By 1919 Aimee and her children had settled in Los Angeles, California, the city that would be her home for the rest of her life and that she used as a base for her itinerant evangelism. She always called her house on Orange Grove Drive in Los Angeles the "House That God Built," because the land, the house, its furnishings, and the landscaping—all just a half block away from a school for her children—had been donated to her by people attending her meetings.[8]

The year 1921 was one of remarkable meetings for Aimee, beginning in San Diego, California, in January. The meetings were held in the 3,000-seat Dreamland Arena, which very quickly proved inadequate to contain the crowds that turned out each day. Aimee conducted both preaching services and healing services, and the public response to both was phenomenal. Thousands had to be turned away every day, causing Aimee to institute a reservations system, giving free tickets to and reserving half of the building for those who had not yet been able to attend a service.[9]

Unlike many other evangelists of the time who stressed "hellfire and brimstone," Aimee focused on a message of love and acceptance. This was undoubtedly one of the major reasons for her enormous appeal. Aimee's message was, in her own words, "the simple story of Jesus' love, and the outpoured Holy Spirit who has come to convict us of sin and draw us to the cross of Calvary, where, as we confess our sin, Jesus…cleanseth us from all unrighteousness."[10]

She believed that the secret of her success was her emphasis on Christ. Originally scheduled for two weeks, the meetings were extended twice. Even after five weeks there was no ebb in the tide of people coming for prayer, especially prayer for healing. Aimee tried at first to pray personally for as many as possible, but the demand was too great. In response to the overwhelming need, two outdoor healing services were scheduled in Balboa Park. San Diego police, augmented by US Marines and US Army personnel, handled traffic and crowd control. A Salvation Army band, an orchestra, and a large combined choir were on hand. Aimee also depended on a group of local ministers present to assist in anointing the sick with oil, the laying on of hands, and praying for healing.[11]

As many as 30,000 people crowded into the park. The service began at 10:30 in the morning and by nightfall the sick were still coming. The January 1921 meetings in San Diego are just one example of the enormous popularity and influence that Aimee Semple McPherson enjoyed throughout her ministry, particularly in the early years.

The Foursquare Gospel

On January 1, 1923, Aimee Semple McPherson dedicated the Angelus Temple, the church building in Los Angeles that would become the hub of the wide-ranging ministries of her Echo Park Evangelistic Association. The full, or official, name of the church was the International Church of the Foursquare Gospel. The name "foursquare" referred to a four-point theme or emphasis that had become the doctrinal core of Aimee's preaching by the summer of 1922. The church history gives these details:

Aimee Semple McPherson explained Ezekiel's vision in the book of Ezekiel, chapter one. Ezekiel saw God revealed as a being with four different faces: a man, a lion, an ox and an eagle.

To Sister Aimee, those four faces were like the four phases of the gospel of Jesus Christ. In the face of the man, she saw Jesus our Savior. In the face of the lion, she saw Jesus the mighty Baptizer with the Holy Spirit and fire. In the face of the ox, she saw Jesus the Great Burden-Bearer, who took our infirmities and carried our sicknesses. In the face of the eagle, she saw Jesus the Coming King, who will return in power and victory for the church. It was a perfect, complete Gospel. It was a Gospel that faces squarely in every direction; it was the "Foursquare Gospel." The four symbols perhaps most identified with Foursquare today are the cross, cup, dove and crown which stand for Jesus the Savior, Jesus the Healer, Jesus the Baptizer with the Holy Spirit, and Jesus the Soon-Coming King, respectively.[12]

From the outset, Angelus Temple was one of the largest churches in Los Angeles. Its 5,300-seat sanctuary was filled to capacity regularly. The large platform area was built on hydraulic pistons so it could be raised or lowered to accommodate the needs of Aimee's illustrated sermons, which were an ever-popular feature of the Temple's Sunday night service. A full schedule of services of different types and for different age groups kept the church open seven days a week. Her message was so simple and straightforward, her style so warm, and her methods so innovative, that she attracted a wide and diverse audience: Hollywood actors and actresses, politicians, common folk, African Americans, and even members of the Ku Klux Klan.

The various ministries of the Temple were very practical in focus, seeking to meet human needs in any form. The Temple commissary, which began operation in 1923, provided for the needs of thousands of poor and destitute people in the Los Angeles area. Other ministries extended help to women in trouble, alcoholics, prostitutes, and the uneducated. The Angelus Temple Prayer Tower also began in 1923, receiving and praying for thousands of requests and needs. From its beginning and for decades after Aimee's death, the Prayer Tower operated twenty-four hours a day, every day of the year.

Each of these ministries reflected the heart of the woman who inspired them. Aimee genuinely loved people. She reached out personally to them wherever she went, often laboring far into the night to minister to them. People everywhere responded to her and loved her for her compassion.

Her heart for people also made her bold. She did not hesitate to go into a city's "red-light district" to talk with the prostitutes, to love them and share Jesus with them, and to invite them to her meetings. In San Diego in 1921, Aimee appeared between rounds at a boxing match to challenge those attending to find the "worst sinner in the city" and bring that person with them to the meeting the next night, where she promised to "go into the ring for Jesus."[13]

Aimee had a pioneering spirit and a vision for the future. This was demonstrated by the fact that in February 1924, radio station KFSG began broadcasting, making Angelus Temple one of the first churches in the country to own and operate its own radio transmission facility. Aimee Semple McPherson was also the first woman in America to own a radio-broadcasting license and was one of the first women to preach over the radio.

Another sign of her far-reaching vision was her establishment of a training institute for ministers and other Christian workers. The institute was named L.I.F.E.: the Lighthouse of International Foursquare Evangelism. Through the years (under the names Life Bible College and, today, Life Pacific College), this school has trained thousands of people for Christian ministry.

Aimee's Legacy

When Aimee Semple McPherson died on September 27, 1944, she left behind a remarkable record of accomplishments. The denomination she founded, the International Church of the Foursquare Gospel, still flourishes today with hundreds of churches and thousands of members worldwide. The Angelus Temple in Los Angeles still serves as the headquarters for the denomination and still conducts services with capacity crowds. Aimee was the most well-known and popular evangelist of her day. By all accounts, she was very effective in reaching people with the gospel. During her life she personally baptized over 100,000 people.

Although she is known by many for her healing ministry, her first priority was evangelism: winning people to saving faith in Jesus Christ. Healing was a vital part of what she called "full-gospel evangelism," but preaching Christ to save sinners was foremost.

Although she was a Pentecostal, she de-emphasized many of the more controversial aspects and manifestations of Pentecostalism. She did not prohibit them, but she kept things under control. Because of this and because of her infectious personality, Aimee's ministry enjoyed widespread interdenominational support. At one time or another, she held ministerial credentials from the Assemblies of God, a Methodist exhorter's license, and a Baptist preaching license.

Aimee Semple McPherson was a woman of courage. She overcame the grief and trauma of early widowhood and the stigma of two divorces (one from a later third marriage), and kept working to build a powerful and effective ministry. In a society that still placed significant social and public restrictions on women, Aimee prevailed against significant odds: prejudice against women ministers, the belief that women were not capable of succeeding without male guidance, and the belief that women did not have the ability to head large "business" organizations.

She was not afraid to speak the truth even against powerful people. One evening service at Angelus Temple was attended by hundreds of white-robed Ku Klux Klansmen. Aimee pulled no punches, saying to them plainly:

> You men who pride yourselves on patriotism, you men who have pledged yourselves to make America free for white Christianity, listen to me! Ask yourselves how is it possible to pretend to worship one of the greatest Jews who ever lived, Jesus Christ, and then to despise all living Jews? I say unto you as our Master said, "Judge not, that ye be not judged."[14]

Aimee even overcame the notorious scandal regarding her six-week disappearance in the spring of 1926. Her claim to have been kidnapped was never seriously investigated by the authorities, but their accusations of fraud, lying, and a sexual affair on her part fell to pieces under investigation because no evidence of any kind was uncovered to support them.

What was the secret of Aimee's success in ministry? Perhaps it can be summed up best in these words of triumphant declaration that Aimee herself wrote in 1935:

O'er my head the lightning flashes,
Dark'ning clouds the heavens fill;
But I'm sheltered 'neath the cross-tree,
In the center of God's will;
There I fear no power of darkness,
For tho' man the body kill,
Yet my soul shall live forever
In the center of God's will.[15]

🌿

Chapter 8

Lydia Christensen Prince

THE PEACE OF JERUSALEM

By the time she was thirty-six years old, Lydia Christensen seemed to have it all: a good job, a good salary, a generous inheritance from her late father, a secure future, a growing relationship with a man who cared about her, and the respect of her colleagues in her chosen profession. What more could she want? Lydia had already achieved the personal goals she had set for herself as a teacher. In addition to the standard certificates in history, geography, Danish, and English, she was one of the first teachers in Denmark to complete postgraduate study in domestic science. Now she was the director of domestic science in one of the largest and best-equipped schools in Denmark. Her department was used as a model for similar departments being established in other schools throughout the nation.[1] Lydia Christensen was at the height of her profession.

Like most Danish people of her generation, Lydia was a "good Lutheran"—baptized as an infant into the Danish state church, instructed as a child in its doctrines and beliefs, and settled in her religion as an adult, keeping it and God comfortably at arm's length. She had long since put away the childish things of religious devotion in favor of the sophisticated skepticism of the educated modern adult. Lydia had enough religion to be respectable but not enough to be inconvenienced.

By all normal standards of human measure, Lydia should have been happy, satisfied, and on top of the world. Yet she wasn't. Something was missing.

The Search for Meaning

As the Christmas holiday of 1926 approached, Lydia Christensen was growing more and more restless with her life. She sensed that there must be more than she was experiencing but had no idea what it was. Born into a well-to-do Danish family, Lydia was the youngest of three children and the only one still unmarried. While at home with her family over the holiday break, Lydia discussed her yearnings with her mother. The elder woman felt that what Lydia was missing was a home and children of her own. Although Lydia couldn't explain how she felt, she knew it was deeper than that. Fumbling for the right words, Lydia told her mother, "If there was something special in life that another woman wouldn't do—even if it was difficult or dangerous—that's what I'd like to do!"[2]

After Christmas, Lydia returned to her apartment in the Danish city of Korsor. She still had a week before school began again. Determined to find an answer to her inner restlessness, she gave her housekeeper the week off in order to spend the time completely alone. Bypassing the books of philosophy and literature on her shelf, Lydia pulled down the Bible that she hadn't read since her college days. She opened it to the gospel of Matthew and began reading. The Beatitudes in chapter 5 spoke to her heart, especially the words, "Blessed are they which do hunger and thirst after righteousness: for they shall be filled" (Matt. 5:6, KJV). Hungry and thirsty were just how she felt.

Reading further, she was particularly arrested by Jesus' words in the seventh chapter of Matthew:

> Ask, and it shall be given you; seek, and ye shall find; knock, and it shall be opened unto you: for every one that asketh receiveth; and he that seeketh findeth; and to him that knocketh it shall be opened....Enter ye in at the strait gate: for wide is the gate, and broad is the way, that leadeth to destruction, and many there be which go in thereat: because strait is the gate, and narrow is the way, which leadeth unto life, and few there be that find it (Matt. 7:7–8,13–14, KJV).

Lydia realized that if she were to find the way of peace and fulfillment, she had to enter through the gate. In order to find that gate, she would have to ask God to show her.[3] Kneeling in her living room, Lydia prayed aloud, "O God—I do not understand—I do not understand—who is God, who is Jesus, who is the Holy Ghost?...but if You will show me Jesus as a living reality, I will follow Him!"[4]

God answered Lydia's prayer. She saw a vision of Jesus standing before her, and for the first time in her life she knew—beyond doubt—that Jesus was real and that He was alive. Peace and joy flooded her heart. She developed a constant hunger for the Bible and for prayer. In response to her prayer, God delivered her instantly and completely from her smoking habit. A couple of weeks later, while reading in First John about joy, confession, cleansing, and forgiveness, Lydia was baptized in the Holy Spirit and spoke in tongues, something she had not consciously sought or prayed for because she knew very little about it.

Call to Jerusalem

During the same experience in which she spoke in tongues, Lydia received her second vision. She saw a barefooted woman in a long dress with an earthen jar balanced on her head. The woman was dancing slowly with her hands on her hips and chanting in a shrill voice. She was surrounded by a group of men who were clapping their hands in time to her song.[5] Lydia had no clue either to the woman's identity or nationality, yet she felt as if she were a part of the scene, as if she lived there or belonged there. It would be weeks before Lydia understood what it meant.

Lydia's conversion to Christ and baptism in the Holy Spirit created some difficulties for her professionally. Soon after these experiences she received water baptism by immersion and joined a small Pentecostal church. When word of this got around Lydia's school, she found herself ridiculed by her students behind her back and ostracized by her fellow teachers. There was even a movement begun among some of the faculty to force her to resign. She was called before her superiors to explain her actions. Although a formal review of her case by the Ministry of Education reaffirmed her right to her beliefs and her qualifications to teach, Lydia understood that her commitment to Christ had irreversibly changed many of her relationships.

Throughout this time, Lydia was still trying to understand the meaning of her vision of the dancing woman and was seeking to learn God's will for her future. When her pastor told her about some churches in Sweden where people went to receive spiritual counsel, she decided to devote her summer vacation of 1927 to visiting those Pentecostal churches. One Sunday, at the largest Pentecostal church in Stockholm, Lydia listened to Dr. Bengt Karlsson, a Swedish missionary to the Congo, speak of his work there and his plans to build a small hospital in the jungle. Lydia felt the clear voice of God that she should help. Under the Spirit's leadership she gave $3,000—most of what remained from the inheritance she had received from her father—to help pay for the hospital.

Lydia had an opportunity to speak with the Karlssons later, and she shared her own experiences, particularly her questions regarding her vision. As she described it to them, they helped her see that the dancing woman was dressed in the style of women in the Holy Land. From that moment Lydia began to sense a growing awareness that the Holy Land, and especially Jerusalem, figured significantly in God's plans for her.

As her conviction grew that God was leading her to go to Jerusalem—for what reason she had no idea—Lydia had to face several serious questions. Was she prepared to truly be a woman of faith? Could she trust God to guide her steps and to provide for her every need no matter what it was? She had no inheritance left. If she resigned from her teaching position, she would have no income. Because of her Pentecostal ties, no official Danish missionary society would appoint her. If she went to Jerusalem, she would be leaving behind everything and everyone she had ever known and would be *totally* dependent upon God. Was she ready to make those sacrifices? Did she have the faith to take that step?

Two events helped Lydia resolve these questions. On December 4, 1927, during a special day of prayer at her church in Korsor, Lydia received another vision: the face of a baby girl staring up at her with solemn black eyes. Lydia sensed that this child was a member of the growing family in Jerusalem—a family yet unknown to her—that she felt an increasing burden to pray for. The second event was a precise answer to a specific prayer. Even though Lydia did not need money, she prayed, "Please God, I want someone to give me five dollars before midnight tomorrow. If you will do this, then I will know that you can cause people to supply my needs even in Jerusalem."[6]

At 9:30 p.m. the next night, the school librarian, who was a Christian, stopped by and gave Lydia five dollars, saying that she had felt an unusual urging from God to do it. The next day, when she saw Lydia at school, the librarian gave her another fifteen dollars, explaining that God had laid on her heart all along to give twenty dollars, but for some reason she had only given five dollars the first time. Lydia realized that God had answered her prayer in the precise terms that she had requested. She no longer had any doubt that she was to go to Jerusalem.

During the spring school term of 1928, Lydia submitted her resignation, effective with the end of the term in July. Still not knowing *why* God wanted her in Jerusalem, Lydia began making preparations for her move. She sold her furniture, bought her steamship ticket, and arranged to be met in Palestine by a Swedish woman living in Jerusalem whose name Lydia had gotten from a missionary magazine.

Lydia sailed from Marseilles, France, on October 8, 1928, and arrived in Tel Aviv, Palestine, ten days later, where she was met by the Swedish woman as arranged. They took a taxi to Jerusalem, where Lydia spent the night with her new friend. The next day Lydia found a place of her own to rent. It was a small, sparsely furnished basement room, which had a separate door and stairway leading to the street above, in the home of a British missionary named Lorna Ratcliffe. Lydia settled in with all her worldly possessions: two suitcases and a little more than a hundred dollars in cash. Now it was up to God to supply her needs and reveal to her why she was there.

Care for the Children

As the first few weeks went by, Lydia's money dwindled and she was no closer to understanding why she was in Jerusalem. However, her conviction that God had led her there and had a purpose for her continued to grow. Her first impressions of the city of Jerusalem had been shocking, even frightening.

Only ten years before, at the end of World War I in 1918, thirteen centuries of Muslim rule in Palestine—including the previous two hundred years under the Ottoman Turks—had ended with the establishment of the British Mandate that now governed Palestine and the adjacent land of Transjordan. Relations between Arabs and Jews in the region—never very good to begin with—were strained even more under the new government. Tensions ran high. Yet early on Lydia began to develop an unshakable love for the ancient city. She discovered two passages from the Psalms that opened her eyes to God's attitude toward Jerusalem:[7]

> If I forget thee, O Jerusalem, let my right hand forget her cunning. If I do not remember thee, let my tongue cleave to the roof of my mouth; if I prefer not Jerusalem above my chief joy. (Ps. 137:5–6, KJV)

> Pray for the peace of Jerusalem: they shall prosper that love thee. (Ps. 122:6, KJV)

On Friday, December 28, 1928, a little more than two months after Lydia had arrived in Jerusalem, there was a knock on her door. Upon opening it, Lydia met a man named Eliezer Cohen. Mr. Cohen and his wife had a baby daughter named Tikva, who was dying. He asked Lydia if she would take Tikva.

Lydia was mystified. Was this her mission in Jerusalem, to care for a sick and dying child? Besides, how had Mr. Cohen even heard of her? At first Lydia put Mr. Cohen off, promising to pray about the situation. She then discovered why Mr. Cohen had come to her. An old, blind Arab woman named Nijmeh, a Christian who also lived with Lorna Ratcliffe, had met Tikva's mother earlier in the day and upon hearing of Tikva's condition, had recommended that they give the baby to Lydia. Nijmeh then explained that she had prayed for years for God to send someone to Jerusalem to care for children who had no home. Nijmeh believed that Lydia was that person.[8]

As Lydia prayed, she became more and more certain that God wanted her to take Tikva into her care. That very same day Lydia hurried over to the Cohen's house to pick her up. Tikva, though more than a year old, looked much younger because she was so thin and frail from illness. Her little body was burning with fever. Back at her basement room, Lydia placed Tikva in her wicker trunk and suddenly realized that Tikva was the baby she had seen in her vision during the church prayer meeting in Korsor. God had once again confirmed Lydia's calling to Jerusalem.

Lydia prayed for Tikva, claiming the promise found in James: "Is any sick among you? let him call for the elders of the church; and let them pray over him, anointing him with oil in the name of the Lord: And the prayer of faith shall save the sick, and the Lord shall raise him up" (Jas. 5:14–15a, KJV). She took some olive oil and anointed Tikva's forehead. Lydia then went to find Nijmeh, and the two women prayed together for Tikva. After a few hours Tikva's fever broke, and it became clear that she would recover.[9]

Eventually, after being returned to her parents, whose marriage had dissolved in the meantime, the little girl stayed with Lydia permanently and called her Mama.

Lydia's Legacy

Lydia Christensen's life in Jerusalem is a wonderful example of a life truly lived by faith. She left behind all she had known and, like Abram centuries before, traveled to an unknown land simply by God's direction. Her circumstances demanded complete trust in God for the provision of every need. Time after time her resources ran low, only to be replenished by the unexpected arrival of letters or cards containing gifts of money. Some came from her mother, some from her former colleagues at the school in Korsor, some from other friends she knew. Some of the gifts were anonymous. Whatever the source, Lydia continually found her needs met by a bountiful and faithful God.

Lydia's absolute faith in God also gave her courage. She endured much hardship, privation, hunger, thirst, and also physical danger in a city and land torn by the centuries-old hostilities and strife between Jews and Arabs. In time, she came to understand that her calling was not only to care for the homeless children of the city, but also to intercede in prayer—to pray continually for the "peace of Jerusalem."

Lydia lived in Jerusalem for more than twenty years, becoming "Mama" to scores of Arab and Jewish children she kept and loved and cared for in her home. In 1945 she met Derek Prince, a British soldier stationed in Jerusalem. At this time Lydia's "family" consisted of eight girls: six Jewish, one Palestinian Arab, and one English.[10] Derek had become a Christian several years before in the early days of World War II. After the war he took his discharge in Jerusalem, entered full-time

Christian ministry, and married Lydia. They remained in Jerusalem until 1948, witnessing the rebirth of the nation of Israel and enduring the new nation's war for independence.[11]

After leaving Israel, Lydia and Derek labored faithfully together through thirty years of marriage. Together, their Christian service ranged from pastoring churches in England, to running a school in Kenya, to heading up a large and expanding international Christian teaching ministry based in the United States. Their adopted daughters grew up and made their own lives.

Lydia died suddenly of heart failure in 1975 when she was in her mideighties. She left behind a legacy of countless lives changed by the power of God and the living Christ. This is particularly true for those children who lived with her during her years in Jerusalem. Another, perhaps even more important legacy is her heart for Jerusalem and its people and her insight into God's plan for Israel, gained through many years of faithful prayer and loving service. This insight is best understood in Lydia's own words from a letter she wrote to her mother:

> You ask what you can do to help....We Christians have a debt that has gone unpaid for many centuries—to Israel and to Jerusalem. It is to them that we owe the Bible, the prophets, the apostles, the Savior Himself. For far too long we have forgotten this debt, but now the time has come for us to begin repaying it—and there are two ways that we can do this. First, we need to repent of our sins against Israel: at best, our lack of gratitude and concern; at worst, our open contempt and persecution. Then, out of true love and concern, we must pray as the psalmist tells us, "for the peace of Jerusalem," remembering that peace can only come to Jerusalem as Israel turns back to God.[12]

Lydia Christenson Prince is not the only woman who has been called to be a burden bearer for Jesus, taking up her cross in a foreign land. She is also not the only one called to be an intercessor for Israel. Learning about her obedience and courage in the face of deprivation and unknown perils can infuse new strength to anyone who may be considering (or already following) the summons of Jesus.

Jesus, I am convinced that you are truly the Good Shepherd, and that you do not take your eye off even one of your sheep, but that you send trusted undershepherds to help protect them and care for them. I want to be sturdy and strong enough in my faith to qualify for your service. I want to be ready when you beckon to me to turn to the right or the left, to pick up or to lay down the burdens you give to me. Here I am; use me! Amen.

Chapter 9

Bertha Smith

WALKING IN THE SPIRIT

For two years Bertha Smith had endured the buzzing in her ears. Although it was not constant, it was always irritating. Usually it would start in one ear and then move to the other. A specialist had diagnosed her condition as a degenerative "growing in" of her eardrums, a condition for which there was no cure. He told her that she would eventually go deaf. During the two years after the diagnosis, Bertha prayed daily for God to heal her ears, but nothing had happened. At that time she was the only Baptist missionary in the town of Tsining in the Shantung province of China. The church there had no pastor, so Bertha, although she did not believe in women preachers, had taken up that responsibility out of necessity.

A Chinese pastor from a large church in another Chinese city was invited to preach for a week in Bertha's church in Tsining. Pastor Fan Wei Ming had a reputation for praying for the sick, so on his first day in Tsining, Bertha asked him to pray for healing for her ears. He put her off until later in the week. The preaching theme for the week was personal holiness for Christians. Pastor Fan preached about the Feast of Unleavened Bread, urging all who heard to search their hearts for any leaven (sin) that was there.

During this week Bertha became increasingly convinced by the Holy Spirit that she was going to be healed. The Spirit also led her into a deep awareness of the leaven in her own heart, particularly how she had used her ears to sin, always craving the compliments of others and the praise of men. Her conviction was so strong that for a time she could not eat or sleep. She confessed her sin to the Lord and committed her ears to Him for cleansing, also surrendering her whole being to Him.

On the last Sunday of the meetings, several people gathered in Bertha's living room for prayer. Pastor Fan asked Bertha if she still wanted prayer for her ears. When she said that she did, he read from the book of Exodus: "And the Lord said unto him, Who hath made man's mouth? or who maketh the dumb, or deaf, or the seeing, or the blind? have not I the Lord?" (Ex. 4:11, KJV). As they read, Bertha felt a physical sensation on each side of her face, as if a tight tendon was being loosed. Pastor Fan read from chapter 5 of James and then prayed.

Although Bertha knew in her spirit that she would be healed, healing did not come immediately. The buzzing continued, this time with a painful aching that became almost unbearable.[1]

After a month of this aching, Bertha prayed, "Lord, you know that these ears are not mine! They were definitely given over to you, and since they are yours, they cannot hurt unless you let them hurt. Now if you do, it will be for some purpose and you will enable me to stand it, I know."[2]

Within two weeks the pain and buzzing were completely gone. Two years later, when Bertha was in the United States on furlough, a physical examination confirmed that her eardrums were in perfect condition with no evidence that there had ever been a problem.[3]

Called to China

Bertha's healing occurred in 1935 and is just one of many remarkable events in the life of a remarkable woman who lived in revival for seventy years. For nearly forty-two years she gave herself to China as a missionary, witnessing and participating in one of the greatest revivals in history as it swept across China in the 1920s and 1930s. Retiring in 1958 at the age of 70, Bertha returned to the United States, where she undertook another ministry of almost thirty years, awakening American Christians to their need for revival and inspiring them to pray for it.[4]

Olive Bertha Smith was appointed as a missionary to China by the Foreign Mission Board of the Southern Baptist Convention on July 3, 1917.[5] She was twenty-eight years old. Her life since her conversion to Christ in 1905 had been marked by several deepening experiences in her walk with the Lord. The first came in 1907 when, during a revival service in her hometown of Cowpens, South Carolina, Bertha surrendered herself completely to the lordship of Jesus Christ for anything that He might choose for her. She determined that nothing would be too much for Him to ask of her.[6]

At this time she received her first "in-filling" of the Holy Spirit. As Bertha understood it, both then and to a greater degree later, being filled with the Holy Spirit was meant to be a continual and repeated experience for the Christian. It was dependent upon a believer's cleansed life, free of all unconfessed and unrenounced sin, and upon a constant yielding of oneself to the Spirit's leadership. It was the practical working out of Paul's instruction to the Galatians: "If we live in the Spirit, let us also walk in the Spirit" (Gal. 5:25, KJV).

Another deepening experience for Bertha came in 1910, when she answered God's call on her life for mission service. A college student at the time, she struggled with the issue for several weeks, considering what sacrifices such a commitment would require. It would mean leaving home for many years, perhaps for life. Would her family approve? What settled it for her was the realization that Jesus Christ had given up the glories of heaven, lived on the earth, and died a shameful death for her, all because it was the Father's will. How could she do any less than obey His will?

When she yielded to God's call, a joy filled her heart that never left her.[7]

Prelude to Revival

When Bertha first arrived in China, she quickly became concerned about the low level of spirituality and commitment among Chinese believers. This was a burden shared by all the other missionaries as well.[8] They believed that a genuine revival was the only answer. Their conviction about this was strengthened as many of the missionaries experienced personal revivals in their own lives.

God was moving in the Shantung province of China, preparing the land for a great outpouring of the Holy Spirit. He began by working in the hearts and lives of the missionaries. During the summer months the missionaries had opportunities to attend annual conferences on various themes related to the spiritual life. These conferences were character-ized by dynamic speakers and teachers and a powerful moving of the Holy Spirit to such a degree that many of the missionaries received deep refreshing and significant spiritual renewal. Bertha was one of these.

The most significant change for her was learning the secret to con-sistent victory in her Christian life—victory over her "old self." The key was in not trying to *overcome* the flesh—an impossible task—but in regarding it as *dead,* crucified with Christ. She realized that she had been wrongly struggling to crucify herself, rather than considering it already dead in Christ.[9]

It was the truth that Paul taught the Romans when he wrote, "Likewise reckon ye also yourselves to be dead indeed unto sin, but alive unto God through Jesus Christ our Lord" (Rom. 6:11, KJV). Bertha explained the truth this way: "You cannot consecrate the old sinful self to God; you assign it to death."[10]

Bertha and the other missionaries felt an increasing burden from the Lord to pray for revival in China. This became so intense that they set aside the first day of each month for that specific purpose. They maintained this practice faithfully for several years before revival came. This committed, consistent discipline of prayer was one of the cata-lysts for the great revival that swept across the Shantung province, and indeed all of China, in 1927.

Another catalyst in the revival was an Evangelical Lutheran mis-sionary from Norway named Marie Monsen. God used this deeply spiritual woman to spark revival fires wherever she went. In March 1927, she fled to the Chinese port city of Chefoo to escape political unrest farther inland. Many other missionaries had taken temporary refuge in Chefoo also. Among them were Bertha and the other Southern Baptist missionaries with whom she worked. They invited Marie to share her testimony with them, and she told of her experiences in Bible teaching and evangelism in the field, and also of the many instances she had seen of sick people being healed by the grace of God. The testi-mony of divine healing was a new and unusual concept for the Baptist missionaries, yet they were profoundly moved and touched by Marie Monsen's words.[11]

Marie believed that a great revival was coming to China and that it would come through the Baptists. When Dr. Charles L. Culpepper, one of the Baptist missionaries and the president of the small Baptist seminary in Shantung, asked her why it would be the Baptists, she answered, "Because you, more than any others, have fulfilled the promise of 2 Chronicles 7:14."[12] This verse reads:

> If my people, which are called by my name, shall humble themselves, and pray, and seek my face, and turn from their wicked ways; then will I hear from heaven, and will forgive their sin, and will heal their land. (KJV)

The Shantung Revival

If any single event can be said to be the "beginning" of the Shantung revival, it was the powerful prayer meeting in March 1927 that involved Marie Monsen and the Baptist missionaries. The Holy Spirit inspired brokenness and deep confession of personal sin on the part of the missionaries. They resolved differences between one another, and the result was a great cleansing of their lives and hearts.

The primary purpose of the prayer meeting was to pray for the physical healing of Mrs. Ola Culpepper, Dr. Culpepper's wife, who had suffered for many years from optic neuritis—the decay of the optic nerve. It was a painful and degenerative condition. Although she was slowly going blind, Mrs. Culpepper could still see relatively well with glasses. After the time of confession and cleansing, the missionaries laid hands on Mrs. Culpepper and prayed for her. The Spirit was so strong that when two Chinese cooks who worked at the mission, and who had great animosity toward each other, walked into the room, they were immediately brought under deep conviction. They confessed their sins to each other and accepted Christ as their Savior on the spot.

After this Mrs. Culpepper testified that her pain was completely gone. It never returned. Although the vision in her most severely damaged eye was not completely restored, her vision in both eyes improved significantly and permanently.[13]

Although everyone in the group rejoiced at the goodness and grace of God, Bertha suddenly felt convicted by their behavior. She told the others how inconsistent it seemed to spend so much time in confession, soul-searching, and prayer for each other when they had never done so in order to pray for the spiritual awakening of the Chinese people. Bertha's words hit the group like a thunderclap. As Bertha described it:

> Our mountaintop of ecstasy suddenly became a valley of humiliation. We all went to our knees in contrite confession for having been so careless as to have gone along supposing that we were right with the Lord, while holding all kinds of attitudes which could have kept the Lord's living water from flowing through us to the Chinese.[14]

From this beginning, the revival began to spread as the missionaries returned to their various mission stations. It next affected the Chinese pastors and Bible-teaching women in the mission schools, and from there it spread into the general Chinese population. Confession of sin, restitution, and a strong emphasis on verifying one's genuine conversion to Christ by being "born of the Spirit" were hallmarks of this tremendous awakening. The progress of the revival demonstrated the spiritual principle that "cleansing precedes fullness, and the in-filling of the Holy Spirit precedes joy and effective service."[15]

The Holy Spirit moved mightily until every church in the Shantung province had been affected. Many nominal church members who had never truly trusted Christ for salvation were genuinely converted. Many other believers in the churches experienced significant deepening in their relationships with Christ. There was a renewed burden for evangelism and a greatly increased hunger for God and for His Word. Thousands of believers experienced the joy of the Lord as never before and were filled with the Spirit, discovering for the first time the power of God for evangelism, discipleship, and service. As believers got their lives right with God and with each other, relationships were healed and true Christian fellowship became possible.

People outside the churches saw the change that occurred in the lives of the revived believers. As a result, countless numbers of Chinese were brought to Christ.[16]

The Shantung revival made a significant impact on the Chinese churches throughout the land. The direct and immediate effects of the revival continued into the 1930s and beyond. In many ways, the effects are still being felt. Nothing that God does occurs without a purpose. The awakening of the Christian church in China came at just the right time to strengthen it and prepare it for the dark years ahead—years of danger and oppression first by the Japanese occupiers before and during World War II and then by the Communists. Without the awakening, the Christian Church in China probably would not have survived.

Days of Occupation

Bertha's experiences in China both before and during the Shantung revival set the tone and pattern for the rest of her life. Once she understood the principles of dying to self and how to be filled with the Spirit on a continuing basis, her life was never again the same. The secret was to keep her "sins confessed up to date." It was important to keep a short sin account before God—to confess and renounce sin as soon as the Holy Spirit revealed it to her. This is the same principle that she taught countless believers through the remaining years of her life.

When the Japanese invaded China in the spring of 1937, Bertha faced a dilemma. The two primary missionaries, a married couple with whom she worked with in Tsining, were in the United States on furlough; she was the only missionary in the town. The American government had urged all Americans to leave the country and declared that it would not be responsible for the safety or welfare of any who decided to stay. Bertha debated what to do. Through prayer she became convinced that she should stay. It was God who had placed her in China, not the American government. She could not bear to leave the Chinese people, particularly the Chinese Christians who would be undergoing such hardship.[17]

While war raged in the countryside in every direction from Tsining, Bertha labored faithfully and courageously. She opened the church for daily services, focusing on sharing the gospel to win people to Christ. She opened her home for any who wanted personal help in making decisions to receive Christ. Bertha knew that many of these Chinese would soon be fleeing from the Japanese; she knew that many of them would die. She was deeply concerned that they come to Christ and be firmly established in the faith while there was time. She regularly visited the local hospital to talk with the wounded soldiers and tell them about Jesus.[18]

Bertha made a practice of seeking God's specific, direct guidance for every move she made. There were so many needs, that effective ministry was possible no other way. She could not address everyone, so she depended on God to show her where to go, what to do, and whom to talk to. In this way, walking with God, she was led to the people in whom He was already working.

After Tsining fell to the Japanese, the mission compound where Bertha lived and worked housed many refugees, most of them women. Japanese soldiers were constantly looking for girls and young women for illicit purposes, and more than once Bertha squared off face-to-face with the soldiers, protecting those whom God had placed under her care. She had a holy boldness born from many years of prayer and fellowship with Christ. Bertha was totally surrendered to God and trusted Him absolutely, and He protected, provided, and guided her steps.

After the United States entered the war, Bertha and other American missionaries were interned for a time in the mission compound. Eventually, Bertha was given an opportunity to return to the United States. This time she took it and did not return to China until after the war.

Bertha's Legacy

After the Communist takeover of China, all Christian missionaries were forced to leave the country. This is when the Lord opened a door for Bertha, now sixty years old, to become the first Southern Baptist missionary on the island of Formosa (Taiwan). There she labored faithfully for another ten years, planting churches, teaching seminary classes, and helping to firmly establish the mission work on the island.

In December 1958, she retired from active missionary service and returned to her hometown of Cowpens, South Carolina. God was not yet through with Bertha Smith, however. For almost thirty years, until her death in 1988 (just five months short of her one-hundredth birthday), Bertha was in demand to speak at churches and conferences all over America.

She felt that God had told her to "go home and tell" Christians in America about revival and being filled with the Spirit, and to encourage them to seek and pray for spiritual awakening in America such as had occurred in China during the Shantung revival. During her travels and constant speaking engagements, she touched thousands of lives. She was totally surrendered to Jesus Christ to the very end. A month before her death, she led a Chinese businessman to Christ in Spartanburg, South Carolina.[19]

In addition to a legacy of changed lives in China, America, and other parts of the world, Bertha Smith left a legacy in the form of the Peniel Prayer Center, a retreat center for spiritual life conferences that was created near her childhood home in Cowpens. Until 2004, the Center provided opportunities for believers to learn the principles of revival, the Spirit-filled life, and spiritual victory that Bertha Smith so exemplified throughout her life.

The secret of Bertha's courage and effectiveness throughout a century-long life is that she learned how to die to self—to regard herself as being dead to sin but alive to God through Jesus Christ (see Rom. 6:11). That is the key to spiritual victory, to personal revival, and to effectiveness in ministry. Bertha Smith lived her life with spiritual courage and holy boldness because, like the apostle Paul, she knew that "to live is Christ, and to die is gain" (Phil. 1:21 KJV).

> Saving Lord, along with Paul, I declare that I have been "crucified with Christ and I no longer live, but Christ lives in me. The life I now live in the body, I live by faith in the Son of God, who loved me and gave himself for me" (Gal. 2:20). Search my heart and show me what doesn't belong there. Give me the courage to confess my specific sins to You, asking for forgiveness and cleansing that will result in a new infilling of your Holy Spirit. Keep me by Your side, Lord, in holy love. Amen.

Chapter 10

Corrie ten Boom

NO PIT SO DEEP

As arrests of Jews in the streets became more frequent, I had begun picking up and delivering work for our Jewish customers myself so that they would not have to venture into the center of town. And so one evening in the early spring of 1942 I was in the home of a doctor and his wife....The Heemstras and I were talking about the things that were discussed whenever a group of people got together in those days, rationing and the news from England, when down the stairs piped a childish voice. "Daddy! You didn't tuck us in!" Dr. Heemstra was on his feet in an instant. With an apology to his wife and me he hurried upstairs and in a minute we heard a game of hide-and-seek going and the shrill laughter of two children. That was all. Nothing had changed. Mrs. Heemstra continued with her recipe for stretching the tea ration with rose leaves. And yet everything was changed. For in that instant, reality broke through the numbness that had grown in me since the invasion. At any minute there might be a rap on this door. These children, this mother and father, might be ordered to the back of a truck. Dr. Heemstra came back to the living room and the conversation rambled on. But under the words a prayer was forming in my heart. "Lord Jesus, I offer myself for Your people. In any way. Any place. Any time." And then an extraordinary thing happened. Even as I prayed, that waking dream passed again before my eyes. I saw again those four black horses and the Grote Markt. As I had on the night of the invasion I scanned the passengers drawn so unwillingly behind them. Father, Betsie, Willem, myself—leaving Haarlem, leaving all that was sure and safe—going where?[1]

This is how Corrie ten Boom, a fifty-year-old unmarried Dutch watchmaker, described the turning point in her life. Shortly after this Corrie and other members of her family put their lives on the line to harbor and assist frightened people who had become enemies of the state for no other reason than that they were Jews. In defiance of the repressive Nazi government that occupied their beloved Holland, the Ten Boom family hid fugitive Jews in their home and helped them escape to freedom. By the time it was all over, Corrie's father, oldest sister, and a nephew had died in concentration camps. Other family members spent time in jail, and Corrie herself survived ten months of imprisonment, first in a Dutch prison, then in a concentration camp in Holland, and finally in the infamous Ravensbruck camp in Germany, where 96,000 women died.

A Pattern of Preparation

From all external appearances, there was little about Corrie ten Boom's first fifty years of life that would lead anyone to expect that she would ever become involved in such dangerous activities. She lived all those years in the same house where she was born: an ancient structure known as the Beje, which housed her father's watch and clock shop on the first floor and the family's living quarters on the floors above. With her oldest sister, Betsie, Corrie helped her father in the watch shop. She took such an interest in the work that she eventually became the first licensed woman watchmaker in Holland.

Corrie and her family were active members of the Dutch Reformed Church. These early years were characterized by a regular, comfortable routine to everyday life. Yet within this familiar sameness of day-to-day life, God was preparing Corrie and her family for the great acts of courage and devotion that they would be called upon to perform during the years of Nazi oppression.

Corrie was only five years old when she accepted Jesus Christ as her Savior and Lord. When the great crisis came in her life, she had already spent forty-five years walking with Him. For more than twenty of those years, Corrie had planned and led weekly worship services for the retarded children of the city. The daily routine of life in the Beje included family Bible reading and prayer at breakfast in the morning and before retiring for the night. Despite the family's modest means, the Ten Booms opened their home to people in need. Consequently, the presence of guests and strangers around the Ten Boom dining table was a familiar sight to Corrie.

The Ten Boom family believed that the Christian faith was to be lived out, not just believed and talked about. Day by day their lives were focused on relating to people through the ordinary circumstances of life, just as Jesus did. Such Christlike living became almost as natural to them as breathing. When the Nazi occupation of Holland forced extraordinary circumstances upon them and brought scores of desperate people their way, the Ten Booms responded according to the pattern established over a lifetime of faithfulness to God. Corrie came to understand later how God prepares us for what lies ahead. She said, "I know that the experiences of our lives, when we let God use them, become the mysterious and perfect preparation for the work He will give us to do."[2]

Working for the Underground

After the Germans began occupying Holland in the spring of 1940, conditions of life for the Dutch people gradually deteriorated and grew more and more repressive. Every person was required to carry identification at all times, and it had to be presented at the demand of any member of the occupying forces. Food and other goods were severely rationed. Young men between the ages of sixteen and thirty were subject at any time to be hauled off to work as virtual slave laborers in German factories. Even minor offenses could mean imprisonment without trial for indefinite periods.

The most oppressive of all was the increasing persecution of Jews. All Jews were required to wear a Star of David made of bright yellow cloth that was prominently displayed on their outer clothing. Verbal abuse and ridicule on the streets led to the routine vandalism of Jewish businesses. Before long, Jews were being rounded up on the streets without warning. Jewish homes were raided in the middle of the night and families carried away in the darkness.

The Ten Boom family became directly involved for the first time in November 1941, when Mr. Weil, the Jewish furrier across the street, was ejected from his shop by four German soldiers who smashed his display cases, threw his clothing and personal belongings into the street, and carried off his furs. During all this activity, Corrie and her sister Betsie quickly ushered the man to shelter in the Beje. That same evening, with the assistance of their brother Willem and his son Kik, Mr. Weil was taken to safety.[3]

By the summer of 1942, the Beje had become the center of an underground operation that focused on harboring Jews who were hiding from the Nazis and helping them escape to safety. All of the Ten Booms were involved: Corrie, Betsie, and their father, all of whom lived in the Beje, as well as Corrie's brother Willem and his family and her older sister Nollie and her family, who lived in homes of their own. Corrie was regarded as the "leader" of the operation in the Beje. It began on a small scale, harboring two or three fugitives for a day or two until arrangements could be made to lead them to safety.

Within a short time the operation grew to a more sophisticated level: an illegal radio carefully hidden beneath the stairs; extra ration cards to provide escapees a means of getting food; an electrical buzzer system to warn of approaching trouble; a visual warning system to let outsiders know whether or not the coast was clear; and their personal telephone secretly reconnected even though it was illegal for private families to have phones.

Eventually, the Beje became the permanent home for seven Jews who could not be placed elsewhere. They took their meals regularly at the Ten Booms' table. A false wall was constructed in Corrie's bedroom on the top floor of the house, concealing behind it a crawl space only eighteen inches wide yet large enough for all seven "houseguests" to hide for several days if necessary. Practice drills were held until all seven could be concealed without a trace in just over one minute. Such care was crucial to their survival in the event of a raid.

One of the things that sustained the Ten Booms' underground

operation was their sensitivity to God's leadership. Corrie learned to trust the direct leadership of God for specific decisions, particularly with regard to people. In a social and political environment in which the wisest human course was to trust no one, it nevertheless was necessary on occasion for Corrie to seek help from someone who could supply a particular need. The risk was in not knowing whether the person approached would be sympathetic or would betray the operation to the Nazi authorities.

Time after time Corrie received what she called the "gift of knowledge" when these decisions were needed.[4] Her brother Willem had told Corrie to develop her own sources. When reflecting on this, Corrie realized another value of having lived quietly in the same place for years: they knew someone in every business and service in the city![5] As Corrie remembered:

> We didn't know, of course, the political views of all these people. But—and here I felt a strange leaping of my heart—God did! My job was simply to follow His leading one step at a time, holding every decision up to Him in prayer. I knew I was not clever or subtle or sophisticated; if the Beje was becoming a meeting place for need and supply, it was through some strategy far higher than mine.[6]

On February 28, 1944, after about eighteen months of underground activity, the inevitable happened: the Beje was raided. The Ten Booms had been betrayed by a Dutch man working for the Nazis who had posed as a Jew needing help. During the raid, Corrie, Betsie, and their father were arrested, along with numerous others who appeared at the Beje, unaware that anything was wrong. The seven Jews sheltered there were not discovered, however; all had made it into the secret room in Corrie's bedroom. After several days in hiding, they were able to escape to safety.

The Ten Booms and the other prisoners were taken to the local police station for processing, where they spent the night under guard in a gymnasium. The next day they were taken to the town square and put on a bus for prison. In all, several dozen people in the underground were taken, including Corrie's brother Willem and sister Nollie. The scene at the square seemed strangely familiar to Corrie. Then she realized that she had seen it twice before in a vision: once on the night Germany invaded Holland and once on the night of her "turning point," during her visit to the Heemstras.[7]

Neither Corrie nor any of the others knew what was in store as they were driven away from their homes by their captors. They knew only that their lives were in God's hands. In reality, the next very difficult phase of God's plan for them—the plan for which He had been preparing them all through the years—was about to unfold.

If I Make My Bed in Hell...

Ten years after the family's arrest, a Dutch policeman still remembered the Ten Booms' first night when they were held in the police station gymnasium. He told Corrie:

> I shall never forget that night. There was an atmosphere as if there were a feast, even though most of you were on your way to die in prison. I remember that just before your father tried to sleep, he said, "Children, let us pray together." Tired from the ordeal, but with a radiance on his face, he offered comfort from God's Word, Psalms 91:1 [KJV]: *He that dwelleth in the secret place of the most High shall abide under the shadow of the Almighty.*[8]

It was the family's faith and confidence in God's protection that would sustain them through the horrors that lay ahead. The next day the prisoners were transported to a Dutch prison in the coastal town of Scheveningen. There Corrie and Betsie were held for several months. While in prison they received word that Willem, Nollie, and all the others taken in the raid at the Beje had been released after a few weeks. They eventually learned that their father, who was well into his eighties, had died after only ten days in prison.

In the late spring of 1944, Betsie and Corrie were transferred to Vught, a concentration camp on Dutch soil. There, using a small Bible they had received from Nollie while they were in prison, Corrie and Betsie held secret prayer meetings in the barracks at night, sharing the light and hope of Jesus Christ with the other women. It was during this time also that Corrie found in Christ the power to forgive the man who had betrayed them to the Gestapo. In fact, the final letter Corrie wrote from prison before being sent to Ravensbruck was to this man. Her letter declared her forgiveness and pointed him to Jesus Christ as the source of eternal salvation.[9]

As the Allied forces advanced after the invasion of Europe in June 1944, the camp at Vught was evacuated. Corrie and Betsie and hundreds of others were transported by freight train to Ravensbruck, a larger and much more brutal camp in Germany. If any place could have earned the designation of "hell on earth," it would have been Ravensbruck. Yet it was here, in the midst of the darkness of human sin and brutality, that the light of Christ shone brightly in the lives and witness of the Ten Boom sisters.

God encouraged them by confirming His continuing presence with them through several miraculous events. First, He made it possible for them to smuggle their Bible, a bottle of vitamins, and a sweater past the careful eyes and searching hands of the guards.[10] Betsie's health, never very good, was deteriorating, and she needed the sweater for warmth and the vitamins for strength. The Bible they needed for their own faith and as a means to share the love of God in a place where love appeared to be dead.

Second, the tiny bottle of liquid vitamins served not only Betsie's needs, but also the needs of other sick women in the barracks. Day after day, week after week, dose after dose, the vitamins kept coming long after the contents should have been exhausted. It was a miracle that paralleled the biblical story of the poor widow of Zarephath, who gave the prophet Elijah a room in her home. She gave Elijah food when she had none to spare for herself and her son. By the providence of God, her small supply of meal and oil did not run out until the drought ended in Israel (see 1 Kings 17:9–16). In Ravensbruck, the very day a prisoner who worked in the camp hospital smuggled a supply of vitamins to the Ten Booms' barracks, not another drop appeared from their bottle.[11]

Third, the barracks were heavily infested with fleas. Corrie could not understand why Betsie insisted on thanking God for the fleas, but they did anyway in accordance with Paul's admonition, "In every thing give thanks: for this is the will of God in Christ Jesus concerning you" (1 Thess. 5:18, KJV).[12] They soon discovered that the camp guards rarely came into the barracks because of the fleas. Corrie and Betsie were free almost without hindrance to pray, witness, and read the Bible to the ever-increasing circle of women who gathered to hear the words of hope and life.[13]

As Corrie and Betsie walked with God in Ravensbruck, He used them to bless hundreds of other prisoners. He also spoke to them, especially Betsie, regarding the future. They had a vision of a beautiful home in spacious surroundings; a home where concentration camp survivors could come for spiritual, emotional, and psychological healing; a home where they could live until they were ready to return to the normal world.[14] Another vision was of a German concentration camp, transformed after the war into a home where people warped by the philosophy of hate, force, and violence taught by the Nazis, could learn of love, peace, and the forgiveness of Christ. [15]

Betsie's health continued to decline until she was released from outside work and eventually was put in the camp hospital in December 1944. While in the hospital, Betsie shared with Corrie a final dream:

> We must tell people what we have learned here. We must tell them that there is no pit so deep that He is not deeper still. They will listen to us, Corrie, because we have been here....By the first of the year, Corrie, we will be out of prison![16]

Betsie's words came true. The very next day she died in the hospital. When Corrie came to see Betsie's body, she witnessed another miracle. The day before, Betsie's face had been hollow from hunger and disease and deeply lined from care and grief. Now, in death,

> her face was full and young again. All signs of disease and pain were gone. As Corrie described her: "In front of me was the Betsie of Haarlem, happy and at peace. Stronger! Freer! This was the Betsie of heaven, bursting with joy and health."[17]

Three days later, Corrie received her notice of discharge. Her release was delayed for several days while she was treated for swelling in her legs. Finally, on January 1, 1945, she walked out of Ravensbruck a free woman. Both she and Betsie had been released, Betsie to heaven and Corrie to the outside world.

Now it was time for her to tell the world what she and Betsie had learned.

Corrie's Legacy

As soon as she was free and had returned home, Corrie began to speak wherever she had opportunity. God immediately opened the door for the home for concentration camp survivors to become a reality. A wealthy Dutch widow donated her elegant suburban estate, and the home received its first residents in June 1945. It remains in operation today under the auspices of the Dutch Reformed Church.[18]

In 1946, Betsie's second vision, the home for rehabilitation and renewal for Germans, was fulfilled with the reopening of Darmstadt, a former concentration camp in Germany. Under the direction of the German Lutheran Church, it remained in operation until 1960.[19]

Corrie embarked on another journey of nearly forty years, traveling the world as a self-described "tramp for the Lord," visiting sixty-one countries on both sides of the Iron Curtain with her gospel message. Wherever she went, to whomever she spoke, she shared the truth that she and Betsie had learned in Ravensbruck: that Jesus can turn loss into glory.[20]

During the remainder of her life, she influenced countless thousands, perhaps even millions, by the testimony of her life and her witness to God's faithfulness. As a "tramp for the Lord," Corrie sought God's direct guidance concerning where to go and how long to stay, trusting Him to provide for her every need. She never appealed for money or other kinds of financial support. This was part of her absolute trust in the God who had sustained her so absolutely throughout her life and particularly in Ravensbruck.

Corrie ten Boom's courage came from a source beyond herself. It lay in the One for whom she had lived exclusively since the age of five; the One whom she had met daily in the pages of the Bible; the One to whom she prayed regularly. In all her years she never found Him to fail. Corrie ten Boom found courage because she knew that God is good and that God is faithful. He never puts on us more than we can bear.

Whatever He requires of us, He equips us to do. Corrie walked with God and in His strength bore the unbearable and prevailed to victory.

Let's ask for the grace to walk the crucified life that this woman on the front lines lived for the glory of her Master.

Father God, You know the present challenges that I am facing, and You are the only one who knows what my future holds. I trust you implicitly for every detail, believing that whenever You chose to allow a seeming tragedy to penetrate Your protection over me, you will supply the grace and faith to carry on without wavering. Your ways are above our ways, but You are utterly faithful to Your children. Once again, I entrust my whole life into Your more-than-capable hands. Amen.

Chapter 11

Jackie Pullinger

LIGHTING THE DARKNESS

I loved the dark city. I loved wandering down the narrow lanes which were like some exaggerated stageset. It upset me to see twelve- or thirteen-year-old prostitutes and to learn that these girls were not free, having been sold by parents or boyfriends. It troubled me to meet their minders—the aged mamasans who sat on the orange boxes in the streets luring the Walled City voyeurs with promises of "she's very good, very young, very cheap." I noticed their hands, which were scarred on the back with needle marks from the heroin injections which made the job bearable. Or maybe the job was to pay for the heroin. There were bodies at that time lying in the streets near the drug dens: they could have been alive or dead after "chasing the dragon" (a popular way of inhaling heroin through a tube held over heated tinfoil). There were the "weather men" who guarded the alley exits and the entrances to the heroin huts where up to a hundred people "chased" in lonely chorus. I saw thousands of poor people living in one-room dwellings: many were so crammed that they had to sleep in shifts because they could not all lie down at the same time. I saw some who still lived with pigs, neither able to see the light of day….I loved this dark place. I hated what was happening in it but I wanted to be nowhere else. I dreamed of walking into heroin dens, laying hands on men and seeing them set free. I dreamed of praying with the blind in the dark lanes, touching them, and watching their eyes open. It was almost as if I could already see another city in its place and that city was ablaze with light. It was my dream. There were no more crying, no more death or pain. The sick were healed, addicts set free, the hungry filled. There were families for orphans, homes for the homeless, and new dignity for those who had lived in shame. I had no idea how to bring this about but with "visionary zeal" imagined introducing the Walled City people to the one who could change it all: Jesus.[1]

Jackie Pullinger had talked about being a missionary since she was five years old, even though for many years she had no real idea what a missionary was. She had a conventional English upbringing—attending a boarding school and being confirmed in the Church of England. Higher education followed at the Royal College of Music, where Jackie studied piano and oboe.[2]

Upon completing her degree she began a career teaching music. However, she could not escape the feeling that she needed to give her life to something. Although she had been confirmed in the Church of England, the Christian faith did not become real to Jackie until she was in college. She encountered a group of friends who obviously enjoyed their relationship with Jesus and could discuss their experience and feelings about it with ease and joy. This concept intrigued Jackie. She states,

> This was the first time that I had met Christians who did not look unhappy, guilty or grim, and my music college Christian Union…had only served to confirm my worst fears and impressions of earnest organists trying to get to heaven. I preferred brass players. I avoided the Christians while unable to avoid the unhappy conviction that at some time God himself would nail me for my shortcomings and I would have to account for my life.[3]

From Music Teacher to Missionary

Through her new Christian friends, Jackie was confronted with the reality of Jesus Christ, His sacrifice on the cross, and the good news of God's love and forgiveness that was available through Jesus. It changed her life dramatically. After accepting Jesus as her Lord and Savior, she found herself filled with a great joy, and rather than becoming more limited and grim, her life became more fun than ever before. Sharing this good news with others became a spontaneous outpouring of her newfound joy and peace. She developed a great burden for those who did not know this joy and personal relationship with Jesus and who were lost and bound for hell.

God reawakened within Jackie her childhood dream of becoming a missionary, but she was a single woman and too young and unqualified to be accepted by any of the conventional missionary societies. Every door seemed shut, and she wondered if she had heard God correctly. Desperate for answers and direction, Jackie attended a special prayer meeting with friends, and there God spoke to her. He said, *Go. Trust Me, and I will lead you. I will instruct you and lead you in the way in which you shall go; I will guide you with My eye.* At that, Jackie knew that she must take action and obey.

After much prayer and godly counsel, Jackie decided that God had doors to open for her that she had not yet seen. She decided to allow God to lead her directly and go on a daring adventure. She bought the cheapest boat ticket that stopped at the greatest number of countries and prayed for God's direction to know where to get off and how He wanted her to proceed from there. So with this great act of faith, Jackie found herself stepping off a boat in Hong Kong in 1966, after traveling halfway around the globe.

She had no missionary agency or organized support back in Great Britain, no job, and no contacts. She had very little money and no clear direction of what God had in store for her, but she had the assurance that God had called her and would continue to direct her.

The Walled City

Soon after her arrival in Hong Kong, Jackie was hired to teach music three afternoons a week in a primary school operated by a Mrs. Donnithorne. The school was located within a six-acre enclave of Hong Kong known as the Walled City. One of its Chinese names is "Hak Nam," which means "darkness." Cramped, secluded, and filthy, the Walled City was home to anywhere from 30,000 to 60,000 people—no one knew for sure how many—and it was a haven of opium dens, heroin huts, brothels, pornography theaters, illegal gambling, smuggling, and all other kinds of vice.

Virtually ignored by the rest of Hong Kong, the Walled City was accessible only through dark, narrow alleys between shops located on its outer edges. There were no sanitary facilities—refuse and excrement were simply dumped out in the streets and alleys—and electricity was illegally tapped from supplies outside the City.[4]

Daily life in the Walled City was defined by a number Triad gangs who controlled all aspects of vice, extortion, and crime. The boundaries of each gang's territory were clearly defined, and violence between rival gangs was frequent. Gang membership provided a sense of family and acceptance that young Chinese men rarely found elsewhere in "Hak Nam." The city called "darkness" was in great need of the light of Jesus, and Jackie's teaching work gave her access to the Walled City, where she began trying to relate to the people she met there, seeking to share the light of Christ as she had opportunity. Externally, the Walled City was one of the most revolting places on earth, yet every time she entered it, Jackie felt a profound sense of joy. This confirmed for her that she was where God had called her.[5]

At first Jackie met with little success. She had a lot of zeal, but could show few obvious results. This was made apparent one day as she tried to share Jesus with a young corner prostitute who looked old before her time. She squatted all day long over a sewer, attracting no customers:

> She had no radio; she could not read. She looked dead before her life had even started. I tried the "Jesus loves you" routine on her and touched her to show her I meant it. She looked terrified. "You've made a mistake. You don't know who I am. You're not supposed to touch people like me." Looking back now I can see how ridiculous it was to be walking down alleyways talking intensely of Jesus. Of course, no one could respond to words about Christ. They had never met him and had no evidence of his love. When I checked, I found he had never done it that way either; instead of declaring "I love you," Jesus had shown his love through action. He opened the eyes of the blind man,

caused the lame to leap for joy and fed five thousand hungry people full to bursting.[6]

She Showed Them Jesus

This thought planted a dream deep within this radical disciple. She wanted these desperately needy people to know Jesus, but in order for them to meet Him, she realized that she must first show Him to them. Jackie began a youth club to reach out to the young people of the Walled City. This club enabled her to befriend young people who were members of the feared Triad organizations. God touched her in a new way, and she began to pray intensely for the people within the dark Walled City. Suddenly light began to break through the darkness around her and lives began to be changed one by one.

Jackie took seriously her call to help the people at their point of need. She went to bat for the poor and helped them obtain assistance and housing from government agencies. She planned activities to give the young people alternatives to the vices around them. She looked for ways to help and minister to the most "poor in spirit and body" of those around her, which ultimately led her to preaching Jesus and ministering to the needs of the drug addicts. Jackie discovered that a sincere heart, prayer, and praise could often help an addict go through withdrawal in a short and relatively painless way.[7]

It was not long after this that Jackie found herself sitting across a tea table from one of the most powerful Triad bosses in the Walled City. He had become frustrated with the problem of addiction among his own followers. Although the Triads regularly dealt in drug trafficking, actual addiction often made their members useless to their gang. He made the amazing proposal to give Jackie the addicts of his group so she could get them off drugs.

Jackie, however, refused. She wouldn't help the young men break free of their heroin addiction only to return to their lives of violence and crime. The leader then made her an offer never heard before; he told her that he would release from the Triad any of its members who wanted to follow Jesus. (Triad membership was always considered a lifetime commitment, and persons attempting to leave it often would be severely punished.) What an offer! What an opportunity for her Lord!

St. Stephen's Society

This arrangement gave Jackie an even greater "green light" for ministry to the drug addicts of the Walled City. She found that many of the people she helped among the addicted, poor, crippled, and homeless literally had nowhere to go and no way to start a new life. Eventually this led to the development of special homes for them and to the founding of what became the St. Stephen's Society, a ministry actively involved in all aspects of help and rehabilitation to the people of Hong Kong who were in need.

Jackie's one-woman crusade within the Walled City not only led to the development of a very successful drug rehabilitation program but also gave birth to an active, vibrant, Spirit-empowered church within the confines of the Walled City. Special group homes and ministries were formed, and after a while the government gave them facilities in which to continue their work and house the needy on a greater scale. These facilities became known as Hang Fook Camp, and they served as base of operations for Jackie and the St. Stephen's Society for several years. But her emphasis stayed the same: the preaching of the cross, holy abandonment, and the power of prayer.

The Power of Prayer

Jackie's modern-day exploits with God rival the stories in the book of Acts. Her keys are the cross of Christ and a revelation of our dependency on God through prayer.

This power of prayer is well demonstrated in her story about a young man named Alie:

Alie...was studying to be a Buddhist monk. Alie was also facing court charges as an alleged accomplice with seven other men in the murder of a rival drug lord. Jackie began to visit this particular Hong Kong jail every week to minister and to testify to these men, and specifically to Alie. Four of the men came to the Lord almost immediately. But though Jackie visited the jail every day for nine months testifying to Alie about Jesus through a thick glass partition, he was unmoved. Alie wouldn't admit it, but he was very afraid of dying for a crime that he did not do. Week after week, Jackie...continued to minister to him. "I know that you are afraid, Alie. I know that you are terrified of death, but I want to tell you that there is a loving God. There is a God of justice who knows all things and He is a Father of mercy. And I have enlisted Christians from all across the world to pray and fast on every Wednesday for you, Alie."

Although Alie heard and understood the things Jackie was saying, he still refused to come to the Lord because his heart was hard. One day the governor of the jail and a jail attendant passed by Alie's cell and remarked to one another that they smelled something. They did not know what the strange fragrance was, but they thought it was some kind of delicate perfume with a fragrant odor. They began asking Alie questions about the fragrance, but Alie said, "What smell?" Perplexed, the two men asked other inmates about the smell, as the entire jail cell took on the fragrant odor of this strange perfume. Finally, the governor of the jail sent authorities into Alie's cell. They searched his body and found nothing. When they sniffed the air around him, they nodded and said, "Yes, the smell is here." Yet Alie still smelled nothing.

When the guards left, Alie began to ask himself, *What is that smell?* Then a little word trickled down inside him. It was this simple message: "Oh, it is Wednesday!" Suddenly, he remembered Jackie's words. *He was smelling prayer!* He realized his entire jail cell was filled with the fragrant aroma of the prayers of the saints.[8]

As a result, Alie eventually accepted Jesus as his Savior. Such stories are common in Jackie's ministry, due to the prayers of faithful saints.

Transitions with Hong Kong and with Jackie

The Walled City itself was torn down in 1992, and the Kowloon Walled City Park was opened in 1995. In 1996, Jackie and her organization were requested to leave Hang Fook Camp. Because no alternative accommodations became available, the St. Stephen's Society had to disperse and decentralize its activities. At last report, this seeming "dispersion" has actually sparked greater life and activity among the people and churches of Hong Kong, and many individuals have risen up to continue the society's ministry on a one-to-one and house-to-house basis. It has become a wonderful expression of the body of Christ in action.

As Jackie has stated, "All of this is what I've been sharing and teaching on for years, and with the loss of a big centre it's meant that people have taken more responsibility for their own groups and lives....we are [also] continuing on a regular basis to do outreaches, feeding the poor, the old people, street sleepers, etc."[9]

In 1997, Hong Kong was turned over to the Chinese government. Yet lives continue to be changed as a result of the work Jackie began in the late 1960s. The St. Stephen's Society also has broadened its vision to include missions and ministry throughout Asia. Jackie travels periodically to Britain and the United States to speak and to teach. She actively exhorts believers that "every Christian must be directly involved with reaching out to the poor—meaning: people with needs which they are unable to help themselves, such as addictions, abject poverty, victims of child abuse or spouse abuse,"[10] and as a result, even more lives continue to be transformed.

Eventually, after years of serving her Lord as a single white "proper" British woman in an Asian crime-ridden society, Jackie's life took another radical shift in 1992. She married a tall Chinese convert to the faith, John To. Sadly, after only seven years of marriage, John died of cancer. Jackie's ministry, however, continues to this day.

Jackie's Legacy

Through Jackie's ministry in the Walled City over the years, hundreds of Chinese came to Christ: drug dealers, drug addicts, prostitutes, gang members, and gang bosses. God was able to do a mighty work among the lost and outcast people of the Walled City in Hong Kong because a young English woman had the faith to believe that He would lead her and the courage to act on that faith. Jackie Pullinger entered Hong Kong with no human resources to fall back on. She followed the Spirit's leading to Hong Kong and knew that she was totally dependent upon God for her protection, resources, and success. Her life is a testimony to the truth that there is no limit to what one person can accomplish when he or she commits him or herself completely into the hands of the Lord.

Taking the Baton

Jackie Pullinger, and these other valiant women warriors—these healers, brave souls, and pioneers whose lives we have just read about—are only a few of the many whom God has used through the years. Regardless of their differences in calling and life work, all have them have carried the same banner—passion for Jesus and compassion for people.

But simply reading about them is not enough. I hope that these chapters don't just inspire you; I hope they unsettle you. It's time now to get up from your chair and "seize the day."

> Jesus, You are the Savior of the world, and in order to reach the lost ones in this vast world, You need the hands and feet and voices—and hearts—of many, many passionate people. I volunteer mine to You, for Your purposes. Whether You keep me right in my neighborhood or send me far away, I want to follow where You lead. Show me what to do, when to do it, and how to do it. Surround me with like-minded others who can pray and help. Above all, help me to stir up the heart of compassion that comes from Your Spirit, so that everything I do will express Your love to each individual I meet. Unquestionably, I need You. Unquestioningly, I follow You. Amen and amen!

Part Three

Seize
the Day

Chapter 12

✿

YOU ARE CHOSEN

Consider for a moment the nine women whose lives we have profiled in this book. They are so different from each other in race, nationality, culture, background, and time in history. What is the common bond between them? What connects Joan of Arc, Vibia Perpetua, Sojourner Truth, Harriet Tubman, Aimee Semple McPherson, Lydia Christensen Prince, Bertha Smith, Corrie ten Boom, and Jackie Pullinger? Very simply, they are all *ordinary women* who knew an *extraordinary God*. When they gave to Him their very ordinariness, when they came to Him in their human weakness, He showed Himself strong on their behalf and used them in extraordinary ways.

You may feel that you are the least qualified for God to use and the most unlikely candidate for His Spirit to fall upon. But you know what? You are just the kind of person He chooses! God makes a point of choosing the weak things of the world to shame the mighty and the foolish things of the world to shame the wise (see 1 Cor. 1:27). God is revealed and glorified in your weakness. The apostle Paul himself knew this. He wrote to the Corinthians:

He has said to me, "My grace is sufficient for you [My lovingkindness and My mercy are more than enough—always available—regardless of the situation]; for [My] power is being perfected [and is completed and shows itself most effectively] in [your] weakness." Therefore, I will all the more gladly boast in my weaknesses, so that the power of Christ [may completely enfold me and] may dwell in me. (2 Cor. 12:9, AMP)

Do you fall into the category of the weak, the ordinary, the least likely? If you do, take heart! You are a prime target for the Lord to come and wrap Himself around you. Isn't that great news?

Chosen Ones

Years ago I had a dream in which I was entering a large coliseum. It was in a foreign country, and the king's court was about to convene. Every woman who entered the building was given a number. Mine was number 29. The king had not yet come out, so I sat down to watch the proceedings.

I ended up sitting next to a woman who simply despised me, no matter how hard I tried to be nice. For some reason I just irritated the daylights out of her. Anything nice I tried to do or say was like rubbing salt into a wound. She became extremely hostile to me and was constantly reviling me—putting cigarette ashes on my head and that kind of thing.

In this dream, during the preliminary proceedings prior to the king's appearance, someone was calling out the different numbers assigned to the women in the room. Whoever's number was called had to go spend the night with a man, whether or not she wanted to.

The hateful woman next to me called out my number. I was so sickened at the thought of what I was supposed to do that I simply got up and ran out of the auditorium as fast as I could. Unknown to me at the time, the king's son had come out and was going to choose his bride that day. He had heard my number—number 29—called and had seen me run away. He put his fingers to his lips and said, "I like that. She ran away from evil. I choose *her!*" Everyone began looking around, saying, "Where is she? Where did she go?"

Suddenly, I came back in, dressed in regal robes. My face looked totally different. I knew it was me, but I didn't recognize myself. I approached the court and stood in front of the king's son. He kissed me and gave me a scepter. There were two thrones and we both turned around and sat down in them. That's how the dream ended.

I have come to understand since then that this dream wasn't just for me, but for all of us—the Bride of Christ. It is a dream of where the Lord wants to take us. We are His chosen ones, set apart before we were ever born. Paul told the Ephesians:

For he chose us in him before the creation of the world to be holy and blameless in his sight. In love he predestined us for adoption to sonship through Jesus Christ, in accordance with his pleasure and will—to the praise of his glorious grace, which he has freely given us in the One he loves. (Eph. 1:4–6)

For years I asked the Lord, *God, what's the deal about number 29? What does it mean?* He answered my question by showing me Scriptures such as "'For I know the plans I have for you,'" declares the Lord, "'plans to prosper you and not to harm you, plans to give you hope and a future'" (Jer. 29:11); "But you are a chosen race, A royal priesthood, a consecrated nation, a [special] people for God's own possession, so that you may proclaim the excellencies [the wonderful deeds and virtues and perfections] of Him who called you out of darkness into His marvelous light" (1 Pet. 2:9, AMP); Esther 2:9 (which tells how Esther is given the choice place in the king's harem); and Psalm 29 (which describes the voice of the Lord thundering, causing the deer to calf, stripping bare the forests, echoing across the waters, and *breaking open the way*).

Then there is Acts 29. Now, I know there is no chapter 29 in the book of Acts, because it ends with chapter 28. But *we're writing it.* That's what we're called to come into. We have been chosen. That's what the number 29 means—chosen.

Being a Chosen One Carries Responsibilities

When you accept yourself as among those whom God has chosen, you must understand that your position carries great responsibilities as well as privileges. I am so thankful that the Lord is bringing a release for women in ministry today. He is setting us free and unshackling our voices, our arms, our legs, and our hearts. In the midst of it all, though, we must be careful to keep our focus pure. In the days ahead we will have opportunities for far more battles than we can possibly endure. Therefore, we must choose wisely and carefully discern the battles that the Lord has given us to fight.

You see, the issue isn't the Lord's releasing women. The issue is the lordship of Jesus Christ. We're not here to promote our own camp. Constant harping on "equality for women" comes from the wrong spirit. We want to build the body of Christ, and that means focusing on *unity.* It means repairing the breach between men and women. We have to be very careful when we as women stand before anyone that we are not guilty of self-exaltation.

Jesus told us in Luke 14:10 to take the lowest seat and to let the host invite us to a higher place. We should not assume that higher place ourselves. I know that in many cases women have taken leadership or responsibility because men have failed to do so. Women have seen the need and jumped in. Unfortunately, many times they have done so out of a wrong spirit and have taken an inheritance that was not meant for them.

God doesn't intend for it to be an "either–or" setup but a "both–and" arrangement. We are to be laborers *together* with God, as Paul says in 1 Corinthians 3:9. Whether we are men or women, we are to take our stations on the wall and do our jobs, thankfully receiving the inheritance that God has given us and running with it, all the while helping those next to us to do the same. It's called servant leadership, and it requires a humble heart. You must be willing to take the low place and let God be the one who raises you up.

If you want to be able to walk in the authority God wants to release to you, then you must learn how to walk *under* the authority that is over you—the Lord's authority. If you want to see release in your own life, then you must be in right relationship with the Lord and with those whom He has placed in authority over you. When you are in your proper place, doing God's will and exercising the gifts and function that He has given you in the body of Christ, then you experience victory and effectiveness and can impart to others their sense of destiny and calling.

You must find the place that God has for you and work there in partnership with others, both men and women. You must also be humble and discerning in your spirit lest you usurp an inheritance meant for others. Each of us has a great responsibility to the generation that will follow us—our children. If they are to fully realize their place in God's plan, then we must give them a pure stream from which to drink—a stream unpolluted by bitterness, contention, division, unbelief, and fear; a stream where the way ahead has been cleared by pioneers and heroes who have gone before.

A Time for Heroes

The book of Nehemiah describes how the exiled Jews who returned to Jerusalem rebuilt the walls of the city and repaired many of the buildings. In the third chapter we find an interesting reference: "Beyond him, Nehemiah son of Azbuk, ruler of a half-district of Beth Zur, made repairs up to a point opposite the tombs of David, as far as the artificial pool and the House of the Heroes" (Neh. 3:16).

What was the "House of the Heroes"? According to historians, it was probably a barracks that had a special section set aside to honor the memories and exploits of the great heroes of the faith and of the Israelite nation. It probably contained artifacts or other memorabilia such as scrolls, carvings, shields, swords, and the like. The House of the Heroes was where the memory of the great ones was not only recalled, but also perpetuated and imparted to succeeding generations. An integral part of the restoration of Jerusalem and the returning of the people of God was the restoration of the House of the Heroes. These people recognized the importance of keeping alive the memories of the heroes of God.

Today there is a heroic anointing that God wants to place on His people. We have not been set free simply to celebrate our freedom; we have been set free for a purpose. God is restoring in this generation the heroic anointing of His male and female leaders to shape a generation that will walk in power. A hero is someone who breaks through a barrier in one generation so that other people, another generation, can go even farther. A hero is someone who lifts a canopy of oppression in one generation so that others can stand up under it.

For example, for centuries no man or woman on earth had ever broken the four-minute mile. In 1954 a British medical student by the name of Roger Bannister developed some new ways of training and broke the four-minute mile for the first time in history. You might think that a record that took so long to achieve would stand for a long time. However, less than two months later, someone else broke the four-minute mile. By the end of the year, thirteen people had done it. Once someone proves that something can be done, it creates an environment of the possible, an impartation of hope and possibility that enables others to do it. It is a natural principle. The person who first breaks through the barrier makes it possible mentally and physically for others to break through. That's what being a hero means.

We have had many singular pioneers in past generations. What is different about today is that God has issued a call and is raising up thousands upon thousands of people like you and me to be the heroes and the pioneers for the generations that will follow us. It's great to be free in Christ, but if we celebrate that freedom for its own sake and hoard it for our own private benefit, then we will miss the ultimate calling that we have as heroes in our generation.

We are guardians of a deposit that God is pouring out on this generation. It's like the Niagara Falls—a great, thunderous flow of power and anointing that begins with us is meant to flow on to the next generation. How we walk today in our power and anointing will determine whether our children will inherit a pure or a polluted stream. If we do not cleanse our stream now, our impurities will be perpetuated and magnified in the next generation. We live in an age that is sorely lacking in heroes. Think about it. Who can we look at today and regard as a hero? Certainly there are some, but they sure are hard to find.

Isaiah the prophet said that when a people comes under judgment, God takes away wise leadership from the land—the hero, warrior, judge, prophet, elder, and others (see Isa. 3:1–4). During a time of restoration, the Lord restores these to the land. We are now entering such a time of restoration, and the Lord is calling us to be heroes. He is preparing us for a time soon to come when the world will cry out for leaders who are in touch with the heart and mind of God.

If you are going to accept your calling as a hero, you must be prepared to live vicariously. That is, you must be ready to live your life for the sake of others. That is just what Jesus did. His death on the cross for all our sins was a vicarious atonement—a substitutionary death on our behalf. True heroes don't perform for themselves or for personal gain, but for the good of others. They give themselves for the sake of others. That's what Joan of Arc did. That's what every truly great person does.

Vicarious living is a truth that every true leader understands. God wants us to understand that we are to live today for the sake of our children and for a generation yet unborn. He has called us and anointed us to live heroically beyond the immediate and beyond the personal.

Keeping the Stream Pure

How can you be sure to maintain an unpolluted stream to pass on to those who follow? It requires hard work, a lot of prayer, and constant vigilance. There are seven general principles that we all need to take to heart that will help us keep our stream pure.

1. *Develop a passion for God's Word.* First Peter 3:15 says, "But in your hearts set Christ apart [as holy—acknowledging Him, giving Him first place in your lives] as Lord. Always be ready to give a [logical] defense to anyone who asks you to account for the hope and confident assurance [elicited by faith] that is within you..." (AMP). Paul wrote to Timothy, "Do your best to present yourself to God as one approved, a workman who does not need to be ashamed and who correctly handles the word of truth" (2 Tim. 2:15).

Being prepared to give an answer to those who ask about the hope we have requires more than just the testimony of our walk with God. It also requires knowledge of God's Word. Solid grounding in the Scriptures is needed if we hope to correctly handle the Word of truth.

How important is the Bible in your daily Christian life? Do you read it devotionally and let it go at that? Do you study it vigorously, trying to understand everything you can? Have you been hurt by the way others have used the Bible in the past to tie you down or hold you back and keep you from realizing God's call on your life? Because of this, have you distanced yourself from the Bible, telling yourself that you want to focus on being "spiritual" rather than biblical?

If you are interested in accepting the anointing of a hero and living vicariously for another generation, understand that God is calling you to be *exactly* what Scripture teaches. None of us can afford to distance ourselves from Scripture, to settle for anything less than learning and understanding everything we can. For the sake of future generations, we have to hammer into the Scriptures and ask God for the understanding. If you've left being biblical for the sake of being spiritual and pursuing your calling, come home. You don't have to neglect the Word to pursue your calling from God as a woman.

The Word and the Spirit always agree. If the Holy Spirit is the One who both empowers you and releases you, then His Word is consistent with that. When you welcome a heroic anointing, when you welcome the call of God to be the heroic woman that you're called to be, then you welcome the responsibility to launch the rising generation out on the firmest biblical foundation possible.

2. *Expect to be wounded.* David the psalmist said to God, "For they persecute those you wound and talk about the pain of those you hurt" (Ps. 69:26). Have you ever been hurt because you were trying to stand up for Jesus? Do you carry deep pain over something that another person, even another Christian, said or did to you?

Wounds are an occupational hazard for heroes. Whenever you accept the calling of God, whenever you stand up against the norm, you will be wounded. Wounds hurt. Sometimes they hurt very badly. Our theology of victory does not exempt us from bruises and wounds. God uses them to make us into the heroes that He has called us to be. Even if the wound comes from someone who is not in the Lord, the wound itself is something that God wants us to embrace redemptively.

Anything of value costs something. King David said that he would not offer to the Lord that which cost him nothing (see 2 Sam. 24:24). Everything we do as Christians takes on more meaning when we have paid a price for it. It's one thing to worship God on the good days when everything is going great. It's quite another thing to do so when we're under attack and hurting deep inside. Carrying the heroic anointing will cost us a price in hurt and pain. Many of you are already paying that price where you are. Take courage! The pain is worth the price if it means you can pass on an untainted stream to those who come after you. Embracing the pain for the sake of others is part of being a hero.

3. *God wounds you to develop your character.* To many people today, character means not doing certain things. That's not what it means in the Bible, however. In the Scriptures, the word "character" means to bear up under suffering and difficulty. In Ruth 3:11, Ruth is called a woman of noble character because she bore up under difficulty. God will use the hard things in your life to prepare you for the anointing that He wants to place upon you. The writer of Hebrews said of Jesus, "Son though he was, he learned obedience from what He suffered" (Heb. 5:8).

Think of what Jesus suffered: rejection by His family, the death of His earthly father, ridicule, crucifixion, and death. Through all this He learned obedience and thus became a source of new life for His generation. In the same way, the Lord uses the hardships of your life to build in you pillars of character that can sustain the anointing that will rest on them. God's anointing must work *on* you before it can work *through* you.

4. *Don't give place to bitterness.* Hebrews 12:15 says, "See to it that no one misses the grace of God and that no bitter root grows up to cause trouble and defile many." The Greek word for "defile" carries the idea of a dye for coloring clothes. If you allow roots of bitterness to spring up in your life, they will dye or taint everything you do. Have you ever heard someone speak where the words were great and the message solid, but there was something about his or her spirit that just didn't sit right with you? There may have been a root of bitterness or some other negative force that tainted the flow of that person's lives.

As believers, each of us ministers out of the flow of our spirit and out of the Holy Spirit in us. If we allow bitterness to dwell in our lives, we pollute that flow and produce weakened, diseased fruit. Anytime we take offense at a wrong or a hurt, we open ourselves up to be trapped by the enemy. The Greek word in the New Testament for "offense" is *skandalon,* from which we get the word "scandal." It literally refers to a trap-stick or snare—that part of an animal trap that sets off the trap when the animal steps into it. Our bitterness, our offense, can become the trigger that snares us in the enemy's trap.

What do you do about bitterness in your life? When the Israelites in the wilderness complained to Moses because the water was too bitter to drink, Moses threw a piece of wood into the water and the water became sweet (see Ex. 15:23–25). When you throw the wood (that is, the cross of Jesus!) onto your waters of bitterness, they will become sweet.

5. *Submit to one another.* A lot of us get uncomfortable with the words "submit" and "submission," and with good reason. There is no doubt that men have treated women wrongly throughout history. There's also no question that men often have acted as though they could go it alone without the gifts that women could bring. The great danger that lies in the current release of women into ministry is that it will degrade into a feministic Holy Spirit women's movement that is at

odds with the men. All of us, men and women, need to reexamine the Scriptures to understand the model that God intends.

The apostle Paul summed up that model very well for the Ephesians: "Submit to one another out of reverence for Christ" (Eph. 5:21). What God wants now is not an independent women's movement and an independent men's movement, but a *team movement* that unfortunately most men and women in the church don't yet understand. Submitting to one another out of reverence for Christ is the context for everything that follows.

It's bad theology that has held women in bondage, not good theology. There is a place in certain contexts and situations for men to submit to women. There's a mutual deferring to gifts. There's a way women are created to carry certain things, and to do certain things, and a way men are created for certain things. If a man will love and protect his wife, if he will encourage her, she can be a tremendous fount of wisdom, revelation, and insight for him.

The quickest way to pollute the stream for the next generation is to make it an independent movement filled with harshness and unsubmissive spirits. God didn't intend for women to go it alone any more than He intended for men to do so. He intended for us to participate in a godly merging. We can't afford to pass on to the next generation an ungodly spirit of independence.

6. Don't compromise your call. There is a tendency among Christian women today, when the traditional and normal corridors of power and ministry are closed to them, to seek alternative routes, especially the ones men aren't interested in. Let's take intercession, for example.

Frankly, most men aren't interested in intercession. There are many more women than men in the intercession ministry. Now, if that's your calling, get after it. Don't hesitate. But don't choose that route simply because it's a well-worn path for women—especially if your calling is somewhere else. You may be called to pastoral ministry or to evangelism. Don't let yourself be diverted. Don't compromise your call. The path of least resistance may *not* be the *right* path! If you settle for what's easy or open to you right now, you may miss out on God's higher calling on your life.

However, this doesn't mean engaging in guerrilla warfare either, blowing down doors and toppling walls in order to take your "rightful place." We as women need to let the Lord be our defense and open those doors to us in His time and in His way. As we walk in the character we're called to walk in and as His anointing rests upon us, He will break those yokes. Don't compromise the high call in your heart. The Lord will prepare the way.

7. *Drive a stake into the heart of the fear of man.* Quite often the fear of man stems from the fact that we have too lofty a picture of humanity and too limited a picture of God. Man and his institutions seem so big and substantial while our concept of God is restrained by sin and unbelief. But as you grow in your walk with the Lord, as you learn to worship Him and behold His presence, and as you cry out to Him, He will give you such a high view and a holy transforming vision of who Jesus is, and a high and transformed view of who you are and what you are called to be, that the opinions of men fade in comparison. Chapter 40 of Isaiah has some powerful descriptions that compare mankind with God:

> "All people are like grass, and all their faithfulness is like the flowers of the field. The grass withers and the flowers fall, because the breath of the Lord blows on them. Surely the people are grass. The grass withers and the flowers fall, but the word of our God endures forever."…Surely the nations are like a drop in a bucket; they are regarded as dust on the scales; he weighs the islands as though they were fine dust.…Before him all the nations are as nothing; they are regarded by him as worthless and less than nothing.…He sits enthroned above the circle of the earth, and its people are like grasshoppers. He stretches out the heavens like a canopy, and spreads them out like a tent to live in. He brings princes to naught and reduces the rulers of this world to nothing. No sooner are they planted, no sooner are they sown, no sooner do they take root in the ground, than he blows on them and they wither, and a whirlwind sweeps them away like chaff.…Do you not know? Have you not heard? The Lord is the everlasting God, the Creator of the ends of the earth. He will not grow tired or weary, and His understanding no one can fathom. (Isa. 40:6b–28)

How do you deal with the fear of man? Realize that the God who created the universe is the same God who has commissioned you. You are small, but He is BIG! He will strengthen and empower you in your adventure of faith. Yes, exchange your fears. Cast off your fear of man and receive in its place the reverential fear of the Lord. Look at the Lord and see how awesome and omnipotent He is. Then look at yourself—you'll be overwhelmed by your smallness in contrast. But then take a look again—this BIG God is personally cheering you on. This everlasting God is on your side. As you understand this, the snare of the fear of man fades into the background, and courage will rise up within you. With another piece then put into place, we are ready to seize the day!

Carpe Diem—Seize the Day

Take courage! You are chosen. The King of heaven and earth has selected you to be His very own. He has called you to courage and to be a hero in this generation, living for the sake of the next. You are in good company. The Spirit of the Lord is with you, the same Spirit who led, inspired, and gave courage to Joan of Arc, Perpetua, Sojourner Truth, Harriet Tubman, Aimee Semple McPherson, Lydia Christensen Prince, Bertha Smith, Corrie ten Boom, Jackie Pullinger, and countless other women throughout the ages—women who heard God's call and seized the opportunity in their day. May we in this generation rise up and join this exalted company of the called, the chosen…His beloved!

Let us enter the House of the Heroes. Let us look on the scrolls, carvings, shields, and swords. Let our eyes look into the faces and the hearts of heroes past. Let us lean forward, quiet in our souls, and listen for what advice and counsel they would give us. These stories of Joan of Arc, Perpetua, Harriet Tubman, and all the others are not just good "stories" or "legends." Their memorabilia is not just rotting cloth and rusting iron.

Listen close and look deeply for what you can glean from them. They would say to you, *Serve the Lord with all your strength. Love Him with all your being. Do not miss the day of your visitation. While it is yet your day, seize it. Seize your destiny, your calling, your opportunity.* Seize the day! Yes, there is a call to courage being pronounced in our day. Warriors are being searched for, and are desperately needed. Do you hear the call? If so, sign up right now!

> Father, I surrender my life to the call to courage. Here I am. Change me. Use me. Drive fear out of me. I volunteer freely to be on the front lines in Jesus' name. Be glorified through my life. Amen.

ACKNOWLEDGMENTS

First we want to thank our family, for without their love and support we could never have attempted these projects. Thank you, dear children: Justin, GraceAnn, Tyler, and Rachel, for all that you have sacrificed for our sakes and for the sake of so many others. Hugs!

Thanks always go to our faithful staff and intercessors over the years at God Encounters Ministries. You have always been the most wonderful, dedicated team there could possibly be. We count ourselves most fortunate to work together with these dear friends. Thank you all for your watchful prayers on our behalf, as well as for your practical assistance. Your sacrifices on our behalf are seen in heaven.

I (James) also want to express my thanks to some special spiritual leaders who have invested in our lives over the years. First, I give honor to my adopted Papa in the faith, Don Finto, of the Caleb Company in Nashville, Tennessee. What an honor to know and walk with you. Second, I want to honor some of our dearest friends and mentors, Mahesh and Bonnie Chavda. Where would we be without you? Third, I want to express gratitude for the years of investment that the late prophetic seer Bob Jones poured into our lives. Last, I want to thank the Lord for the years of relationship with Che and Sue Ahn, for their care, love, and making room for us among the HIM apostolic team. You and others have provided a place of shelter for us—to be pioneers for Christ's kingdom's sake.

Most important, I want to thank our Lord and King, Jesus Christ, who has opened the door of freedom for us and who cares more about our destiny and future than we could ever possibly imagine.

We worked on this series of books for You, Jesus. And we pray that they will be used to release Your kingdom life into the lives of many, many men and women across the globe for generations yet to come.

A Call to Courage NOTES

Chapter Three: Joan of Arc

1. "Joan of Arc: Biography," Bio., (www.biography.com/people/joan-of-arc-9354756).
2. C. M. Stevens, *The Wonderful Story of Joan of Arc and the Meaning of Her Life for Americans* (New York: Cupples and Leon Company, 1918), 28.
3. Stevens, 29.
4. "Joan of Arc: Biography."
5. Herbert Thurston, "St. Joan of Arc," The Catholic Encyclopedia, vol. 8 (New York: Robert Appleton Company, 1910), http://www. newadvent.org/cathen/08409c.htm.
6. Ibid.
7. Ibid.
8. Ibid.
9. Francis W. Leary, *The Golden Longing* (New York: Charles Scribner's Sons, 1959), 31.
10. Thurston.
11. Leary, 42.
12. Thurston.
13. Leary, 44.
14. Thurston.
15. Ibid.
16. Ibid.
17. Ibid.
18. Ibid.
19. "Joan of Arc Trial Transcripts," Gavel2Gavel, http://www.re-quest.net/g2g/ historical /trials/joan-of-arc/. Stevens, 300.
21. Stevens, 302.
22. "Joan of Arc: Biography."

Chapter Four: Vibia Perpetua

1. Alban Butler, "Saints Perpetua, Felicitas, and Companions—Martyrs," *The Lives of Saints* (New York: John J. Crawley & Company, 1954), provided courtesy of EWTN library (http://www.ewtn.com/library/mary/perpetua.htm).
2. "Sts. Perpetua and Felicity," Catholic Online, http://www. catholic.org/saints/saint. php? saint_id=48.
3. Peter Dronke, trans., "Perpetua," *Women Writers of the Middle Ages* (New York: Cambridge Univ. Press, 1984).
4. Butler.
5. W.H. Shewring, trans., *The Passion of Perpetua and Felicity* (London: Sheed and Ward, 1931). *Internet Medieval Sourcebook* (http://legacy.fordham.edu/halsall/source /perpetua.asp).
6. Butler.

Chapter Five: Sojourner Truth

1. W. Terry Whalin, *Sojourner Truth: American Abolitionist* (Uhrichsville, OH: Barbour, 1997), 195.
2. Arthur Huff Fauset, *Sojourner Truth, God's Faithful Pilgrim* (New York: Russell & Russell, 1971), 57–63.

3. Harriet Beecher Stowe, "Sojourner Truth, The Libyan Sibyl," *Atlantic Monthly* 11(April 1863), 473–481 (http://www.theatlantic.com/magazine/archive/1863/04/sojourner-truth-the-libyan-sibyl/308775/).

4. Whalin, 55–56.

5. Victoria Ortiz, *Sojourner Truth, A Self-Made Woman* (Philadelphia, PA: J.B. Lippincott, 1974), 44.

6. Whalin, 87.

7. Stowe.

8. Whalin, 94.

9. Ibid., 101.

10. Ibid., 152.

11. Ortiz, 62.

12. Whalin, 118.

13. Frances D. Gage as quoted in Elizabeth Cady Stanton, Susan B. Anthony, and Matilda Joslyn Gage, eds., *History of Woman Suffrage*, vol. 1 (Reprinted, New York: Arno Press and the *New York Times*, 1969), 2.

14. Patricia McKissack, *Sojourner Truth: Ain't I a Woman?* (New York: Scholastic, 1994), 112–114.

15. Stanton, et al., 2.

16. Ibid.

Chapter Six: Harriet Tubman

1. Ann Petry, *Harriet Tubman: Conductor on the Underground Railroad* (New York: Thomas Y. Crowell, 1955), 214–217.

2. Judy Carlson, *Harriet Tubman: Call to Freedom* (New York: Fawcett Columbine, 1989), 79–81.

3. Ibid., 29.

4. Ibid., 4.

5. Sarah Bradford, *Harriet: The Moses of Her People* (New York: George R. Lockwood & Son, 1886), 30 (http://docsouth.unc.edu/neh/harriet/harriet.html).

6. Ibid., 61

7. Ibid., 49–51.

8. Ibid., 83–84.

Chapter Seven: Aimee Semple McPherson

1. Edith L. Blumhofer, *Aimee Semple McPherson: Everybody's Sister* (Grand Rapids, MI: William B. Eerdmans Publishing Company, 1993), 108–109.

2. Don Taylor, "Aimee: A Short Biography," Liberty Harbor Foursquare Church, 1998, 1 (http://www.libertyharbor.org/aimee.htm).

3. Daniel Mark Epstein, *Sister Aimee* (New York: Harcourt Brace Jovanovich, 1993), 47–50.

4. Blumhofer, 102–103.

5. Taylor, 4.

6. Ibid.

7. Blumhofer, 107.

8. Lately Thomas, *Storming Heaven* (New York: William Morrow and Co., 1970), 20.

9. Blumhofer, 160.

10. Ibid., 159–160.

11. Ibid., 161.

12. The Foursquare Church, "Our Story: The History and Future of the Foursquare Church," http://www.foursquare.org/about/history.

13. Epstein, 206–207.

14. Blumhofer, 277.

15. Ibid., 359.

Chapter Eight: Lydia Christensen Prince

1. Lydia and Derek Prince, *Appointment in Jerusalem* (Grand Rapids, MI: Chosen Books, 1975), 21. Used by permission. Derek Prince Ministries-International, P.O. Box 19501, Charlotte, NC 28219-5901.

2. Ibid., 30.

3. Ibid., 31–33.

4. Ibid., 33.

5. Ibid., 45–46.

6. Ibid., 71.

7. Ibid., 102, 107.

8. Ibid., 119.

9. Ibid., 123–125.

10. Derek and Ruth Prince, *God Is a Matchmaker: Seven Biblical Principles for Finding Your Mate* (Grand Rapids, MI: Chosen, 2011), 25–33.

11. Ibid., 33.

13. Prince, *Appointment in Jerusalem*, 174.

Chapter Nine: Bertha Smith

1. Lewis Drummond, *Miss Bertha: Woman of Revival* (Nashville, TN: Broadman & Holman Publishers, 1996), 100–102.

2. Bertha Smith, *Go Home and Tell* (Nashville, TN: Broadman & Holman, 1995), 90.

3. Drummond, 102.

4. Ibid., 5–6.

5. Bertha Smith, *How the Spirit Filled My Life* (Nashville, TN: Broadman Press, 1973), 22.

6. Drummond, 17.

7. Ibid., 24.

8. Ibid., 46.

9. Smith, *How the Spirit Filled My Life*, 29.

10. Drummond, 40.

11. Ibid., 48–49.

12. Ibid., 49.

13. C. L. Culpepper, *The Shantung Revival* (Dallas, TX: Crescendo Publications, 1971), 13–14.

14. Smith, *Go Home and Tell*, 40.

15. Drummond, 54.

16. Culpepper, 72–73.

17. Smith, *Go Home and Tell*, 96–98.

18. Drummond, 121–123.

19. Ibid., 285.

Chapter Ten: Corrie ten Boom

1. Corrie ten Boom, *The Hiding Place* with John and Elizabeth Sherrill (Grand Rapids, MI: Chosen Books, 1984), 69–70.

2. Ibid., 29.

3. David Wallington, "The Secret Room: The Story of Corrie ten Boom," *Soon* Online Magazine, Soon Ministries, United Kingdom (http://www.soon.org.uk/en/stories/series -9/the-secret-room.html).

4. Ten Boom, 85.

5. Ibid., 77.

6. Ibid.

7. Ibid., 114.

8. Joan Winmill Brown, *Corrie: The Lives She's Touched* (Old Tappan, NJ: Fleming H. Revell Company, 1979), 49.

9. Ten Boom, 158ff.

10. Ibid., 153–154.

11. Ibid., 160–161.

12. Ibid., 157–158.

13. Ibid., 165.

14. Brown, 63.

15. Carole C. Carlson, *Corrie ten Boom: Her Life, Her Faith* (Old Tappan, NJ: Fleming H. Revell Company, 1983), 117.

16. Ten Boom, 171.

17. Ibid., 172.

18. Elizabeth Sherrill, "Since Then," from *Guideposts* Magazine, 1983, in Ten Boom, *The Hiding Place*, 226–228.

19. Ibid.

20. Ibid.

Chapter Eleven: Jackie Pullinger

1. Jackie Pullinger, *Crack in the Wall* (London: Hodder & Stoughton, 1997), 7–8.

2. Jackie Pullinger, *Chasing the Dragon* (Ann Arbor, MI: Servant, 1982), 137.

3. Pullinger, *Crack in the Wall*, 8.

4. Pullinger, *Chasing the Dragon*, 34–36.

5. Ibid., 39.

6. Pullinger, *Crack in the Wall*, 18–19.

7. Ibid., 26–32.

8. Jim Goll, *The Lost Art of Intercession* (Shippensburg, PA: Revival Press, 1997), 36–37.

9. Jackie Pullinger, "Where We Are Now," Worldscope Communigram, http://www. churchlink.com .au/churchlink/worldscope/communigram/jackie.html.

10. Jackie Pullinger: "Caring for Kowloon," "Report on the Meetings with Jackie Pullinger-To," Street Level Consulting and Counseling, http://streetlevelconsulting.ca / compassion/biographies/jackie-pullinger-caring-for-kowloon/.

Chapter Twelve: You Are Chosen

1. The former senior pastor of Belmont Church, Stephen Mansfield, is a man who firmly believes in women in ministry. This material is adapted from the message he gave at a 1998 "Women of Valor" conference. I am deeply grateful for his allowing me to include it in this book.

A Call to Compassion

Taking God's Unfailing Love to Your World

James & Michal Ann Goll

DEDICATION

First and foremost, I (Michal Ann) dedicate this book to Jesus, who comes to us with His heart filled with compassion to fulfill every promise. And I want to dedicate this particular book to my grandmother, Ann Lucinda McCoy, whose prayers kept me on the path, always loving Jesus and living for Him every day—and who also had a dream in her heart, to be a missionary to China. In addition, I dedicate *A Call to Compassion* to the many women who have ventured into closed countries with the Good News and were never heard from again. To the keepers of the flame, the champions of compassion, those who have gone on silently before us, whose stories we will not know until we meet in heaven.

Together with Michal Ann, I (James) dedicate this book of the Women on the Frontlines series to our four miracle children. Your mom now worships God on the other side, but you know she gave everything she had to bring you forth and you were her joy. Her lineage and legacy are deposited in you, Justin, GraceAnn, Tyler, and Rachel. All of us will meet again someday at the waterside.

FOREWORD

Patricia King

The world is full of victims: victims of war, poverty, terrorism, sex trafficking, slave labor, abuse, sickness, and disease. Where are these victims? They are everywhere. They could be as visible as your neighbor, coworker, or family member, but they could be as hidden from your sight as a young child chained to a bed in a dark brothel, or a young man abducted and recruited into an army where he is trained and commanded to brutally kill the innocent. They could be desperate mothers weeping in the midst of a famine- and drought-afflicted region, unable to feed their children, or they could be the elderly being taken advantage of and abused behind closed doors. Victims are everywhere, and it is compassion that will motivate and empower us to reach them.

Compassion is the response to the suffering of others that motivates a desire to help. When Jesus was "moved with compassion," the blind saw and those with defiled flesh became clean (see Matthew 20:34 and Mark 1:41). His compassion was both the motivator and the conduit through which God's power flowed to bring transformation in lives.

It was God's compassion for mankind in our sinful estate that motivated Him to give all that He is and all that He has for our redemption. "For God so loved the world, that He gave His only begotten Son, that whoever believes in Him shall not perish, but have eternal life" (John 3:16, NIV).

Oh, what a gift! He did not close His eyes or His heart to our need. We had become victims of the power of sin and we could not help ourselves. We could not change our destined end if we remained in that helpless state. God could have judged and condemned us but He did not. He freely demonstrated heartfelt compassion and love that has transformed us. A divine exchange takes place through the power of

His compassion and love so that we are no longer victims but victors in Christ when we receive this glorious gift from His heart.

I remember the first time I visited Bangkok, Thailand. Our ministry had not yet been involved in anti-trafficking, but that night in Bangkok transformed my life and our ministry. Sitting at a table right beside me in a restaurant was a man in his mid-fifties with a young girl he had "bought" for the weekend. She was a sweet Thai girl appearing to be around fifteen to eighteen years of age. She looked very nervous but tried to smile.

Confused emotions erupted in me. I felt so much love and compassion for her but anger toward him. I wanted to "punch his lights out" and rescue her. In the midst of this emotional in-burst, the Lord spoke very tenderly, "Patricia, they are both victims." Suddenly God's compassion was filling me for both of them as I was reminded that our battle is not against flesh and blood but against powers of darkness (see Eph. 6:10–12). Although my emotions remained confused and somewhat helpless, I knew God was giving me a perspective that I had not yet considered.

Over the next few days in Bangkok and Pattaya, I had numerous emotional wrestlings due to similar situations, but in the midst of each of them, compassion from the Lord filled me. As a result of that short-term visit, our ministry launched into a successful and fruitful anti-trafficking outreach assignment through which many children and young women have been rescued. Anti-trafficking policies are now established in nations that did not have them before, and many have dedicated their lives to the cause.

Compassion was the motivator and the conduit for such activation. I have seen entire crowds moved with deep compassion when we have shared just one testimony of a child being rescued. Many have wept at the altars, offering their lives, gifts, prayers, voices, and finances to serve the afflicted. Compassion moved them as His compassion moved me years ago. It is so beautiful to give God such a gift. He sowed compassion and now He is reaping through His people who carry His heart.

Michal Ann Goll is one of my heroes of the faith. She is in glory now, but she both knew and responded to the compassion of God while living on earth and led many to step into acts of compassion.

I am currently serving Michal Ann's vision for Women on the Frontlines, and one of the mandates we carry is the mobilization of women to serve the poor, the afflicted, and the needy. Michal Ann set the bar high for us, and she has left a rich legacy behind. Many are living out the trumpet call she heralded and the example she set. I am one of those. This book is filled with perspective, teaching, testimony, and "heartbeat"—God's heartbeat.

Oh, that we would be compassionate as He is compassionate. Digest the message in this book and you will connect with the power of His compassion that can transform victims into victors—through you—for His glory.

—Patricia King
Founder of Patricia King Ministries and XP Ministries
www.patriciaking.com

INTRODUCTION

Michal Ann Goll

My personal journey leading to the school of compassion started long ago. It began on the day I was born, when God touched my life with His amazing love and grace.

As my mother was giving birth to me, my body was turned around in the breech position. The labor and delivery process had begun during the early morning hours, so the doctor was not immediately available, though he had been called and was hopefully on the way. The contractions increased in frequency and the transition came, but still no doctor. I began to emerge from the birth canal feet first, but my head had not yet appeared. As a result, from the lack of oxygen, my body began to turn blue. The nurse, who had been there the whole time and had witnessed the entire labor process and the beginning of my delivery, was now faced with a life-or-death decision. She knew the law, which stated that a doctor had to deliver the baby, but she also knew that if she did not do something, I would die from suffocation.

The moment of truth had arrived. Should she follow the requirements of the law, or should she act in compassion and save my life? It did not take her long to make this choice, for she put her hand inside the birth canal, found my mouth, put her fingers in my mouth, and pulled me out.

So, I knew the Lord's lovingkindness from the moment of my birth. I was born on February 14—Valentine's Day—and each birthday I celebrate is like receiving a special valentine from my heavenly Father, a personal affirmation which says, "I love you!" Yes, He is full of loving compassion.

Like Christian in *Pilgrim's Progress,* God is taking me on a journey. When I found myself in the valley of intimidation, He introduced me to a "hall of heroes" like the ones described by the prophet Nehemiah and the writer of the book of Hebrews (see Neh. 7 and Heb. 11).

First, as He introduced me to many heroines of courage, I was drawn to the life of Joan of Arc. She taught me that the darkness of the age we live in does not really matter, because God's light is eternal and He will open every door for us if we truly love Him and desire for His will to be done. As a result, my heart became a flame of passion that filled me with the courage I needed to sever the chains of intimidation that had held me captive for so long; my appetite for more of God became truly insatiable.

Next, I began to devour books about other great women of faith and courage: Vibia Perpetua, Sojourner Truth, Harriet Tubman, Aimee Semple McPherson, Lydia Christensen Prince, Bertha Smith, Corrie ten Boom, and Jackie Pullinger. I wrote about these great women in my book, *A Call to Courage*, and they laid the foundation of my own hall of heroes.

As I built upon that foundation and continued walking through the hallway, the fierier my heart became, and I fell more deeply in love with my heavenly Father, who began helping me build the second level of my hall of heroes. The Lord gave me fresh insights and showed me how He had always been with me, even during the most trying times of my life. I know that He will always be with me.

Through the writings of Madame Jeanne Guyon, I received further spiritual enlightenment and new understandings of God and His ways. Her profound wisdom helped me firmly establish Jesus as the center of my life; when this happened, everything in my life began to fall into place and I discovered a wonderfully deep peace in Him. This brought great healing and strength to my soul.

As I continued on, I studied the lives of Teresa of Avila, Susanna Wesley, Fanny Crosby, Basilea Schlink, Gwen Shaw, and Elizabeth Alves. Oh, the riches I gained from these special women. Like Susanna Wesley, I determined that my prayer closet could be as simple as my apron. I basked in the anointing that rested upon the famous blind hymn-writer Fanny Crosby, whose inspiring and stirring hymns ushered in a vital spiritual awakening in her time and continue to minister personally to people everywhere. These new friends were brought together in my second book in the Women on the Frontlines series, titled *A Call to the Secret Place*. This book releases a sweet fragrance of God.

I am convinced that if we have truly experienced the transformation that always occurs when we abide in His presence, it will cause us to turn outward to bring this powerful transformation to the world. After all, this is the power of the love of God that we have known and experienced. His heart is always reaching out to anyone who will receive Him. If I have truly been set free from fear and intimidation and have been filled with a courageous spirit, and if I have truly found my resting place in the heart of God, I must stir myself to action and move my heart to act on behalf of others.

Therefore, I next looked into the lives of other women who knew this same compelling call and who followed through. These trailblazers are Catherine Booth, Nancy Ward, Florence Nightingale, Gladys Aylward, Mother Teresa, Amy Carmichael, Katharine Drexel, Phoebe Palmer, Hannah More, Elizabeth Fry, and Heidi Baker. These ladies have challenged the prevailing systems and have met the circumstances of life and even governments with gutsy determination, overcoming anything that resisted God's love and power.

I love these women. I want their don't-tell-me-I-can't determination, and I hope you do too. Let's continue our journey with them, and let's bring with us many men and women who desire to love the Lord with all their hearts and to love their neighbors as themselves.

Now I have a few questions for you. What is your heart telling you? Do you want to break open whole regions of the earth for the Lord's heart? Do you want to make a difference in someone's life? Do you want to overcome the limitations that have bound you up and paralyzed you? Then come along with me. Join me on this exciting journey.

As Heidi Baker would say, let's build a whole of company of "laid-down lovers" for Jesus' sake. The Father is waiting for us to fill His house. He is waiting and longing for you and me to take action.

—Michal Ann Goll
Franklin, Tennessee
August 2006

Part One

The Journey Begins

This book is a journey into the heart of God. The journey begins with a look at the source of all compassionate action—God's compassionate heart. You will discover that our compassion is a reflection of the All-Compassionate One. John writes, "The one who does not love has not become acquainted with God [does not and never did know Him], for God is love. [He is the orig-inator of love, and it is an enduring attribute of His nature.] (1 John 4:8). Our love, replicated in our actions toward others, is a reflection of the depth of our relationship with God.

Yes, God is love, and the essence of His being is manifested in His acts toward us. His conduct toward people reveals His compassion for people. Those who bear His nature will also reflect His character in their actions in the human city. He longs for us to become love and compassion in the midst of a world starving for just a little love. In order to do so, however, we must get to know Him intimately and personally, as Jesus did. We must be connected to the Source and allow His love to flow through us. As that love begins to freely flow to us from our Father, it will eventually flow through us to others in loving words and compassionate acts.

In this first section you will learn what compassion is, how God's compassion works, and the power of tears. Jesus frequently wept when He saw the needs of the people and was moved with compassion to do something about them. He sowed in tears and reaped in joy, and you can do the same, for His power and anointing rest upon you.

We must unite our hearts to go forth in compassion to the world. We realize, though, that we still have a lot to learn about converting desire into deed. In many ways our journey has just begun.

Each step of the way, we have learned to look to Jesus, who truly is the personification of compassion. The lives of those who have gone before us will also serve as a source of great inspiration. They will encourage us to reshape our world as they reshaped their world by the love of God.

Our prayer for you is this:

> …that the God of our Lord Jesus Christ, the Father of glory, may grant you a spirit of wisdom and of revelation [that gives you a deep and personal and intimate insight] into the true knowledge of Him [for we know the Father through the Son]. And [I pray] that the eyes of your heart [the very center and core of your being] may be enlightened [flooded with light by the Holy Spirit], so that you will know and cherish the hope [the divine guarantee, the confident expectation] to which He has called you, the riches of His glorious inheritance in the saints (God's people), and [so that you will begin to know] what the immeasurable and unlimited and surpassing greatness of His [active, spiritual] power is in us who believe. These are in accordance with the working of His mighty strength (Eph. 1:17–19).

So, let the journey begin!

Chapter 1

GOD'S HEART
OF COMPASSION

(Michal Ann Goll)

On a trip to Thailand, I found myself sitting in a Mexican restaurant in Bangkok. The young ladies who worked as servers were wearing cowboy hats, cowboy boots, and other western wear. I thought it was funny to see such outfits in Bangkok, never mind in a "Mexican" restaurant.

I had been in Thailand for a couple of weeks and had eaten a variety of dishes, some of which caused me to wonder about their ingredients, and I was gaining a little skill in eating with chopsticks. This Mexican restaurant represented my first opportunity to taste more familiar foods and flavors.

My friends and I were having a delightful conversation—a nice respite from our hectic schedule of prayer meetings, travel, sleeping in different hotels, and many, many meetings. As I looked around the room and through the front window, I noticed a young man standing outside. He was holding a sign, and he had several little toys dangling on fine strings all around him.

From the booth where we were sitting, I could read his sign; he was deaf and had created these little toys, which were crickets, out of bits of bamboo. He was selling them for a modest price of twenty baht (approximately fifty cents) apiece so he could buy food.

Though he was a simple and needy young man, he didn't look like he was begging. He stood upright, showed no emotion, and was not really trying to sell us anything. He did not have the typical pleading eyes of a beggar, and he did not gesture for our attention.

I was impressed by how he stood with an air of quiet self-respect and seeming uprightness of heart. We did not exchange a word between us, but our hearts touched each other that day as we peered into each other's souls. I believe I gave him something that day—something far more than the twenty baht it cost me to buy a cricket. I gave him my promise to do all I could with my life, to make a difference in his life and in the lives of others like him.

At the same time, he gave me something, something I desperately needed. He gave me the privilege of touching his life, of making a difference. I caught a glimpse into the heart of God. This young man showed me that you don't have to be somebody who is important or famous; you just have to be available. You have to be willing to engage in the journey and walk the path that Jesus walks every day. This is what the journey of learning God's ways is all about.

Whenever I looked at the little cricket I bought from this young man, I remembered this treasured experience and renewed my commitment to the Lord Jesus Christ. Thus, I continued on the journey that had been set before me.

Do you want more of Jesus? Is your heart engaged with the things that move His heart? Do you want more of the Father's love deposited in your heart?

How can we understand this amazing love that He so deeply desires for us to experience? His love is beyond our mental abilities to comprehend. Many of us have tainted understandings of what a father is like. Our understanding of fatherhood is shaped by our childhood experiences with our earthly fathers. So, we have to ask ourselves, "What do I really know about God and His heart? What do I really know about His mercy and compassion?" To know His mercy and compassion, we must open our hearts to Him. We must go to the one place where He exposes the tenderness of His heart—into His written Word, the Bible.

Act Justly and Love Mercy

In the book, *The Justice God Is Seeking,* author and our friend David Ruis writes, "Steeped in humility, we are called to act justly and to love mercy. Don't miss this! Justice is an action, to be done in and through the power of Christian community, but mercy is to be loved. It is not an action; it is a passion."[1]

True compassion and mercy stem from a passion for the Father's heart. Do you love mercy? When we learn to truly love mercy and compassion, out of our passion for God's heart, we will be motivated to act justly.

Justice and righteousness form the foundation of the Father's throne. The psalmist writes, "Righteousness and justice are the foundation of Your throne; lovingkindness and truth go before You" (Ps. 89:14).

Go to God's throne of grace as we begin, and ask Him for a grace of impartation and a spirit of revelation to come upon you. Ask God to enlighten your mind and to fill your heart with His fire. Open your heart to the Holy Spirit and let Him speak to you, guide you, teach you, and move you. Let the river of God, which is always full, flow forth in all its energy and power.

The writer of the book of Hebrews says, "Let us then approach God's throne of grace with confidence, so that we may receive mercy and find grace to help us in our time of need" (Heb. 4:16, NIV).

Consider the Weak and the Poor

Did you ever consider the fact that happiness comes from walking in compassion? This is what David meant when he wrote, "Happy are those who consider the poor; the Lord delivers them in the day of trouble" (Ps. 41:1, NRSV). What a glorious promise this is.

The psalmist then goes on to list some of the other benefits to be derived from considering the weak and the poor (see Ps. 41:1–4):

> The Lord will protect us.
> The Lord will keep us alive.
> We shall be called "blessed in the land."
> We will not be given over to our enemies.
> The Lord will sustain us.
> The Lord will refresh us.
> The Lord will strengthen us.
> The Lord will turn, change, and transform us.

These are just some of the things that happen when we are filled with compassion and reach out in love to others. Doesn't this make you want to really be in tune with God's heart as you begin your journey?

God's Heart of Compassion

God's compassions never fail. In fact, they are renewed every day (see Lamentations 3:22). He wants us to keep our hearts open to Him each day as well.

We must be careful to guard against any bitterness or hardness of heart that may try to creep into our lives. God actually commands us to never let our hearts and minds grow hard or cold:

> If there is a poor man among you, one of your fellow Israelites, in any of your cities in the land that the Lord your God is giving you, you shall not be heartless, nor close-fisted with your poor brother; but you shall freely open your hand to him, and shall generously lend to him whatever he needs. Beware that there is no wicked thought in your heart, saying, "The seventh year, the year of release (remission, pardon), is approaching," and your eye is hostile (unsympathetic) toward your poor brother, and you give him nothing [since he would not have to repay you]; for he may cry out to the Lord against you, and it will become a sin for you. You shall freely and generously give to him, and your heart shall not be resentful when you give to him, because for this [generous] thing the Lord your God will bless you in all your work and in all your undertakings. (Deut. 15:7–10)

What does God want from us? Open hands and open hearts and a willingness to help those in need. He wants us to give freely and cheerfully. This is mercy in action, the love of God reaching out to the oppressed.

This passage refers to the seventh year—the year of Jubilee—when all the lands would lie fallow and the slaves would be set free. He warns the people against looking to the seventh year as the time when their needs would be met instead of getting involved in the here-and-now. In fact, God calls such a consideration "a base thought," something that actually leads to sin.

Notice how God tells us to open our hands wide to the needy and the poor in "your land." What is your land? Everyone will have a different answer, depending on the work of God in their hearts. But this we know, "our land" is local; it's home. We are to start at home, but not to stop there. We must enlarge our hearts and do all we can to reach the peoples of every nation, tribe, and tongue.

True Justice

True justice involves both kindness and compassion. Zechariah writes, "Thus has the Lord of hosts said, 'Dispense true justice and practice kindness and compassion, to each other; and do not oppress or exploit the widow or the fatherless, the stranger or the poor; and do not devise or even imagine evil in your hearts against one another" (Zech. 7:9–10).

Do you see the relationship between justice and compassion that is portrayed here? In order to understand God's plumb line of justice, we have to know what He values. In fact, the Lord showed me something I had never seen before (story just below), and when He did so, He said to me, "Mercy without justice enables thievery!"

This helped me to understand that our concept of mercy and compassion is limited. In fact, many times it is askew. All too often people think that mercy, simply stated, is *pity*. Though pity is certainly an element of mercy, true mercy and compassion involve so much more.

God always acts from both justice and mercy, and you really can't have one without the other. Sometimes the most merciful thing is to say no to someone who is seeking something from you, particularly if you are looking at the person's stated need through the eyes of both justice and mercy.

The boundaries of the field of mercy and compassion must be firmly established and clearly delineated. We don't ever want anything to encroach on territory that belongs to the Lord and is set apart for the poor and needy.

While I was in Mozambique one time, I observed some children who were beggars from a nearby village. There are many needy children there, since disease, war, poverty, and drought have ravaged the land and torn families apart. Many children have no parents because they have died from AIDS or other causes. Many children beg, but some have learned how to "work the system."

In a church service one Sunday morning, a few boys entered the tent (sanctuary) for the sole purpose of seeing what they could get from people. They could spot the new visitors. These unsuspecting people gathered these young boys in their arms, not engaging in spiritual discernment. They just wanted to bless these children.

The problem was that this particular group of boys was looking for things they could steal and sell later. They worked their plan, getting into camera cases and people's bags. While one would occupy a person, one or two others would look for what they could steal. As I watched this situation unfolding, I began to understand that some of them were actually operating out of demonic activity in order to steal from people.

This is where discernment comes into play. We need to be sure that the one in front of us has a genuine need before we attempt to respond to that need. Did the boys have a legitimate need? Yes. And as food was always served in that place, they could have had the opportunity to fill their stomachs. But what was the condition of their hearts? They also had the opportunity to come to know Jesus; but they were on a different mission. They were in church to steal. The attention that was given to those boys denied other dear children who really could have used that love, those hugs, that attention. The children who were really needy, with open loving hearts to the Lord, suffered because of the others' thievery.

Here's another story. One man who was with us had brought several deflated soccer balls to Mozambique because he knew the children there rarely get to see one. One boy came up to him and began begging for money. The man gave him a soccer ball instead. A short time later, the boy returned. He had ruined the ball, and he began to demand money in exchange for it. Even if he couldn't use the ball, or didn't want it, he had no concept of giving it away to someone else. His mind was consumed with the love of money. This was true thievery. The boy had destroyed the ball so nobody else could enjoy it.

We need to understand what mercy and compassion are according to God's standards, not according to the standards of humans. From His point of view, compassion must always involve justice.

True Judicial Government

God wants governments to rule with justice, righteousness, and compassion, but we all know that this is not always the case. The psalmist writes:

God has taken his place in the divine council; in the midst of the gods he holds judgment: "How long will you judge unjustly and show partiality to the wicked? Give justice to the weak and the orphan; maintain the right of the lowly and the destitute. Rescue the weak and the needy; deliver them from the hand of the wicked." (Ps. 82:1–4, NRSV)

Here we see God's heart concerning true judicial government. Such a government should not show partiality, and it should always do justice to the poor, the fatherless, the afflicted, and the needy. In fact, it should even deliver the poor and needy and rescue them from the wicked.

As followers of Jesus, we should do everything within our power to make sure that this is the kind of government we have. We should vote for godly candidates, and we should vote the wicked out of office. God might even call us to run for public office ourselves so that His justice, righteousness, and mercy can take hold where we live. It is time to stand up in the seats of government and let our lights shine.

God's Heart Concerning Honor

The following Scripture shook me to the core of my being as its truth penetrated my spirit: "Whoever oppresses the poor shows contempt for their Maker, but whoever is kind to the needy honors God" (Prov. 14:31, NIV). I don't know how this could be any clearer.

Do you want to honor God? If your answer is yes, you must operate in kindness and mercy to the needy. To do otherwise brings contempt, mockery, and insult to God.

God's Heart Concerning Lending

Proverbs 19:17 (NIV) says, "Whoever is kind to the poor lends to the Lord, and he will reward them for what they have done." This reminds me of what Jesus said: "Truly I tell you, whatever you did for one of the least of these brothers and sisters of mine, you did for me" (Matt. 25:40, NIV).

What you give to the poor, you give to God, and He promises to repay you.

God's Heart Concerning Righteousness

God equates righteousness with care for the rights of the poor: "The righteous man cares for the rights of the poor, but the wicked man has no interest in such knowledge" (Prov. 29:7). Look at the contrast that is painted for us here. Whereas the righteous person knows and cares for the rights of the poor, the wicked person is completely uninterested in anything like that.

I would like to think of myself as a righteous person, but there have been many times when I've had to repent of my lack of mercy and my unwillingness to tune my heart to God's heart. My desire is to be like the woman who is described in Proverbs 31: "She opens and extends her hand to the poor, and she reaches out her filled hands to the needy" (Prov. 31:20). This verse shows a righteous woman in action.

God's Chosen Fast

Once I had a dream in which I saw twenty or thirty people standing all around me. It seemed that they had been witnesses of my life. One particular man who was standing over me had a spirit of prophecy resting on him. He reminded me of an old-fashioned water pump, the kind where you prime the pump first and then start moving the handle up and down. I sensed that, as this man moved from side to side, the water of God's Word was building up inside him.

In this dream I was very sick. My body was crumpled over an old stone wall, and I was crying, "Will someone get me a doctor? I'm very, very sick!"

Everybody stared at me, and the man I mentioned said, "Don't you know you've been called to prayer and fasting?"

I said, "I need help. Will someone please get me a doctor?"

Again, he said, "Don't you know you've been called to prayer and fasting?"

I whimpered, "Please! Somebody help me! Please! I need help!"

The man stood in front of me and repeated, "Don't you know you've been called to prayer and fasting?" Then he added, "Don't you know that if you would enter into prayer and fasting, you would extend the orphan's bread from three to five days?"

This question hit me hard. I began to see that what I needed was not a doctor after all. What I really needed was to obey the Lord by entering into prayer and fasting.

I have always been really terrible at fasting. God's chosen fast, however, goes beyond the issue of food and flesh; it goes deep into your heart. God's chosen fast becomes a lifestyle that we are called to embrace. What is His chosen fast? The Bible tells us, "[Rather] is this not the fast which I choose, to undo the bonds of wickedness, to tear to pieces the ropes of the yoke, to let the oppressed go free and break apart every [enslaving] yoke?" (Isa. 58:6). Now that's a powerful fast.

Have you entered a fast that shares your own bread with the hungry? Have you brought the homeless into your home, covered the naked, and provided for the needs of your family and all those around you? (See Isa. 58:7.) This is God's chosen fast, and it is truly an exciting fast in which to get engaged, for this is always its result:

> Then your light will break out like the dawn, and your healing (restoration, new life) will quickly spring forth; your righteousness will go before you [leading you to peace and prosperity], the glory of the Lord will be your rear guard. (Isa. 58:8)

The Compassion of Jesus

David Ruis writes, "As followers of Jesus, we cannot ignore what moved Him to send out the first of His disciples, what moves Him still to send us out today: compassion. Biblical compassion is a uniquely Christian virtue."[2]

Jesus always saw the need first, then He was moved with a compassion so strong that it always led Him to do something in response to the need. Matthew writes, "When he saw the crowds, he had compassion for them, because they were harassed and helpless, like sheep without a shepherd" (Matt. 9:36, NRSV).

He then went on to tell His disciples to pray that God would send laborers into His harvest. We need to engage in the same kind of prayer today, for so many people are confused like sheep without a shepherd. God is looking for people who will go out into the fields that are now white unto harvest (see Matt. 9:37–38).

The Greek word for compassion (pity and sympathy) that is used here is *splanchnizomai,* and it means to be moved deep within. It involves a sense of yearning in behalf of others.

If you have compassion, you will be moved to take action, as Jesus always did and still does. God wants you to know His compassion, receive His compassion, live His compassion, and share His compassion with others.[3] All the Scriptures within this chapter open God's heart to you. He is your loving heavenly Father, and He wants you to share in His compassion. I agree with David Ruis, who writes:

> To touch Christ is to touch compassion. Far beyond a guilt-trip, a tweaked conscience or a pale sense of pity, compassion reaches into the very guts and demands action. It compels prayers that will move heaven, intercessions that cry out for workers to be thrust into this weighted-down harvest. It motivates one to move—to go and set it right—to administer justice through the power of the Kingdom.[4]

Compassion will move so deeply within your being that many times you will find yourself moved to the point of tears and agony. God places great value in your tears, and as we turn to the next chapter, you will discover this is a deep well that moves heaven on behalf of others.

> Heavenly Father, I come to You right now in the name of Jesus. I ask You to light the fire of passion in my life and let it become the kind of compassion that doesn't just look at the need, but looks to You. Help me to become so passionate for loving You and knowing Your heart that I will move in compassion to all those in need. I ask that You will bring about a corporate shift of thinking and acting in the entire body of Christ, that Your people would become passionate about compassion by being passionate for You. I ask that You would take the Scriptures in this chapter and drop their truths deep within my heart. Let Your Word continue to flow within the depths of my spirit so I will be able to receive all the spiritual nutrients you have for me. Drop Your plumb line of justice through all of my thoughts and feelings, all of my traditions and training, and let me learn to do justly and to love mercy and to walk humbly with You. In Jesus' name, amen.

Chapter 2

THE COMPASSIONATE POWER OF TEARS

(James W. Goll)

Jesus frequently used the word "behold" when He was teaching His disciples the truths about His kingdom. In so doing He was telling them to open their spiritual eyes and see the truth He was conveying.

When Jesus saw the throngs of people who were suffering as a result of their sins, He was moved with compassion for them. Often, He even wept over them. The shortest verse in the Bible says, "Jesus wept" (John 11:35). What was He weeping over? First, He saw the need, which was the death of Lazarus.

Then He heard the cry of Martha's heart: "Master, if You had been here, my brother would not have died" (John 11:21). At this point Martha expressed her faith in the Master's ability to heal. She said, "Even now I know that whatever You ask of God, God will give to You" (John 11:22).

Next, Jesus heard the piercing cries of Mary, the sister of Martha and Lazarus, and "When Jesus saw her sobbing, and the Jews who had come with her also sobbing, He was deeply moved in spirit...and was troubled" (John 11:33).

Because He saw and listened actively to the heart cries of Martha, Mary, and the assembled Jews, and because He was tuned in to the resonance of the heart of Father God Himself, Jesus was moved with compassion. In turn, He ministered effectively to the urgent need at hand—Lazarus came forth from the tomb, demonstrating resurrection power.

Tears preceded this power encounter. Perhaps compassion and

power are inevitably linked. Yes, our tears have the power to cleanse, to enable us to see, and to thrust us into action in behalf of those in need.

Whenever we hear God speaking to our hearts, we need to obey His inner promptings. As good parents raising their children frequently say, "Just listen and obey!" Obedience brings action to our feelings. Obedience demonstrates commitment to our inner convictions and moves us beyond ourselves.

Bowels of Mercy

Jesus was frequently moved with pity, sympathy, and compassion for the people He saw around Him. He really saw them, and He saw their needs. This means He was fully aware, perceptive, understanding, and responsive to them.

Often, the Lord saw people as being bewildered, like sheep without a shepherd, and this deeply troubled Him, as we see in the Gospel of Mark: "When Jesus landed and saw a large crowd, he had compassion on them, because they were like sheep without a shepherd. So he began teaching them many things" (Mark 6:34, NIV).

It has been accurately said that when a need is presented to us, we really have three options:

- To be inactive—to do nothing. Like the proverbial ostrich, we can choose to stick our heads in the sand and hope the problem will go away.
- To be reactive—this is an emotional response, usually in the form of anger, to a troubling situation.
- To be proactive—this involves taking positive steps to rectify the problem.

Jesus, when He was moved with compassion, was always proactive. In the case just cited in the Scripture, we see that He responded to the disorientation He saw in the people by commanding kingdom order in their lives.

As we go forth in compassion, we need to do more than express only sympathy or pity. As Jesus did, we need to do something concrete to help others. Perhaps the best help we can give others is to teach them how to overcome through faith, prayer, and spiritual understanding.

We need to exemplify kingdom authority right out in the open, as Jesus did, for all to see. The kind of compassion Jesus walked in was not weak and passive; it was tender yet tough, sensitive yet confrontational.

Jesus' heart was (and is yet to this day) filled with compassion. Jesus modeled compassionate living in personal ways for both individuals and for the masses. He practiced what Paul preached:

> Therefore, as God's chosen people, holy and dearly loved, clothe yourselves with compassion, kindness, humility, gentleness and patience. Bear with each other and forgive one another if any of you has a grievance against someone. Forgive as the Lord forgave you. (Col. 3:12–13, NIV)

Can there be any more vivid portrayal of compassion than this? This is a verbal picture of what God expects from each of us. It is the "bowels of mercy" that the King James Version of the Bible tells us to "put on."

The "bowels" are found deep within us, and the fountain of tears that flows when our hearts are filled with mercy comes from deep within our spirits, where the Holy Spirit, who groans in compassion with "unspeakable yearnings and groanings too deep for utterance" resides (see Rom. 8:26).

So, listen and obey. Let compassion flow forth from your innermost being—your bowels of mercy. Remember, it is out of practicing His presence that compassion is born. The love of God works inward (within you), but, as it works inward, it always begins to move outward.

Seven Doors

One evening, my friend Marcus Young and I were waiting on the Lord together. I received a remarkable spiritual vision of seven consecutive doors, which I told about in full in my book *The Lost Art of Practicing His Presence.* Let me give you an overview of that God encounter:

I saw in the spirit a succession of seven doorways, and over each one there was a word written. The word "Forgiveness" was engraved over the first door. As I crossed over the threshold of that first door, I was able to see what was written over the second door: "Cleansed by the Blood."

This helped me to understand that sometimes, though we know

we are forgiven, we might not have fully realized or experienced the reality of total cleansing through the blood of Jesus Christ. As I passed through the second doorway, I experienced the cleansing power of the blood in a new and total way. I knew I was truly cleansed by His blood.

I went on through the third and fourth doorways; they dealt with areas of holiness and sanctification through the power of the Holy Spirit. Then I came to the fifth doorway and noticed that its title was "Grace." As I walked through that portal, a new revelation of the grace of God came upon me.

I learned much as I continued in this interactive vision. I discovered that grace empowers the believer with the anointing, and I also learned that all of God's giftings are received by grace. These are what I call "gracelets," little drops of grace. I learned that the degree of anointing one has comes from passing through God's doorway to grace. It is then that the oil of the Holy Spirit begins to fall on us.

The word "Mercy" was prominently displayed over the sixth doorway. Whereas grace had dealt with God's action toward me, I now learned that mercy had to do with our actions toward others.

This was a very long passageway, but at its end I could make out what was written over the seventh door: "Union With Christ." I wanted so desperately to get to the seventh door, but I knew I couldn't do so until I had completely passed through the sixth corridor—the realm of mercy. This realization filled my heart with anguish.

All I could do was cry, "Lord, teach me your mercy," for I knew then that the only way I would ever be able to enjoy complete union with Christ would be by walking in mercy and compassion at all times.

Sympathetic Consciousness

Compassion involves a sympathetic consciousness toward others. More simply stated, it is being stricken in your heart with a sensitive spiritual awareness of others' hurts, positions, distresses, and dilemmas. More than that, it involves having a divine motivation to do something about their situation. The following verse gives us insight into the heart of compassion at work:

Brothers, if anyone is caught in any sin, you who are spiritual [that is, you who are responsive to the guidance of the

Spirit] are to restore such a person in a spirit of gentleness…
(Gal. 6:1)

The Lord Jesus has a heart of compassion toward each one of us, as
we see in Hebrews 4:15:

For we do not have a high priest who is unable to empathize
with our weaknesses, but we have one who has been tempted in
every way, just as we are—yet he did not sin. (Heb. 4:15, NIV)

Jesus knows about our struggles. He shares our feelings and bears
our burdens with us. He truly understands what we are going through.
It is this knowledge that enables us to "approach God's throne of grace
with confidence, so that we may receive mercy and find grace to help us
in our time of need" (Heb. 4:16, NIV).

We really do have a High Priest who sympathizes with us and gives
us His mercy. He is our compassionate Lord and Savior. The psalmist
puts it this way: "The Lord is good to all; he has compassion on all he
has made" (Ps. 145:9, NIV).

His Compassions Fail Not

Jeremiah wrote, "Because of the Lord's great love we are not consumed,
for his compassions never fail. They are new every morning; great is
your faithfulness" (Lam. 3:22–23, NIV).

These verses give us a clear understanding of the heart of our Father
and the way He deals with His children. The late John Wimber shared a
revealing testimony in his outstanding book, *Power Healing*[1:]

One day, as he was praying, he was discussing an observation with
the Lord about how many people, including himself, are sometimes
afraid to pray for the sick. As he contemplated this idea, he began to
understand that this may well be due to the fact that many do not
understand God's nature and how He works. Then the Lord spoke to
John and told him that most people are hesitant and even fearful about
praying for another's healing because they misunderstand His compassion and mercy. The Lord told him that many know *about* Him but
they do not really *know* Him.

This word from the Lord empowered John to go forth in faith and
compassion and, as a result, God used him as a vehicle through which

His healing mercies flowed, but his joy was tempered somewhat when he received a rather disturbing vision from the Lord. As he was driving, he saw what looked like a cloud bank in the sky. He pulled his car to the side of the road. Then he realized it wasn't a cloud that he was seeing after all; it was a honeycomb filled with honey, and it was dripping on the people below.

Some people were eagerly gulping down the honey, loving its sweet taste and offering it to others. Other people, however, were irritated by the sticky honey that was being poured all over them, trying to wipe it off and complaining about "the mess."

The Lord explained to John that the honey was His mercy, which to some is a blessing and to others is a hindrance. He told John that there was plenty for everyone and that we shouldn't beg Him for healing, because the problem isn't on His end; it is with the people.

Like Jesus, we need to weep over the people who are wandering like sheep without a shepherd. Often they just do not understand who God is, what He has already accomplished on Calvary, and what He wants to do for them.

Try Tears

General William Booth, who founded the Salvation Army with his wife, Catherine, received several letters from people who were lamenting over the seeming lack of progress in their ministries. In their letters they expressed little hope about saving the lost. They said that things were too hard and that it appeared as if nothing was happening.

Booth's response to them was very simple. He tore off a piece of a brown paper, wrote a note on it, and sent it to the seekers. Poignantly, it stated, "Try tears."[2]

We need to let our hearts be broken with the things that break the heart of God. One pastor put it this way: "My church will never grow while my eyes are dry."

What a splendid way this is of expressing the strong burden that comes when our hearts are broken before God. Basilea Schlinck wrote, "The first characteristic of the kingdom of heaven is the overflowing joy that comes from contrition and repentance, tears of contrition soften even the hardest hearts."[3]

Tears of contrition come from our brokenness before God. They express our utter abhorrence of our sinfulness and our complete dependence upon the Lord for everything. David Brainerd, a well-known missionary to American Indian tribes, recorded the following entry in his diary on October 18, 1780:

> My soul was exceedingly melted and bitterly mourned over my exceeding sinfulness and vileness. I never before felt so pungent and deep a sense of the odious nature of sin as at this time. My soul was then carried forth and loved to God and had a lively sense of God's love to me."[4]

This was an experience that Brainerd had as he was praying while standing in the snow on a bitter winter day. He was smitten with a great revelation of His utter dependence upon and absolute need for God, and he saw his own sinfulness in a new light. But God didn't leave him there; He gave him a greater revelation of Himself and His great love for him.

The Prayer of Tears

Compassionate praying, as David Brainerd's experience shows, is prophetic praying. It deals with the deep-seated desires of the spirit, a craving for that which does not presently exist. It is deep calling unto deep (see Ps. 42:7). This involves profound yearning, crying, groaning, longing, and earnestness that come from deep within you. It is the beginning of the prayer of tears.

The prayer of tears is a form of compassion in action. It works in an intercessory and prophetic fashion, touching the lives of those we pray for. As we engage in compassionate praying, God puts His heart within us. We actually receive an impartation of something that is not of ourselves, and we are moved with tenderness, sensitivity, and mercy. This allows us to actually feel the pain of another person at least for a while. We could say that this is the "gift of pain," a gift in the sense that it is a supernatural impartation of compassion, the ability to suffer with those who suffer (see 1 Cor. 12:26).

My dear brother Mahesh Chavda was praying for me one time, and the Holy Spirit began to speak to me. He said, "I am going to give you the gift of pain." Now, this was a message that I wasn't too sure about, as you can well imagine. The Holy Spirit went on, "I'm going to give you the gift of pain, and you will feel my feelings temporarily in your being, your body."

The word "temporarily" helped to ease my anxiety over this message a little bit. It was then that an entirely new spiritual understanding came to me. I began to realize that it is possible to feel the sufferings of others for a while when we are interceding for them. I think what happens is that God actually puts His heart, which breaks with compassion for others, within us for a while so that we will be truly able to bear their burdens before His throne.

As you wait before the Lord and give Him your heart, He will touch you with a portion of His burden and give you His heart to enable you to carry others at least for a while before His throne. When this happens, it's as if you become a little donkey—a beast of burden—for Him. In this way God puts His burden upon you.

The Holy Spirit concluded what He was saying to me with this sentence: "I'm going to give you the gift of pain, and you will feel the fellowship of My sufferings, and you will feel the pains of others, and then, as you release this and bring it back to Me, the pain will lift."

Then I realized how glorious it is to be smitten with the things that break God's heart. Indeed, it's one of the greatest privileges we could ever have. To think that God in all of His glory and grandeur would share His heart with us and give us His pain is mind-boggling. It truly is an honor to be a donkey for Him.

The Fellowship of His Sufferings

Paul writes that his determined purpose is, "...that I may know Him and the power of His resurrection, and the fellowship of His sufferings, being conformed to His death" (Phil. 3:10, NKJV). We can join the fellowship of Christ's sufferings. This enables us to rejoice with those who rejoice and to weep with those who weep (see Rom. 12:15). The God of compassion and all comfort is always there to help us (see 2 Cor. 1:3–4). David writes, "My sacrifice, O God, is a broken spirit; a broken and contrite heart you, God, will not despise" (Ps. 51:17, NIV).

The great evangelist and writer Charles Finney knew and practiced the truth of this verse. He had a weeping heart. He often went into the woods north of his village to pray, and he confessed that he did this so that others would not see him. He writes, "An overwhelming sense of my wickedness in being ashamed to have a human being see me on my knees before God took such a powerful possession of me that I cried at the top of my voice, and I exclaimed that I would not leave, and I proclaimed that I would not leave this place, that if all the men on earth, and all the devils in hell surrounded me. I prayed until my mind became so full that before I was aware of it I was on my feet and tripping up the ascent towards the road."

Though he had gone into the woods at dawn, when he reached town it was already noon. He had been so deep in prayer that time had lost all meaning to him. He later went to dinner but discovered that he had no appetite for food, so he went to his office to play hymns on his bass viola, but he found that he couldn't sing without weeping.

He shares what happened as that night progressed: "All my feelings seemed to rise and to flow out, the utterance of my heart was, I want to pour out my whole soul to God. The rising of my soul was so great, I went…back to the front office to pray, I wept like a child, and made such confession as I could with my choked utterance. It seemed to be as though I bathed His feet with my tears."[5]

This weeping servant sowed precious seed into the lives of two and a half million people who came to know the Lord Jesus Christ as their personal Savior. Research tells us that at least 75 percent of these converts remained true to Christ till their deaths.

This is what we need today—men and women of God who learn the power of tears, the compassion of Christ, the importance of prayer, and the fire of the Holy Ghost.

Do What Matters

A few years ago, in one of those times of transition that God loves and we tend to disdain, I was fervently seeking the Lord. Like a shepherd guiding His sheep, Jesus my Great Shepherd responded to my passionate prayer and gave me a dream of wisdom and guidance. In this enlightening dream, I was soaring through the heavens like an American kestrel, a bird that is noted for its ability to hover in the air against even strong winds. Sometimes the kestrel appears to be standing still in midair. So, here I was, flying like a bird through the air when suddenly everything stopped. Next, I received a tremendous revelation.

I saw a beautiful garden next to a great stone wall and an attractive stucco-covered house. It was as if I was looking at this scene through a camera's zoom lens. I saw a spectacular array of multicolored flowers and then saw a woman in a red dress; she was bent over, working in the garden.

Somehow I knew this woman was my Aunt Mae, a wonderful, godly woman who had inspired my life at a very early age. I remembered the details of her scarlet red dress. She looked up at me and slowly said, "Do...what...matters." That's all I heard in the dream, and then the revelation was over.

This was a pictorial representation of my mother's oldest sister, and she was giving me a very important message as she worked in her garden as she had always loved to do. Aunt Mae gave her life to serve others. She remained single all through her life, and fully presented herself to God so He could use her as He desired. This wonderful lady impacted my life in so many important ways in my youth, and I still miss her today, though she has been with the Lord for many years now.

In the dream her voice said, "Do what matters," and I knew immediately what the Lord was referring to. What's important in this life? Paul says, "...The only thing that counts is faith expressing itself through love" (Gal. 5:6, NIV).

As you get the heart of God, which is love, you can't help but do what matters.

Brought Back by the Tears of a Friend

When I was in Prague some time ago, I learned that one of the main pastors, Evald Ruffy of a Moravian church, would not be able to be with us because he had suffered a heart attack while ministering in Sweden, and he was in a coma.

His best friend, Peter, called for Christians throughout the Czech Republic to pray for Pastor Ruffy. As he traveled to Sweden to be with the pastor, Peter felt as if he was actually taking the prayers of the saints with him. He said that he could definitely feel the power of their prayers as he walked into the hospital.

An eruption of the Holy Spirit took place within Peter in the entranceway of the hospital, and he was stirred with compassion deep within. Meanwhile, Pastor Evald had already spent three days with God in heaven, where he discovered many spiritual mysteries. He was able to look down upon the earth from his heavenly vantage point, and he saw dark clouds all over Central and Eastern Europe. While beholding this scene, he noticed white lights going up and down through the black clouds. He asked his Guide, the Holy Spirit, "What is this?"

"Well, the dark clouds are the territorial spirits of darkness that are over Central Europe."

The pastor raised another question: "What are those white lights?"

"Oh, those are My angels, and they are breaking up the powers of darkness over Central Europe."

"How does this happen?" the pastor asked.

"Oh, this happens in answer to the prayers of the saints."

Pastor Evald was greatly enjoying this special experience that God was giving to him unbeknownst to Peter, who was now standing by his friend's bed feeling somewhat helpless. In his weakness, Peter began to cry, weeping profusely over his friend. When his tears streamed down his face and fell onto his friend's face and body, something amazing happened.

Those tears that splashed upon Evald's face caused him to realize that his work on earth was not over. He still had more to do as a husband, father, and pastor. His eyes opened, and he was instantly released from the coma that had imprisoned and immobilized him. In fact, he was totally healed. Even his doctors declared that what happened to him was a miracle.

The power of tears had brought healing to a man of God, a modern-day apostle who went on to establish many Spirit-filled evangelical Moravian churches in Eastern Europe.

Intercessory prayer combined with compassionate weeping is a powerful force that truly brings change in our world today. As William Booth declared, "Try tears!"

Do you want to move in compassion? Then receive compassion.

Do you want to move in healing? Then receive healing. Do you want to move in deliverance? Then receive deliverance. Whatever you receive by faith through the love of God you will be authorized to give away.

Stop by the gateway of the sixth door as I have, and drink deeply from the brook of mercy. This will enable you to continue to move forward in your walk of being more like Jesus and to empower you to do the works of Christ.

Jesus said, "Freely you have received, freely give" (Matt. 10:8, NKJV).

Heavenly Father, your Word declares that you welcome those who have a broken and a contrite heart. Give me your great grace so that I can walk in unison with Your heart. Help me to humble myself before you, leaning on Jesus. Lord, grant me the gift of tears and a compassionate heart, so that I can see life spring forth where it seems hopeless and lifeless. I desire your heart, Lord, and I cry with streams of tears, as Joel did so long ago, "I rend my heart in hope that You will bring forth newness of life, victory, healing, joy, and compassion to those in need." In Jesus' great name, amen.

Part Two

Lives of
Compassion

Part Two is devoted to eleven women who have spent their lives in compassionate service to God and others. These women and many others have pioneered the way so that God's compassion might be expressed in new and creative ways in the lives of countless millions of people around the world.

May your heart be stirred as you read these stories, and may they become sources of inspiration so that you will live a life of compassion in your own world.

Chapter 3

🌿

Catherine Booth

THE MOTHER OF THE SALVATION ARMY

(Michal Ann Goll)

A true heroine of faith and compassion, Catherine Booth, paved the way for the liberation and deliverance of women, children, the downtrodden, the forgotten, the lost, and the dying. And from her courageous example we can learn so much.

In Catherine's time very few women ever rose to speak to a church congregation. One day, however, as Catherine was sitting in the Gateshead Bethesda Chapel, she felt a strong urging to rise and speak. As she prepared to do so, she heard an inner voice say, "You will look like a fool and have nothing to say!"

She recognized the voice as being the devil, and she countered with, "That's just the point! I have never yet been willing to be a fool for Christ. Now I will be one!"[1]

I love this lady and the wonderful determination she exhibited in the face of seemingly insurmountable odds, although it is difficult to separate her life and accomplishments from those of her husband, William. William and Catherine exemplify a "Barak and Deborah" kind of anointing. Their ministries blended together and overlapped; the ministry and anointing of one made the other's possible.

"God shall have all there is of William Booth!"

William Booth was born on April 19, 1829, in Nottingham, England. His father, Samuel, was a builder, but the economic conditions were very poor in England at this time, which meant that the homes he built were not selling. He could neither sell nor rent the homes he built, so he eventually lost everything, including the mortgage on his own house.

Though he had great plans for William, including a good gentleman's education, Samuel did not have enough money to make this happen for his son. Therefore, when William was thirteen years old, he was apprenticed to a pawnbroker in a horrible part of Nottingham, where homeless people had to live in the streets.

Less than a year later, Samuel Booth died, so William was faced with the dismal prospects of having to support the family, which included his mother and his sisters. Eventually, his mother was able to find a job running a small shop, and between their two incomes, they managed to keep food on the family table.[2]

As a result of working in such a poor part of the city, William saw firsthand how the poor had to live and how miserable most of them were. He responded to the misery he saw around him with a sense of gloom and despair until one night in 1844, when he was walking home after work.

Suddenly, a sense of spiritual exaltation flooded his entire being. This was very much like John Wesley's Aldersgate Chapel experience, when the founder of the Methodist Church felt his heart "strangely warmed." In William's case he responded by renouncing his sin and turning his heart and life over to the Lord. This was the earnest declaration he made that night: "God shall have all there is of William Booth!"

Soon thereafter, William began to blend his social consciousness with his newfound faith, and a great desire grew within him to see an organization formed that would have the salvation of the world as its supreme ambition and goal. His perspective was a practical one; he wanted to meet the real needs of people. Therefore, he wasn't very much concerned with ecclesiastical creeds, rituals, and forms.

Several preachers, including the American revivalist James Caughey, held evangelistic meetings in Nottingham in 1846, and they became William's mentors. He learned a great deal about God from these men. He also read the sermons and books of John Wesley, George Whitefield, and Charles Finney, particularly Finney's *Lectures on Revivals of Religion*.

William and his friend Will Sansom joined their hearts and hands together by determining to make a difference in the lives of the people of the Meadow Platts neighborhood, another very poor section of the city. Theirs was a roll-up-your-sleeves kind of faith that wasn't afraid to reach out and touch the actual needs of people. The compassion these men had in their hearts for the "down and outers" of society made them unafraid to act on behalf of others.

These two men did more than just hold meetings; they went on to visit and encourage those who made decisions for Christ, and they visited the sick in the community as well.

This was a time when the average life expectancy, due to disease and other factors, was short—only thirty-five to forty years of age. Unfortunately, Will Sansom died soon after the two men began their ministry. It was then when William began conducting open-air meetings for the poor in Red Lion's Square and "down in the bottoms," one of Nottingham's cruelest neighborhoods.

Booth wrote, "I saw terrible sights—ragged, shrieking people, little children foraging for food, dirty women, some clad only in soiled petticoats, more little children—these appeared drunk, with their mothers forcing beer down their throats—whimpering, hungry dogs, men's faces with animal passion written all over them as they watched dancing women in the street."[3]

Later, in a letter he sent to Catherine from London, he wrote,

I've been told that there are 3 million souls in London, and 100,000 paupers. After what I've seen this week, I know it's true. Many of these people are on the brink of starvation.... Catherine, the people are sick, some of them dying, some are already dead. And the smell...the whole city stinks, I couldn't escape it.... I've found my destiny. It's a human jungle out there. I've been walking in the midst of it.... It's as bad as any tiger-infested jungle in darkest Africa.

Because of his hard work and his passion for the poor, William Booth became known as "Willful Will." He was very much like the American evangelist Dwight L. Moody, who ministered in Chicago later in that same century. Moody said that the world had yet to see what would happen when one man gave his life unreservedly to the Lord, and he said he intended to be that man.

"My God, I am Thine!"

Now let's take a closer look at the life of Catherine Booth, who was born on January 17, 1829, in Ashburn, Derbyshire. Her maiden name was Mumford, and her father was a rather unstable individual who exhibited very erratic behavior. At one time he had been a lay preacher in the Methodist Church, then he became a temperance advocate who preached vigorously against alcohol, but finally he became an alcoholic himself. He was prone to wild swings of uncontrollable emotions, which created an environment of disorder and uncertainty for his daughter as she was growing up.

As the child of an alcoholic, Catherine knew firsthand what happens to families affected by alcoholism. By the time she was twelve, she was able to attend a girls' school and became the secretary of the Juvenile Temperance Society, and she had read the Bible all the way through eight times. Catherine's mentors included Charles Finney and John Wesley, and she read many of the same works that her future husband had read.

When Catherine was fourteen, she developed a spinal curvature; then, four years later, she was diagnosed with incipient tuberculosis. She was home-schooled during much of this time. Because she was isolated from other children her age, she was able to cultivate her relationship with her heavenly Father. She read the Bible and also studied church history and theology. This was when her writing career began, as it was while she was sick in bed that she began writing magazine articles that warned of the dangers of alcohol, and she became a supporter of temperance societies.[4]

When Catherine was sixteen, she had a radical conversion experience in church on a Sunday morning. This happened because she took to heart the words of a hymn written by Charles Wesley: "My God, I am thine, what a comfort divine, what a blessing to know that Jesus is mine." She surrendered her life to the Lord Jesus Christ, and she knew that He took up His residence in her heart.

Catherine and her mother were attending a Wesleyan Methodist

Church at this time, but like so many others, including William, they got caught in the division between the Wesleyan Methodists and the Reformers, who had broken from the Methodist Church because they perceived it to be cold and lifeless, too conservative for their tastes. Both William and Catherine were expelled from the Methodist Church because they favored the Reformers.

Their relationship with the Reformers did not last long, however, for the Reformers stressed strong organization and a lot of committee work, which many perceived as detrimental to the more important work of revival.

She became a strong advocate for the unlimited involvement of women in all aspects of worship, teaching, and leadership in the church. In that regard, Catherine Booth was definitely a woman who was ahead of her time.

What God Has Joined Together

In 1852 Catherine met William Booth, a Methodist minister. By this time the Methodist church had lost some of the fervor it had known during the previous century, when the Wesleys—John, Charles, Samuel, and their mother, Susanna—had been instrumental in bringing great change to the church.

William Booth, however, was on fire for God, and he believed that ministers should be involved in "loosing chains of injustice, freeing the captive and oppressed, sharing food and home, clothing the naked, and carrying out family responsibilities." He was a man who was committed to compassionate reform.[5]

Though they loved each other deeply, William and Catherine did have their differences. One of these involved the role of women in the church. These were days in which women were not permitted to minister in the church. Even William Booth regarded them as "the weaker sex," and this aggravated Catherine very much. She could not believe how prejudiced her husband was with regard to women, and she said, "Oh, prejudice, what will it not do, that woman is in any respect, except physical strength and courage, inferior to man, I cannot see cause to believe, and I am sure no one can prove it from the Word of God."

Initially William was strongly opposed to the idea of women preachers, and he based this position on what Paul had written: "Let your women keep silent in the churches, for they are not permitted to speak; but they are to be submissive, as the law also says" (1 Cor. 14:34, NKJV). I believe that this Scripture has been misinterpreted for centuries, not taking into account that Paul was referring to women who had previously been temple prostitutes, or who were newly converted to Christianity, and therefore untaught in appropriate behavior and customs for a Christian context.

However, Catherine believed that God loved women as much as He loved men and that He had endowed women with qualities and gifts that were equal to those He gave to men.

As time went on, William began to rethink his position on this issue, and he said, "I would not encourage a woman to begin preaching, although I would not stop her on any account." His focus was on the salvation of the world, so he said, "I am for the world's salvation; I will quarrel with no means that promises help." Here we see his attitude concerning the role of women beginning to undergo some change.

Catherine said, "What can we do to wake the Church up? Too often those who have its destinies in the palm of their hands are chiefly chosen from those who are mere encyclopedias of the past rather than from those who are distinguished by their possession of Divine Power. For leadership of the Church something more is required."[6]

This couple, despite their differences, was sold out to God. Catherine once wrote these words to her husband: "The nearer our assimilation to Jesus, the more perfect and heavenly our union." They knew that for their marriage to work, they had to put God first.

William was now beginning to learn things about his wife that he had not known before. He discovered that in conversation she was someone who could hold her own with anyone. She was a very intelligent lady who was conversant about many different things.

For example, she was able to discuss current trends in the churches of England, and she was very much concerned about the controversy swirling between the Revivalists and the anti-revival movement. In addition, Catherine understood the plight of the poor.

Sometimes William would fall victim to fits of gloom and depression. At such times Catherine would stir him up again and give him fresh reasons for battling on. He began to recognize her as his equal and to see that her capacity for work and self-sacrifice was as strong as his. She was both a stimulant and a stabilizer for her husband.

Catherine's compelling and heart-touching writings became well-known throughout England, and she became known simply as "the woman preacher." In the early days of her public ministry, she spoke these strong words about her role: "I dare say many of you have been looking on me as a very devoted woman, but I have been disobeying God. I am convinced that women have the right and duty to speak up; yes, even to preach! I have struggled with this for a long time, but I'll struggle with it no longer."

When William heard his wife preach, he completely changed his mind about women preachers. He did so in spite of the fact that many people judged him for doing so and continued to feel that women preachers were unbiblical.[7] Lord Shaftesbury, a well-known politician and evangelist, actually declared that William Booth was the antichrist due to his attitude toward women preachers. This did not seem to faze William, however, for he commented, "The best men in my army are the women."[8]

Catherine went on to teach Bible studies, visit in the homes of the poor, and reach out to women who were greatly abused and oppressed. She made this observation, "The plight of the women is so pathetic."[9] Here we see the birth of a woman preacher, who became a heroine and mentor to thousands of women, but she was never ordained. Nonetheless, during the first few months of 1861, while the Civil War was raging in America, Catherine began accepting invitations to preach in public.

She and William served in several different communities, including Gateshead, a town of 50,000 that is located just across the River Tyne from Newcastle, on the northeastern coast of England.

When William became sick during the summer of 1860, Catherine had to take over all his duties, for it took him several months to recover. As a result, her remarkable abilities became known to many and her fame as "the woman preacher" grew far and wide.

Trailblazer for Women

In nineteenth-century England, as a result of the Industrial Revolution, poverty, crime, disease, corruption, prostitution, alcoholism, and immorality were rampant. We read about some of these conditions in the socially realistic novels that were written by Charles Dickens.

The Beer Bill of 1830 allowed pubs to be legally open from 4:00 A.M. to 10:00 P.M., and many people would spend their meager wages on beer and ale. Decades of beer drinking brought forth an entire generation of drunkards who lost sight of all moral values. Mothers would even serve beer to their small children, who became alcoholics before they reached puberty.

Working conditions were horrendous for everyone, especially women and children. While working with the poor in London, Catherine Booth learned about "sweated labor," women and children who had to work long hours for very low wages in the worst imaginable conditions.[10] In certain London tenements Catherine found seamstresses, for example, who had to hem and stitch for eleven hours or more each day, and their pay was abysmally low.[11]

Catherine's work among the poor grew into a ministry that seemed as powerful as her husband's preaching, and she continued to preach the gospel despite the many criticisms she and her husband received.

When she became aware of a pamphlet that was written by a Rev. A. A. Reese, which was a diatribe against the ministry of Phoebe Palmer (who ministered in both England and America and who had written *The Way of Holiness and Faith and Its Effects)*, Catherine responded by writing a booklet of her own titled *Female Teaching: or the Reverend A. A. Reese vs. Mrs. Palmer, Being a Reply to a Pamphlet by the Above Named Gentleman on the Sunderland Revival,* in which she voiced her support of Phoebe's ministry.

Catherine Booth was a true trailblazer for women, and she was a model of Christian compassion at work in the world.

The Fruit of Their Labors

The Booths' first evangelistic work began on August 11, 1861, in Cornwall County. Originally planned as a seven-week revival, the crusade was extended to an eighteen-month campaign, unparalleled in that part of England at least since the time of John Wesley.

At least seven thousand Cornishmen found peace with God during this year and a half. It was even reported that fishermen sailed ten miles across dark and choppy waters to hear the young couple preach. Similarly, it was not unusual for villagers to walk several miles to attend the meetings. As a result, many shop owners experienced a great decline in sales, because people's hearts were turning away from material things.

There was a great hunger for God in the hearts of the people. This included Catherine's father, who returned to the Lord. The Booths' outreach was not limited to church people, and they discovered that people who frequented the pubs were "more likely to go through a tent flap than through an oaken church door to find God."

William Booth recognized the fact that clergymen weren't reaching the people who had the greatest needs, and he wondered how he would be able to unite his ministry with that of the local church. Many of the new converts, when they went to churches, were greatly disappointed by the stale traditionalism they found there. He wanted his converts to be able to find a "church home."

Therefore, the Booths began to look for ways to connect evangelism to the local church.

Bringing the Poor and the Wealthy Together

Another cry in the hearts of William and Catherine Booth was to find a way to bring the poor and wealthy together. Therefore, William boldly took the poor into the wealthiest churches of Nottingham. His approach was not well-received by the established church.

As a result of the friction, the Booths left the Reformers and joined a group called the Methodist New Connection, which had a strong Wesleyan foundation, supported revivalism, and encouraged lay people to get involved in the decision-making. This organization's magazine provided Catherine a great opportunity to continue her writing ministry.

Then in the spring of 1857, at the annual conference of the Methodist New Connection, William was removed from his position as a full-time evangelist because some of the leaders of the organization were no longer comfortable with his methods. They had made him take a regular preaching circuit in an effort to force him to focus on pastoral responsibilities rather than evangelism. The particular circuit to which they assigned William was obscure and unsuccessful. The leaders must have felt that this was the perfect place to "keep him out of trouble." William endured this assignment but did not really like it, and in the meantime Catherine's ministry continued to flourish.

The following year William was ordained as a minister, and his next pastoral assignment was in Gateshead. This was when real release began to happen in the Booths' ministry and their evangelistic outreach began to surge. At this point the young couple began to experiment with publicity, and they distributed handbills door to door throughout every neighborhood. They also conducted street meetings, which consisted of hymn-singing, exhortations, and invitations to attend church services.

In an effort to meet the needs of people where they were, the Booths began to take the popular melodies and tunes of their day and adapt them for use as gospel songs. They made their ministry relevant to the needs of the people.

Before their meetings would begin, the Booths would set aside an entire day of prayer, and this had a great impact on the services, paving the way for the Spirit of God to find entrance into the prepared hearts and lives of the people who attended. William and Catherine loved the people, and the people responded to their love, which reflected the Father's heart to them.

The Salvation Army Is Born

On August 7, 1878, William declared his vision for the Salvation Army. He said, "To postpone action any further will be an act of disobedience to what we both sense is the divine will of God."

Catherine was in full support of this declaration. She said, "William, don't hold back because of me. I can trust in God and go out with Him, and I can live on bread and water. Go out and do your duty. God will provide if we will only go straight on in the path of duty."

At this point they broke with the Methodist New Connection and began their own independent evangelistic ministry. The distinguishing features of this ministry were authority, obedience, the adapted employment of everyone's abilities, the training and discipline of all workers, and the combined action of all.

They adapted army jargon in their work. William believed very much in the chain of command, and he became a general, whose job was to oversee the ministry. They trained the people who worked with them and taught them how to endure and rise above the mocking of the crowds in the street, which sometimes occurred. The idea of uniforms began to emerge at this point as well, and the bonnets for the women were designed in such a way as to protect them from rotten eggs and garbage that were sometimes thrown at them.

The Booths expected their workers to go into the most distressful situations and love the most needy, the most hurting, and sometimes even the most hateful. They also believed in the importance of combining their forces like a mighty army as they reached out to those in need.

At this stage in their lives, William and Catherine Booth were both only thirty-two years old. They had five children and very little money. They settled in Leeds, a town in the English midlands, and began to conduct separate campaigns so as to increase their effectiveness.

Hundreds of adults and children responded to the invitation to find Christ under Catherine's preaching ministry. Her preaching, along with the success William was experiencing in his ministry to the poor, came to the notice of *The Revival*, England's premier evangelistic journal. As a result, William was invited to preach in White Chapel in early 1865. White Chapel was a poor section in the notorious East End of London. He asked Catherine to preach there as well.

Soon thereafter, Catherine became aware of the Midnight Movement for Fallen Women, an agency that combined evangelism with social redemption. Her experience with this organization opened her eyes to the need for social concern to become a part of their ministry. Catherine began to see a need to champion the cause of women, and she advocated for them to be placed in positions of responsibility and usefulness within the church. Through her preaching in the West End, she touched the hearts and lives of people who could help provide financial support for the struggling work William was doing in the East End.

When speaking publicly, Catherine never minced her words. She spoke with boldness and righteous indignation as she confronted the evils of her day. In so doing she made the comfortable less comfortable, and she even went so far as to accuse affluent Christians by saying that they were responsible for the sweatshops and the filthy working conditions in which women and children found themselves.

Once she made this statement: "It will be a happy day for England when Christian ladies transfer their sympathies from poodles and terriers to destitute and starving children."

The Booths then created the East London Christian Revival Society, which became known as the East London Christian Mission or, more commonly, the Christian Mission. The name was later changed to the Salvation Army. Catherine became the primary promoter of this ministry, while William continued to work among the poor in the East End. What a team they were, with Catherine doing the preaching and raising the funds, and William in the slums ministering to the needs of the poor.

Early on, their children learned what ministry was all about. Their oldest child, William Bramwell Booth, was dedicated to God when he was born. Catherine said, "I held him up to God as soon as I had strength to do so, and I remember specially desiring that he should be an advocate of holiness."

Ballington, their second son, began to see himself as a preacher when he was eleven. He even preached to his sisters' dolls. One of his "new converts" was a pillow in a chair. Looking at this pillow, he was heard commanding, "Give up the drink, brother!"

The younger children were Kate, Herbert, Emma, and Marion, who was an invalid, and then along came Evangeline Corey, who eventually became the first woman general of the Salvation Army, and Lucy. The Booths had a total of eight children, and each became active in the work of the Salvation Army. Their children said that Catherine not only patched their clothing, but she even made them proud of the patches.

Bramwell recalled that his father once took him into a pub in the East End of London where he saw the men's alcohol-inflamed faces and observed drunken, disheveled women nursing their babies. Although he was nauseated by the pungent aroma of gin, tobacco, and sweat, his father turned to him and said, "These are our people; these are the people I want you to live for and bring to Christ."

Catherine Booth organized Food-for-the-Million shops, where the poor could afford inexpensively priced hot soup and three-course dinners. On special occasions such as Christmas, she would sometimes cook more than three hundred dinners that were distributed to the poor.

By 1882 there were almost 17,000 people worshiping under the auspices of the Salvation Army, far more than the attendance in mainline churches. This caused the Archbishop of York, the Rev. Dr. William Thornton, to comment that the Salvation Army was reaching people that the Church of England had failed to reach.

Since those early days and more than a century later, the Salvation Army remains a vital force in the world. As a result of the army's ministry, new laws protecting women and children were enacted in England. The impact of the Salvation Army was reached around the world, and its ministries have included prison work, youth work, rescue homes for women, ministry to alcoholics and drug addicts, rescue missions, salvage operations, disaster relief, and men's hostels.

The Salvation Army has earned the respect of the White House, the United States Supreme Court, embassies around the world, the U.S. Congress, and governments in many nations.

Catherine Booth was the mother of the Salvation Army—a true "mother in Israel." She knew that *compassion acts.* She knew that it is born out of passion for the Father's heart. She wrote, "Don't let controversy hurt your soul. Live near to God by prayer. Just fall down at his feet and open your very soul before him, and throw yourself right into his arms."

Father God, thank You for the wonderful example of Catherine Booth. Help us to be like her, people who fall at your feet and open our souls before you. I throw myself into Your arms, dear Father, and ask You to light the fires of passion in my heart, that I would be aflame with Your love and go forth in compassion to those who need to know how much You love them. Let me become a true agent of change in the world, as I act in mercy to others. Give me Your wisdom, Lord, so I can see things from Your point of view. Help me not to lean upon my own insight, but to trust You for all things. As I acknowledge You, I know You will direct my path. In Jesus' name, amen.

🌿

Chapter 4

Nancy Ward

Nan-ye-hi (Nancy Ward), Ghighau (Beloved Woman)
of the Ani-Yunwiya (Principal People)

BELOVED WOMAN
OF THE CHEROKEE

(Ada Winn, with Dr. J. Mark Rodgers)

A fresh wind is blowing within the body of Christ. Across denominational, racial, and political lines the Spirit of God is exposing the roots of ritual-based, Christian religion. This exposure is showing many of us ways in which our religious expressions have supplanted an authentic relationship with the Father.

Whether or not we like to admit it, the cultures that most dramatically shaped our nation as we know it were those of the Greeks and Romans. Even in this modern era, their societies continue to influence government structures, health care delivery systems, educational institutions, and, perhaps most importantly, religious structures in America. The third-century Roman Church is responsible for when we worship, where we worship, how we worship, and with whom we worship. It is said that Christian faith conquered Rome and then Rome conquered Christianity. It is out of a conquering mind-set that most people view American history. Could it be that God views the United States differently?

Over the millennia, European societies exploited environmental conditions for the purpose of gaining greater wealth and opulence.

Wealth represented power, and power, in turn, control. During this same time period, Native American societies lived in cooperation with their environment; in contrast to exploitation, they practiced stewardship. When Europeans arrived on the continent of North America, they found a pristine environment that showed little impact from thousands of years of human habitation. It is out of those thousands of years of stewardship that we examine the life of one Native American we know as Nancy Ward.[1]

Her native name was Nan-ye-hi. In the custom of many Europeans, white people anglicized her name to Nancy. Out of respect for her, I will use her native name for the remainder of this chapter.

Nan-ye-hi was born sometime around 1737 in Chota, the capital of the Cherokee Nation. She was described as a strikingly beautiful woman with a tall, erect figure, prominent nose, piercing black eyes, and silken black hair. Because her skin was tinted like a reddish-pink rose, she was given the nickname Tsistuna-gis-ka, or Wild Rose. As she grew older, Nan-ye-hi matured with a stately but kind disposition, carrying herself in a queenly and majestic way.

Cherokee societies were matrilineal. Warriors received their status in the tribe from their mother's lineage, not from their father's. In this matrilineal society, women were stewards of the land, not the men. The women enjoyed more matrimonial rights than men; upon marriage, the men became members of their wife's clan, with their homes along with the contents belonging to the women. Children belonged to the mother's clan. It was into matrilineal lines of the tribal leadership that Nan-ye-hi was born.

Her mother was said to have been Tame Doe. Tame Doe was a niece of Old Hop, who was a principal chief. One of Tame Doe's brothers was Attakullakulla, a celebrated peace chief. Historians rated him as one of the most influential leaders among the southern tribes. He was named Little Carpenter by the whites because of his diplomatic skills, which included fitting parts of peace treaties together into a workable diplomatic document.

Nan-ye-hi married early by today's standards. She married Kingfisher when she was only sixteen years of age. Kingfisher was a leader within the tribe, and his leadership was tested during one of the fiercest battles recorded in Cherokee history, the battle of Taliwa in 1755. Led by their great war chief, Oconostota, the Cherokee were determined to drive the Creeks out of their land. Creek opponents reportedly outnumbered a five-hundred-man Cherokee war party. In support of her husband during this battle, Nan-ye-hi was chewing the musket balls for his rifle, in hopes that they would become more jagged and lethal.

There were war whoops and screams, the sound of musket fire, and the yelling of commands over the din of the battle. In the midst of the fight, Kingfisher was struck down with a mortal wound. I imagine that husband and wife glanced at each other for one brief moment realizing the tragedy that had befallen them. When this sixteen-year-old bride witnessed the flicker of life leave her husband, Nan-ye-hi distinguished herself from other women. Even though it was common for a woman to support her warrior husband, it was very uncharacteristic to join in the battle and continue the fight. Her unwavering bravery that day rallied the Cherokee warriors and routed the Creeks from northern Georgia.

After the appropriate time of mourning, the tribe celebrated Nan-ye-hi's efforts in this nationally significant battle by bestowing upon her the honor of Ghighau or "Beloved Woman." Nan-ye-hi was in her teens when vaulted into her high position—an honor ordinarily bestowed on older women.

Ghighau was more than a term of endearment; it enabled Nan-ye-hi to participate in negotiations for treaties, to commute death sentences passed upon by tribal leadership, and to prepare portions of ceremonial offerings given to the men of the tribe. The Beloved Woman title was a lifetime distinction. During state council meetings in the townhouse, Ghighau sat with the peace chief and war chief in the holy area near the ceremonial fire. As head of the women's council, she would represent the view of women in the tribe. The female council did not hesitate to vote to oppose the decisions made by the ruling headsmen, particularly if they felt that the welfare of the tribe was at stake. It was during the lifetime of Nan-ye-hi that tribal leadership passed all but two of the land cession treaties with the Cherokee.

During the 1700s, European settlers began in earnest to encroach upon Cherokee lands. The surge of newly arriving immigrants increased annually. These newcomers pressed westward as settlements grew crowded in the east. They saw vast stretches of wilderness seemingly uninhabited except for scattered tribal villages, and all native people were viewed as inhabitants with no recorded claim or title to the land. As rising unrest was apparent (the colonies were preparing for war against British rule), westward expansion continued.

Trade between the native people and Europeans was more like exploitation than marketplace equality. English traders' demand of animal skins increased yearly. Up until 1750, an average of 54,000 deerskins per year were shipped from Charles Town (today known as Charleston, South Carolina). By 1759, it is said that over 1.5 million deerskins were shipped annually through the Charles Town port. This "big kill," as it is called, almost exhausted the deer population in the South.

The fledgling independence movement found its way across the Appalachian Mountains into what is now eastern Tennessee. Having to face either the tyranny of British rule or hostile tribes, some chose to face the Cherokee. Despite stern warnings from the Crown of England for all white settlers to leave native land west of the Appalachian Mountains, settlements at Watauga and Nolichucky were created.

The Cherokees' first reaction was not war. The Cherokee tribal council negotiated a ten-year lease agreement with the Wataugans. In exchange for this land lease, they were to receive the equivalent of a $1,000 per year in trade goods. Their desire was to live peacefully alongside the white settlers while they remained stewards of the land. The Wataugans also agreed to no further encroachment on native lands. There was a peaceful coexistence during the early years of the lease, but this peace was short-lived when the settlers annexed more land without providing trade goods as promised.

After many violated treaties by the settlers, a battle erupted with the Wataugan and Nolichucky settlements during the summer of 1776. Nan-ye-hi sent messages to Fort Watauga and the surrounding communities warning of an attack. Some might question her motives in warning the settlers; however, her desire was to live peacefully with the white population. The Cherokee, led by Dragging Canoe, Nan-ye-hi's cousin, were defeated by the settlers due to her warning before the attack, and the attack on Fort Watauga was repelled.

During this battle, Chief Old Abram captured two prisoners who were taken back to Cherokee villages. One of the captives was a Mrs. William Bean. Tied to a pole with leather thongs, she had dry tree branches laid around her feet and lit on fire. When Nan-ye-hi learned of the planned execution, she kicked the burning branches away, stomped out the remaining small flames, and cut the throngs, freeing Mrs. Bean. She then addressed the angered warriors and spoke with harsh words, "It revolts my soul that Cherokee warriors would stoop so low as to torture this woman. No woman shall be tortured or burned at the stake while I am Honored Woman."

This incident shows Nan-ye-hi exercising her official position as Ghighau. Nan-ye-hi led Mrs. Bean to her home in Chota, the town of sanctuary, and asked Mrs. Bean to teach her and the members of her family how to process cow's milk to make butter and cheese. She was hoping to encourage interest in her people for raising their own meat and farm crops, since dependence solely on dwindling wildlife, resources of the forest, and expensive supplies would spell certain failure for her people. Nan-ye-hi also learned the art of weaving cloth, or "homespun," from Mrs. Bean. When it was safe to do so, Nan-ye-hi sent Mrs. Bean back to her home. Nan-ye-hi's son, Fivekiller, and her brother, Longfellow, escorted Mrs. Bean to protect her during the journey.

It was sometime during this time when Nan-ye-hi met a trader named Bryant Ward. Some believe that she and her friends protected the life of this trader during a time of hostility. Bryant Ward and Nan-ye-hi were married shortly thereafter. As a woman in a matrilineal society, she had rights to take a husband as she pleased, even when her choice was outside of her race. What is more interesting is that she took his last name in direct conflict with her cultural upbringing. You may recall that the men took their wife's heritage after marriage. Nan-ye-hi was sending yet another message that it was possible to make changes in order to preserve a way of life.

Throughout Nan-ye-hi's life, her tribe was approached many times about additional acquisitions of land. Very few of the treaties signed with the native peoples of America were kept by either the British or American governments. Hostilities continued to flare as native warriors retaliated for white encroachments, and white settlers exacted their revenge on native populations for what they felt were atrocities. Nan-ye-hi found herself continuously in a place of attempting to mediate between warring factions.

One time when the Cherokee were going to war against the white settlers, Nan-ye-hi again found herself forewarning frontier settlers of an imminent attack by Dragging Canoe. She saw that every time the Cherokee were on the warpath, her nation suffered tragically. She had witnessed indiscriminant killing on both sides. Perhaps she hoped that by sending her warning, much bloodshed could be avoided.

Nan-ye-hi never acted alone in any of these warnings to frontier settlers. Her tribal leadership had met and voted to continue peacefully, but the warring chiefs would not listen to those who were in leadership. In sending warning of attack, Nan-ye-hi was representing what she thought was the true nature of official tribal leadership.

A new treaty was demanded by the Cherokee in order to prevent future battles with the new American colonies. Nan-ye-hi rose from the negotiations and eloquently addressed both parties present: "You know that women are always looked upon as nothing, but we are your mothers. You are our sons. Our cry is all for peace. Let it continue. This peace must last forever. Let your women's sons be ours, our sons be yours, let your women hear our words." The sincerity and appeal of her words reached the hearts of her listeners.

Colonel William Christian was chosen to answer Nan-ye-hi's comments. He said, "Mothers, we have listened well to your talk. It is humane. No man can hear it without being moved by it. Such words and thoughts show the world that human nature is the same everywhere. Our women shall hear your words and we know how they will feel and think of them. We are all descendants of the same woman. We will not quarrel with you because you are our mothers. We will not meddle with your people if they will be still and quiet at home and let us live in peace." This is one of the very few treaties, if not the only one, that did not ask for land.

Her speech placed Nan-ye-hi in the ranks of great women of America. The time of her talk was July 1781. Nan-ye-hi had witnessed the burning and pillage of her tribe. She had every right to be bitter in seeing everything she loved destroyed; however, she chose a different path—the path of peace. It took fortitude and character for any woman warrior not to strike back.

By 1784, Nan-ye-hi Ward's home in the beloved town of Chota could no longer remain a prominent place in Cherokee history. It was burned and pillaged first by the British and later by American colonists. Legend has it that prior to Nan-ye-hi moving from Chota, she opened her home to orphaned native children (mostly outcast and abandoned children of white traders and native women), perhaps the only real sanctuary these youngsters ever enjoyed. A Lieutenant Francis Marion wrote with eloquent terms what he saw take place:

> We proceeded by Colonel Grant's orders to burn the Indian cabins....I saw everywhere around the footsteps of little Indian children where they had lately played under the shade of their rustling corn. When we are gone, thought I, they will return and, peeping through the weeds with tearful eyes, will mark the ghastly ruin where they had so often played. 'Who did this?' they will ask their mothers, and the reply will be, 'The white people did it, the Christians did it.' Thus, for cursed mammon's sake, the followers of Christ have sowed the selfish tares of hate...

Nan-ye-hi remained an advocate for her country and nation for several years. She continued to speak of the necessity of her people to devote more attention to farming and raising stock as a means of survival. One of Nan-ye-hi's last treaties with the Cherokee, Article 14 of the Holston River Treaty, guaranteed their ability and assistance in husbandry and agriculture as they would continue to prosper in their land.

Nan-ye-hi Ward addressed her nation for the last time on May 2, 1817:

> The Cherokee ladies now being present at the meetings of the chiefs and warriors in council have thought it their duty as mothers to address their beloved chiefs and warriors now assembled.
>
> Our beloved children and head men of the Cherokee Nation, we address you warriors in council. We have raised all of you on the land which we now have, which God gave us to inhabit

and raise provisions. We know that our country has once been extensive but by repeated sales has become circumscribed to a small tract, and never have thought it our duty to interfere in the disposition of it until now. If a father or mother was to sell all their lands which they had to depend, on which their children had to raise their living on which would be indeed bad, and to be removed to another country, we do not wish to go to any unknown country which we have understood some of our children wish to go over the Mississippi. But this act of our children would be like destroying your mothers. Your mothers, your sisters ask and beg of you not to part with any more of our lands we say ours. You are descendants and take pity on our request, but keep it for our growing children, for it was the good will of our creator to place us here and you know our father, the great president will not allow his white children to take our country away. Only keep your hands off of paper talks, for it is our own country. For if it was not, they would not ask you to put your hands to paper for it would be impossible to remove us all. For as soon as one child is raised, we have others in our arms, for such is our situation and will. Consider our circumstance.

Therefore children, don't part with any more of our lands but continue on it and enlarge your farms and cultivate and raise corn and cotton and we your mothers and sisters will make clothing for you which our father, the president, has recommended to us all. We don't charge anybody for selling any lands, but we have heard such intentions of our children. But your talks become true at last and it was our desire to forewarn you all not to part with our lands.

Nancy Ward to her children: Warriors take pity and listen to talks of your sisters. Although I am very old yet cannot but pity the situation in which you will hear of their minds, I have great many grandchildren, and I wish them to do well on our land.

This address was taken to the council meeting by Nan-ye-hi's son, Fivekiller, and accompanied by her distinctive walking cane, which represented her official vote and authority in her absence.

Nan-ye-hi made one final attempt to stay on her land prior to her death. One stipulation of the 1817–1819 treaty had a reservation clause: "Each head of a Cherokee family residing on lands herein or hereafter ceded to the United States who elects to become a citizen of the United States shall receive a reservation of six hundred and forty (640) acres to include his or her improvements for life, with reversion in fee simple to children, subject to widow's dower." Nan-ye-hi's Reservation number 767 was registered with United States government, but the state of Tennessee flatly refused to recognize these individual reservation grants.

Nan-ye-hi died in the Amovey district near the Ocoee River at the home of her brother, Longfellow. Her white husband had left her for other relationships, although they continued to be friends. Ward's white family reportedly received her with great respect when she visited on occasion. She lived a long and fruitful life, and was called by some Princess and Prophetess.

Nan-ye-hi and those she represented planted many seeds in her nation that would not come of age until after her death. By the time of the Indian Removal Act of 1838, the Cherokee Nation had a form of government similar to that of the colonies. They had a supreme court, a tribe-elected leadership, a written language, a newspaper, and had adapted many of the ways of the colonists. It was against the Cherokee constitution for anyone to hold official office within the nation who did not have a belief in God. The unofficial Cherokee national anthem became "Amazing Grace."

I had the privilege of visiting Nan-ye-hi's homesite near Benton, Tennessee. Her gravesite is now a Tennessee Historic Site. There is a tangible, honorable stillness there. This chapter about the life of Nan-ye-hi is not simply a historic visitation for me as an individual. My family was in Fort Watauga during the time period of Dragging Canoe's attacks. Nan-ye-hi's two warnings to these settlements may well have saved my family's life—and ultimately, my own. Could it be that neither my children nor I would enjoy this life without her compassion for the early settlers of Tennessee?

As I walked her land, my heart was grateful for the compassionate acts of this wonderful lady I have never met. Who else walks this country today who does not know they are alive because of Nan-ye-hi? I felt as if people were watching from past generations.

Nan-ye-hi might have never worshiped in a church. Yet Scripture challenges us that authentic relationship is evident by visible fruit of the outward life we lead.

Less than 5 percent of native people profess a true relationship with Christ; they see Christianity as white man's religion. Many more than this, though, offer a yes to the response of being a Christian. This yes is tempered with generations of those who have been given the choice of being seen as "civilized" Christians or being killed. Most tribal people cannot find cultural identity within traditional Roman Christendom. Roman Christendom defines all facets of the Christian faith currently in America, from Roman Catholics to the independent charismatic church.

Fire is important to the Cherokee. Women were keepers of the fire in their homes. Each year the women ceremoniously extinguished all flames within the tribe. One of the roles of the Ghighau was to reintroduce new fire. In countless ceremonies Nan-ye-hi would have helped in rekindling the fire within her tribe. It was said that if the principal people kept the fire burning, the Creator God would reveal truth. An eternal flame now burns at Red Clay, Tennessee, which was the last capital of a united tribe called the Cherokee prior to the Trail of Tears.

Jesus, you are part of the tribe of Judah. You are a man of color, not a white man. You wore traditional clothing, and power was associated with it. You celebrated the many feasts of your Father. Your tribe's calendar is kept in cycles of the moon. Your Bible is a tribal book. You celebrated your ancestors. Your nation was led by tribal elders. Throughout your tribe's history, animals played important roles. Your Bible celebrates the created order.

You celebrated the land of your inheritance. You took nothing from it you did not need. Your nation fought fiercely all those who attempted to take your land from you. You upheld all your tribal laws. Your Father held your nation accountable to past generations who did not keep their covenants. You are a person who always keeps your word. You allowed false counsel to be spoken of you, without taking revenge, for the sake of your tribe.

You died a tortured death at the hands of a conquering nation to save your people. All who come to you for their salvation are not saved apart from being engrafted into your tribe.

Chapter 5

❧

Florence Nightingale

THE LADY WITH THE LAMP

(Michal Ann Goll)

Florence Nightingale was known as "the lady with the lamp," a nickname that was given to her by British soldiers who were wounded during the Crimean War in the mid-1850s.[1] They called her this because they always saw her carrying her lamp as she walked the halls of the hospital each night. Now this name has become a symbol of all that Florence stood for—care for the sick, concern for soldiers' welfare, and freedom for women to choose what kind of work they want to do.

This founder of the modern nursing profession was not the romantic, gentle, retiring Victorian woman that some people might imagine. She was a bright, tough, driven professional who became a brilliant organizer and one of the most influential women of the nineteenth century.

Florence was named for the city where she was born—Florence, Italy. Her date of birth was May 12, 1820, and her wealthy parents were on a two-year-long honeymoon trip through Italy when she was born.

She spent most of her childhood on the family estates in England with her mother, Fanny; her sister, Parthenope; and her father, William. Both of the girls were taught at home by their father, who was a graduate of Cambridge University. He tutored them in languages, history, and philosophy, while their mother taught them the social graces.

Florence excelled in her studies, and she was a very lively and attractive young lady. Her parents probably expected her to be a refined woman of class and distinction who would eventually marry a rich young man—but the Lord had different plans for her.

When she was seventeen years old, God spoke to her heart at Embley, the family's winter home. She wrote, "On February 7, 1837, God spoke to me and called me into His service."[2]

She felt strongly that He had given her a special mission in life. She suspected that this mission would involve helping others, something that Florence had always enjoyed doing. Often, she would care for the babies of her parents' visitors, and she would help care for caretakers on her father's estates when they got sick. Later in life, she wrote: "O God, Thou puttest into my heart this great desire to devote myself to the sick and sorrowful. I offer it to thee. Give me my work to do."[3]

She became a single-minded young lady and even turned down offers of marriage from various suitors, including one young man for whom she felt great love. Instead of attending parties to which she was invited, she would spend her time studying health and social reforms for the poor. Her mother had a hard time with this, because such things were simply not proper for wealthy young women of her day.

Florence had deep compassion in her heart for women and children who had to work in deplorable conditions. She was concerned about the poor in her own land and the economic and political situation in Ireland. It is clear that she cared about every social issue of her day.

She made regular visits to the sick in nearby villages and began to study the nursing systems of hospitals. Nursing wasn't really a formal profession at this time, and many of the people who helped in hospitals were prostitutes, former servicemen, and drunks. Therefore, nursing was not considered a noble profession.[4] In light of this, you can imagine how horrified Florence's parents were when she told them that she wanted to be a nurse. They tried to discourage her from going out to help the sick.

The Call Gets Clearer

In the spring of 1844, Florence became convinced that her calling was to nurse the sick, but she had her own health struggles to deal with first. In 1850, her family sent her to Egypt in order to recuperate, and while she was there she kept a diary, which details her dialogue with God about His calling in her life. Some of her journal entries follow:

March 7, 1850—"God called me this morning and asked me would I do good for Him, for Him alone without the reputation?"

March 9, 1850—"During half an hour I had by myself in my cabin settled the question with God."

April 1, 1850—"Not able to go out, but wish God to have it all His own way. I like Him to do exactly as He likes without even telling me the reason."

May 12, 1850—"Today I am 30, the age [when] Christ began his mission, now no more childish things, no more love, no more marriage, now, Lord, let me think only of Thy will, what Thou wouldst me to do, oh, Lord, thy will, thy will."

June 10, 1850—"The Lord spoke to me. He said, 'Give five minutes every hour to the thought of Me, couldst thou but love Me as Lizzy loves her husband, how happy wouldst thou be.' But Lizzy does not give five minutes every hour for the thought of her husband, she thinks of him every minute, spontaneously."[5]

God had given Florence this time to draw closer to Him. She heard Him speaking to her, and she was ready to go forth in full-flowered compassion to help those in need.

At St. Bartholomew's Hospital in London, Florence met Elizabeth Blackwell, the first woman who ever qualified to be a physician in America. Dr. Blackwell had to overcome all kinds of opposition to enter the medical profession, and Florence was greatly impressed by her. Blackwell encouraged Florence to keep on pursuing her goals.

Eventually her father reluctantly agreed for her to train as a nurse, so, when Florence was thirty-one years old, she went to Kaiserwerth, Germany, in order to be trained at the Lutheran Institute of Protestant Deaconesses, which was running a hospital there. Her training period lasted two years.[6]

Obedience to the Call

Upon her graduation from the nurses' training, Florence went to work at a hospital for invalid women that was located on Harley Street in London. She was appointed as the resident lady superintendent there.

While in this position, the new nurse began to think of innovations that might be employed to help the sick. For example, she developed a system of dumbwaiters, which enabled food to be delivered directly to each floor. Previously, nurses had to carry trays of food up several exhausting flights of stairs.

Florence also invented and installed a system of call bells that would enable patients to ring for nursing help from their beds. The bell would sound in the corridor and the valve that was attached to it remained open, enabling the nurses to see who had called for help. She also had the water heater for the hospital installed on the top floor so that hot water would run down, making it much more accessible to the nurses.[7]

The Crimean War

In March 1853, Russia invaded Turkey. Britain and France were concerned about the rise of the Russian Empire, so they responded to the invasion by declaring war on Russia in March 1854. This was the beginning of the Crimean War.

Many soldiers had to endure great hardships as they fought in this bloody war. The death rate was very high due to wounds, typhus, cholera, malaria, and dysentery. Within a few weeks after the conflict began, eight thousand men were in medical facilities.

The *London Times* exposed the poor medical care that was being given to the British soldiers. This caused a public outcry for greater medical care, and Florence Nightingale responded to this need by offering her services. There was still considerable prejudice against women being involved in medicine in any capacity, so the British government officials rejected her offer at first. As time went on, however, they changed their minds because the need was so great.

Florence was given permission to take a group of thirty-eight nurses to the military hospitals in Turkey. When she arrived at the Barak Hospital in the suburbs of Constantinople on November 4, 1854, Florence found the conditions appalling. The doctors who were there seemed to resent having female nurses, so they said, "Don't do anything until we tell you."

Florence reported that many of the men did not have blankets or nutritious food. They were unwashed and still in their uniforms, which were "stiff with dirt and gore." Many were infested with lice, and conditions there permitted only thirty men to be bathed each day—with the same sponge. Florence calculated what this meant: each patient would get bathed only once every eighty days, and it was a very poor bath indeed. She remarked, "Perhaps it was a blessing not to be bathed!"[8]

As the number of wounded increased, the doctors decided that they needed the new nurses after all, though they still objected to many of Florence's views with regard to reforming the system.

Blankets were rotting in warehouses instead of providing warmth for the men because no one had issued the proper paperwork to allow them to be distributed to the patients. The lavatories in the hospitals had no running water, and the latrines were open tubs that had to be emptied by hand, but they were never emptied because no one knew which department was responsible for them.

This resulted in a foul stench wafting throughout the hospital—a sickening odor that could be smelled far outside the hospital walls as well. The sewers did not function properly and were frequently backed up, spewing human waste into the hospital wards. War wounds accounted for only one death in six; most deaths were caused by diseases due to the unsanitary conditions in the hospital.

The army doctors gave the nurses five cramped rooms in which to work. They found the decaying corpse of a Russian general in one of those rooms. The central yard of the quadrangle was a virtual dump inhabited by rats.

Each patient received a daily ration of only one pint of water. There were no cooking facilities, and only thirteen five-gallon copper pots were available for cooking the food to feed two thousand men. There were no vegetables; meat and flavored water were the patients' daily fare. The meat came from butchered animals, and the cooks would simply throw the meat chunks into water that wasn't hot enough to cook anything. As a result, that the patients were eating raw meat.

The soldiers came into the hospital with all kinds of wounds. They were ripped, torn, and mutilated. Many of their body parts were missing, and these were replaced with filthy, blood-clotted rags. The patients lay in rows on broken tile floors.

Florence observed the terrible conditions but did not complain. She took the words of a verse from Proverbs to heart: "A fool vents all his feelings, but a wise man holds them back" (Prov. 29:11, NKJV).

Sometimes the doctors wouldn't let the nurses get too involved in actual medical care, so the nurses would spend part of their time making slings, pillows, and mattresses in their efforts to help the ill and wounded. Florence was able to obtain vegetables from the local markets, and she got portable stoves that allowed the nurses to cook meals properly. She also bought tables and screens for the hospital. Many of these things were purchased from her private funds.

Charge of the Light Brigade

When wounded troops arrived from the Battle of Balaklava (where "the charge of the light brigade" had taken place), Florence and her nurses were ready. She wrote these words: "On Thursday last, we had 1,715 sick and wounded in this hospital (among whom were 120 cholera patients) and 650 severely wounded in the other building, called the General Hospital, of which we also have charge, when a message came to me to prepare for 510 wounded on our side of the hospital, who were arriving from the dreadful affair...at Balaklava, where were 1,763 wounded and 442 killed besides 96 officers wounded and 38 killed....We had but half an hour's notice before they began landing the wounded. Between one and nine o'clock, we had the mattresses stuffed, sewn up, and laid down...the men washed and put to bed, and all their wounds dressed....Twenty-four cases [died] on the day of landing. We now have four miles of beds, and not eighteen inches apart....As I went my night-rounds among the newly-wounded that night, there was not one murmur, not one groan....These poor fellows bear pain and mutilation with an unshrinking heroism which is really superhuman, and die, or are cut up without a complaint....We have all the sick cookery now to do—and I have got in four men for the purpose....I hope in a few days we shall establish a little cleanliness. But we have not a basin, nor a towel, not a bit of soap, not a broom. I have ordered three hundred scrubbing brushes."[9]

In the face of such seemingly insurmountable odds many people would have despaired. Not Florence Nightingale; she persevered in her drive, compassion, and hard labor. She was able to work with the kitchen in such a way as to accommodate those patients who had special dietary needs. She and her nurses scrubbed the wards. They washed the patients and dressed their wounds regularly, and they emptied the chamber pots daily.

Out of her own money Florence purchased six thousand hospital gowns, two thousand pairs of socks, and hundreds of nightcaps, slippers, plates, cups, and utensils. She hired two hundred Turkish workers to restore the burned-out corridors, thus making room for an additional eight hundred patients.

Florence was passionate about what she knew God had called her to do, and she moved in unfeigned compassion among the sick and dying. She became compassion in action to those in need. She hired destitute women, many of whom were prostitutes, to serve as laundresses. She recommended a new system, which would require each bed to have tickets that would identify the patients' names and any dietary restrictions that applied to them. She wanted every patient to have his own bed with proper bedding.

Sometimes she would write letters home on behalf of the men and would send their meager wages to their families. Previously, many of them would squander their wages on alcohol. The army actually cut their wages when they got sick, and Florence assumed the role of their advocate in this matter as well as many others.

She introduced reading rooms into the hospital and secured the services of schoolmasters to give lectures to the men. Attendance at these lectures usually caused the halls to overflow.

One night, as Florence carried her lamp while doing her regular rounds, she found a man who was lying in the corridor. She realized that this soldier had never been attended to at all. In all the confusion he had been missed, and now he lay there dying. He could not make a sound, and she noticed that a bullet had penetrated one of his eyes. She later wrote, "Praise God! I found a surgeon, and the surgeon was able to save him."[10]

Awhile later, as she was out on the battlefield, she saw this man again. He had recuperated from the trauma and was back fighting on the field. He brought Florence a bouquet of flowers.

Whenever she went out among the men, they would rally around her. To them she was a true heroine, for she had given dignity, care, and honor to them. One of them said, "Behold the heroic daughter of England, a soldier's friend." Florence responded to this accolade with these words, "Give God the praise."[11] For her part, this valiant nurse had raised the image of the British soldier from a brawling low-life to a heroic working man.

Many days she would spend eight hours on her knees dressing wounds and comforting men who were scheduled for surgery. She had a wonderful presence about her that imparted peace to their hearts and calmed their nerves. She personally ministered to at least two thousand patients during the Crimean War.[12]

The mortality rate, which had been extremely high in the Barak Hospital, went below 10 percent under her care. Sometimes Florence herself worked so hard that she would pass out from sheer exhaustion. She always got back on her feet again, though, and continued her important service to the British soldiers.

When she had to return to England due to exhaustion and illness, Florence wrote these words about her service: "Oh, my poor men who endured so patiently, I feel I have been such a bad mother to you, to come home and leave you lying in your Crimean grave. Seventy-three percent in eight regiments during six months, from disease alone, who thinks of that now? But if I could carry any one point which would prevent any part of the recurrent of this, our colossal calamity, then I should have been true to the cause of those brave dead."[13]

Her extreme exhaustion led to a serious long-lasting illness. She developed a fever that was so high that the doctors had to shave her head in an effort to help release the heat from her body. For two weeks she suffered from delirium and bone-aching pain. She couldn't get out of bed, and this frustrated her greatly because she continued to sense the need of "her men."

By this time Florence Nightingale was famous, and even Queen Victoria worried about the state of her health. Eventually Florence was able to return to the hospital in Turkey, where she remained until the war was over two years and four months after it has started.

Four months after the peace treaty was signed, Florence returned home again. She hid herself away from the public because she didn't want any of the praise that she strongly felt belonged to God. About her service during the war and her feelings about longevity she said, "It matters little, provided we spend our lives to God, whether like our blessed Lord's they are concluded in three and thirty years, or whether they are prolonged to old age."

A Worker Approved

Paul, writing to Timothy, urged, "Study and do your best to present yourself to God approved, a workman [tested by trial] who has no reason to be ashamed, accurately handling and skillfully teaching the word of truth" (2 Tim. 2:15).

Florence Nightingale was such a worker. She had studied, was eager, and certainly did her utmost to present herself to God as one who was approved. She had been tested by trial and had no reason to be ashamed. Through her marvelous example we can learn so much, because she showed us what it means to be a worker approved by God.

After the war she got involved in several other matters, including writing, even though she was never completely well again and was often confined to her room. Nonetheless, she was a national heroine, and she began a campaign to improve the quality of care in military hospitals.

In October 1856, she had a long interview with Queen Victoria and her husband, Prince Albert. In 1859, she published two books that gave her opinions about the need for reform in hospital care: *Notes on Hospital* and *Notes on Nursing*. She raised funds to support her campaign to improve the quality of nursing. In 1860, Florence founded the Nightingale School and Home for Nurses at St. Thomas's Hospital in London. She also became involved in the training of nurses for employment in workhouses.

This valiant woman addressed the subject of women's rights in her book, *Suggestions for Thought to the Searchers after Religious Truths*. In this work she argued for the removal of restrictions that prevented women from having careers. Another book she wrote was titled *Suggestions for Thought to the Searchers after Truth among the Artizens of England,* which she kept revising until it seemed that God had spoken to her. He said, "You are here to carry out My program. I am not here to carry out yours." About this word from the Lord she wrote, "I must remember that God is not my private secretary!"

She served on the Indian Sanitary Commission by gathering documentation relating to the health and sanitary administration of the army in India. Her conclusion was that the death toll from disease in the Indian army was appallingly high, with sixty-nine out of every thousand dying annually due to a lack of sanitation.[14] Her findings resulted in the formation of the Army Medical College.

She revolutionized the public health system of India without ever leaving England, by writing pamphlet after pamphlet in which she used pie graphs to point out the most frequent causes for disease and death. She may well have been the first person to use such graphic displays to show statistics to people in an easy-to-understand manner. She was always careful to document her research.

Florence went on to study new designs for modern hospitals all over Europe. In Paris she found a revolutionary design in which separate units or pavilions made up one large hospital, and each pavilion was a light and airy self-contained unit. This design helped to minimize infections among the patients.

She began an anthology of mystical writings, which she called *Notes from Devotional Authors of the Middle Ages.* She believed that mystical prayer was for everyone, not just for monks, nuns, and priests. Prayer was a vital part of life for her, and it is clear from her writings that she relied on the power of prayer throughout her life. She wrote the manual *Notes for Nurses and a Set of Instructions for the Training of Nurses,* which emphasized the importance of nurses maintaining a daily schedule of prayer in their lives.

Her expertise gained her a reputation in America and Britain. The United States asked for Florence's help in establishing military hospitals for soldiers in the Civil War, and she was the first woman to receive the Order of Merit from the British government.

Due to continued overwork, her health continued to decline and she spent the last half of her life as an invalid. When she was sixty-five, she wrote this on Christmas Day: "Today, O Lord, let me dedicate this crumbling old woman to thee; behold, the handmaid of the Lord. I was thy handmaid as a girl, since then I have backslid."[15]

Florence Nightingale died at the age of ninety, and asked that the epitaph on her tombstone would read simply: "FN 1820 to 1910." She said that it would be a great honor for her to be buried in a casket that would be like those in which common soldiers are buried.[16]

Lioness Among Women

Florence Nightingale was a lioness among women—one whose faith, strength, and courage allowed her to live a compassion-acts lifestyle wherever she went.

We find a summation of her life and philosophy in these often-quoted words that she wrote long ago: "Life is a hard fight, a struggle, a wrestling with the principle of evil, hand to hand, foot to foot. Every inch of the way must be disputed. The night is given us to take breath, to pray, to drink deep at the fountain of power. The day, to use the strength which has been given to us, to go forth to work with it till the evening."

This is how compassion begins, how it grows, and how it keeps on going. So, drink deep at the fountain of power, and remember these words of Paul: "In conclusion, be strong in the Lord [draw your strength from Him and be empowered through your union with Him] and in the power of His [boundless] might" (Eph. 6:10).

Dear Heavenly Father, teach me to put You first in all that I do. Open my heart to serve the ones you put in my path. As I serve them, I serve you—my Redeemer and my Provider. May I look to You for guidance and not be satisfied with earthly wealth or status. My strength comes from you. May I use it to further Your kingdom in our world. In Jesus' name, amen.

Chapter 6

🌿

Gladys Aylward

REJECTED BY MAN, APPROVED BY GOD

(Michal Ann Goll)

will be glad to be of service, sir," she grudgingly muttered, despite the fact her heart had just been ravaged by the harsh words spoken by the principal of the Women's Training Center of the China Inland Mission. Gladys Aylward was twenty-seven years old and, according to the staff of her mission preparatory school, too old to begin training to become a missionary in China. Sure, she knew her record wasn't the most impressive, but she was willing to do what was needed to get to China.

China. Her heart ached for China. While working as a parlormaid, she had attended a religious meeting, and by the end of the night, she had given her heart to Jesus. He gave it back to her with a deep-rooted love not only for Himself but also for the people of China.

She had read an article in a *Young Life Campaign* magazine about the millions of Chinese who had never heard the name "Jesus," and had felt an overwhelming compassion and desire to take action.[1] She tried to convince some of her Christian friends and relatives to take on the cause, but no one seemed very concerned. Surely if she asked her brother, he would understand her concern and move to China. Instead, he bluntly replied, "Not me! Why don't you go?"

Good question. Why didn't she go? If no one else would travel thousands of miles to a country she knew practically nothing about, she would be forced to go herself. She was told she would need to enlist in a certain missionary society and after completing training, she would be sent as a missionary to China. And now, sitting in the office of the man she had hoped would help fulfill her dreams, she was being told she was too old and too far behind the rest of the class. Instead of going to China, she was being offered another parlormaid position, this time caring for retired missionaries in need of a housekeeper.[2]

Questions flooded Gladys' mind. *Did I do something to upset God? Did I even hear God? Maybe I'm not called to China at all...*

Shaking off those thoughts, she held on to what she knew. God longed to embrace the Chinese people, and He wanted to use Gladys' hands and feet to do it. And in the meantime, if God wanted to use her hands and feet to serve an older missionary couple, who was she to stand in the way?

Early Missions Work

During Gladys' time in Bristol, England, caring for Dr. and Mrs. Fisher, she learned many valuable lessons from the couple's simple, extravagant faith in Jesus. While Gladys enjoyed the stories that filled the small house, she still longed to go and love the people of China. Next, she moved from Bristol to work for the Christian Association of Women and Girls, where she worked as a rescue sister. Each night she waded through the dark, gloomy streets near the docks, looking for girls that the sailors had made drunk, and took them back to the hostel. While she did enjoy this work and she knew God was using her, the faces of "her" people of China were etched in her heart and mind. She went to London to inquire of families in need of childcare—anything to earn her way to China. The responses she found were anything but helpful. Still, she refused to lose hope.

Diving into the Word for encouragement, she found herself under great conviction for her lack of faith and action concerning China. If she was so confident God had called her to China, why didn't she just act on it?

She read the story of Abraham. "Now the Lord had said unto Abram, Get thee out of thy country, and from thy kindred, and from thy father's house, unto a land that I will shew thee: and I will...make thy name great; and thou shalt be a blessing" (Gen. 12:1–2, KJV).

Then she read about Moses' absolute faith to obey God, to defy the might of Egypt and the despotism of Pharaoh. Nehemiah's life also called out to her. She saw that not only was he a butler of sorts and had to obey his employer, as she did—but he went. She heard a clear voice speak inside her soul asking if her God was the same one as the God of Nehemiah or not. God was building a whole series of confirmations that released a surge of courage that raced through her mind and spirit.[3] The issue was settled as far as she was concerned. She knew she had received her marching orders from heaven.

The Journey

Just as quickly as Gladys' heart surrendered to God's heart, provision and direction followed. She moved to London and began to save money for a ticket to China. But when Gladys arrived at Muller's Shipping Agency, she discovered the difficulty was not only in the price of the ticket but in the journey itself. The cheapest ticket would take her by rail through Europe, Russia, and Siberia to Tientsin in Northern China. At the time, war was raging between Russia and China. Fighting was over Manchurian soil and there was no guarantee she would get through safely. The clerk at the desk insisted traveling that distance was too great a risk, but Gladys knew in her heart she had to follow the heart of her God. That was the way to China.

Against the advice of the clerk on duty, she opened an account with the Muller's Shipping Agency with a deposit of three pounds toward a ticket to China, leaving forty-four pounds and ten shillings yet to pay. Within a few months, God had provided enough funds for her to travel to China. She worked extra hours, often taking on the serving for special socials and dinners. At one of these meetings, Gladys was introduced to a lady who shared interest in China and who told Gladys of her friend, Mrs. Lawson, an elderly missionary working in China who needed some "younger bones" to carry on her work. Gladys immediately wrote to Mrs. Lawson, offering her services. After a long wait, a reply arrived. If Gladys could travel to Tientsin, Mrs. Lawson would meet her. It was time.

She left Liverpool with two old battered suitcases that contained, among other things, a bedroll, a small alcohol stove, canned fish, crackers, boiled eggs, instant coffee, baked beans, and lots of tea. She tied on the outside of the suitcase a large pot and a kettle. She wore a bright orange dress and a huge fur overcoat with the sleeves cut out. Under her clothes she wore one of her mother's old corsets, into which she had sewn secret pockets to carry her train tickets, her passport, a fountain pen, her money (a grand nine pennies and two one-pound notes), and her Bible.[4] How she had waited for this day to come.

As the train jolted across the tracks, the day turned to night and the night back into day, and Gladys' excitement slowly dwindled into sadness and nervousness. She knew no one. She had no money. She was already tired.[5] What exactly was she thinking when this seemed like such a good idea?

She crossed the border into Manchuria and discovered fighting had intensified, blocking a crucial junction where Gladys had to change trains. After several stops, the lights in the train blackened and thundering gunfire broke the silence. She quickly grabbed her belongings and climbed onto the station platform, shivering in the bitter cold. The station seemed deserted, except for a few guards and uniformed officials who informed her she must walk through the howling wind and stinging cold to Chita, the previous stop on her route.

Gladys walked for several days to arrive back in Chita, stopping only to nap and nibble on the few crackers she had managed to save from the train. When she arrived in Chita, officials questioned her and attempted to persuade her to stay and work in Russia. While sitting in the train station, alone and cold, she questioned God and her own sanity for venturing on this journey alone, wondering if it would ever be worth it. But when she looked over and saw fifty people chained together by their hands and feet and being dragged onto trains to be taken to forced labor camps in Siberia, she knew her answer.

Of course it was worth it. She would pay any price and endure any suffering to get to China, the land where her heart longed to be so she could lavish hungry souls with the love of Jesus. With renewed energy and determination, she trekked on. After another detour, she found herself in Vladivostok, where an interpreter stole her passport and, with a manipulative smile and friendly voice, offered her a decent place to stay in a nearby hotel and a tour around the city. Although honored and appreciative at first, after a few days she began to feel anxious and ready to continue her journey to China. Unfortunately, the interpreter disagreed and insisted she stay. Since he still had her passport, she had no choice.

As she left the hotel in frustration, a woman appeared from behind the door and summoned her aside. In a hushed voice, the mysterious woman informed Gladys that the man who seemed hospitable had no plans of allowing Gladys to leave Russia and instructed her to quickly gather her things and wait for an old man to arrive at her door.

When a knock came a few hours later, Gladys jumped to her feet, anxious and nervous to open the door. The interpreter stood in the doorway, her passport in hand and a grim expression on his face. She grabbed the passport and slammed the door shut just in time. Looking at her passport, she saw it now read "Gladys Aylward, British subject; Profession: machinist." The mysterious woman was telling the truth; the interpreter had tried to change Gladys' passport to force her to stay in Russia.

Gladys was overwhelmed with gratitude for the angel God had sent to help her, but she knew she was not safe until she was out of Russia. In the early morning, another knock came at the door. An old man stood silently and held out his hand to carry Gladys' suitcase, leading her down a dark alley to the docks where they met the mysterious woman from the previous night. Again, her instructions were short and simple. Gladys must go down to the captain's hut and beg and plead, whatever it takes, to get on the boat for Japan.

With no valuables or money, Gladys had only one thing to offer the captain as a bargain: herself. Gladys agreed to become his prisoner, as long as they left Russia.[6]

In the darkest hour, Gladys knew she had a choice. She could forget why she had had traveled such a dangerous journey and become consumed with hopelessness and sadness at her terrible situation, or she could choose to believe. And she knew she must choose to believe in the goodness and faithfulness of her precious God and faithful King.

Touching the Soil

Eventually, the boat reached Japan and she found herself in the hands of the British Consulate. Relieved by the familiar language and comforting words of the officials, she was filled with joy and comfort. God was so faithful! He had once again delivered her from the enemy's hands and placed her in safe territory. On Sunday, November 5, 1932, three weeks after her departure from London, she stepped onto her last train ride into Tientsin to finally meet Mrs. Lawson.

Three days later, her feet touched the soil of a land she immediately called home. Her heart fell in love with the beautiful countryside, high mountains with snow-covered tops, and bright green and red trees. China.

When Gladys arrived in China, exhausted and dirty, she was relieved the journey was complete but nervous about the long-awaited meeting with Mrs. Lawson. Feeling unworthy and insignificant due to her unsightly appearance, she once again realized she had only one thing to offer: herself.

Mrs. Jeannie Lawson was from Scotland and rarely showed any sign of emotion. Rather harshly, Gladys was ushered into what was soon to be her new home. Gladys realized her hopes for a comfortable bed and warm bath were a bit premature when she walked into a dilapidated house where a cement floor was her bed. When asked where she should change clothes, Mrs. Lawson politely told her to sleep in her clothes with all her belongings within hand's reach—having her things close made them harder to steal. Gladys couldn't hide her frustration and anxiety, and again began questioning her sanity for moving to China.

Apparently, the news of her arrival had spread around town and she awoke with dozens of faces peering into the open windows. At any rate, she was grateful for the advice of Mrs. Lawson to sleep in her clothes.

Gladys was surprised at the bleak and poor conditions she and Mrs. Lawson faced on a daily basis. Ministry was not glamorous, she realized. Mrs. Lawson had little money; Gladys had nothing. So when Mrs. Lawson informed Gladys of her plans to transform the house into a working inn, Gladys was indeed relieved to know another source of income was on the way.

The inn was in Yangcheng, a little country Chinese village that sat on the ancient mule track where muleteers, the newsmen of North China, would travel on a regular basis. Excited about the opportunity to love and minister the good news of Jesus to the muleteers, Gladys was less than thrilled when she was assigned her task. Her job was to stand in the streets and, when the mules started to pass, grab the head of the first mule and drag him inside. Apparently, once this was done, the rest of the mules would follow and the muleteers would stay in the inn.

On her first day, Gladys stood shaking with fright as she waited for the mules to pass. Her first attempt failed miserably; the owner was so frightened he ran away. But soon Gladys perfected "the grab" and their home became known along the route as a clean inn where the foreign ladies told long stories at night, free of charge. The nighttime was Gladys' favorite part of the day because it was during these late hours Mrs. Lawson would begin to tell wonderful stories of their sweet Jesus. Gladys would listen carefully, trying to learn the language from Mrs. Lawson's stories, longing for the day it would be her turn to share.

Gladys completed all her daily tasks, no matter how mundane they seemed, to the best of her ability, knowing God could use even the smallest deeds of the day to His glory. She followed Mrs. Lawson faithfully, doing just as she was instructed and using any opportunity to learn more Chinese. Her days were often spent cleaning inside the inn, and during the night, Gladys could usually be found outside, cleaning and caring for the mules.

On weekends the duo would travel to villages, wait until crowds gathered to gaze in curiosity at the foreign ladies, and then begin to preach the gospel. The villagers would stare in amazement, as some had never before seen a white person. They stared especially at their feet. Chinese custom required all women to have their feet bound, so the "free feet" of Mrs. Lawson and Gladys always brought much attention.

Mrs. Lawson and Gladys were indeed a unique pair. Gladys' youthful energy was a definite contrast to the elderly Mrs. Lawson, who was strong in spirit but growing weaker physically by the day. What united the two was an unshakeable belief that God had called them to China; their love for the Chinese people was strong enough to fill any gap. Gladys often wondered what would happen to her if Mrs. Lawson died—would she be sent back to London or would she venture on alone?

Later on in the year, while Gladys was away from the inn, Mrs. Lawson had a terrible accident; having fallen from the second-story balcony, she had lain outside for over a week, exposed to the weather, without any assistance from anyone. When Gladys returned, she found dear Mrs. Lawson lying on top of a pile of coal, where she had fallen. Gladys cared for her and nursed her, but it became evident she was not going to recover. Shortly before she passed into heaven, Mrs. Lawson whispered to Gladys, "God called you to my side, Gladys, in answer to my prayers. He wants you to carry on my work here. He will provide. He will bless and protect you."[7] Mrs. Lawson's funeral was the first Christian burial ever to be held in Yangcheng.[8]

Launching Out

Now alone, Gladys kept the inn running and held gospel meetings in the evenings. She traveled around to villages, caring for and giving medical aid as well as she could. Funds were extremely low, but that wasn't all. Mrs. Lawson had never told Gladys about a yearly tax due to the mandarin. This was a large amount, which Mrs. Lawson had paid out of her small monthly income. Now those funds were no longer available, and the payment was due.

Alone and tired, Gladys wondered how the she would meet the needs of her workers, her guests, and her beloved Chinese people. She felt weak and helpless, knowing God must truly work a miracle if she were to continue her work in China. Unable to bear the thought of closing the inn and leaving China, she knew the only place to go was to the feet of her Jesus and offer the only thing she had to give: herself.

She thought perhaps she should go and bow before the mandarin, but this idea presented several problems. Since Mrs. Lawson and Gladys were the first two foreigners to live in Yangcheng, there were no set rules as to how many times a foreigner should bow to the mandarin, or what she should say, or in what order either of these things should be done. Making just one mistake pertaining to proper protocol could be deadly, as the mandarin was the highest official in the district. The more she thought about this idea, the more she realized it just wouldn't be appropriate. She did not have any clothes suitable to seek an audience, having only her quilted blue trousers and jacket. No, there had to be some other way to deal with paying the taxes.

About a week later, Gladys had an unexpected surprise. The mandarin was seen coming to the inn. What could be the problem? Had she done something wrong? There was no time to make any preparations;

she would just have to receive him with all the honor she held in her heart, and hope it would make the difference.

She bowed twice and waited, but the mandarin seemed focused on a mission. As he began speaking with her, the reason for his visit became clear. A new government had been formed in Nanking, and they had established a new law. This law addressed the ancient custom of foot-binding.

In those days, small feet were considered the ultimate in sexual appeal, and a woman's eligibility for a good marriage depended solely on this criterion. Depending on how affluent they were, Chinese families would bind the feet of their girl children with tight linen bandages while the little bones were soft and pliable, between the ages of three to seven years. The feet would slowly double over until the toes and front half of the foot were tucked underneath. By the time a girl was twelve or thirteen years old, her feet would be permanently doubled in half. Those who were less wealthy held off binding their daughter's feet for as long as they could so that their daughter could be useful longer around the house and the fields. Once her feet were bound, she would have difficulty getting around.

But now a new law challenged this custom. The new law required the mandarin to retain a foot inspector. This, in itself, presented two obstacles. First, the inspector could not be a man, as men were not allowed to look at a woman's feet. That meant the inspector had to be a woman. But all the women had already had their feet bound and they would not be able to travel on foot over mountains and rough roads to reach all the villages. These two issues narrowed down his search to the woman now standing in front of him. Who else was there who spoke the Yangcheng dialect, had unbound feet, and was a woman? There was only one in the entire Yangcheng district, and it was Gladys. She had made herself available, and now God was about to open to her a large field ready to be harvested.

The mandarin offered to pay her for this service, which would take care of the needed monies for the taxes. This would also give her the opportunity to tell every village throughout the entire district about Jesus, as well as help enforce the end of this terrible, torturous custom.

She found herself replying to him that if she took on this responsibility of representing his Excellency, she would speak of the love of God to everyone and lead as many to Jesus as she could. After thinking a few minutes, he in turn responded that if the women became Christians, they would want their daughters to have unbound feet like Gladys, and that would be a good thing.

This audience, which only took a few minutes, was the beginning of what would later become a crucial piece for the complete fulfillment of God's purposes in Gladys' life. As she went from village to village, house to house, she gathered each little girl in her arms and unbound the little feet that had turned white from lack of blood, sometimes with the toes already folded over. She gently massaged the feet until a pink color began to return and the toes began to uncurl, and then soundly threatened that if she came back and found the girl's feet bound again, that person would surely be put in prison. Many times she would be invited to the home of the elder of the village, where she would spend the night and tell stories about Jesus, her wonderful friend and Savior.

After several months, she had reached every village and every family, and unbound every girl's foot. She reported to the mandarin her progress, and he urged her to continue her rounds, making sure everyone was complying. Once the girls' feet were unbound, the parents often decided they were glad the old custom was abolished. This freed Gladys' time so that as she traveled, she was able to spend her time telling the people about Jesus. The villagers anticipated her visits, and as time passed, small bands of Christians began forming in the villages. Gladys visited the mandarin regularly, giving him updates on the region. He was greatly impressed with her work.

The Next Assignment

Some time later, another task was assigned to the "foot inspector." This time inmates in the prison had started a riot. They were killing each other. The mandarin, not knowing anyone else with as much courage or ability, summoned Gladys to the prison. Feeling totally overwhelmed and unprepared to face murderers and robbers, once she reluctantly arrived at the prison, she argued with the governor of the prison. What did she know about fighting, herself being a woman? Surely she would be killed.

The governor looked at her, and with a smile told her that she had been telling everyone that the living God lived inside her, so how could anyone kill her? Faced with the realization that this was the moment of truth, and that she had to stand on her faith in God, she silently prayed for God's protection and strength. She walked through the iron gate and down the pitch-black tunnel into the prison courtyard. She saw blood splattered everywhere as men lay dead or dying all over the ground. Others were running around with machetes, attacking each other.

In this den of violence, anger, and hate, Gladys stepped out of the shadows and ordered the men to stop at once, hand over the weapons, come together, and clean up the mess they had created. As she talked with them, she saw the desperation they were living in. Their bodies were so very thin, covered with oozing, open sores. They had lice in their hair, and what clothing they owned was completely worn out.

The men were dependent on their relatives to bring them food, and if they had no relatives, well, there was no food supplied for them. Gladys heard the stories of their situation and determined in her heart to do something about it. Who wouldn't riot living in such conditions? She corrected the governor of the prison, and told him things could not stay the way they were. She arranged for two old looms to be brought in so the prisoners could weave their own clothes, with local merchants supplying yarn. She begged for a miller's wheel so they could grind their own grain, and she taught the men how to breed rabbits for sale.

Within a few months of the riot, the men were dressed warmly and eating well. They gave her a new name: Ai-weh-deh, which means Virtuous One. Soon the name caught on, and everyone was calling her by her new name.

Serving the Children

As her understanding of the culture in this region grew, Ai-weh-deh became aware of the trade of buying and selling children. Her heart was continually being enlarged with every plight she discovered. How could she leave these little ones to suffer when she could do something on their behalf? One by one, she began adopting children. The first was Ninepence, followed by Less, Boa-Boa, Francis, and Lan Hsiang. Having adopted these children, she felt she needed to become a Chinese citizen so she would never be separated from them. The mandarin helped her fill out many papers, and in 1936 Gladys Aylward became the first foreign missionary to become a Chinese citizen.

The mandarin came to her regularly for help in solving problems. She started a school at the request of the prison governor. These were days of fulfillment and becoming really established in the region. However, there was a shadow of a problem in the distance that would soon knock on her door. War was about to envelope Yangcheng.

War

The Japanese had invaded Manchuria and set up their government there. But now they were moving farther into northeastern China. One morning in the spring of 1938, their beloved village was bombed. (Very few even knew what a bomb was.) Instantaneous devastation. The streets had huge craters in them, shops and houses were just piles of rubble. People were in shock.

Gladys gathered everyone together and set them to work. She had been working long hours caring for the wounded when she realized the mandarin was standing over her head. He had brought word to her that the Japanese were only about two days away from Yangcheng. The destruction that lay around them was only the beginning.

Several years of conflict between Japan and China followed. The conflict weakened the Chinese nationalist government to such an extent that the Communist government was able to slowly gain strength. During these years, regions went back and forth between Chinese and Japanese control.

Yangcheng was emptied on several occasions. The first time, under the counsel of Gladys, the prison governor, and the mandarin, everyone was told to leave the village, taking their food and livestock, giving the Japanese no reason to stay. Gladys, because of her extensive travels throughout the region, knew a perfect hiding place—Bei Chai Chuang. It was ideal, as there was no road that led to it, it was not on any map, and most importantly, the surrounding hills housed several large caves that were almost impossible to spot from the outside. This would become home to Gladys and her children for some time. Local people brought in food and supplies. A slow trickle of sick and wounded found their way to Gladys, knowing she would care for them. The cave was transformed into a hospital.

Things seemed to settle down in the beginning days of 1939, almost seeming normal. But once again the Japanese were on the move, and this time the Chinese felt the best way to defend the land was what they called a "scorched earth policy." They left nothing—no food, no crops, no buildings intact. Everything was destroyed or burned. This meant that the people of China would be left with nothing as well.

On the eve before all was destroyed, the mandarin held one last feast at his home and invited Gladys to attend. She was given the seat of honor. All the important people of Yangcheng were there. The mandarin stood and spoke of the many things Ai-weh-deh had done for him and for the people, going on for more than twenty minutes. Finally, at the end of his speech, he looked her directly in the eye, called her his dear friend, and told her he had seen all she was and all that she did. He wanted to become a Christian like her. How grateful Gladys was to the Lord, that He would do such a work in the mandarin's heart.

Places of Hiding

The war went on and on, and the scorched-earth policy left many in need. The caves continued to be a place of safety, and many came to receive the kindness and care of Gladys. When the number of children with her reached 150, Gladys stopped trying to keep count of them all. She endured many close calls with the Japanese. She ran through gunfire, wormed her way through wheat fields to escape, traveled along dangerous mountain trails, hid in clefts of rocks through the night, and endured a blow from the butt of a rifle on the side of her head, from which she never fully recovered.

She traveled from village to village, encouraging the churches there. Because of her extensive knowledge of the area, the general of the Chinese army requested any troop movement information she could give him. She was glad to do this, and knew she had become a spy for the land she loved. In the midst of all of this, she just kept doing what she could, many times not knowing if she would succeed. One of the prayers she had learned from Mrs. Lawson was, "If I die, let me not be afraid of death, but let there be a meaning, O God, in my dying."

In 1940 or 1941, she was interviewed by an American freelance journalist named Theodore White. Her compelling story was published in *Time* magazine and was read by millions of people, which unfortunately included the Japanese army. This ended up endangering her life and the lives of those under her care, as the Japanese put her on their wanted list—offering a reward for her, dead or alive.[9]

Two Hundred-Mile Journey

A possible option came up in regard to providing care for the two hundred children who were now in her care. It would require dividing them into two groups, and sending each group on a two-hundred-mile journey across the Yellow River to Sian in Shensi province. The first group, led by one of the new converts, made it safely, but on his way back to get the second group of children, this new convert, named Tsin Penkuang, was captured by the Japanese, robbed, and killed. The *Time* magazine article, by this time, had fallen into Japanese hands. Now the remaining children were at greater risk, just by being with her. What should she do? What could she do?

"Flee ye! Flee ye into the mountains! Dwell deeply in the hidden places, because the King of Babylon has conceived a purpose against you!" Her eyes read the verses from her Chinese Bible. Now she knew what she must do. She gathered all the children together, and they put on every piece of clothing they had and tied around their waists every spare pair of shoes they could find. Their shoes were made of cloth and would barely last a day on the rugged trails they would climb. Everyone had to carry his or her own bedroll. The oldest children were around fifteen years old, the youngest barely four years of age. She wrapped all the food she had in a rag, barely enough millet for two days' rations, and carried the old iron pot herself, to cook the millet in. No one had any idea how long a journey they were embarking on.

They slept in Buddhist temple courtyards, in the open air, in small homes, wherever they could find shelter. The older girls, whose feet had been bound previously, had great difficulty because of weakness and the abnormal bone formation. Finding enough food to feed one hundred children every day was more than just a challenge. They trekked over mountains with bruised and cut feet, the younger children in great despair, crying for lack of food and afraid. Gladys herself was dealing with a strange tiredness, a result of the rifle blow to her head. But she had to keep going.

Sometimes they sang hymns; sometimes they were silent, except for the children crying. There were many Japanese in the area, and they always had to be on the lookout, not knowing what they would do if they ran into any of them. There were the soldiers on the ground, but also they had to watch for the Japanese war planes that could suddenly appear. At times, they ran into Chinese soldiers, who sometimes carried sugar treats and food the children had not seen for months in Shansi province.

The soldiers were glad to share their provisions, missing their own beloved children. As food supplies dwindled, they picked twigs and leaves and brewed "tea"—anything to fill all the hungry stomachs. They had to cross the Yellow River, but when they arrived Gladys noticed that everyone had fled and there was no way to cross. All of the boats were gone. They sat by the river for four days before a Chinese soldier overheard them singing. There was one boat available to ferry the children across, but it would be very dangerous. If a Japanese war plane happened over the area at the wrong time, all would be lost. Gladys was slipping in and out of consciousness. Trying to stand up made her feel dizzy. They prayed, and after three trips across the river, all were safely on the other side. Relief was close at hand now—or was it?

The next morning they boarded the train and rode for three days only to discover that the bridge had been blown out. To get to Sian, they would have to climb over another mountain and catch another train on the other side. It would take four or five days to make this leg of the journey. How were they going to make it?

They got off the train and gazed at the steep grade of the climb before them. Gladys sat down on a rock and started to cry. One by one, they all joined in and cried together for several minutes till Gladys stopped, wiped her eyes on her sleeve, and told the children it was okay to cry but now it was time to move. It was time to sing, and time to march.

At every promise of being "almost there," there was always farther to go, it seemed, more miles to walk. "This train can't carry passengers. You can't stop here; no more refugees are being accepted." The delays were many. Finally, after three weeks or more, they arrived at Fufeng, a city that was still receiving refugees.

By this point Gladys, who didn't know it at the time, was suffering from fever, pneumonia, typhoid, and malnutrition. She delivered safely every child; not one of them had died or become seriously ill. She hardly knew who or where she was, and two days after getting the children to safety in an orphanage, she fell into a coma that lasted two weeks.

Need For Rest

It was time for recuperation. Gladys would require much time. She got stronger, and was able to resume her missionary work. She visited the head lama in Tibet, who told her they had been waiting for three years for someone to come who could tell them more about God. He showed her the Scripture John 3:16: "For God so loved the world that He gave His only begotten Son," which had been glued to the wall. She preached to the Lamaist monks and prayed with them. She worked in a leper colony and preached in a local prison. Everywhere she went, many Chinese people were searching for the one true God.

She witnessed among university students the ugliness of the communist regime, as they were given the choice to either support the communist government or not. One by one, these fiery students, who knew of a higher allegiance, having made their declaration for Jesus, were promptly shoved to their knees and beheaded, right there on the spot.

Gladys went back to England for a while to recuperate some more from the physical rigors she had endured. She was not prepared for how famous she had become. She traveled to many places, using her notoriety to call Christians to pray for China and send relief to the Chinese people. Hollywood made a movie about her life called *Inn of the Sixth Happiness,* and the big London newspapers interviewed her. She was introduced to heads of state, met Queen Elizabeth, and worked with the many refugees who streamed into England.[10]

Desire to Go Home

After ten years in England, she traveled back "home." Entry into mainland China was not allowed, and her Chinese citizenship was not honored at this time, so in 1957 she landed in Formosa (modern-day

Taiwan). She picked up her life where she had left off. Her heart was full, and her hands were never empty.

On New Year's Day in 1970, Gladys simply did not wake up. She was sixty-seven years old, and her heart just stopped beating. Beside her bed was a newborn baby, sleeping peacefully. The baby had been abandoned and brought to Ai-weh-deh, where it had been received with open, loving arms.

Memorial services were held around the world for this amazing woman, and over a thousand people attended her funeral service in Taipei. Gladys' body was buried on a hilltop at Christ's College in Taipei, with her tomb facing the Chinese mainland.

Father, I come to You in the name of Jesus. I pray that I would know Your voice and Your Word so well that I would be totally transformed by Your Word and become a living epistle to the world. Oh Lord, may I be so in love with You that no obstacle would keep me from doing all I can do for Your name's sake. May man's opinion not sway or affect my focus and determination to do all You have deposited in my heart. May I always remember that it is Your approval, not that of other people, that counts. In Jesus' name, amen.

Chapter 7

✿

Mother Teresa

THE HUMBLE ROAD

(Michal Ann Goll)

If you asked people, "Who was the most compassionate person of the twentieth century?" I'm sure many would answer without hesitation, "Mother Teresa." She moved in compassion among the poor in her beloved Calcutta, India, and among the rich and famous around the world as well. She was a flesh-and-blood example of what compassion looks like, and she seemed to exhibit the qualities of humility and love wherever she was.

Indeed, she obviously took joy from her service to others and this seemed to fill her heart with peace. This was reflected in her radiant, smiling countenance.

There is much we can learn from Mother Teresa, and I feel as if I have actually gotten to know her as I researched and wrote this chapter. I hope you are inspired as you read these pages about her life and ministry.

Mother Teresa of Calcutta (Agnes Gonxha Bojaxhiu) was born on August 27, 1910, in Skopje, which is in modern Macedonia. Her family was of Albanian descent, and she was the youngest of three children. Her father was a builder.

At the age of twelve, Agnes strongly felt the call of God on her life, and she knew that she was destined to become a missionary. The overarching desire of her life from then on was to spread the love of Jesus Christ, particularly among the poor, the sick, and the outcasts of society.

When she was eighteen years old, Agnes left home to join the Sisters of Loretto, an Irish community of nuns who managed mission schools in India. As a novice in this order, she took the name of Sister Teresa. She served her novitiate in Dublin, and after several months of training was sent to India. On May 25, 1931, she took her initial vows as a nun.

From 1931 to 1948, Sister Teresa taught at St. Mary's High School in Calcutta. While there, she was moved with deep compassion for the poor and suffering people she saw outside the walls of the convent. Thousands of destitute people lived there with little hope that the basic necessities of life—food, shelter, health, cleanliness, and income—would ever be theirs.

In 1946, Sister Teresa developed a suspected case of tuberculosis. To get her out of the crowded city into the mountain air, she was sent by train to the village of Darjeeling, in the foothills of the Himalayas. While sitting on the train, she heard God speaking to her and telling her that He wanted her to serve Him "among the poorest of the poor."

Soon, she recovered from her illness and received permission to leave her order. She moved to Calcutta's slums to set up her first school for slum children in an open-air mission. She had no funds for this work, so she had to depend on faith in God's provision. Clearly, she knew the truth of this Scripture: "And without faith it is impossible to please God, because anyone who comes to him must believe that he exists and that he rewards those who earnestly seek him" (Heb. 11:6, NIV).

Before long, volunteers joined with her, and people who saw what she was doing began to provide financial support for her fledgling ministry. This allowed her work and ministry to grow.

Calcutta, India

Calcutta (Kolkata) is the capital of the Indian state of West Bengal in eastern India. It is the fourth largest city in India, with a population that currently exceeds five million.

After India declared its independence from Great Britain in 1947, the city went through an extended period of economic stagnation and many of its inhabitants were the "poorest of the poor." The city's port had been bombed by the Japanese twice during World War II. Millions had starved to death during the Bengal famine of 1943. In 1946, demands for the creation of a Muslim state had led to massive violence in the city, and more than two thousand people had died.

When the subcontinent was divided between India and Pakistan in 1947, a flood of over one million destitute refugees poured into Calcutta. Most of these people were Hindus who had no concept of a personal God who was their heavenly Father. The majority of people who lived in Calcutta during the 1940s lived in the worst possible conditions of extreme hunger, deprivation, squalor, and filth.

Sister Teresa went through these great trials with the Indian people, so she knew how intense their suffering and hardships were. She gathered the city's "throwaway children" from rubbish heaps. Many were orphans. She explained, "We do our best to nurse them back to life."[1]

This valiant nun could see the life of Jesus in every child and adult, and she approached each one as if he or she was the Lord himself. She was their servant, an obedient follower of the One who said:

> For I was hungry, and you gave Me something to eat; I was thirsty, and you gave Me something to drink; I was a stranger, and you invited Me in; I was naked, and you clothed Me; I was sick, and you visited Me [with help and ministering care]; I was in prison, and you came to Me [ignoring personal danger]. (Matt. 25:35–36)

When Jesus' disciples asked Him when it was that they had done these things, He said, "Truly I tell you, whatever you did for one of the least of these brothers and sisters of mine, you did for me" (Matt. 25:40, NIV).

Sister Teresa gave food to the hungry, hospitality to the strangers, clothes to the naked, and healing and practical help to the ill. She explained, "In the slums we are the light of God's kindness to the poor. To the children, to all who suffer and are lonely, [we] give always a happy smile...not only [our] care but also [our] heart."[2]

In spite of its poverty, violence, and bloodshed, Calcutta came to be known as "the City of Joy," and Sister Teresa was able to help turn suffering into joy for many people who lived there.

Saint of the Gutter

On October 7, 1950, Sister Teresa was given permission by the Holy See to found a new order of Catholic nuns—the Missionaries of Charity. She was now Mother Teresa of Calcutta, the Mother Superior of this new order.[3]

She saw the order's primary task as being the provision of love and care for needy persons who had no one to help them.[4] Mother Teresa described their mission as follows: "…[to care for] the hungry, the naked, the homeless, the crippled, the blind, the lepers, all those people who feel unwanted, unloved, uncared for throughout society, people that have become a burden to the society and are shunned by everyone."[4]

The Missionaries of Charity began with only twelve members in Calcutta. Today there are more than four thousand nuns in the order throughout the world, and they minister to orphans, AIDS victims, refugees, the blind, the disabled, the aged, alcoholics, the poor, victims of natural disasters, and the hungry. They can be found working in Asia, Africa, Latin America, North America, Poland, and Australia.

Mother Teresa always emphasized service to others. She believed and followed these words of Jesus: "And whosoever of you shall be the chiefest, shall be servant of all" (Mark 10:44, KJV). She became a leader because she was a servant, and her Sisters of Charity truly are the servants of all. These are some of the reasons why Mother Teresa became known as "the saint of the gutter."

Her Spiritual Life

Pope John Paul II admired Mother Teresa, and he said that she was one of the greatest missionaries of the twentieth century. He explained, "The Lord made this simple woman who came from one of Europe's poorest regions a chosen instrument (see Acts 9:15) to proclaim the gospel to the entire world, not by preaching, but by daily acts of love towards the poorest of the poor. A missionary with the most universal language: the language of love that knows no bounds or exclusion and has no preferences other than for the most forsaken….Where did Mother Teresa find the strength to place herself completely at the service of others? She found it in prayer and in the silent contemplation of Jesus Christ…"[5]

In his first encyclical, Pope Benedict XVI echoed John Paul's observations by stating, "In the example of Blessed Teresa of Calcutta we have a clear illustration of the fact that time devoted to God in prayer not only does not detract from effective and loving service to our neighbour but is in fact the inexhaustible source of that service."[6]

Angel of Mercy

Mother Teresa was also known as an "angel of mercy" to the poor. This is an apt description of her work, for an angel is a messenger, one who is always ready to come to the aid of others. She opened Nirmal Hriday ("Pure or Immaculate Heart"), a home for the dying, in 1952. This hostel became the focal point of her ministry for a couple of years. The government leaders of Calcutta gave her the use of a building for this purpose.

Writer Eileen Egan describes her work there as follows:

> I watched Mother Teresa as she sat on the parapet next to the low pallets of men, patting their heads or stroking their stick-like arms, murmuring to each one. Sometimes only the eyes seemed alive in men whose skin was drawn so tightly that the skull seemed struggling to burst through. Some were even smiling, as though amazed to be alive. It was the same in the women's hall. Seeing me, they held out their wasted hands to me, searching for human consolation. I turned away in fear and shame. I wondered how she could face day after day caring for those who were brought in covered with the filth and spittle of the gutter. Mother Teresa explained that her work and the work of the Sisters called for them to see Jesus in everyone, including the men and women dying in the gutter.[7]

Mother Teresa said that in the earlier days of their ministry they did little planning. They simply responded to the needs, and she stated that God showed them what to do. She said, "Keep giving Jesus to your people not by words, but by your example, by your being in love with Jesus, by radiating his holiness and spreading his fragrance of love everywhere you go. Just keep the joy of Jesus as your strength. Be happy and at peace. Accept whatever he gives—and give whatever he takes with a big smile. You belong to him."[8]

I love this simple statement of faith. We should never forget that we are God's property, as Paul pointed out to the Corinthians: "You were bought with a price [you were actually purchased with the precious blood of Jesus and made His own]. So then, honor and glorify God with your body" (1 Cor. 6:20). Knowing that we are no longer our own, that we have been bought with a price, helps to clarify many things in our lives. It helps us to see what God wants us to do. It makes us realize that we do not have to do anything in our own strength.

Pure Religion

The apostle James wrote, "Pure and unblemished religion [as it is expressed in outward acts] in the sight of our God and Father is this: to visit and look after the fatherless and the widows in their distress, and to keep oneself uncontaminated by the [secular] world" (Jas. 1:27). Mother Teresa's life was characterized by this kind of "external religious worship."

After opening her free hospice for the poor, Mother Teresa opened a home for lepers, which she called Shanti Nagar ("City of Peace"). Then she opened an orphanage, Shishu Bhavan. She became a true mother to the precious children who lived there.

About her work in the orphanage, Mother Teresa wrote:

One of the abandoned children we had in our Shishu Bhavan I gave to a very high-class and rich family. After a few months I heard that the child had become very sick and completely disabled. So I went to that family and said, "Give me back the child and I will give you a healthy child." The father looked at me and said, "Take my life first, then take the child." He loved the child from his heart. In Calcutta, every night we send word to all the clinics, to all the police stations, to all the hospitals, "Please do not destroy any children; we will take them all." So our house is always full of children. There is a joke in Calcutta: "Mother Teresa is always talking about family planning and abortion, but every day she has more and more children."[9]

How did Mother Teresa learn to be such a giving parent? She developed her parenting skills by getting to know her heavenly Father. She often spoke of His tenderness to her and quoted these verses from the prophet Isaiah:

> But now, thus says the Lord, who created you, O Jacob, and He who formed you, O Israel: Fear not, for I have redeemed you; I have called you by your name; you are Mine. When you pass through the waters, I will be with you; and through the rivers, they shall not overflow you. When you walk through the fire, you shall not be burned, nor shall the flame scorch you. (Isa. 43:1–2, NKJV)

She knew that God was her loving heavenly Father and that He would always be with her. She stood upon His promise that He would never leave her nor forsake her. It was obvious to all who knew her that she knew God personally and intimately.

Mother Teresa understood that God had adopted her into His family, that she was His child. Like Paul, she believed, "For all who are allowing themselves to be led by the Spirit of God are sons of God. For you have not received a spirit of slavery leading again to fear [of God's judgment], but you have received the Spirit of adoption as sons [the Spirit producing sonship] by which we [joyfully] cry, 'Abba! Father!'" (Rom. 8:14–15).

I'm sure this is why she respected life so much and was adamantly opposed to abortion. She always encouraged people to adopt children so that they could experience family love, nurturing, and support. She frequently spoke against abortion and artificial contraception. When she accepted the Nobel Peace Prize in 1979, she said, "I feel the greatest destroyer of peace today is abortion, because it is a direct war, a direct killing—direct murder by the mother herself....Because if a mother can kill her own child—what is left [but] for me to kill you and you kill me—there is nothing between."[10]

To her, abortion was infanticide—a blatant disregard for God's gift of life—and in 1994, at the National Prayer Breakfast in Washington, D.C., she said, "Please don't kill the child. I want the child. Please give me the child. I am willing to accept any child who would be aborted and to give that child to a married couple who will love the child and be loved by the child."[11]

This is complete compassion—a willingness to do all that could be done for those in need. Her offer to take any unwanted child had no limits; it was an open-ended and heartfelt invitation from a true mother who knew how much Jesus loves the little children. Her offer reminds me of what Jesus said: "Leave the children alone, and do not forbid them from coming to Me; for the kingdom of heaven belongs to such as these" (Matt. 19:14).

Forgiveness

Mother Teresa believed in the importance of forgiveness. She said:

I once picked up a woman from a garbage dump and she was burning with fever; she was in her last days and her only lament was: "My son did this to me." I begged her: "You must forgive your son. In a moment of madness, when he was not himself, he did a thing he regrets. Be a mother to him, forgive him." It took me a long time to make her say: "I forgive my son." Just before she died in my arms, she was able to say that with a real forgiveness. She was not concerned that she was dying. The breaking of the heart was that her son did not want her. This is something you and I can understand."[12]

Forgiveness is an important part of compassion, for it is only as we are able to empathize with and understand the person who has wronged us that we will be able to forgive them and find peace for ourselves. Paul writes, "Be kind and helpful to one another, tender-hearted [compassionate, understanding], forgiving one another [readily and freely], just as God in Christ also forgave you" (Eph. 4:32). This is the lifestyle of compassion, and these qualities are desperately needed in society today.

Mother Teresa expressed her feelings about life and her relationship with Jesus Christ in the following poem:

He is the Life that I want to live,
He is the Light that I want to radiate.
He is the Way to the Father.
He is the Love with which I want to love.

He is the Joy that I want to share.
He is the Peace that I want to sow.
Jesus is everything to me.
Without Him, I can do nothing.[13]

Something Beautiful for God

In 1969, Malcolm Muggeridge produced a documentary about Mother Teresa's life titled *Something Beautiful for God*. In 1971, he wrote a book with the same title. These two works helped to spread the name of Mother Teresa around the world. She became the best-known missionary in the world, and people everywhere respected her life and her work.

She received many accolades and awards, including the first Pope John XXIII Peace Prize (1971), the Kennedy Prize (1971), the Albert Schweitzer International Prize (1975), the Balzan Prize for humanity, peace, and brotherhood among peoples (1978), the United States Presidential Medal of Freedom (1985), the Congressional Gold Medal (1994), honorary citizenship of the United States (1996), the Nobel Peace Prize (1997), and honorary degrees from numerous colleges and universities.

Hers was a life well-lived, and she became "something beautiful for God" indeed. In 1999 a Gallup poll found that Mother Teresa was the most admired person of the twentieth century.

In 1982, Mother Teresa was successful in persuading the Israelis and Palestinians to stop shooting long enough to enable her organization to rescue thirty-seven retarded children from a hospital in Beirut. The love and compassion she exhibited is needed in the Middle East today.

In the 1980s and 1990s her health began to decline. She suffered her first heart attack in 1983 while she was visiting Pope John Paul II in Rome. She received a pacemaker after her second heart attack in 1989. When she was in Mexico in 1991, she developed pneumonia, which led to further heart problems. In the face of her deteriorating health, Mother Teresa offered to resign as the head of the Missionaries of Charity, but the sisters had a vote, and all of them voted for her to remain in leadership, so she continued on with her ministry.

In 1996, Mother Teresa suffered a fall that caused her to break her collar bone. In August of that same year she suffered from malaria, and the left ventricle of her heart failed, causing her to undergo heart surgery. On March 13, 1997, she stepped down as the head of her order, and she died later that year, on September 5, 1997. She was eighty-seven years old.

At the time of her death there were more than 4,000 sisters serving with the Missionaries of Charity around the world. In addition, 300 brothers had become associated with the order, along with over 100,000 lay volunteers. These devoted servants of God operated 610 missions in 123 countries, including hospices, homes for people with HIV/AIDS, leprosy and tuberculosis sanitariums, soup kitchens, children and family counseling programs, orphanages, and schools.

This humble woman who came from an obscure village in Macedonia had risen to become the most respected woman in the world because she was faithful to the call God gave to her. In devoting her life to serving others, she became a role model of compassion for all of us to follow.

Peace and Joy

Mother Teresa has often been compared to Saint Francis of Assisi, the thirteenth-century friar who found his joy in serving others. She loved his lifestyle of compassion, poverty, and service, and she learned a great deal from him.

She was fond of praying (and living) St. Francis' well-known prayer:

> Lord, make me an instrument of your peace;
> Where there is hatred, let me sow love;
> Where there is injury, pardon;
> Where there is despair, hope.
> O Divine Master, grant that I might seek
> Not so much to be consoled, as to console;
> To be understood, as to understand;
> Not so much to be loved, as to love another.
> For it is in giving that we receive;
> It is in pardoning that we are pardoned;
> It is in dying that we are born to eternal life.

Mother Teresa was an instrument of peace in the world. The former Secretary-General of the United Nations, Javier Perez de Cuellar, said about her: "She is the United Nations. She is peace in the world."

"Do small things with great love"

One of Mother Teresa's best-known mottos is, "Do small things with great love." This simple but profound advice is what the world needs today. She also said, "Never forget you are co-workers of Jesus." These two quotations form the framework of Mother Teresa's life and ministry, and, when we apply them to our own lives, we will see exciting changes taking place in our life and ministry.

As we let the peace and compassion of Jesus fill our hearts, we follow the trail that Mother Teresa has blazed, and we walk in the footsteps of Jesus: "To this you were called, because Christ suffered for you, leaving you an example, that you should follow in his steps" (1 Pet. 2:21, NIV).

In conclusion, I offer a simple quote from Mother Teresa that seems to reveal the secret of her success in service to others. I ask you to reflect on her words and apply them to your life: "When there is a call within a call, there is only one thing to do, to say 'yes' to Jesus. That's all. If we belong to him, he must be able to use us without consulting us....I had only to say a simple 'yes.'"[15]

Dear Heavenly Father, in Jesus' name I come before You to offer my life to help Your children, young and old, in whatever way is right and lovely in Your eyes. May I follow the example of Jesus when He ministered to them out of love and compassion. Your example is the only example I need; Your love is the only love I need to share with others. It is pure and holy, nourishment to body and spirit. In the precious name of Jesus, amen.

Chapter 8

ᔥ

LITTLE WOMEN—BIG GOD

(Michal Ann Goll)

This chapter focuses on the lives and ministries of five little ladies who became great women of God: Amy Carmichael, Katharine Drexel, Phoebe Palmer, Hannah More, and Elizabeth Fry. Each one of their hearts was filled with compassion, and they spent their lives in service to God by helping others.

As I have studied their lives and writings, I have been deeply stirred to become more like them, for these women lived close to God and shared His life with the people He brought to them. I'm sure you will be impressed, as I was, by their uncompromising devotion to the Lord. God called each of these women to acts of compassion and uncommon valor. They were women after God's own heart, ladies of character who lived their lives in sold-out commitment to the Father.

As you read their stories, may you respond to His call as well, for He is looking for those who will obey Him by going forth into the whitened harvest fields during these last days of human history.

Abandoned to God—Amy Carmichael

Amy Carmichael was born on December 16, 1867, in Millisle, a small village in Northern Ireland. As its name implies, this was a place of mills (flour mills), where Amy's father acquired considerable wealth. Unfortunately, her father died when Amy was eighteen years old, and this resulted in financial uncertainty for the Carmichael family, which was subsequently forced to move to Belfast.

Amy was the oldest of seven children. One wintry Sunday morning, as the family was returning home from the Presbyterian church they attended, Amy and her two brothers saw an old woman who was carrying a large bundle. All the children wanted to help her, but they felt somewhat embarrassed about asking her if they could help. Nonetheless, they went to her aid.

Amy writes, "This meant facing all the respectable people who were, like ourselves, on their way home. It was a horrid moment. We were only two boys and a girl, and not at all exalted Christians. We hated doing it. Crimson all over (at least we felt crimson, soul and body of us) we plodded on, a wet wind blows in about us, and blowing, too, the rags of that poor old woman, till she seemed like a bundle of feathers and we unhappily mixed up with them."[1]

As they kept walking, they came to a beautiful Victorian fountain. Just as they were passing this fountain, Amy heard a voice that was speaking the words of a Scripture verse: "Now if any man build upon this foundation gold, silver, precious stones, wood, hay, stubble; every man's work shall be made manifest; for the day shall declare it, because it shall be revealed by fire; and the fire shall try every man's work of what sort it is. If any man's work abide…" (1 Cor. 3:12–14, KJV).

Startled by this message, Amy turned around to see who had spoken it to her, but no one was there, and all she heard then was the bubbling and splashing of the fountain and a few distant passersby who were talking with each other.[2] She knew then that God was calling her to "settle some things with Him."[3] Prior to this she had been primarily preoccupied with her social life.

The death of her father caused Amy to reevaluate her values and beliefs, and she began to think seriously about her future and God's plan for her life. As a result, she began to work in an inner-city mission in Belfast.

The Carmichaels traveled to Cumbria County, England, in order to attend a Keswick Conference in England's Lake District. The convention had begun a decade or so earlier as an important gathering of evangelical Christians. It was the center of what came to be known as the Higher Life Movement in Great Britain. Personal holiness was the major emphasis of this movement.

Amy Carmichael was greatly influenced by her experience there. She writes, "The hall was full of a sort of gray mist, very dull and chilly. I came to that meeting half hoping, half fearing. Would there be anything for me?...the fog in the Hall seemed to soak into me. My soul was in a fog. Then the chairman rose for the last prayer...'O Lord, we know Thou art able to keep us from falling.' Those words found me. It was as if they were alight. And they shone for me."[4]

This was the moment when Amy realized that she must dedicate her whole life to the Lord Jesus Christ, who had given His life for her. In her heart of hearts, she understood that she had to do the same in return and give her all to Him.

Amy began to realize that she had to die to the self-life in order to follow the Lord's leading. She knew the meaning of Paul's words, "I am crucified with Christ: nevertheless I live; yet not I, but Christ liveth in me: and the life which I now live in the flesh I live by the faith of the Son of God, who loved me, and gave himself for me" (Gal. 2:20, KJV). Nothing but complete surrender to Jesus could satisfy her now, and she determined to give her life in total abandonment to Him.

In 1887, Amy heard a speech by China Inland Mission founder Hudson Taylor, and his compelling message ignited her passion for missions. In 1893, she left for Japan with the support of the Keswick Convention, but this initial introduction to foreign missionary service was a big disappointment to her, because she felt there was little difference between the missionaries she worked with there and people in the world.

She wrote, "...we are here just what we are at home—not one bit better—and the devil is awfully busy...There are missionary shipwrecks of once-fair vessels."[5] Amy wanted more of God, and her desire to live a holy life before Him pushed her away from her work in Japan. She decided to return home, but on her way back to England, she stopped in Ceylon to help care for a sick family friend.

Upon returning home, she continued seeking God and His will for her life. After less than a year back home, she decided to return to the mission field. This time she went to India—the place God had picked for her. It was 1895 and she was commissioned by the Church of England Zenana Missionary Society to go to Dohnavur, India, where she subsequently served for fifty-six years without a furlough.

In time, Amy Carmichael founded the Dohnavur Fellowship for Girls, which was a ministry devoted to rescuing girls whose families had dedicated them to become temple prostitutes. Through her ministry, more than a thousand children were rescued from abuse and neglect. The children called her "Amma," which means "mother" in the Tamil language, and Amy truly became a mother to them.

She wrote:

There were days when the sky turned black for me because of what I heard and knew was true....Sometimes it was as if I saw the Lord Jesus Christ kneeling alone, as He knelt long ago under the olive trees....And the only thing that one who cared could do was to go softly and kneel down beside Him, so that He would not be alone in His sorrow over the little children.[6]

Amy Carmichael was a devout woman of prayer, and her life was characterized by total commitment, all-out compassion, obedience, and selflessness. One of her most heart-felt prayers, a prayer that became the theme of her life, was expressed in the following poem:

O Father, help, lest our poor love refuse
For our beloved the life that they would choose,
And in our fear of loss for them, or pain,
Forget eternal gain.
Show us the gain, the golden harvest there
For corn of wheat that they have buried here;
Lest human love defraud them and betray,
Teach us, O God, to pray.
Teach us to pray, remembering Calvary,
For as the Master must the servant be;
We see their face set toward Jerusalem,
Let us not hinder them.
Teach us to pray; O Thou who didst not spare
Thine own Beloved, lead us on in prayer;
Purge from the earthly, give us love Divine,
Father, like Thine, like Thine.[7]

Amy Carmichael wrote thirty-five books, many of which continue to inspire people around the world today. She was crippled by a fall in 1931, and four years later she became bedridden. She remained an invalid until her death in 1951, and she was buried in her beloved Dohnavur.

For more than fifty years Amy's overarching goal in life was: "To save children in moral danger; to train them to serve others; to succor the desolate and the suffering; to do anything that may be shown to be the will of our heavenly Father, in order to make His love known, especially to the people of India."

The "Millionaire Nun"—Katharine Drexel

Katharine Mary Drexel was born in Philadelphia, Pennsylvania, in 1858. She was the second daughter of a wealthy Philadelphia banker, Francis Martin Drexel, and his wife, Hannah Langstroth. Her mother died approximately one month after Katharine was born.

Katharine's sister, Elizabeth, was three years older than she. When her father remarried, another sister, Louise, was born in 1863. Francis's new wife, Emma Bouvier, became a very devoted mother to Katharine and her sisters.

The Drexel girls did not go to school; they were home-schooled by governesses. Nonetheless, Katharine was well-educated and her natural intelligence became obvious to all when she was very young. As she grew up she was able to travel extensively with her family, and this broadened Katharine's understanding of the world and its people. On one trip to the Southwest, Katharine saw firsthand the deprivation of Native Americans and was appalled to see the deplorable conditions in which they lived.

This caused her to resolve to do something to help the poor when she got older, and this may well have been the time when her heart for missions began to develop. Around this same time, she also began to become deeply concerned about the plight of African-Americans.

Katharine's parents instilled in their children the concept that wealth was a gift from God that He wanted them to share with others.[8] Jesus said, "freely ye have received, freely give" (Matt. 10:8, KJV), and this was Katharine's approach to life and ministry when she became a nun in 1889. She entered the Sisters of Mercy convent in Pittsburgh, Pennsylvania, and while preparing for her vows, she began to sense that God was calling her to a ministry to the poor.

Katharine had a personal visit with Pope Leo XIII in 1883. She asked him what could be done for the American Indians and blacks in the United States. The pope answered, "Daughter, why don't you become a missionary?" His question stirred something deep inside her; she felt she had heard God's challenge, and she began to weep.[9]

As a result, she began to envision a new order of nuns who would serve Native Americans and African-Americans in particular. When she returned to America, she consulted with her spiritual director, Bishop James O'Conner. He advised her to start her own religious community.

The new order—the Sisters of the Blessed Sacrament for Indians and Colored People—was founded on February 12, 1891, and Katharine Drexel took the name of Mother Katharine Drexel. Because she was a multimillionaire and had taken the vow of poverty, Archbishop Patrick Ryan of Philadelphia reminded her that she needed to be willing to surrender her funds to the Lord's work.

From then on, she lived a very austere life, using money for herself only to provide for the basic necessities of life. Though she was rich, she voluntarily became a poor woman who ministered to the poor, much like Jesus Himself:

> For you know the grace of our Lord Jesus Christ, that though He was rich, yet for your sakes He became poor, that you through His poverty might become rich. (2 Cor. 8:9, NKJV)

Using her money for God, Mother Katharine began by building a convent in Bensalem, Pennsylvania, not far from her native Philadelphia. In her lifetime she freely gave nearly twenty million dollars from her parents' estate to the poor. She established sixty missions to provide education for American Indians and blacks, and she and her sisters dedicated their lives completely to the welfare of these disadvantaged people.[10]

Along the way, Mother Katharine and her sisters encountered great opposition, particularly from people with racial prejudices. She never wavered in the face of conflict, however, and eventually won the respect of many people, even former enemies. She always stood stalwartly for justice, mercy, and peace.

Katharine was a woman who believed in the power of prayer. She asked God to intervene in the lives of Native Americans and African-Americans and to stem the tide of racism in the United States. Though the Civil War had ended a few decades earlier, she realized that many blacks were still not free and had to live in substandard conditions as sharecroppers and menial laborers.

She recognized that American Indians and blacks were denied the rights of full citizenship and equality in many places and that those who were able to attend school received poor educations. As a result, she developed "a compassionate urgency to help change racial attitudes in the United States."[11]

In 1915, Mother Katharine was responsible for the establishment of Xavier University in New Orleans, which was then the only Catholic university for blacks in America.

Throughout her long and devoted life, Katharine Drexel held true to the stated goals of the order she founded:

1. The primary object which the Sisters of this religious congregation purpose to themselves is their own personal sanctification.

2. The secondary and special object of the members of the congregation is to apply themselves zealously to the service of Our Lord...by endeavoring to lead the Indian and Colored races to the knowledge and love of God, and so make them living temples of our Lord's divinity.[12]

The Roman Catholic Church canonized Mother Katharine Drexel in 2000. In her lifetime of service to God and His Church she accomplished:

- The founding of forty-nine convents for her sisters.
- The establishment of training courses for teachers.
- The building of sixty-two schools, including Xavier University.
- Numerous writings.
- Helping to change the attitudes of church people toward the poor and disenfranchised.
- A life of holiness, prayer, and total giving of herself.
- An example of courage, mercy, justice, and compassion.

The Vatican News Service described her life as follows:

> In her quiet way, Katharine combined prayerful and total dependence on Divine Providence with determined activism. Her joyous incisiveness attuned to the Holy Spirit, penetrated obstacles and facilitated her advances for social justice. Through the prophetic witness of Katharine Drexel's initiative, the Church in the United States was enabled to become aware of the grave domestic need for an apostolate among Native Americans and Afro-Americans. She did not hesitate to speak out against injustice, taking a public stance when racial discrimination was in evidence.[13]

Katharine Drexel died on March 3, 1955, after living for Jesus and walking in compassion for almost a century.

The Mother of the Holiness Movement— Phoebe Palmer

Phoebe (nee Worrall) Palmer was born in New York City on December 17, 1807. Her father, Henry Worrall, was a devout Methodist who had experienced a radical conversion during the Wesleyan Revival in England before he immigrated to America. He married an American, Dorothea Wade.

Phoebe's parents made sure that they had family worship twice a day in their home. They placed high value on "religious conversion and holy living" for themselves and their children.[14]

When she was only eleven years old, Phoebe wrote this poem on the flyleaf of her Bible:

> This revelation—holy, just, and true
> Though oft I read, it seems forever new;
> While light from heaven upon its pages rest,
> I feel its power, and with it I am blessed.
> Henceforth, I take thee as my future guide,
> Let naught from thee my youthful heart divide.
> And then, if late or early death be mine,
> All will be well, since I, O Lord, am Thine![15]

Throughout her life Phoebe kept the Bible as her guidebook, and the power of the Word motivated her to spread the concept of holiness throughout America in great love and compassion for everyone she met.

Phoebe married a homeopathic physician in 1827. His name was Walter Clarke Palmer, and he, like Phoebe, was an active member of the Methodist Episcopal Church. His parents, Miles and Deborah Clarke Palmer, had helped establish the denomination in New York City.

The young couple shared a commitment to Christ and each other, but their marriage and faith were severely tested by a series of hardships and tragedies, including the deaths of three of their children. At first, Phoebe felt that the deaths of her children were evidence of God's displeasure with her, and she began to question her salvation as she struggled with despair, guilt, and remorse.

This thrust her into a deeper pursuit of God and His ways. After the death of her second son, she wrote, "I will not attempt to describe the pressure of the last crushing trial. Surely I needed it, or it would not have been given. God takes our treasure to heaven, that our hearts may be there also. The Lord had declared himself a jealous God, he will have no other gods before him. After my loved ones were snatched away, I saw that I had concentrated my time and attentions far too exclusively, to the neglect of the religious activities demanded. Though painfully learned, yet I trust the lesson has been fully apprehended. From henceforth, Jesus must and shall have the uppermost seat in my heart."[16]

Phoebe's sister Sarah Lankford began having weekly prayer meetings with Methodist women. Within two years or so, Phoebe assumed leadership of these meetings, which became known as "the Tuesday Meeting for the Promotion of Holiness." Eventually men began to attend these gatherings as well. As word of these meetings spread around the country, a great interest began to develop in what became known as the Holiness Movement.

Phoebe and her husband became itinerant preachers, and they received invitations to speak on holiness—the "deeper work of grace"—from churches, conferences, and camp meetings. Phoebe's work encouraged many other women to start meetings for the promotion of holiness throughout America.

In the autumn of 1857 the Palmers went to Hamilton, Ontario,

Canada, to speak at an afternoon prayer meeting. This prayer meeting turned into a ten-day revival in which hundreds of people chose Christ as their Savior.

When they returned to New York, they preached to standing-room-only crowds, and then they traveled to England, where many found faith in Christ. They remained in England for a few years, and it is estimated that more than 25,000 people came to the knowledge of Christ through Phoebe's ministry.

The Palmers believed in a deeper work of grace that would lead to holiness, and this concept was based on John Wesley's idea of Christian perfection, a belief that a Christian can live a life free of serious sin. This "deeper work of grace" was what the Palmers called "entire sanctification."[17]

Without any question, Phoebe Palmer played a prominent role in spreading the concept of Christian holiness throughout America and around the world. She wrote several books on this topic, including *The Way of Holiness*, a foundational book in the Holiness movement. She was very influential in the lives of several women, including Frances Willard, a leading advocate in the Temperance movement, and Catherine Booth, the cofounder of the Salvation Army.

In her book *The Promise of the Father,* Phoebe Palmer took a strong stand for the role of women in Christian ministry. She based this on Acts 5:29, which urges us to obey God rather than men. She said, "It is always right to obey the Holy Spirit's command, and if that is laid upon a woman to preach the gospel, then it is right for her to do so; it is a duty she cannot neglect without falling into condemnation."[18] Her teaching opened the door for many women preachers to respond to God's call in their lives.

Phoebe's holiness was reflected in every aspect of her life, and it impelled her to help found the Five Points Mission in a slum area of New York City in 1850. She also served as a leader in the Methodist Ladies' Home Missionary Society. Her faith had "legs," as it moved in compassion among the dregs of society.

Other influential books by Phoebe Palmer include *Entire Devotion to God* and *Faith and Its Effects,* both of which were published in the 1840s.

When her daughter Eliza was accidentally burned to death as the result of a fire in her nursery, Phoebe wrote these words that prophetically described what her life and ministry truly became:

> While pacing the room, crying to God, amid the tumult of grief, my mind was arrested by a gentle whisper, saying, "Your Heavenly Father loves you. He would not permit such a great trial, without intending that some great good proportionate in magnitude and weight should result. He means to teach you some great lesson that might not otherwise be learned."...My darling is in heaven doing an angel service. And now I have resolved that the service, or in other words, the time I would have devoted to her, shall be spent in work for Jesus. And if diligent and self-sacrificing in carrying out my resolve, the death of this child may result in the spiritual life of many.[19]

Phoebe Palmer held true to this commitment until her death on November 2, 1874, and as a result, thousands came to know Christ personally, walking in holiness throughout their lives.

Champion of the Disenfranchised—Hannah More

Hannah More was born at Stapleton, near Bristol, England, in 1745, the youngest of the five daughters of Jacob More, who had been a Presbyterian but became a member of the Church of England. Jacob was a teacher, and his older daughters followed in his footsteps by founding a boarding school at Bristol. Hannah became a pupil in her sisters' school when she was twelve years old and eventually became a teacher there as well.

Hannah began writing for publication when she was still a teenager. Her early works were mostly pastoral plays written for young ladies. She became engaged to William Turner, a wealthy squire who was twenty years older than she, but the couple never married. Even so, William provided Hannah with an annuity that enabled her to become financially independent.

By the mid-1790s, Hannah had become closely involved with the Clapham Sect of evangelical Christians, a group that was very involved in the abolitionist movement. Well-known anti-slavery advocate

William Wilberforce and former slave captain John Newton attended this group's meetings as well. She was the most influential female member of the Society for the Effecting the Abolition of the African Slave Trade, and wrote a number of religious tracts, several of which opposed slavery and the slave trade, that eventually led to the formation of the Religious Tracts Society.

Hannah became friends with Wilberforce and other anti-slavery leaders, including John Newton, who wrote "Amazing Grace," and in 1788 she published a poem titled "Slavery." In the late 1780s Hannah and her sister, Martha More, conducted philanthropic work in the Mendip area, a poor coal-mining region. They had set up twelve schools by 1800, and in these schools, reading, the Bible, and Christian teaching were central. They encountered considerable opposition along the way, because many farmers felt that education would become fatal to agriculture.[20] At the same time, the Anglican clergy of the area accused Hannah of having "Methodist tendencies."[21]

Clearly, Hannah blazed a trail for women in her day. She believed in justice for all people and was a pioneer in the abolitionist movement, which eventually brought an end to slavery in Great Britain and the United States. She was also instrumental in the establishment of Sunday schools in the Wrington, England, area, and in these schools poor children were taught reading, religion, and personal hygiene. She chose to get involved in the world instead of living a life of quiet obscurity.

In her life we see a woman who was a great "…example of balance: the hearts of Mary and Martha beating within the same bosom. Hannah More proves that you can be passionate about His presence and at the same time be a servant to fellow man. She earned credibility in two realms, so that both worlds would heed her invitations. If you build it He will come…and they will come to see Him."[22]

As a prolific writer of dramas, poetry, and prose, she became quite wealthy as a result of the publication of her numerous books, plays, poems, and tracts. In fact, she developed a "cottage industry" that enabled her to print millions of religious tracts, which were distributed around the world.

Many of her works were spiritually and ethically influential in the lives of women: *Strictures on Female Education* (1799), *Character of a*

Young Princess (1805), *Practical Piety* (1811), *Christian Morals* (1813), *Character of St. Paul* (1815), and *Moral Sketches* (1819). Even though most of her writings have been forgotten now, they were extremely popular and highly marketable during her day, and they had a great impact on women throughout the English-speaking world. She wrote, "Prayer is not eloquence, but earnestness; not the definition of helplessness, but the feeling of it; not figures of speech, but earnestness of soul."[23]

When she died in 1833, Hannah More left the equivalent of three million dollars to charities and religious societies. In one of her poems, she writes about her heavenly home, where she now resides:

> The soul on earth is an immortal guest,
> Compelled to starve at an unreal feast;
> A pilgrim panting for the rest to come;
> An exile, anxious for his native home.[24]

Prison Reformer—Elizabeth Fry

Elizabeth (nee Gurney) Fry was born in Norwich, England, on May 21, 1780. Her father was John Gurney, a successful businessman who was a member of the Society of Friends (Quakers). He was a partner in the Gurney Bank and the owner of a wool-stapling and spinning factory. Elizabeth's mother, Catherine Gurney, was a member of the Society of Friends as well, and she was extensively involved in charity work among the poor. Catherine required her children to spend two hours a day in quiet worship of the Lord.

Elizabeth was twelve when her mother died soon after the birth of her twelfth child. As one of the older daughters, she was required to help in the raising of her younger siblings, which caused Elizabeth to grow up fairly quickly. She became familiar with the writings of Mary Wollstonecraft, who wrote *Vindication of the Rights of Women,* and studied the writings of the abolitionists of her day. At this point in her life, Elizabeth seemed to be heading in a non-religious direction.

However, when she was eighteen years old, Elizabeth heard an American Quaker named William Savery preach in Norwich. She was so impressed by what Savery had to say that she begged her father to invite the preacher to dinner. Her father did so, and after her meeting with Savery, Elizabeth wrote these words: "Today I felt there is a God. I loved the man as if he was almost sent from heaven—we had much serious talk and what he said to me was like a refreshing shower on parched up earth."[25]

This was a dramatic turning point in Elizabeth's life. She wrote, "After we had spent a pleasant evening, my heart began to feel itself silenced before God and without looking at others, I felt myself under the shadow of the wing of God....After the meeting my heart felt really light and as I walked home by starlight, I looked through nature up to nature's God."[26]

The "showers" from heaven that Elizabeth experienced that night led her to make a momentous decision in her life. From then on she determined to devote her energies to helping needy people. She began to collect used clothing for the poor, she visited the sick, and she opened a Sunday school in her home where she taught poor children to read.

She wrote, "Since my heart was touched...I believe I never have awakened from sleep, in sickness or in health, by day or by night, without my first waking thought being, 'how best I might serve my Lord.'"[27] Clearly, her conversion to Christ went deep, and its repercussions were felt around the world. Soon thereafter she was appointed to the committee that was responsible for running the Society of Friends' school at Acworth.

In the summer of 1799, Elizabeth met Joseph Fry, a Quaker who was the son of a prosperous merchant in Essex. They were married in the summer of the following year, and God blessed the young couple with eight children.

In March 1811, Elizabeth became a preacher for the Society of Friends. A friend, Stephen Grellet, told Elizabeth about the horrific conditions that existed at Newgate Prison, which he had recently visited. He was particularly shocked by the way the women who were incarcerated there were being treated. They had to sleep on the floor without nightclothes or any kind of bedding, and three hundred women were huddled together in only two wards. These prisoners had to cook, wash, and sleep in the same cell.

Elizabeth decided to visit the women of Newgate Prison herself, and she did so on a regular basis thereafter. She took clothing to them, would often read the Bible to them, and started a school and chapel in the prison. As time went on, she established a new system of administration there as well, and this included matrons and monitors who supervised the women.

Meanwhile, Elizabeth continued her duties as a wife and mother, and three more children were born, although she grieved the loss of her five-year-old daughter, Betsy.

Elizabeth and eleven other Quakers founded the Association for the Improvement of the Female Prisoners in Newgate. In her address to the House of Commons, Elizabeth described the conditions of the women in Newgate Prison: "...each with a space of about six feet by two to herself...old and young, hardened offenders with those who had committed only a minor offence or their first crime; the lowest of women with the respectable married women and maid-servants."[28]

Her work influenced major changes in the penal system in Great Britain, which punished prisoners harshly. Richard Huntsman writes:

> For misdemeanours such as causing a nuisance, the culprit would expect physical punishments such as being whipped, branded or put in the stocks. For minor offences, such as stealing a teaspoon or merely begging, one could, before 1775, expect transportation to North America for 7 or 14 years to serve as an indentured labourer or servant. During that period some 40,000 men and women were transported to North America and the West Indies. For what were seen as serious offences ranging from murder, forgery or stealing any object worth over 5 shillings (a week's wage for a maid 'living in'), one would expect to be hanged. Hence the advice that you might as well be hanged for stealing a sheep as a lamb! In all, over 300 offences attracted the death penalty.[29]

It was these unjust penalties and unfair conditions that caused Elizabeth Fry to get fully involved in prison reform. Between 1818 and 1843, Elizabeth visited prisons throughout the British Isles and the continent of Europe. It was an exhausting and dangerous journey. She would seek the approval of local officials before entering the prisons, and after her visits, she would organize a ladies' association to continue her work in each local prison.

She also became involved as an advocate for women who were sentenced to death. Often she was able to save them from being hanged. Her constant prayer was, "O Lord, may I be directed what to do and what to leave undone."[30]

In 1824, Elizabeth visited Brighton and was shocked by the number of beggars and poor people she encountered there. This led her to form the Brighton District Visiting Society, a group of women who would visit in the homes of the poor and provide them with physical, emotional, and spiritual help and comfort. She campaigned for the homeless in London and tried to improve the care that was given to mental patients in the asylums throughout England. She also worked arduously for the reform of workhouses and hospitals throughout her country.

Nursing care became another one of Elizabeth's concerns. She established a training school for nurses in 1840. Florence Nightingale once wrote to Elizabeth to let her know what a great influence she had been in her life. In 1840, Fry founded the Protestant Sisters of Charity, an organization of nurses who made themselves available to families in need. She often met with Queen Victoria, and the monarch contributed money to her ministry. The queen wrote that she considered Elizabeth Fry to be a "very superior person."[31]

In 1827, Elizabeth published a book, *Observations on the Visiting, Superintendence and Government of Female Prisoners,* in which she showed the need for prison reform and called for greater opportunities for women. She also condemned the death penalty.

After a short illness, Elizabeth Fry died on October 12, 1845. Over a thousand mourners stood in silence as she was buried at the Society of Friends graveyard at Barking. She was a woman of eminent compassion and strong faith who surely believed these words of Paul: "The only thing that counts is faith expressing itself through love" (Gal. 5:6, NIV).

Dear Father in heaven, as did the saints who have lived before me, may I find those who need Your touch of compassion and may I share with them the goodness of Your love. May I find the lost, feed the hungry, speak for the voiceless, and provide shelter for the homeless. Please give me the courage I need to seek out those in the greatest need. In Jesus' name, amen.

Chapter 9

Heidi Baker

BLESSED ARE THE POOR

(Julia C. Loren)

There are those who talk the talk, and there are others who walk the walk. Heidi Baker is a modern-day apostle of compassion who is living the call—right now.

Heidi is "Mama Ida" to thousands of displaced, abused, and orphaned children who have been raised alongside her own two children, Elisha and Crystalyn. She is truly one who radiates the love, compassion, and joy of the Lord to all she meets. She calls herself a "laid-down lover of God"—one whose life is wholly given over to the Lord, one whose life also inspires others to surrender themselves more completely to the love and service of Jesus. At a Voice of the Apostles conference in 2005, Heidi said, "Fully possessed by the Holy Spirit we become lovers and we do radical things because we know who we are."

In a world that glamorizes the achievements of men, Heidi Baker shuns the spotlight. When she speaks at conferences, those attending tend to see and hear more of Jesus and less of her. Her joy is to fade into the background and let Jesus take over. People weep as the Spirit of God tenderizes their hearts with His compassion for the lost, the broken, and the hurting ones all around the world. Fluent in several languages, she is a gifted communicator with advanced educational degrees.

She also has seen astounding miracles during her thirty years of ministry, especially in Mozambique, where she and her husband, Rolland, and their Iris Ministries team have planted more than seven thousand "bush churches," five Bible schools, and four children's feeding centers since 1990.[1]

Astounding miracles are common to Heidi and Rolland. The blind receive their sight, the deaf hear, and children with AIDS seroconvert to normalcy. Children traumatized by war, severe neglect, and abuse, full of hate, who can barely speak or trust, rapidly respond to their love. Today these same children can be found dancing and ministering with joy. The Bakers have seen God supernaturally multiply food to feed hungry orphans and crowds who gather for meetings. African pastors who have been trained by the Bakers have raised fifty-three people from the dead in Mozambique as of this writing.[2]

The Bakers' lives display the full meaning of Jesus' death and resurrection as they embrace the cross daily—a cross that includes suffering and sacrifice for the sake of releasing healing and reconciling the world to Jesus. It is a cross of compassion and a cross of love.

They spend countless hours soaking in the love of God and interceding for those to whom they minister. Heidi, as a result, has learned that worship is the key to releasing love. And their "intimacy with God provokes confidence that releases faith to stand in God's presence and see Him as big as He is." They live in a place rife with the external evidence of demonic control—war, disease, famine, and corruption. Yet their internal dwelling is "...the place of refuge, a fortress, a secret place of worship and communion. They access a place of blinding, coruscating light. From that place they embark on their mission, to magnify the Lord in the world of men."[3]

Heidi's Calling

Tenacity characterizes this petite blonde, who is originally from Laguna Beach, California. At the age of sixteen, when most Laguna teens were lounging on the beach enjoying the party atmosphere of the era, Heidi was accepted as an American Field Service student. She was sent to a Choctaw Indian reservation in Mississippi, where she was exposed to an environment of poverty that she had never seen before. It was here that she gave her life to Jesus and, after a five-day fast, encountered the Lord in a dramatic way:

On the night of the fifth day, I expectantly went to the Roark's little Pentecostal church in the country and was drawn to the altar. I knelt down and lifted my arms to the Lord. Suddenly, I felt taken to a new heavenly place. Pastor Roark was preaching, but I couldn't hear his loud, powerful voice at all. God's glory came to me again, wrapping me in a pure and brilliant white light. I was overwhelmed by who He is. I had never felt so loved, and I began to weep. This time He spoke to me audibly. "I am calling you to be a minister and a missionary," He said. "You are to go to Africa, Asia, and England." Again my heart was pounding and racing. I thought I might die.

Then the Lord Jesus spoke to me and told me I would be married to Him. He kissed my hand, and it felt as if warm oil ran down my arm. I was overcome with love for Him. I knew at that moment that I would go anywhere anytime and say anything for Him. I was ruined for this world by His intense love and mercy in calling me to Himself.[4]

Full of the presence and love of Jesus, Heidi started telling everyone about Him—on the reservation and later at her high school. She talked the local Episcopal priest into letting her start a Christian coffeehouse in the parish hall and ministered every Friday night for several years—praying for the drug addicts, alcoholics, homeless, and demon-possessed people. In the meanwhile, she attended Southern California College (now Vanguard University).

During her last year in college in 1980, she met her husband, Rolland Baker, grandson of well-known missionaries to China who had gained a place in the Church history books for their vital part in launching a revival among Chinese youth in the pre-Maoist years (see H. A. Baker's *Visions Beyond the Veil*).

True to both Rolland's heritage and Heidi's calling, they discerned that they were called together to help bring revival among the poor. Their ministry would be incarnational. They would live like the people, learn the language and the culture from those on the street, suffer with them and earn trust in the process. They married six months later and have since traveled as missionaries to Hong Kong, England, and Mozambique. Their work has extended from Africa into many other countries of the world.

Launched Into Fields of Poverty and War

Their work in Africa began in 1990, when Rolland saw a *Time* magazine article that described the poverty in Mozambique, naming it the poorest country in the world. God knew He needed tenacious and seasoned missionaries and launched them out to start Iris Ministries—working among the Muslims and the poorest of the poor, who were ravished by war, starvation, and disease. The following excerpt best describes their introduction to the mission field:

> At the time, the country was involved in a prolonged civil war, and it wasn't until 1995, after a cease-fire was declared between the Renamo (north) and the Frelimo (south), that the Bakers were invited by South African missionaries to go into the war-torn country. They and their friends loaded a few supplies into a red Nissan truck and drove to the border of Mozambique.
>
> To their dismay, the truck sputtered and lost power until, finally, the engine stopped just in front of the border gate between South Africa and Mozambique.
>
> Suddenly, helicopters began flying over them, and people started yelling. The truck in front of them was riddled with bullets from bandits. But as soon as the bandits left and the air cleared, the truck the Bakers were in mysteriously started, so they were able to continue their journey to Maputo, the nation's capital.
>
> The countryside they saw on their way was desolate in the aftermath of the civil war. There were no hospitals or ambulances, but many lay sick or injured as a result of the conflict.
>
> The Bakers struggled to begin a church and an orphanage in a rundown building. In these grim conditions, the Bakers say God displayed His power over poverty one day by multiplying a small amount of chili and rice—originally intended to feed only four people—to such a degree that it was sufficient for not only the Baker family but also 80 orphaned children.[5]

Stopping for One

Stopping for "the one"—the child on the street, the boy scavenging for food in the dump, the girl languishing under forced prostitution—has always been the focus of Heidi's ministry. In the early days after their arrival in Mozambique, they took in dozens of children, many of whom were extremely sick, dying, or angry to the point of violence. Some were healed instantaneously. Others were loved into total emotional, physical, and spiritual health. Others experienced the love of God for a brief time until heaven called them home.

Currently the Bakers and their team care for thousands of orphans living in several children's centers and in the "foster" homes of pastors and widows. Every Iris Ministries pastor, whether he leads a church in a city or in the bush, is encouraged to adopt at least ten orphans. Local widows are summoned to feed and care for the overflow of homeless children who flock to the love offered by the Christians. Many of the children have lost their parents to AIDS in a country where more than 180,000 children are AIDS orphans.

An article in *Charisma* magazine describes the differences in the children before and after Heidi's touch:

> Gitou was an AIDS orphan and a tough street kid when Heidi Baker met him. "He said he was 12, but he looked around 8. His heart was ha7rdened, and he continued telling me off whenever I came near," she recalled. "But I just kept loving and loving Gitou until his heart melted. Now he preaches out on the street and leads many to the Lord."
>
> Constancia was a scared little orphan girl of around 5 who was left on the steps of Iris Ministries' orphanage. "She didn't speak and couldn't communicate," Heidi said. "The Lord just told me to chase her…with His love. I'd chase her and hold her until she fell asleep in my arms.
>
> "The same day Constancia was baptized; she began to speak and even asked to lead the choir. She told us then that she'd been mute since seeing her parents brutally murdered right in front of her."[6]

Ever praying about what to do with the overwhelming needs of so many thousands of children and the growing ministry, Heidi received an amazing strategy from the Lord: "The Lord had showed me thousands and thousands of children, and I believe we are called to care for millions of children. At first I was absolutely overwhelmed with that vision, and I thought, 'God how could that ever happen? How could we ever do that, just stopping for the one? I don't know how we could ever, ever do that.' I was praying, crying, fasting and asking God, and He said that He would bring a great revival, and in this revival He would touch the hearts of pastors, and they would become fathers of the fatherless. He said that was His answer for these children. They would be literally cared for by these Mozambican pastors. And then He told me that the widows would cook for them and feed them, that the widows would help farm and that we were to build indigenous buildings made of mud and straw, buildings that fit in with every church. We would see these children cared for in families."[7]

From Struggling Missionary to Apostolic Anointing

Heidi and Rolland labored for years in Africa, and this lifestyle eventually took a toll on Heidi's spirit. Yet her ever-expanding heart of love ached to do more. She tells what happened next:

"Now in Africa we were seeing the sequel to the revival Rolland's grandfather saw among his orphans in China. That was not an isolated outpouring without further fruit. In it Rolland and I saw the heart of God. We saw how He feels about the lost and forgotten. We saw how He delights to use the helpless and hopeless to accomplish His best work. We saw His pleasure in revealing Himself to those humble and poor in spirit enough to appreciate Him. We saw His ability to use simple children to ignite revival. Now we are seeing Him do the same thing in Mozambique. And what He was doing in our children's center fired our appetites all the more for revival.

"We were simply desperate for more of God.

"In January of 1998, Randy Clark was [in Toronto] preaching about the apostolic anointing, laying down our lives and the holy fire of God. He pointed to me and said, 'God is asking, Do you want Mozambique?' I experienced the heavenly fire of God falling on me. I was so hot I literally thought I was going to burn up and die. I remember crying out, 'Lord, I'm dying!' I heard the Lord clearly speak to my heart, 'Good, I want you to be dead!' He wanted me to be completely emptied of self so He could pour even more of His Spirit into my life.

"For seven days I was unable to move. Rolland had to pick me up and carry me. I had to be carried to the washroom, to the hotel and back to the meeting. The weight of His glory was upon me. I felt so heavy that I could not lift my head."[8]

Unable to speak or move for seven days, the presence of God changed Heidi's life. She had never felt so humbled, poor, and vulnerable. Engulfed in the presence of the Lord, she listened as God spoke to her about relinquishing control of her life and the ministry to Him. He spoke of planting hundreds of churches in Mozambique. Where Heidi and Rolland labored for several years with seemingly little fruit, God would burst in with His power and unleash His presence over the region.

"It had taken us seventeen years to plant four churches, and two of them were pretty weak. As I lay there, engulfed in His presence, He spoke to me about hundreds of churches being planted in Mozambique. I remember laughing hysterically, thinking I would have to be two hundred years old before that promise was fulfilled!

"God showed me that I needed to learn to work with the rest of His Body...

"I thought I had been depending on Him to plant churches, when in reality I depended a lot on my own abilities. Naturally, things moved pitifully slowly. It's comical to think we can do God's work for Him. It's all grace. He allows us to participate with Him, and so there is always enough. He showed me how much I needed Him and the body of Christ. He is calling us to complete humility and gentleness. It is never about us; it is always about Him."[9]

After that transforming encounter, everything in Heidi's ministry changed. She returned to Mozambique and began releasing people into ministry, recognizing potential ministers even in young children. She relinquished control and started delegating responsibilities. In return came the apostolic anointing to heal the sick, cast out demons, raise the dead, see blind eyes open and deaf ears hear, and train and launch hundreds of pastors into the largely Muslim fields of Mozambique, where they had labored for years to plant a handful of churches. Now they were shocked to discover the Lord empowering them to plant thousands more in record time.

Keys to Fruitfulness

The Bakers say that one of the keys to becoming a successful ministry lies in relinquishing complete control to God, a concept the Western church needs to learn in order to sow effective ministry throughout the earth. Another key to fruitfulness, the couple says, is intimacy with God. "Revival breaks out when people are desperate for God. When they become intimate with Him and lose sight of themselves, then anything can happen," says Rolland.

One of the most important keys to sustaining successful ministry, however, is tenacious faith to persevere through opposition. Heidi and Rolland Baker articulate the price they pay as they come against the demonic strongholds—a price that includes theft of ministry resources, sickness, malicious lies, and political backlash. They have faced guns and violence. Not one New Creation Power Broker on the mission field today leads an easy life coasting along in a bullet-proof bubble of the Holy Spirit, untouched by human suffering and demonic attack. They need the miraculous power of God every day.

Here is the Bakers' mission-field perspective: "Some who hear us in conferences may come away with the impression that we lead a charmed, tribulation-free life of endless miracles! We do prefer to give Jesus and His glorious power most of the attention in our ministry, but it may encourage you to know that, like Paul, we are jars of clay who glory also in our weakness. When we are weak, then we are strong (2 Cor. 12:10). We do encounter fierce, demonic opposition, and its intensity is almost incomprehensible. This Mozambican province where we live has been a pagan, occult stronghold for centuries, and the evil we encounter shocks us over and over. Our time, energy, funds, and resources are viciously attacked and drained as the devil aims to turn our hearts away from this great revival in which God has graciously placed us.

"Together with Paul, we understand that these things happen that we might not rely on ourselves but on God, who raises the dead (2 Cor.

1:9). We resist the devil by overcoming evil with good, and by resting in Him with all the more faith and childlike joy. We cannot lose while secure in His heart. We have no need to shield ourselves, but we entrust our souls to a faithful Creator in doing what is right (1 Pet. 4:19). The God who has raised at least 53 people from the dead among our churches in Africa will also renew and refresh us with His incomparable power. He will not fail us; we are His workmanship!"[10]

It is their tenacious faith that enabled them to remain in Mozambique long enough to see a breakthrough, not only in church plants, but in increasing miracles, as this 2006 report in *Charisma* magazine reveals:

The miracles are a big part of the Bakers' method for winning Muslims to Jesus. Heidi says they do it "by signs, wonders, and caring for the orphan and the widow. It's love and stopping for the one."

According to her report, however, their target audience is not immediately receptive. "At first the Muslims throw rocks," she says, "but once they see signs and wonders and practical love they can't resist. My ministry team are 8-, 10- and 12-year-olds. Barefoot children in raggedy shirts lay hands on the crippled and they walk."

One day, Heidi took some of these children with her to minister to some synchronistic Muslims (who combine Islam with traditional animistic beliefs) in the city of Pemba. "They're not a happy bunch," she says. "My kids were ducking rocks, and one hit me low in the back. I jumped up and said, 'Bring me the deaf! Bring me the blind!'"

The team was led through the darkness to an old man who was both lame and blind. He got saved and then said, "I have a headache."

The Bakers' children prayed over him. He was still blind and crippled. Heidi told him, "When you are healed tomorrow, send me a runner." Heidi returned to their meeting place and again asked, "Anybody else blind?" A blind man was brought to her and she said, "I bless him in the name of Jesus."

Heidi says when the blind man screamed, "Ahhhhh! I can see!" the villagers finally stopped throwing rocks.

The next day a runner came up to the car she was sitting in with one of the most influential Muslim men in Pemba and reported, "The blind man can see! He's at his farm working." The man in the car grabbed Heidi's hand and stuck it on his head, tears running down his face. "Pray for me!" he said.

The explosive growth of their ministry is due to the miraculous power that God has released through them in the past decade. The gospel is advancing whole villages at a time as the Holy Spirit's power is poured out, resulting in healing released through compassion and love.

Faith for Healing

Heidi's faith for healing and refreshing has been tested over and over again, and she has persevered to help bring healing to others even as she herself has struggled to receive God's healing.

In 2006, Heidi lay dying from a methicillin-resistant staph infection in a hospital in Johannesburg, South Africa. It was her seventh hospitalization for the infection doctors attributed to her work among the street children. Her two children, away in the United States attending a ministry school, stood vigil in prayer. Rolland cancelled his commitments to remain by her side and sent out urgent requests for corporate prayer. But Heidi had already decided that, like the apostle Paul, although she would love to be with the Lord, it would be better for her to remain in the flesh and continue the work of the ministry. And, characteristically of her tenacious faith, she cried out, "I'm not going out like this!"

The report from *Charisma* magazine summarizes her miraculous recovery from that last life-threatening bout with the infection:

Heidi checked herself out of the hospital two times. The first time she flew to Pemba, Africa, where hundreds of Mozambicans came to the airport to greet her and sing and dance for her healing. Although she was experiencing incredible pain, she preached to a tent full of people from the Makua and Makonde tribes.

That evening, 55 Makua ran forward to give their lives to Jesus. The Bakers were thrilled with the souls saved, but Heidi's body remained wracked with pain, and following the meeting she flew back to Johannesburg for further treatment.

After returning to the hospital and taking antibiotics for another month, Heidi still had not recovered. The doctors told Heidi there were more advanced drugs in California—her only hope for healing.

Heidi packed her bags and told the medical staff, "I'm going to see a Specialist in Toronto."

She checked herself out of the hospital for the second time and flew to Toronto, to the Toronto Airport Christian Fellowship, home of what is now known as the Toronto Blessing. Heidi lay on the floor with a pillow, soaking in the presence of God, too sick to get up and participate in worship.

When it was time for her to preach, she felt she had to stand. Weakened and suffering with intense pain, she began her message from Zechariah.

"The fire of God pulsated through my body," Heidi says. "I was literally healed as I preached. There was no pain by the end of the service—it disappeared."

At the end of the meeting, Heidi danced across the platform in thanksgiving to God. Rolland claims tenacity is part of the DNA of a good missionary. "If faith is not exciting to you, don't sign up," he says.

Heidi agrees. "Tenacity is part of the kingdom. King Jesus will win, and we stand on His side."[11]

The Future is Jesus

Rather than burning out (physically and spiritually) on the mission field and giving up, consumed with worry over funds and food shortages, and rather than flickering out in middle age after decades of ministry, Heidi and Rolland are burning ever stronger, completely dependent on God. Heidi has come to know of the love of God more keenly through the suffering orphans they minister to daily, orphans who reflect the face and heart of God.

"It is a privilege beyond price to see the joy and affection of the Holy Spirit poured out like a waterfall on people who have known so much severe hardship, disappointment and bitter loneliness in their lives," Baker wrote in her online ministry report. "From the freezing cold gypsy huts of eastern Bulgaria to the 115 degree heat of Sudanese refugee camps, from the isolated native Inuits of arctic Canada to the dirt-poor subsistence farmers along the Zambezi River, we see ravenous desire for God among the poor and lowly. Jesus knows their suffering, and He will make it up to them. He will be their God, and they will be His people. He will use them to shame the wise and make the world jealous of their wealth toward Him."

As for how the Lord is using Heidi, she too is shaming the wise and making the world recognize that compassion releases the anointing of Jesus. For a laid-down lover of God, anything is possible. She says:

"I'm so desperate to stay in this place of abandonment. From this place, nothing is impossible. I have only one message—passion and compassion. We're passionate lovers of God, so that we become absolutely nothing. His love fills us. When it's time to stand up, God stands up with us. We focus on His face, never on our ministry, anointing, or numbers.

"All I want to do is love God and care for His people. I find them in the garbage, under trees dying of AIDS. I'm just really simple. Jesus said, 'Look into my eyes,' and everything completely changed. His eyes are filled with love and passion and compassion. Jesus always stops for the dying man, the dying woman and the dying child. That's all I know, passion and compassion. He calls me to love every single person I see every single day.

"Just focus on His face. You will only make it to the end if you can focus on His face. Focus on His beautiful face. You can't feed the poor, you can't go to the street, you can't see anything happen unless you see His face. One glance of His eyes, and we have all it takes to lie down. We're not afraid to die."[12]

Loving People Back to Life

Having led intercessory and equipping teams on site in Mozambique to co-labor with Iris Ministries, I can give you a firsthand report. I agree with John Crowder's statement in his marvelous book, *Miracle Workers, Reformers, and The New Mystics*, "Heidi has no formula for raising the dead except that she literally loves people back to life. She has held the dead bodies of babies and others, weeping over them for hours, until warmth came back into them and they were supernaturally revived."[13] This indeed is compassion in action.

As she globe-trots the nations spreading the fire of the Father's great love, often you can hear Heidi devotionally singing a song that pierces your heart: "I want to be a laid-down lover!" Want to join the song?

Dear Lord God Almighty, thank You for the strength and courage You have given those who are Your laid-down lovers. Thank You for those who reach out to the poor—one child, one person at a time. Help me to become like those who seek to help and comfort others. I need Your face before me to focus on and to draw power from; I need You to show me the way. In the precious name of Jesus, amen.

Part Three

Living
The Call

This final part of our book is a call to compassion and action to help relieve the horrific conditions of the poor in our world. The Bible says, "Vindicate the weak and fatherless; do justice and maintain the rights of the afflicted and destitute. Rescue the weak and needy; rescue them from the hand of the wicked" (Ps. 82:3–4). This is what the women portrayed in Part Two did, and it is what you and I must do as well.

> Heavenly Father, help us to become a compassionate people. Change our concepts, eradicate our prejudices, demolish our mental strongholds, transform our minds, and give us a strong desire to be merciful and compassionate to all we come in contact with. Let us be agents of change in our world today. In Jesus' name, amen.

Chapter 10

IT'S GOT TO BE PERSONAL

(James W. Goll)

I grew up in a rural area of Missouri, and I have lived in a beautiful country setting in Tennessee with my family. Because of my background of living in rural, agricultural areas, I know something about seed time and harvest. From that vantage point, I realize that there is great power in the hidden seeds that are planted in God's good earth.

Under the direction of my parents, along with my sisters, I helped plant many gardens during the spring of each year. Later, in July and August, I weeded many rows of corn, potatoes, green beans, tomatoes, and many other colorful and leafy vegetables. I often wondered why I had to work so hard in the hot and humid weather, but when fall and winter arrived, I understood and appreciated why I did so. My mom made the best vegetable soup, and to this day, I can still taste its luscious flavor and smell its enticing aroma that filled the entire house.

I learned a great deal from the principle of seedtime and harvest from those garden experiences, and later in life found it to be one of the major guiding biblical principles as well.

Michal Ann also enjoyed the bounty of large gardens when she was growing up. In addition to this, her dad loved using his old cider press to make apple and pear cider. In order to make those delicious natural beverages, however, one first needs fruit. So Michal Ann and the rest of her family would go into the orchards and pick the fruits her father needed to make his favorite recipe. In fact, a Willard family song that is still sung at family gatherings is the "Johnny Appleseed Song." In harmonious unity they sing with all their hearts, giving glory and thanks to God for the harvest He has provided.

Seeds of Compassion

Our job, as believers, is to plant seeds of compassion in a personal way wherever we go, in much the same way that John Chapman ("Johnny Appleseed") planted seeds from apples throughout the United States during the late eighteenth century. We plant the seeds, and God gives the harvest. This is just as true in the spiritual realm as it is in the natural. As we sow seeds of compassion into the lives of others, we look to God to water, cultivate, groom, and prune the emerging seedlings so they will bring forth fruitfulness in due season in the lives of those to whom we minister. There is phenomenal power in the hidden seed.

Sharon Salzberg writes, "Any ordinary favor we do for someone or any compassionate reaching out may seem to be going nowhere at first, but may be planting a seed we can't see right now. Sometimes we need to just do the best we can and then trust in an unfolding we can't design or ordain."[1]

In one of my favorite verses, Paul points out that God will supply the seed for you: "Now He who provides seed for the sower and bread for food will provide and multiply your seed for sowing [that is, your resources] and increase the harvest of your righteousness [which shows itself in active goodness, kindness, and love]" (2 Cor. 9:10). The psalmist David adds for us, "He has dispersed abroad, He has given to the poor; His righteousness endures forever; His horn will be exalted with honor" (Ps. 112:9, NKJV).

If your intention is to know God and serve Him by ministering to others, He will supply your seed to sow. He will make His all-sufficient grace abound toward you, and He will multiply your resources. From His seed fruit will grow the fruit that is called "the fruit of the Spirit" (see Gal. 5:22–23). And there will be a harvest. You can count on that. But remember, the seedlings of love are what will bring a great reward.

Champions of Faith, Hope, and Love

The Holy Spirit is looking for champions in our day. Michal Ann and I have written about many of these valiant heroes in the Women on the Frontlines series, in which the book you are now reading is the third volume. There are many champions, both great and small, who have made it into "God's Hall of Heroes." Some of these good people we may never meet or know until we see them in heaven, but others, such as Rolland and Heidi Baker of Iris Ministries, are modern-day trailblazers and pacesetters from whom each of us can learn a great deal.

All too often we focus on the gigantic exploits that are done by great people of faith, but we must never forget that little acts of love and kindness often precede public displays of power. Each of us must go through a hidden preparation period in which we learn how to walk in compassion and, as in any process, we have to take "baby steps" at first. This is the seed-planting stage.

Michal Ann and I have had the pleasure of knowing Mahesh and Bonnie Chavda for many years. As many already know, it was the healing prayers of Mahesh that paved the way for the Lord to bless us with our four beautiful children. I have often said, "Mahesh is not a show horse; he is a work horse!"

In the earlier days of my ministry, I had the privilege of doing some behind-the-scenes work for Mahesh's meetings as he traveled around the United States and internationally. I remember getting drinks for him, serving as a "catcher," fetching his tennis shoes so his tired feet could be more comfortable after praying with people until 2:00 A.M., and enjoying the fun of fellowship with him.

What always impressed me the most, as I observed and learned from Mahesh, was how he always took time for each individual. He never seemed to be in a rush; he ministered to each person as though every single individual was the most important person in the meetings. The Bakers and the Chavdas are both modern-day examples of the power of taking time for the one—always making it personal. The following is a story that was taken from Mahesh's first book, *Only Love Can Make a Miracle*. It shows how his heart of compassion and his ministry began to bloom.

Only Love Can Make a Miracle

"The Lord gave me an overwhelming love for children. It was hard to explain. It was as though the Lord broke off a little piece of His heart and placed it inside me. I loved those children as though they were my own.

"I used to work a nine-hour shift in Lily, usually with the ambulatory children, those who were able to get around on their own. When I was off duty, I would go to the non-ambulatory wards just to be with the children there. I had such a love for them. The thought of them having to spend the rest of their lives in those cribs almost broke my heart.

"I knew that God loved them, too, and that he wanted to channel that love through me. I didn't really know what to do with them or even how to pray for them. I used to just hold them and pray quietly in the Spirit. Often I would sit in a rocking chair with one of them for hours, just praying and singing in tongues.

"One little girl especially touched my heart. Her name was Laura. Laura's mother had been using hard drugs during pregnancy, and she had been born blind and severely retarded. I used to rotate through the different non-ambulatory wards on my after-hours visits, but in time I began to gravitate more and more to little Laura. She was so precious to me.

"One day I had occasion to go into Laura's ward during the day. It had been several weeks since I had started holding her and praying with her. As I approached her crib, she turned toward me and stretched out her hands to welcome me! There were a number of staff members nearby. They were amazed. They kept saying to each other, 'Did you see that?' Laura had never shown any outward response to anyone before, not even to being touched. Now she was responding to me from across the room. Could it be that she was gaining her sight? Could it be that the Lord was healing her through my prayers?

"Not long after this, I had a similar experience with a little boy who had been born with a terrible birth defect. His spine was deformed so that he was unable to sit up. Again, after I had been praying with him over a period of several weeks, he suddenly became able to sit up. His back was healed!

"As far as I can recall, I never once specifically prayed that these children be healed. I had prayed that way for my mother because I felt the Lord had told me to. Other than that, prayer for healing was not something I was accustomed to doing.

"When I was with the children, I would simply hold them and pray that the Lord would somehow enable them to experience His love through me. I was as surprised as anyone when they started getting better.

"I was learning many lessons in my school of the Spirit. Now I was learning that the power of God was to be found in the love of God. When the Lord sent me to the State School, he did not say, 'I am sending you as my ambassador of power or of miracles.' He said, 'I am sending you as my ambassador of love.' That was the way I saw myself and that was the way I prayed for the children: that the Lord would make His love real to them. The healings came almost as a by-product. I learned that only love can make a miracle."[2]

Any of us can be an ambassador of love for the Father. His love is powerful; it truly is the stuff of which miracles are made.

Revival of Kindness

The world needs a revival of kindness today. Imagine what would happen if God's people began to use their innate creativity to develop ways to show kindness to others. Simple acts of kindness, stemming from the love of God, would effect major changes in people's lives.

Early one morning I was awakened by the voice of the Holy Spirit speaking to me. The dove of God seemed to be gently whispering secrets to me. In the midst of hearing of coming moves of His manifested presence with signs and wonders and displays of great power, what struck me the most that morning was one simple phrase: "I will have a revival of kindness."

I wrote everything down in a journal by my bedside, and later I shared with Michal Ann about it. That one line went deep within her very being: "I will have a revival of kindness." Perhaps this experience was one of those seeds that put language to what was already growing in Michal Ann's heart, so that eventually she would launch a new ministry called Compassion Acts.

I wonder what our society would really look like if instead of our hurried, dog-eat-dog, frantic pace, we actually took time to pause, breathe, and act a little more like Jesus?

Random Acts of Kindness

I wonder what a revival of kindness looks like. We know of some of the characteristics of power evangelism and crusade evangelism by reading and observing the great revivals of the past. But it seems to me that for a genuine revival of kindness to come to pass, it has to be personal.

In fact, I believe the Holy Spirit wants us to have some fun in the process. Why not try some "random acts of kindness" as seeds to sow? For example:

- Give someone a word of encouragement.
- When in the drive-through line of a fast-food restaurant, pay for the meals that were ordered by the people behind you.
- Take time to be a good listener to someone.
- Get trained and participate in healing rooms or prayer rooms in your area.
- Distribute Bibles and Christian books to people you encounter in your day-to-day activities.
- Randomly give out worship CDs to people in a mall.
- Surrender your place in line to someone who seems to be in a hurry, whether in a supermarket, a bank, or elsewhere.
- Participate in an outreach at a public venue.
- Ask others if you could pray for them and invite the Holy Spirit's presence to come so that God's glory will be revealed.
- Give an unusually good tip to a server in a restaurant and leave them a note telling them that God cares.
- Take bags of groceries to a poor family and leave a note that says, "From the Man Upstairs who sees and cares."
- Invite international college students to your home over the holidays.
- Send cards of encouragement and comfort to those who are alone.
- Invite people to attend church or a time of fellowship with you.
- Tell people in practical ways about the love of Jesus.

All of these "random acts" of kindness are seeds of compassion that will truly make a difference in the lives of others in personal, practical, and tangible ways.

True Compassion Is Always Personal

Compassion is always personal. It costs you something and it releases something. In Webster's *New Collegiate Dictionary,* we read that *compassion* is "a sympathetic consciousness of others' distress together with a desire to alleviate it." It is more than just a feeling; it is also an action. Compassion gives you insight into another's need, and it enables you to understand their hurts, pain, and heartache.

God will reveal to you what needs to be done to help alleviate another's situation.

Vine's Expository Dictionary of New Testament Words provides us with many additional insights related to compassion by showing us the Greek verbs that are associated with it:

Oikteiro—to have pity, a feeling of distress through the ills of others. This verb is used to describe the compassion of God, which is one of His central attributes. As you can see, God's compassion is always personal and it is directed to individuals in need.

Splanchnizomai—to be moved as within one's inwards; to be moved with compassion, and to yearn with compassion. This is the verb that is frequently used to describe the way Jesus was moved with compassion toward the multitudes and toward individuals.

Do you remember the story of the widow of Nain? Her only son had died. When Jesus saw her, "...He had compassion on her and said to her, 'Do not weep.'" (Luke 7:13, NKJV). The Lord saw the funeral procession for the young man, and He was moved with compassion for the widow who was experiencing a painful sense of loss. Notice the progression here: first He saw, then He was moved with compassion. But it didn't stop there. It went beyond the feeling level and became an act.

Jesus' primary concern in this example did not appear to be the eternal state of the young man; rather, He was concerned about the mother and what she was going through. He felt compassion for her. Not only did He tell her, "Don't weep," but He also took positive steps to rectify the situation. The Bible says, "And He came up and touched the bier [on which the body rested], and the pallbearers stood still. And He said, 'Young man, I say to you, arise [from death]!'" (Luke 7:14).

Jesus saw. Jesus felt compassion. Jesus spoke words of comfort. Then Jesus moved forward with a touch and a command. The result was: "The man who was dead sat up and began to speak. And Jesus gave him back to his mother" (Luke 7:15).

First we have to perceive (see) the need. Then we speak words of encouragement and comfort, which may often lead us to communicate love and warmth through a touch or an embrace. Next, we take action by doing what we can to provide practical help and assistance to the person in need. One thing we can always do is to pray for him or her, and, as Tennyson said, "More things are wrought by prayer than this world dreams of."

An Eruption of Mercy

Deep within His spirit, Jesus is always in tune with the Father. His intimacy with His Father propelled Him to go out among the people and to be sensitive to their needs. In other words, He looked outside Himself and He saw what others needed. We can do the same, but first we must spend time alone with God in the secret place of the Most High. That is time well-spent, for it empowers us to go forth in love and compassion. A deep yearning arises as we spend time with the Father, and this yearning is focused on helping others.

In his book *Authority to Heal*, Ken Blue tells us that Jesus' compassion for people was not merely an expression of His will, but rather an eruption from deep within His being.[3] This volcanic image shows us how compassion should work in each of our lives, as an eruption of sympathy, empathy, and mercy flowing out to others like lava from a crater. God's mercies are everlasting, and they are constantly flowing from His throne—a throne that is established on the foundation of righteousness and mercy.

Have you ever noticed that when you get emotional about something, you do something in response to your emotions? When your emotions are stirred up, you take action. You may weep, jump up and down, write a letter, or head in a certain direction with a specific goal in mind. It is the same with God. He gets emotional over us, and it stirs Him to take action on our behalf.

Some things stick with you. I remember so very well many of the journeys I have taken as an intercessory missionary praying "on site with insight." Walking in the Cité Soleil, Port-au-Prince, in impoverished

Haiti...how can I forget? The sights, the sounds, and yes, the smells... As I walked through the areas where little boys wore no clothes, where there were no flushing toilets or anything close to it for that matter, my heart broke.

I walked in areas that were not safe according to World Health Organization standards. But God propelled my feet to walk among the poor, praying, caring...and sowing seeds of kindness. I wept as I walked among these precious people. I had a "compassion eruption" that motivated me to go back and forth numerous times from the United States to Haiti, hoping, praying, and longing to make a difference somehow.

Do you want to walk where Jesus did? Then watch out. If you express that desire before God, He might just take you into some really strange and wonderful places. Could it be that the farther we go on our journey with God, the more He wants us to be like Him? Do you want to be like Him? Do you want to follow in the footsteps of the Lord? Do you want His image to be formed in you?

If your answer to these questions is yes, then you must let the necessary ingredient of compassion fill your heart and motivate you to get on the front lines of service for your Lord. God is full of compassion, and His eruptions of love and mercy are yearning to be activated in our lives.

Sweeter Than Honey

Many people do not understand the nature of God—that He is full of mercy and compassion. If we truly understood this, wouldn't it change everything about us? Wouldn't it impel us to get compassionately involved with meeting others' needs, as Jesus was? Jesus certainly understood what is in the Father's heart, and because He does, He was willing and able to go to the cross for us.

As I shared in chapter 2, John Wimber was given a spiritual vision about God's mercy once while driving his car in southern California:

"Suddenly in my mind's eye there appeared to be a cloud bank superimposed across the sky....Then I realized it was not a cloud bank, it was a honeycomb with honey dripping out onto people below. The people were in a variety of postures. Some were reverent; they were weeping and holding their hands out to catch the honey and taste it, even inviting others to take some of their honey. Others acted irritated, wiping the honey off, and complaining about the mess. I was awestruck. Not knowing what to think, I prayed, 'Lord, what is it?'

"He said, 'It's My mercy, John. For some people it's a blessing, but to others it's a hindrance. There is plenty for everyone. The problem isn't on my end, John. It's down there.'

"What God showed me…was that he is much greater than I ever imagined him to be, and with only the smallest act of faith I could experience his compassion and mercy.

"I also realized that God's mercy is constantly falling on us, because everything that He does is related to what He is: the Father of compassion….Psalm 145:9 says, 'The Lord is good to all; he has compassion on all he has made.'

"…But too often I did not see God in the fullness of his mercy and grace. I trusted him to lead me, but I did not trust him to provide for me; I had faith to receive forgiveness of sins and salvation, but I had no faith for divine healing. I never realized God's mercy was as readily and abundantly available to me as the honey was available to all under the honeycomb.

"…In the vision, some people rejoiced, freely received, and freely gave away. The more they gave away, the more they received. 'There is plenty for everyone,' the Lord said. 'Don't ever beg me for healing again.'

"But others, full of unbelief and skepticism, could not receive the grace, blessings, and gifts of God. They could not see that God's mercy and healing are greater than their understanding of how he works."[4]

Want to Make a Difference?

Do you want to make a difference in the world? Then be different from others by walking in compassion wherever you are. Plant seeds of mercy in soil of desperate people's lives. People will see the difference, and they will want to have what you have. Not only that, but they will receive what they need through the grace on your life.

But compassion always has to be personal. It needs to flow from your heart to the person in front of you. As the writer of one the shortest books in the Bible states, "And on some have compassion, making a distinction" (Jude 1:22, NKJV).

We need a revelation of what compassion really is and what it entails. The God of all compassion and comfort wants to be compassionate in and through you. He lives within you, so let Him and His miracle-working love and compassion flow forth from you and propel you, along with others, into action.

Jesus, be big in me! Let Your emotions within me be stirred up. By Your grace, I choose to sow seeds of Your radical transforming love and mercy into the lives of others. I volunteer freely to be a part of Your compassionate army walking throughout the nations to bring a revival of kindness. I want to make a difference. Here I am—use me! Amen.

Chapter 11

COMPASSION ACTS

(Michal Ann Goll)

We have journeyed through Scripture, studying God's heart for justice, righteousness, and mercy. We have looked, up close and personal, at the lives of some amazing women and their impact on the world. Before we go any farther, though, we are going to rest. Rest is very important, especially in regard to this call to compassion.

As we open our hearts to feel God's heart, we may feel pressure to "do" something. Where is this pressure coming from? Is it direction from God, or are we beginning to see legitimate needs but moving out of our mental or "soulish" strength rather than out of our spirit? Ah, this is very important! Take time right now to stop and rest. Let your mind and heart center on His presence and worship Him for just a few minutes.

Compassion ministry, or whatever you want to call it, can be draining and exhausting. But it doesn't have to be. It depends on your motivation and your approach. It should not drive you, but rather, God's heart should lead you. Do you see the difference?

Mary and Martha

Do you remember the story about Mary and Martha? I used to think only that "Mary chose the better part," and that Martha was repri-manded. We need to look at the Scripture again.

Martha, dear Martha! She was the one who received Jesus and wel-comed Him into her house. Now, she did become distracted with much serving, and that was the point that Jesus spoke tenderly to her, redi-recting her heart to "the better part," to worship Him (see Luke 10:40). But I believe He was wooing her, drawing her to Himself, not correcting or belittling her. She had compared her serving and cooking to Mary's "sitting." What a common error that is—a lesson we are still trying to learn.

Yet when Lazarus was sick (see John 11), the sisters sent word to Jesus. By the time He came, Lazarus had been in the tomb for four days. "When Martha heard that Jesus was coming, she went out to meet him, but Mary stayed at home. 'Lord,' Martha said to Jesus, 'if you had been here, my brother would not have died. But I know that even now God will give you whatever you ask'" (John 11:20–22, NIV).

Do you see a pattern here? Not only was it Martha who welcomed Jesus into their house, but when her brother died, she was the one who met Him and asked for her brother's life to be restored. We need Martha. It doesn't have to be, "Are you a Mary or a Martha?" The point is, God wants us to be both. There is no place for comparison in the kingdom of God, and we don't have to choose between either living a life of prayer and devotion, or serving; we are to choose both. It's time for Mary and Martha to come together. After all, they were sisters and they did live in the same house. So should we.

Bowels of Compassion

The bowels are part of the intestinal tract, and though we don't like to talk about that part of the body, we do see an enlightening analogy here. In earlier times the bowels were considered to be the seat of pity, tenderness, and courage. Look at the language of the King James Version: "But whoso hath this world's good, and seeth his brother have need, and shutteth up his bowels of compassion from him, how dwelleth the love of God in him?" (1 John 3:17, KJV).

The bowels are the deepest parts of our bodies, the last stop within our digestive tracts. The food we eat goes through many different processes as it is absorbed by the digestive system, but where we receive the greatest nutrition from our food is as it passes through the bowels.

Similarly, we drink the pure milk of the Word of God (see 1 Pet. 2:2) and we begin to digest its truths, that we might grow. However, we have to get it past our minds. We need to let it find its way into our hearts. It needs to go through every part of our "digestive" process, and if we stop short of the "bowels of compassion," we have missed the greatest release of spiritual nourishment and enrichment. If we listen, take notes, and recite spiritual truth, but never act on it or apply it, all that has happened is that just our brains got bigger and not our hearts.

Paul writes, "Put on therefore, as the elect of God, holy and beloved, bowels of mercies, kindness, humbleness of mind, meekness, longsuffering" (Col. 3:12, KJV). We must *put on* compassion and kindness. This is a decision we must make if we want to follow God's ways. It's a commitment we make to God.

I've had people come up to me at conferences and different gatherings, asking me to pray for them to receive an impartation for compassion. I've thought about this a lot, and I've come to the conclusion that I don't think that is possible. Just as our bodies process the food that causes the bowels to act, so should our spirits, as we process the love of God and His Word, bring our "bowels of compassion" to act. You can't eat food in the physical and not have the process that brings elimination; you can't have one without the other. Compassion acts.

I've been concerned not only about the condition of my own heart, but also the heart of the Church. If we're having a difficult time getting this individually, then how can the kingdom of God advance corporately? The answer is obvious—we can't.

Charles Spurgeon wrote this about compassion: "It is expressive of the deepest emotion; a striving of the bowels—a yearning of the innermost nature with pity....When our Savior looked upon certain sights, those who watched Him closely perceived that His internal agitation was very great, His emotions were very deep, and then His face betrayed it, His eyes gushed like founts with tears, and you saw that His big heart was ready to burst with pity for the sorrow upon which His eyes were gazing. His whole nature was agitated with commiseration for the sufferers before Him."[1]

Jesus Christ is a compassionate Friend to precious souls; His bowels yearn in mercy and pity for those in need. It was this mercy that brought Him from heaven to earth, and it was this mercy that took Him to the cross. His compassion brought Him to action—even dying on the cross for our sins, that we would be forgiven and have fellowship with the Father. His compassion brought action.

Jesus loves you. God the Father loves you. To use a phrase from Graham Cooke, "You can't make Him love you any more, and you can't make Him love you any less." He loves you without reservation, just as you are, right now! That's who He is and what He does. That is the focus of His compassion. He longs and groans for His house to be full, for His table to be full, and it won't be full unless you are there. He desires to draw you to Himself today, and to never be separated from you ever again. He has done it all for you and me.

All you have to do is say yes to Jesus. If you've never said yes to Him before, or maybe He's tugging on your heart in a fresh way, just talk with Him now. Tell him you love Him, you believe in Him, and you want to walk with Him. He will hear you and will answer your prayers.

Paul writes, "Therefore, I urge you, brothers and sisters, in view of God's mercy, to offer your bodies as a living sacrifice, holy and pleasing to God—this is your true and proper worship" (Rom. 12:1, NIV).

This is what is needed today: a decisive dedication of our lives as living sacrifices to God. What better offering can we give to God, in light of all His mercies to us?

The World We Live In

The world is desperate for help. According to recent studies, 75 percent of the world's population lives in poverty. Most of these people live in Third World, or developing, countries. The average annual gross income for individual workers in Western countries is $27,000. Contrast that with the rest of the world, where the average annual gross income is between $450.00 and $2,500.00 per person.[2] What a difference!

Approximately 50 percent of the world's population is female. Women suffer more from poverty than men. Forty percent of the world's population consists of children. They are the ones who suffer more than all others. In fact, over one billion children are at risk today, and many have become victims of extreme poverty, homelessness, the loss of their parents, child labor, abuse, slavery, sexual exploitation, AIDS and other illnesses, and the effects of war and religious persecution.[3]

In certain parts of the world, orphaned children are conscripted into armies, where they suffer sexual, mental, and physical abuse. They are forced to carry guns and trained to kill. At times, the governments involved are willing to "sell off" numbers of these children to ease their financial situations. Finances are needed today for these purposes. I know of dear, precious saints who are working behind the lines to rescue these children, give them hope for their destiny, and restore self-respect and esteem.

Sometimes it can be quite easy to read the words but not engage our hearts in the reality of what they mean. If those children were *our* children, or those people *our* family, don't you think our attitude would be different? I know mine would. That is what the Lord wants to do—to enlarge our hearts to such a degree that "they" become "our family." They are His kids, the love of His heart, and we just don't seem to get it or care. When will we get it? When will we do something about these needs? If there ever was a time for compassion in our world, it is today!

The Deborah Company

There is a need for the Deborah anointing today. (See Judges 5:7 regarding Deborah, "a mother in Israel.") The Israelites were faced with a complete disruption of the entire region. There was no protection for the people. No laws were enforced. The people couldn't even travel on the roads; they had to sneak along hidden pathways because the Philistine army was all about, raiding, killing, plundering their crops and their homes. Then Deborah arose.

The name Deborah means "bee." Like a bee, Deborah was a very industrious woman. She judged Israel, but was particularly devoted to the reestablishment of true biblical worship in the temple. It is said that she spent time making the wicks for the candles that would be used in the temple. How appropriate this is when you realize that the word "Lappidoth," mentioned in Judges 4:4, it is a Hebrew term that deals with light or illumination. Different translations give various meanings to this word. Deborah was either married to a man named Lapidoth, or she came from a region with that name. We see that Deborah, who served as a prophetess and judge in ancient Israel, was a bearer of great light, illumination, and wisdom.

Deborah was a very courageous woman who was not afraid to take risks (see Judg. 4). While she was sitting under her palm tree, a symbol of authority from which she judged, in the hill country of Ephraim, the Israelites came up to her, bringing their grievances concerning the onslaughts from the army of Jabin, the King of Canaan. Then she called for Barak, an army general, and told him to go forth into battle and that God would give him victory over Sisera, the general who was commanding the Philistine army.

Barak responded to her prophecy by saying that he would go to the River Kishon, where the battle would take place, but he would do so only if she would agree to go with him. Deborah said, "I will surely go with you; nevertheless there will be no glory for you in the journey you are taking, for the Lord will sell Sisera into the hand of a woman" (Judg. 4:9, NKJV).

What had Barak seen in Deborah's life that caused him to want her to go into warfare with him? What qualities did she possess that made him feel strengthened in her presence? Why would he ask a woman to take part in the battle with him?

I believe it's because he saw her as a woman of illumination, someone who walked in the light and glory of God. She was a wise, industrious, and brave woman who knew God. Therefore, I believe Barak was saying in effect, "I'm not going to go into battle unless you go with me, unless I have the illumination and presence of God with me."

Deborah had divine illumination and she had the presence of the Lord. Barak, also a prophet, had the administrative ability to raise an army and go out into the field and do the work. Neither one could do without the other, and neither one cared who received the glory. They just wanted to defeat the enemy and to give all the glory to God. And that's what happened (see Judg. 4:22–23). Commerce was restored, villages and families were restored, law and order was restored. When the government of God is set in place, it displaces all other governments.

I believe there is a new release of the Deborah anointing, but this time around it's not given to just one person; it's for a whole company of women who want to see the illumination of God and His kingdom established, and are willing to become breakers in the Spirit—to break it open!

In a similar vein, I believe there is a whole company of Baraks, who don't care if the glory goes to men or women; they just want God to show up—that's all that matters. They are trustworthy and know how to wage war, and how to win.

War Generals

What we're talking about here is the body of Christ coming into formation, becoming connected. In order for us to truly be effective in this battle for compassion, there has to be order, good supply lines, and good communication. I believe the Lord wants to release a whole army of compassionate warriors, and if there is to be a whole army, then there certainly has to be commanders overseeing, directing, and caring for the troops. We need to assemble ourselves together, and gather around those who are farther down the road than we are—ones who are filled with courage, vision, and passion for God. These are men and women who are committed to defending the gospel. They are not afraid of warfare, and they are eager to engage in all necessary battles and are willing to fight.

God wants generals, or breakers, who know His heart. Unlike the world's concept of what a general looks like, God's generals are ones who know authority, yes; but they follow the example of their Master and Savior. They live their lives carrying a towel, ready to love and to serve. They know the meaning of the phrase "lower still." They understand that the authority they carry comes from the greatest servant of all, Jesus.

He calls us to "fight the good fight of faith" (1 Tim. 6:12). With His help we will rise up as the army of God, replete with generals, majors, sergeants, corporals, and privates. We will be "more than conquerors" (Rom. 8:37), carrying our swords, our shields—and our towels.

I hear the sound of horses' hooves pounding the ground and the sounds of victory filling the air. The battle is the Lord's and through Him we will be victorious!

The Innkeeper Anointing

This battle has many fronts. There are some in particular that I feel the Lord is highlighting and sounding a fresh prophetic call. I believe He is releasing specific anointings to accomplish these assignments.

One of them is what I like to call "the Innkeeper anointing." Most of us are familiar with the parable of the Good Samaritan (see Luke 10:30–35). In this story we learn that a certain man had been robbed, stripped, wounded, and left to die. He was slighted by those who should have been his friends and helpers, including a priest who should have known better and a Levite who was supposed to show tenderness and compassion to those in need. When the Levite saw this man, he went over and took a close look at him, then crossed to the other side of the street when he saw the condition he was in. In other words, the Levite got as far away from him as he could.

Another man, a Samaritan, came along, and when he saw the injured man, he had compassion on him. Using his own linen, which he probably tore from his own clothing, he bound up the man's wounds. He poured oil and wine into the man's wounds and then put him on his own donkey. He took him to an inn, put him to bed, and paid the innkeeper for his accommodations.

Previously, I've focused on the Samaritan in this Scripture passage. While the Samaritan anointing is desperately needed and covers a wide range of compassionate acts, I want to acknowledge the innkeeper. He is barely mentioned, but he is also important. We need to have those who will go out into the streets and find the wounded ones, but there has to be some place to bring them in, for full restitution. The innkeeper already has his placement established, rooms available and ready, at a moment's notice. His would be like an extended-care ministry. It may be in the form of recovery facilities, or it could be families who will open up their homes.

This ministry is very practical, and could be very personal. Do you have an extra bedroom the Lord could use? Are you open for a "Samaritan" to come into your life and drop into your lap someone who needs help? This is one of the anointings that God is releasing among His people today. God wants us to provide for all those who are lying alongside the road in a state of hopelessness, despair, and great need. You don't know how much you have to offer until you see how deep the needs of these people are.

Creative Compassion

We need to ask for answers to questions the world has yet to ask. We need to look into the future, and ask the Lord for creative solutions and inventions. We need to look at ways to create entrepreneurial businesses to create jobs for those in low-income areas, and help boost economies. We need to ask for houses, and look for ones that can be salvaged, repaired, and used for places of recovery or rescue.

How about a marriage of compassion with the prophetic? How about building relationships with our police, finding out the needs of our cities, and developing prophetic intercessory teams who will pray and ask for specific answers? We need to see what we can do to rescue and create a net to catch the women and children who have been trapped in sex-trade businesses and prostitution, and who are looking for a way out.

We need to develop water-filtration systems that are inexpensive and easy to set up in Third World countries. We need to develop supply lines so ministries learn to work together and serve each other. We need to cross over boundary lines of denominations and affiliations, reaching into areas that need help. We need to move forward in kingdom understandings and applications, building relationally—in love.

We need to care for the poor and needy, not only within our own regions but internationally as well. Africa is dying right now. Our help is needed right now. They need simple things—beans and rice—by the trailer loads. Whole families are being lost. Here in the United States, most major cities are full of kids who have run away from home; they are living on the streets and using drugs. These are our kids—these are our people. Jesus, open our eyes and hearts!

Preparing Our Fields

Being raised in rural Missouri from birth until James and I were married, I have a great appreciation for the biblical language regarding nature and agriculture. I spent many, many hours in the hot sun with an ever-aching back and sunburned arms, weeding our huge vegetable garden, harvesting those vegetables and preparing and storing them. We kept the kitchen stove running for days at a time, canning beans, tomatoes, and various fruits. We processed countless chickens, cutting them up and freezing them. We processed cherries, peaches, apples, pears, raspberries, and plums.

We spent whole days at my grandmother's house fighting our way through endless blackberry thickets, creating tunnels through the tangled maze of thorny canes, and coming home with tubs and tubs full to put in the freezer. I've worked out in the hayfields with my brothers, running the tractor so they could pick up the bales and stack them on the wagon. That hay was necessary for our cattle to make it through the winter. I've known the necessity and value of tending plants, tending gardens and fields. And God says:

> "When you reap the harvest of your land, do not reap to the very edges of your field or gather the gleanings of your harvest. Do not go over your vineyard a second time or pick up the grapes that have fallen. Leave them for the poor and the foreigner. I am the Lord your God." (Lev. 19:9–10, NIV)

I believe the Lord is issuing a challenge to us, for we all have "fields" that we are laboring in, fields the Lord has given to us. It's in these fields that we must plant the seeds that will bring forth a bountiful harvest. Everyone has a sphere of influence; it may be your workplace, it may be your home, it may be the school you attend, it may be other people who share your ethnic background or the geographical region where you live.

We must prepare our fields in such a way that we allow the poor and the strangers to benefit from the harvest. The times in which we live make this a very urgent matter, for we see a great increase in natural disasters, terrorism, war, and disease around the globe.

Plant good seed in your field, and be sure to plant what God tells you to plant. While you do so, make certain that you leave some fruit in your field so the poor can reap some from your harvest too.

Rest and Rejoice

The seventh year was meant to be a year of rest and rejoicing. The Bible says, "but the seventh year you shall let it rest and lie uncultivated, so that the poor among your people may eat [what the land grows naturally]; whatever they leave the animals of the field may eat. You shall do the same with your vineyard and olive grove" (Ex. 23:11).

As we get to know the heart of God, we need to get our lives in line with His calendar. The seventh year represents perfection and completion, a fulfillment of the will of God, which demands that the land should lie fallow so the poor can reap a benefit, and so the land can rest.

The seventh year was a year of breakthrough and blessing both for the landowners and the poor. Everyone shared in the good things God had provided for them.

In the book of Esther we read: "…as the days on which the Jews had rest from their enemies, as the month which was turned from sorrow to joy for them, and from mourning to a holiday; that they should make them days of feasting and joy, of sending presents to one another and gifts to the poor" (Est. 9:22, NKJV). We need to enlarge our hearts to include the poor as part of our times of celebration. When deliverance, in whatever form it may take, comes to your house—remember the poor. Let your deliverance spill over to those who are still waiting for their own deliverance to be released.

Time is an intriguing element. We have a past, and we speak of a future. But where both become a reality is *right now*. In reality, now is all that we have. We can do nothing about our past, but if we act now, we can establish what will become our past. We can talk about the future, but the problem is, the future is always ahead of us; we can never live in the future.

We must live in the now. If we try to live in the future, we're always dreaming and never realizing. We need to take our dreams and make practical steps today to see them come to pass. We need to move out of any remorse over past mistakes or missed opportunities, and make a decision to get up and act now.

The Poor Man's Watch

When preparing to go on my first trip to Mozambique to serve Iris Ministries with Rolland and Heidi Baker, I bought a simple plastic watch. It was very cheap, but it actually had more bells and whistles than my nicer watch, and was a great tool for the trip. When I got home, I unpacked my clothes, developed my pictures, gave out gifts to my loved ones, and tried to get my life in order again. There was my nicer watch on my nightstand, waiting for me to take it up again, but something inside me didn't want to put it back on. Days went by, weeks went by, and I just couldn't take this simple cheap little watch off my wrist.

I went to the Lord, asking Him what was going on. Didn't I want to go forward? Was I holding onto something I needed to release? Finally one day my friend, the precious Holy Spirit, spoke to me. He said, "You are on the poor man's watch." This word went through my heart like an arrow. I knew it to be true. There was no taking it off; there was no getting my life back in order. In actuality, my life was getting in God's order.

God has a poor man's watch that is perfect for each one of us. It is not a gift; it's part of the kingdom of God. If we want to experience His kingdom, we have to wear the watch.

Looking for Jesus

I'm looking for Jesus; I'm waiting for Jesus. But could it be that Jesus is waiting for me? Could it be that as I engage my heart to not only hear the Word of God, but to live the Word to those who do not know Him, Jesus just might come to me? That sounds like the kingdom of God coming on the earth. I want to be a part of establishing God's kingdom, and raising up a whole army of like-hearted loving warriors who have embraced the call to compassion. He is waiting for you. Will you enlist in this army? I pray that your answer is yes, and that you are stirred to action—because compassion acts.

> Dear Lord Jesus, I come to You this day, volunteering myself to be Your arms, Your feet, Your hands to hurting and needy people. I want to embrace Your heart for the poor, the orphan, and the widow. I want to offer to You the field You have given me, that You would show me how to help provide for those who are less fortunate. Lord, I ask You to speak to me. Lead me into the avenues of service that I am to engage in. Lord, according to James 1:5, give me the wisdom I need to move forward and to connect with the right people. Today I make a commitment in my heart, with my mouth, to show You and the world my faith, by my works—because I love You and I know that You love me. In Jesus' name, amen.

AFTERWORD

The three books in the Women on the Frontlines series—*A Call to Courage, A Call to the Secret Place,* and *A Call to Compassion*—are not just a history tour of great women of God. These books encompass the life journey of a person whose shadow is yet being cast to this day.

First, these books are about the transforming power of the Lord Jesus Christ Himself. None of these women, Michal Ann Willard Goll included, could have made the difference they did without the Son of God, Jesus Christ the Lord, sacrificing His life for us. If you do not know this amazing Savior, then the first thing to do is give your heart to Him. Give your life to Him, as He has already given His best for you.

Second, these books are about the transforming power of the Holy Spirit in lives today. At the time of this writing, Michal Ann has already been worshipping the Lord unabated before His throne for several years. Someday I will join my dear Annie on the other side. I trust you will as well. It will be grand!

But "grand" does not wait till the other side. It is not the length of our days but the depth of our impact that matters. With this eternal life view in mind, I want to give you my own call—*A Call to Do What Matters.* Whether it is to be a man or woman of courage, the secret place, or compassion, just do what matters most. Love God. Love your family. Love your neighbor. Love the world that Jesus died for. Just do it!

The Origins of Compassion Acts and Women on the Frontlines

Compassion Acts first began as a good intention, like most good ideas. However, what made the difference was the woman behind the thought, Michal Ann Goll. She took her good intention of making a difference in the world, and did just that. After she spent months in prayer, seeking clarity on the direction for her ideas, she began networking with friends, and friends of friends.

Through these connections and strong convictions, Compassion Acts was birthed in 2004 as a ministry and humanitarian aid organization to provide help for those in need. Long before this, Michal Ann and I together had started a yearly conference known as Women on the Frontlines. We originally held the conferences in Nashville, Tennessee (the buckle of the Bible Belt), and later we took them elsewhere within the Ohio and Tennessee Valleys. We did this together for eleven years. After her death, I chaired the twelfth year myself.

Passing of Batons—Forward Motion

I then turned to our dear friend, Patricia King of XP Media, and asked her to be the co-chair with me for Women on the Frontlines for the thirteenth year. It was a great fit. Eventually I felt the direction of the Lord to release and empower Patricia to be the international director of Women on the Frontlines and she accepted. Since that time, these gatherings have turned into a global movement, now led by Wendy Peter and team (see WOFL.org). The Lord knows what He is doing, and I am grateful.

Michal Ann founded Compassion Acts, and affected thousands of individuals herself. However, Michal Ann passed away the morning of September 15, 2008, after a five-year battle with colon cancer. Even though she is no longer with us today, we still carry on the heart and soul of Compassion Acts in her stead. In turn, I recognized Mark Roye, Michal Ann's assistant, to become the international director of Compassion Acts. This too has been a wise choice, as Mark loves Jesus and the poor of the earth. To learn more, please see the last page in this book.

Today, Compassion Acts operates in a pursuit of justice, disaster relief, and humanitarian aid work in response to Michal Ann's personal charge found in her last will and testament:

> It has been my goal and desire to love the Lord with all my heart all the days of my life. My desire is to leave with my family, friends and ministry partners a challenge to always love and honor God with all your life. I request that you not forget the poor that Jesus died for and that you carry on my ministry of Compassion Acts to the world.
>
> Michal Ann Goll
> (handwritten on February 4, 2008)

Now It's Your Turn

I now invite you to be a man or woman on the front lines and make a difference for such a time as this. I challenge you to take up the baton and love God with all your heart, soul, and strength. And along with the great cloud of witnesses, I make a request of you: Do not forget the poor that Jesus died for, and carry on this vibrant ministry of Compassion Acts to the world. Does our Father in heaven deserve anything less?

As a small token of commitment, I am dedicating the royalties of this book, *A Call to Compassion,* to the ongoing work of Compassion Acts. Your mere purchase of this book has already made a difference in someone's life, and I thank you for that.

Always remember—together, in Jesus, we make a great team!

ACKNOWLEDGMENTS

Michal Ann was in the beginning stages of her fight with cancer when this project began. Therefore, out of all three of these books, this last book was a definite group effort. It would not have happened without the contributions of Mallory Gabard, Lloyd Hildebrand, Julia Loren, Don Milam, Dr. J. Mark Rodgers, Ada Winn, Kathy Deering, David Sluka, and possibly several others. How wonderful it is to have had a whole company of dedicated believers work together to get this strategic message out.

Then there's the Compassion Acts team. We wish to acknowledge and thank Mark Roye, GraceAnn Goll Visser, Leon Hoover, Dabney Mann, Marcus Young, Kay Durham, Mike and Sisse Phieffer, Ann Bell, Marion Farrar, Justin Goll, all the interns, and those who partnered to see Michal Ann's dream come to pass—and continue to this day. Many thanks also to all the prayer warriors who continually lifted us up in prayer. You have been the guardians, watching over this little baby named Compassion Acts. You have created a safe place for the birth of this message and ministry.

In closing, here is Michal Ann's original statement of acknowledgment: "Most importantly, oh my dear Jesus—thank you for waking me up, and not letting me stay enclosed in my own little world. Thank you for expanding my vision, my dreams, my goals, and my heart."

A Call to Compassion NOTES

Chapter 1: God's Heart of Compassion

1. David Ruis, *The Justice God Is Seeking* (Ventura, CA: Regal Books, 2006), 80.
2. Ibid., 10.
3. From Charles H. Spurgeon, "The Compassion of Jesus," sermon delivered at the Metropolitan Tabernacle, Newington, England.
4. Ruis.

Chapter 2: The Compassionate Power of Tears

1. John Wimber and Kevin Springer, *Power Healing* (San Francisco: HarperCollins, 1987), 47–48.
2. Dick Eastman, *No Easy Road* (Grand Rapids, MI: Baker Books, 1971), 92.
3. From Richard Foster, *Prayer: Finding the Heart's True Home* (New York: HarperCollins, 1992), 39–40.
4. Ibid., 37–38.
5. Eastman, 93.

Chapter 3: The Mother of the Salvation Army

1. "Catherine Booth" (http://spartacus-educational.com/Wbooth.htm). Many of the details in this chapter come from this article.
2. Ibid.
3. Ibid.
4. Ibid.
5. Ibid.
7. Vinita Hampton Wright and Mary Horner Collins, *Women's Wisdom Through the Ages* (Wheaton, IL: Harold Shaw, 1994), 69.
8. "Catherine Booth." (Spartacus.schoolnet.co.uk).
9. Helen K. Hosier, *William and Catherine Booth: Founders of the Salvation Army: Heroes of the Faith* (Uhrichsville, OH: Barbour Publishing, 1999), 58.
10. Ibid., 76–77.
11. "Catherine Booth." (http://spartacus-educational.com/Wbooth.htm)

Chapter 4: Beloved Woman of the Cherokee

1. Pat Aldenman, *Nancy Ward/Dragging Canoe* (Johnson City, TN: The Overmountain Press, 1990). Very little is written about Nancy Ward, and this is one of the only sources. The Cherokee Nation's history, though, is well documented. The author of this chapter, Ada Winn, is a descendant of Nancy Ward.

Chapter 5: The Lady with the Lamp

1. Basil Miller, *Florence Nightingale: The Lady of the Lamp (Women of Faith)* (Bethany House, 1975), 72.
2. Sam Wellman, *Florence Nightingale: Lady with the Lamp: (Heroes of the Faith)* (Uhrichsville, OH: Barbour Publishing, 1999), 58.
3. Mary Ford-Grabowsky, ed., *Sacred Voices: Essential Women's Wisdom Through the Ages* (San Francisco: HarperCollins, 2002), 128.
4. Wellman, 98.

5. Ibid., 123–127.

6. Ibid., 127.

7. Ibid., 140.

8. Ibid., 152–153.

9. Ibid., 156.

10. Ibid., 168–169.

11. Ibid., 169.

12. Ibid., 166.

13. James E. Keifer, "Florence Nightingale, Nurse, Renewer of Society," *Biographical Sketches* (http://justus.anglican.org/resources/bio/158.html).

14. Muhammad Umair Mushtaq, "Public Health in British India: A Brief Account of the History of Medical Services and Disease Prevention in Colonial India," *Indian Journal of Community Medicine* 2009 Jan; 34(1): 6–14. (http://www.ncbi.nlm.nih.gov/pmc /articles/PMC2763662/).

15. Kiefer.

16. Ibid., 202.

Chapter 6: Rejected by Man, Approved by God

1. Janet and Geoff Benge, *Gladys Aylward: The Adventure of a Lifetime, (Christian Heroes: Then & Now)* (YWAM Publishers, 1998), 170.

2. Ibid., 20–21.

3. Gladys Aylward (as told to Christine Hunter) *Gladys Aylward: The Little Woman* (Chicago: Moody Publishers, 1974), 10–12.

4. Benge, 33.

5. Sam Wellman, *Gladys Aylward: Missionary to China (Heroes of the Faith)* (Uhrichsville, OH: Barbour Publishing, 1998), 34.

6. Aylward, 31.

7. Ibid., 42.

8. Benge, 104.

9. Ibid., 169.

10. Ibid., 201.

Chapter 7: The Humble Road

1. Eileen Egan and Kathleen Egan, OSB, eds., *Suffering Into Joy* (Ann Arbor, MI: Servant Publications, 1994), 13.

2. Egan, 21.

3. Nobelprize.org, "Mother Teresa: Biographical" (http://www.nobelprize.org/nobel_prizes /peace/laureates/1979/teresa-bio.html).

4. Words of acceptance for the Nobel Peace Prize, from "Mother Teresa: In Her Own Words," The Associated Press, September 5, 1997, in the archives of the *Washington Post* (https://www.washingtonpost.com/wp-srv/inatl/longterm/teresa/stories/words.htm).

6. John Paul II, "Address of John Paul II to the Pilgrims Who Had Come to Rome for the Beatification of Mother Teresa," 2003.

7. Benedict XVI, *Deus Caritas Est.*

8. Egan and Egan, 14.

9. Ibid., 22.

10. Ibid., 32–33.

11. Nobelprize.org, "Mother Teresa: Lecture" (http://nobelprize.org/peace/laureates/1979 /teresa-lecture.html).

12. Mother Teresa, "Whatsoever you do…" speech to National Prayer Breakfast (http://www.priestsforlife.org/mother-teresa/breakfast-letter.htm).

13. T. T. Mundakel, *Blessed Mother Teresa: Her Journey to Your Heart,* English trans. ed. (Liguori, MO: Liguori Publications, 2003), n.p.

14. Egan, 140–141.

15. Ibid., 65.

Chapter 8: Little Women, Big God

1. Amy Carmichael, Gold Cord (Fort Washington, PA: Christian Literature Crusade, 1932, 1996), n.p.

2. Ibid.

3. Ibid.

4. "Carmichael, Amy (1867–1951), Gospel Fellowship Association (https://www.gfamissions.org/missionary-biographies/carmichael-amy-1867-1951.html).

5. Frank L. Houghton, Amy Carmichael of Dohnavur: The Story of a Lover and her Beloved (Fort Washington, PA: Christian Literature Crusade, 1953, 1979), n.p.

6. Ibid.

7. Amy Carmichael, Thou Givest…They Gather (Fort Washington, PA: Christian Literature Crusade, 1958, 1971), 134.

8. "Mother Katharine Drexel could be the second American canonized saint born in the United States," Catholic World News, as reported in DailyCatholic.org, January 22—24, 1999, Section Three, vol. 10, no. 15. (http://www.dailycatholic.org/issue/archives/1999Jan/15jan22,vol.10,no.15txt/jan22dc3.htm).

9. Ibid.

10. Ibid.

11. Vatican News Service, "Katharine Drexel (1858–1955)" (http://www.vatican.va/news_services/liturgy/saints/ns_lit_doc_20001001_katharine-drexel_en.html).

12. From the 1907 Constitutions of the Congregation of the Blessed Sacrament for Indians and Colored People.

13. Vatican News Service.

14. Barbara Howie, "Phoebe Palmer (1807–1874)" West Virginia University (http://are.as.wvu.edu/phebe.htm).

15. Rev. Richard Wheatley, The Life and Letters of Mrs. Phoebe Palmer (New York: Palmer and Hughes, 1876), 18.

16. Ibid., 26.

17. Howie.

18. Ibid.

19. Ibid.

20. Tommy Tenney, Mary's Prayers and Martha's Recipes (Shippensburg, PA: Destiny Image, 2002).

21. Ibid.Bridget Hill, Women Alone: Spinsters in England, 1660–1850 (New Haven, CT: Yale University Press, 2001), 156.

22. Tenney, 18.

23. Tryon Edwards, ed., A Dictionary of Thoughts (Detroit, MI: F.B Dickerson, 1908), 431.

24. Ibid., 540.

25. Angela Bull, Elizabeth Fry (Newton Abbot, England: David and Charles, 1988), 23.

26. Ibid.

27. Ibid.

28. Richard Huntsman, Elizabeth Fry: Quaker and Prison Reformer (Guist Bottom, Dereham, Norfolk, UK: Larks Press, 1998), 3.

29. Ibid., 27.
30. Ibid., 52.
31. Ibid.

Chapter 9: Blessed Are the Poor

1. Lee Grady, "Heidi Baker's Uncomfortable Message to America," *Charisma* magazine, August 2006.
2. Ibid.
3. Julia Loren, *Shifting Shadows of Supernatural Power* (Shippensburg, PA: Destiny Image, 2006), 91.
4. Rolland and Heidi Baker, *There Is Always Enough* (Grand Rapids, MI: Chosen Books, 2002), 26.
5. C. Hope Flinchbaugh, "Brave Hearts in a Desperate Land," *Charisma* magazine, March 2006.
6. Josie Newman, "Miracles and Church Growth Mark Mozambique Ministry," *Charisma* magazine, March 2004.
7. Baker and Baker, 160.
8. Ibid., 67–68.
9. Ibid., 68–69.
10. Loren, 108.
11. Flinchbaugh, *Charisma*, March 2006.
12. Baker and Baker, 176–177.
13. John Crowder, *Miracle Workers, Reformers, and The New Mystics* (Shippensburg, PA: Destiny Image, 2006), 147.

Chapter 10: It's Got to Be Personal

1. Sharon Salzberg, "The Power of Intention," *O Magazine,* January 2004.
2. Mahesh Chavda, *Only Love Can Make a Miracle* (Ann Arbor, MI: Servant, 1990), 72–73.
3. Ken Blue, *The Authority to Heal* (Downers Grove, IL: InterVarsity Press, 1987).
4. John Wimber and Kevin Springer, *Power Healing* (San Francisco, CA: HarperCollins, 1987), 47–48.

Chapter 11: Compassion Acts

1. Charles Spurgeon, sermon #3438, "The Compassion of Jesus," The Spurgeon Archive (http://www.spurgeon.org/sermons/3438.htm).
2. Ibid., 165–168.
3. Human Rights Watch, "Burma: World's Highest Number of Child Soldiers," October 16, 2002 (http://www.hrw.org/press/2002/10/burma-1016.htm).

WOMEN ON THE FRONTLINES

A Call to the Secret Place

Pursuing the Prize of God's Presence

James & Michal Ann Goll

DEDICATION

We dedicate *A Call to the Secret Place,* this third book of the Women on the Frontlines series to our mothers and grandmothers, who all walked in the faith—our Willard and McCoy and Goll and Burns heritage. These godly women blazed a trail for us, and we have walked in the footsteps of giants. Our desire is that we in turn can blaze a trail for the generations that follow us.

FOREWORD

☙

Elizabeth (Beth) Alves

Someone asked me, "Tell me about Michal Ann Goll. What was she like?" I closed my eyes and thought back. As the memories flooded in, the tears welled up and I couldn't speak.

Michal Ann Goll. The first time I laid eyes on her, she was preaching at a women's conference...while baking bread, no less! She was demonstrating the process of turning raw grain into finished bread; it was an allegory of the Christian walk. As she wiped her flour-covered hands on her backside, I thought to myself, *I'm gonna* love *this girl!*

And indeed I did. This spunky, sweet Missouri-born mother of four always had a smile on her face. I will always remember her walking around singing and worshipping. I never heard a negative word out of her mouth about anyone. Perhaps that was one reason why the secret place seemed always so near to her. Michal Ann didn't just talk about the secret place; she *lived* in it.

The first time I visited in the Goll home, they had just moved into a small house with their four children. It was crowded, but the fruit of the Spirit was everywhere. The first night I was in their home, God had a word that He would give them a lovely house on a hill with lots of green grass on its acreage, with horses on it. Michal Ann began to cry, because she said this had always been her dream.

As with most ministries, their finances were never on the high side. When Michal Ann was asked, "How will this happen?" her answer would be, "I'll discuss it with God." Well, she must have done that, because the house and acreage became a beautiful reality. As she would later say, "It was birthed in my secret place."

Michal Ann has called me a "grandmother of the prayer shield." And indeed I have written books on prayer and intercession. But I have never met a Christian yet who doesn't yearn for that call to the secret place. Some are too afraid to seek it. Some just don't want to take up the challenge. But some are like this deep, passionate, sensitive friend of mine—they don't just visit the secret place. They accept the call, walk the walk, and *live* there.

Six weeks before her death, I saw Michal Ann seated alone at a conference spending time communing with her God. She was very weak and ill, yet her arms and face were lifted up to the Lord in prayer and worship. It seemed such a holy place she was abiding in, enveloped by His presence. Her life truly embodied that high call. This was my friend, Michal Ann Goll...so down to earth, and yet so at home in heavenly places.

If you have a secret place, few, if any, will even know about it. When God calls us to a secret place with Him, it's not something we advertise. Instead, we go quietly into that place where we meet with Him face to face. This book will encourage, teach, and guide you to your own secret place, and it will bless all fellow pilgrims and friends of the secret place.

Thus is the life of my friend and her dear husband, James. Together they lived the message in this book. I miss Michal Ann. But her prayers live on. They live on today in her children, in the Women on the Frontlines movement she birthed, and in her writings. You hold in your hand a key to the best place you will ever know—*A Call to the Secret Place* just for you.

—Elizabeth (Beth) Alves
Founder of Increase International
Author of *Mighty Prayer Warrior*

INTRODUCTION

James W. Goll

(written on behalf of Michal Ann Goll for this edition)

I found my secret place with God in nature. When I was growing up, I used to spend hours sitting in the woods with my dear mother, Dorris Grace McCoy Willard, watching and listening to the chirping birds together. Those were priceless days spent together just "being," with very little talk but a whole lot of observing, patiently waiting, just enjoying nature and God.

Later, I spent hours in our little barn that we rebuilt on our "Field of Dreams" in the beautiful rolling hills of Franklin, Tennessee. I learned many lessons there in solitude in that humble abode. I loved just "being" there with God, in the courts of His presence.

That is what God wants from each of us. Just "being with Him." He has been my closest friend since I was a child, and He will forever be my closest friend. What an honor it is to bring to you, along with the help my devoted husband, Jim (James to most of you), this Women on the Frontlines series of books. These chapters are like pages torn off from my own personal progression of life and ministry. I will take you on a journey from the transformational understandings in *A Call to Courage* to the fundamental essence of life in God found in *A Call to the Secret Place*. It all culminates in my ultimate love and call in life, *A Call to Compassion*.

Will you go on a journey with me? Will you follow in the footsteps of another pilgrim? Come along on an adventure of a lifetime in this series of books—written for men as well as women—Women on the Frontlines.

Part One

"Come
Up Here"

Chapter 1

WHEN I'M CALLING YOU

The gospel is so simple and real. God loves us enormously; it's as though He has decided to leave us love notes everywhere. Whenever you open your heart to see and hear Him, He is there. It's wonderful to look back over your life and see those hidden messages strategically placed—especially when you did not notice them earlier.

I have one such love note I'd like to share with you. When I was growing up, my family enjoyed watching Jeanette MacDonald and Nelson Eddy movies. Jeanette MacDonald had a beautiful operatic voice and she seemed to be a Christian. When her lovely voice was blended with Nelson Eddy's rich baritone, the musical match was just heavenly.

One of their movies was *Rose-Marie,* known for the song, "Indian Love Call." Set in Canada, it is a romantic love story between a Canadian Royal Mounted police officer and a professional opera singer. At one point, the couple stands at a breathtaking scenic high point in the Canadian mountains, looking down into the valley. The Mountie teaches a bit of Indian folklore by singing "Indian Love Call," and the song captures the woman's heart. They fall deeply in love.

When a conflict threatens to separate the lovers forever, the opera singer (Jeanette MacDonald) returns to the same mountain peak. In hope that her voice will be able to find him, tearfully she sings "Indian Love Call" into the depths of the valley below. Her love is expressed in every line. As she sings, the sound of her voice echoes through the valley to the mountain on the other side. The hills echo back each note, each word... "When I'm calling you / Will you answer true? / That means I'm offering my love to you. / To be your own....When you hear my love call ringing clear, / And I hear your answering echo, so dear....You belong to me. / I belong to you!"

Merely typing those words brings such warmth and tenderness into my heart, because I now can see something in those words that I didn't see as a child. I hear a voice calling me; it is asking for a response to a song I've been taught by the greatest romantic of them all. If you listen, you'll hear it too. Can you hear Him singing your name over the mountaintops? He is aching to hear your heart's response to Him. "When I'm calling you…Will you answer true…?" He's calling!

If you learn to listen, and if you are still, you will hear the voice that calls each one of us. And if you follow, you will find the secret place where the One who is love eternal dwells. There alone, in His everlasting arms, will you find strength and peace. There you will be shown the wonders of His love.

The question is: how do we find our way to the secret place where God abides?

Selah

In recent decades, we have been learning great lessons about prayer. Many ministries have sprung up to teach Christians how to be prayer warriors—how to pray for the lost, our schools, our towns and cities, and our nation. Yet, for all our praying, many of us lack a sense of closeness and intimacy with God to whom we pray. We may have no clue how to truly find God in our prayer time. With all our understanding about God's awesome power, it's as if we've lost sight of God Himself and His longing to be intimate with us.

If we want to find God in our everyday experience and sense His real presence throughout life's struggles and joys, we must learn about a kind of prayer few of us understand: the prayer of inner quiet.

In the psalms, we discover long lists of God's amazing attributes and His great and mighty acts. We read, "You are the God who does wonders," "You have demonstrated your power among the people," and "With Your mighty arm You have redeemed Your people, the sons of Jacob and Joseph." We get into the pace of those words, imagining a God who is always on the move. Unfortunately, often we miss the all-important instruction at the end: *selah*—"pause a minute and calmly think about what you've just read."

In this tender instruction, we hear the echo of God's voice calling to us from out of time, calling us to come apart to be alone with Him. But we miss His voice in the midst of our busy days; we run until we drop and then we get up the next day and start all over again.

Although we often complain about our demanding, stressed-out lives, most of us have become accustomed to the frantic pace. We scarcely know what to do with ourselves when things slow down. Some of us are even afraid to slow down, afraid of what will happen. Our running keeps us just ahead of the wind at our backs. And if we should suddenly stop, the whirlwind of promises we've made and responsibilities we've picked up—everything that's swirling in our wake—will catch up with us. Up to now, we've kept just a step ahead, but in a moment it could suddenly overtake us.

At the same time, we sense our own desire to retreat to the wonderful spirit-place, the quiet sanctuary where God abides. Even if we sense His call, we object, "I don't have the time!" when someone encourages us to give prayer greater space in our lives. Giving up in frustration before we even start, we never answer God's love-call.

Learn to Take the Time

No matter how busy your lifestyle has been, you can learn how to enter the secret place with God. You can know His real presence with you every day.

Learning to change the lifestyle you've been living is going to take time. Be patient with yourself. At the same time, learn how to be patient in waiting upon God. Although God is always present with you, coming into the secret place with Him is one thing you cannot hurry. You're not going to get there if you're a speed-reader or if you're a great administrator who lives by a checklist. None of the things you have learned how to do to "make things happen" will help you come into this place in spirit.

You will only find your way to the secret place with God if you learn to take the time.

Nothing Is Impossible

Time is hard to find, it seems. I assure you, I know all about the issue of time...and the lack thereof.

Some years ago, my husband, James, came home on fire after being at a fantastic Christian conference. He could hardly sit down. He walked from room to room, reviewing all the amazing details. "God was so great!" he kept saying. "This amazing thing happened, and that miracle took place."

All the while I was thinking, *Please! Don't tell me another word.* You see, at the time we were between houses, living with our four kids in someone else's basement. I was homeschooling a first grader and getting up in the night with our youngest, in addition to keeping up with the two in between. Every ounce of energy and focus was going to the kids. I was so hungry to be with God, but I didn't have time to go off on a weekend retreat. James was so elated, and all I could do was listen and feel miserable.

When he finally left the room, I leaned my head against the wall and silently cried, my tears releasing to God the depth of my hunger. I felt desperate, because it seemed that I could do nothing to find a spare minute to be alone with Him.

Just then the Lord came to me in my desperation, and in that still small voice inside, He said, *Ann, I know all that. I am the God of the impossible, and what you think is impossible is possible with Me. I will come to you. I will visit you in the night.*

I wasn't even sure I understood what He meant. But the most amazing thing began to happen. Night after night I began to dream. One night I dreamed that a dear, sweet old gentleman came to me. I knew who He was at once. He was so kind and loving, and He loved the fragrance of my hair. He wanted me to simply lean near and hug Him, so He could smell it. I had never noticed that my hair had any kind of scent, but He did. He knew everything about me. In this way, night after night, God came wooing. We went on long walks down country lanes, and He told me how precious I am to Him and revealed how He cherishes me. I was given a gift of seeing myself through His loving eyes.

Of course I believe that perhaps these dreams were unusual. But I know that I am no more unique or specially favored by God than anyone else. He simply had a specific way of revealing His love to me at that time of my life, and I know He has a very special, personal way to reveal Himself to you too.

I'm telling you about my experience so that you will know one thing for sure: with God, nothing is impossible. Even though you may feel like your schedule is too full or too busy, and you don't know how you can squeeze out an additional moment, God Himself can make a way. In fact, He is already seeking out the times and places where He can meet alone with you. He's looking for the tiniest opening in your day or your night, when He can make His wonderful presence known to you.

Entering In

The dreams gave me a very real assurance of God's love and presence, although they did not last. They served as a catalyst, an invitation. They spurred me on in my pursuit of God, because they showed me that intimacy with Him was absolutely possible, regardless of where I was living, how sleep deprived I was, or what kind of daily stress I was experiencing. I wished I could have stayed in that wonderful secret place with Him forever, but it did not happen automatically. I had to learn how to take practical steps to meet with my God who so obviously longs to meet with me.

This is true for each one of us. How do we begin?

First, we must stop assuming that we need to be specially called to times of prayer. Maybe some people are gifted so that they can repeat their prayer lists all the time, but I'm not. Or maybe we've grown up with a distorted view of what prayer is. Do we approach prayer as a form of mental exercise—something that in our own natural power we can "do"? When we read Paul's imperative words, "pray without ceasing" (1 Thess. 5:17, NASB), we may come think of prayer as something meant only for super saints.

The fact is that Paul was addressing you and me—every one of us. God calls each of us pray continually. But we must realize this: before God calls us to prayer, He calls us to Himself. When God says, "Come away, my beloved" (Song of Sol. 8:14a), He is calling every one of us. He is inviting you.

Second, we need to find a place to be entirely alone. Susanna Wesley, mother of John and Charles Wesley and more than a dozen other children, had absolutely no place to go inside her own home to get away from the children in order to be alone with the Lord. So when she pulled her apron up over her head, her children knew it was time to leave her alone. Most of us have better living circumstances than Susanna Wesley. If you have a bathroom, or even a large closet, you can find a place to be alone.

Third, we must learn what it takes to quiet our own spirit. Bombarded as we are by outside noise and information, we get totally out of touch with our own feelings and motives. Begin to be quiet by disconnecting from the ever-noisy TV and radio, and put limits on gab sessions with friends. Then you can take time to search your heart— with the help of the Holy Spirit—to find out what's really going on inside. Sometimes we don't really want to know what's going on in there. But you can't enter the secret place with God unless you enter as your true self. False fronts and masks will hinder you from experiencing God's presence. As David says in his great psalm of confession, only truth and honesty in the inward parts will allow us to enter where God abides (see Ps. 51:6).

Fourth, we need help prevent our minds from wandering. If you've ever tried to spend time alone with the Lord, you know what I mean. You manage to take a quiet break—but the minute you sit down, "the list" takes over your mind. You think, *I can't just sit here. There's wet laundry in the dryer, and I've got to pay this bill, and...and...and...* Failing to get anywhere spiritually, you give up.

For this reason, I recommend you enter into the secret place with God by meditating on His Word. I can think of no better way to corral and direct your straying thoughts than to guide them along the spiritual pathways of truth laid out by God's Spirit. And as you meditate on God's Word, God builds up your faith by revealing Himself to you. There in His Word, you can see Him at work; you can learn about His character. You can see Him act, loving and winning back the world, which includes you, to Himself.

Each of these four steps helps turn your heart toward God. Each step opens you up to the fifth thing that leads straight into the secret place—opening yourself to receive His love.

The need to be loved is the strongest need any of us possess. Most of our arguments and conflicts with other people have to do with the issue of being loved. Yet each of us has a huge void inside that the love of no human being can ever fill. Only God's love can fill it.

In order for God to fill us, our hearts must be wide open to Him—yielded to Him. Therefore, it's absolutely necessary that we learn to pray from our hearts. Praying from our heads, with our understanding, doesn't accomplish anything, because prayer is nothing more and nothing less than turning our hearts fully toward God, opening up all of what we are to Him, and in turn receiving His love in place of our emptiness.

This yielding is not something we do instinctively, and most of us try too hard. What is it like to yield to Him? Consider Adam, just after he was created. There he was, a fine physical specimen made by God, perfect in every way. Yet there was no life in him. As Adam lay there on the ground, God bent down and breathed life into him. God is still doing that today, stopping to breathe life into our empty, needy souls. What did Adam do to receive this life? Nothing. He just lay there and let God do the breathing. In the same way, we must open ourselves to God, yield to Him, and simply allow Him to fill us.

Although I say "simply," that is difficult for our works-based mentality to grasp. We carry around long lists of the things we must do to be worthy enough to approach God. The Christian church has often added to this pressure, making us feel that we need to do more to please God so that He will be "happy" with us.

In actuality, all we are required to do is to relax and inhale the breath of the very Spirit of God, who is always present with us.

My Kingdom Is within You

Jesus promised the disciples that He would send the Holy Spirit so they wouldn't be left alone without Him after His death. He said, "You know him, for *he lives with you and will be in you*" (John 14:17b, emphasis added).

God Himself lives in you! His kingdom, the place where He rules and reigns, is inside of you.

You may have learned about prayer that storms the heavens to tear down strongholds (see 2 Cor. 10:4), and prayer that asks for our daily needs (see Matt. 6:11), but I'm talking about the kind of prayer that allows you to enter the kingdom of God. You can come right into God's presence. The Comforter lives right inside you, and He wants to give you peace.

This is an incredible fact—the kingdom of God is within you, and this makes God Himself accessible to you at any time.

I have studied the great women of faith down through the ages in order to understand how to enter into that secret place with God. God has helped women from every walk of life learn how to draw spiritual strength and courage from the kingdom within so that they could face the hard circumstances that surrounded them. Only in the secret place of prayer could they find inspiration for the dull and dry times, and comfort for the lonely and hurting times as well. These truly noble Christian women knew how to exhale their many worries and surrender their misconceptions about God that might have kept them from approaching Him. They understood what it meant to empty themselves of all worldly preoccupations that can fill up the inner rooms of our souls and push Him out. They also knew how to relax into, and breathe in, His very presence. They knew what it meant to inhale the peace that comes only from Him, like a spiritual fragrance. They knew how to pray, "Father, I want to meet with you in the secret place," and how to follow Him, day after day and year after year.

Prayer is as simple as breathing out and asking God to clear out the clutter and the noise within, asking Him to create that inner room where you can always go to meet with Him in secret.

Have you learned what it's like to have God's very presence fill you the way breath fills your lungs? You can easily enter into the secret place of your soul where God's Spirit dwells if you know the way.

The kind of prayer I am referring to is not about getting it right or about achieving a goal, the motivation for too many of our prayers; neither is it about making yourself presentable to God before you ask to meet with Him. There is a kind of intimate praying that can only come about as we learn to strip away pretense and come, just as we are, into the inner chamber with our Lord and King.

Some of us look at other Christian women, especially "prayer warriors" or "great women of faith" and think, *If only I knew how to pray the way she prays.* When we think this way, we are treating the subject of prayer as if we are going into another woman's home to see her decorating scheme, her lovely fabrics, furniture selection, and colors. We think, *If only I could deck myself out like her. If only I could come before God the way she does—then my life with God would take off and my prayers would become powerful.*

Prayer that brings us into intimate experiences with God does not involve imitating another or reproducing their prayers. You are your own person; you are unique. And there is a place of intimacy with you that God cannot find with anyone else. He wants you to have a relationship with Him that no one else can enjoy. Know this: *God wants you to be just exactly who you are.*

Many of us wish we were someone else. We want to enjoy God's presence, but we think, *God doesn't really want to meet with me.* Listen—you know what? God wants you to take yourself as you find yourself, and start from there. You can't change your history; you can't change mistakes or undo wrong things from your past. *You can't remake yourself into somebody you're not.* So begin with the person you are today. It's like standing in front of the mall-map sign that says You are here. God wants you to say, "God, I am here! Just as I am, I come."

Being able to enter into the deep love and peace of God in prayer is not about getting rid of flaws and faults. If it were, we would spend all our time trying to make ourselves perfect, and that never works. Entering your secret place requires nothing more than coming, for He says, "Everything and everyone that the Father has given me will come to me, and I won't turn any of them away" (John 6:37, CEV). Anytime, you can come as you are into the presence of the wonderful God who has said, "I am with you always..." (Matt. 28:20b).

What is the only requirement for finding your way to the secret place with God? Just begin. Begin by abandoning yourself to God, which means learning to rest in His divine presence no matter what your circumstances may be.

In abandoning yourself to God, you train your soul to rest in Him. You trust that He is in control of your life not only when everything goes well, but also when everything goes wrong. You learn to trust that He has not abandoned you and that He knows what's best for you when He allows different situations and circumstances into your life.

You make a deliberate choice to believe that He is working something bigger into you than what you could accomplish by yourself.

I am not saying this is easy. It's not. But it works.

The Narrow Way

To find the peace of God that only He can give, we must abandon ourselves completely to Him. Abandonment is the key that unlocks the entry door into the secret place where our King and heavenly Bridegroom dwells.

In the secret place, God reveals His mysteries to us. He is our Bridegroom, and He longs to reveal His secrets to us, His bride. One of the greatest mysteries is the way God transforms us into people who bear the marks of Jesus Christ. Paul referred to this mystery when he wrote, "I bear on my body the marks of Jesus" (Gal. 6:17b). If we love and abandon ourselves to God, as Paul did, we will be transformed into His image.

Paul was describing Jesus' "narrow way" (see Matt. 7:13–14), a way that stands open before each one of us. Finding your way to this place in God requires giving Him the keys to everything: children, husband, family, home, possessions, friends, job, and dreams. We must place everything into His hands and leave it there for Him to do with as He sees fit.

What will it take to produce this kind of abandonment in us? It does not come easily, and it takes great faith. The greater our faith, the more we know God, and the better we know Him, the easier it will be to abandon ourselves freely without the slightest hesitation or holding back. What Jesus said is eternal truth: God is our center, and His kingdom is within us (see Luke 17:21).

The more we become completely united with Him in spirit, soul, and body (see 1 Thess. 5:23), the more the barriers of doubt, fear, and pride will melt in the warmth of His love. We will come into a place where peace, love, and eternal strength are ours because we are one with Him, peacefully resting in the wonder of His love.

Great Women of God Show Us the Way

Throughout history, great men and women alike have found their way into the secret place where God dwells. They have entered that place by learning the secrets of quiet prayer, and how to abandon themselves completely to God. They learned what it means to become His bride, and they were consumed with the love of God as they yielded themselves completely to His presence. In this book, we'll look at the lives of a few of these amazing women. From them, we can learn much about answering God's call to the secret place.

As we begin, I offer this prayer on your behalf:

Father, lead us out of the storms and stresses of life that distract us and keep us from knowing You. More than anything else, we want to know You. We want to open our hearts and our lives wide to You. Guide us by Your precious Holy Spirit to the secret place, where You can reveal Yourself in wonder, majesty, and holiness, in us and through us to a lost world. In Jesus' name, amen.

Chapter 2

🌿

THE DEPTHS OF GOD

"C ome up here!" the heavenly voice commanded (see Rev. 4:1b). When Jesus Christ calls you into the secret place of prayer, it's an invitation like no other. That call from the depths of God's presence signals an unspeakable privilege, an open door to a revelation of God Himself. My one major goal in life is to be like the apostle John and to answer the call of God to come into the secret place. What about you?

In the book of Revelation, the veil is pulled back for a moment and we are afforded a glimpse of what John saw when he was called into the secret place. The apostle tells us: "On the Lord's Day I was in the Spirit, and I heard behind me a loud voice…" (Rev. 1:10).

When John turned to see who was calling, he was amazed. The One who commanded his attention was none other than Jesus. But it was not the Jesus he'd seen before—the itinerant Jewish rabbi in a robe and sandals. Here was the shining, resurrected Son of God, summoning John to come up with Him in the glorious heavenly sanctuary where He stood in the midst of fiery candlesticks. From His feet to His hair He was a blazing fire, so that "His face was like the sun shining in all its brilliance" (Rev. 1:16b).

John was so overcome by this shining revelation of God that he "fell at His feet like a dead man" (Rev. 1:17a, NASB). But Jesus placed His right hand on John and lifted him up—and went on to unfold one of the greatest revelations of God that anyone has ever received.

I don't expect to be another John, but I too want to meet with Jesus Christ in the secret and holy place where He dwells in Spirit and, like John, be taken into the depths of God. I want to be a vessel that reveals the awesome mysteries of God's grace and truth to the world. Is that the goal of your life too?

Battle and Blessing

The problem for most of us is that the busyness of life crowds out the time we could otherwise spend alone answering God's call. For example, one Sunday morning I was trying to find even ten minutes to be alone with God, but it seemed that it was not to be. I went into one room after another, and one of my children followed me wherever I went. At every step, I heard, "Mom, I need this," or "Can we do that?"

I was doing my best to see them merely as innocent children and I was trying to maintain a good attitude, but I felt bombarded. I kept thinking, *Why is it such a battle to get to the blessing?*

Interestingly, I've learned that God is not absent from such circumstances. In fact, God is actually very present in these circumstances, allowing them to happen for a reason. As we're being pressed, he grants us an opportunity to see ourselves as we really are. Far from setting up these situations to hurt us or keep us away from Himself, He allows such circumstances to help us see aspects of ourselves that we would otherwise miss. We don't necessarily enjoy that. Our human natures aren't eager to be exposed to His light, but that's the first step toward transformation. He is allowing us to see (through trial and testing) our need for His help.

Besides, God is God. It makes no difference what circumstances surround us; He can still meet with us, and He can still provide for our every need.

I am writing this to you, not because I merely *hope* that it's true or because it sounds like the spiritual thing to say. I'm writing to tell you, as one who has received the true grace of God, that there is a way into the secret place where He dwells—*even in the midst of whatever kind of bombardment or fiery furnace you are going through.* The way is not to try to escape the flames, but to go through them.

Let me tell you how I learned this truth.

My Own Personal Fire

God made sure that I could learn, in the midst of the hot flames of testing around me, to walk in the burning presence of God. He showed me things that I hadn't understood before—events from the past that were hurtful to me; times when I felt spiritually dry; and long stretches in which I had felt alone, forgotten, left out, and overlooked. He redeemed those times by showing me that, from His perspective, I have never been apart from His great love for me. He has brought me out of the unpleasant place where I felt stuck for many years.

For years I was at home all the time, and everyone knew me only as "Jim Goll's wife" or "the pastor's wife." Sometimes it's difficult to live with a person who is really well-known and liked. (For some people, that person may be a parent or sibling, or a coworker.) I think it's the most difficult to be left behind as the one who's holding down the fort.

People would call our home and say, "Oh, you have the most wonderful husband. His meetings are so awesome, and he is so anointed. You must feel so blessed to be married to him."

While I agreed with them that, yes, James is an awesome vessel of God's grace and truth, something in my heart wanted to say, *But what about me? Where is the affirmation I need to feel valued for my contribution to 'our' ministry?* I felt like an appendage. I could try to be "more spiritual" and want to please only God. Yet, honestly I had to admit that I, like anyone else, wanted to be known and to feel valued and respected for my labors.

What made it worse in those early years was our desperate desire to have children, but we were unable to conceive. I was barren for seven years, but then God dramatically and miraculously touched and healed me. I was absolutely ecstatic and filled with indescribable wonder and thanksgiving.

My pregnancy with Justin, our oldest, went well, except for some mild morning sickness in the early months. Then, during my second pregnancy with our daughter, GraceAnn, I became very, very ill. I spent months lying in bed. I was too sick and weak to even hold up my Bible because it was too heavy. I couldn't eat anything; I could barely keep down a tablespoon of liquid at a time. I looked terminally ill. It was truly by the grace of God that GraceAnn was born a totally healthy baby, weighing nine pounds, six ounces.

But my body was so depleted. Shortly thereafter, I became pregnant with our son Tyler. Again I became very ill, not quite as bad but serious enough that I lay in bed for months. My stomach seemed to be over generating digestive juices that were eating me up from the inside out.

And so it went through the pregnancies for three of our four children. I was left alone all day, except for my babies and toddlers. I didn't see or talk to other adults. I didn't watch TV or listen to the radio. I couldn't read anything because I couldn't hold up a book. All I did was take care of little children, rest, and hope in God.

That's how things became clear spiritually. God visited me in quiet ways during those long days. With no other distractions in the way, God began to speak to me, connecting the dots of my life, so to speak. I didn't know it then, but there was more testing ahead.

While we were living in Kansas City where James was serving on a church staff, we entered into a season of unusual spiritual warfare. Suddenly one morning, James got incredibly sick. I found him delirious, hallucinating in our bedroom. I rushed him to the doctor, but for two weeks the doctor could not figure out what was going on.

Almost as soon as James pulled through, I got slammed. In the midst of this, we were trying to sell our home (without a realtor). Suddenly, I became severely ill with a dangerously high temperature. I kept on showing the house to potential buyers, working constantly to keep it perfectly clean and taking care of my small children. After a few weeks of this frantic pace, I started to realize that there were periods of time I could not account for. My temperature was so high that I was blacking out.

That was when my doctor said, "Okay, let's put you in the hospital."

After I was admitted to the hospital, things got worse. They put me in an isolation room where everyone who came to see me was required to wear a mask. The physicians started asking me the most bizarre questions. What kind of sexual relations had I had? What was my lifestyle like? Nothing was sacred, and I felt completely humiliated—stripped down to my very soul.

My lowest point came when my doctor stood at the head of my bed rattling off to himself a list of deadly diseases that I might have. Bewildered with my symptoms, he was saying, "Well now, if it's cancer we can expect to see this symptom…" He went on to catalog just about every terrible life-threatening disease I'd ever heard of. Then he walked out without reaching a diagnosis.

My kids had been farmed out to friends and family. They were able to visit me a few times, but the masks and robes produced a fearful experience for them. I longed to see them and hold them but wasn't sure what this experience was doing to them. On his own, my husband was trying to sell our home, while his wife was lying in the hospital bed, still sick as a dog. Not to mention miserable, scared, empty, and feeling totally alone.

I have to say that no spiritual enlightenment came my way in the long hours of that dark night. I heard no comforting statements from God's throne room like, *Yes, I am with you, Ann,* to carry me through, at any time during those long days. I felt numb spiritually and mentally, as though I had taken my head off my shoulders. I couldn't think or try to process anything. I remembered that God had promised He would always be with me, but I couldn't feel Him, hear Him, or sense His presence.

The Fire Bride

Through that terrible ordeal I learned what treasure can be deposited within us as we pass through the fire—when we keep our hearts open to God and to His deeper workings in our lives. Some of us think that God's greatest goal is to make everything easy and comfortable for us. While it's true that He wants to bless us with good things, He desires something else even more. He yearns for deep friendship with us. He longs for true intimacy.

Intimacy with God…hmm…sounds romantic, doesn't it? But our God is holy and His holiness is a consuming fire (see Deut. 4:24). He draws us closer to Himself by kindling a fire that draws us like moths out of the darkness toward its great light. Drawn by a force that's beyond ourselves, we come closer.

As we get closer, the fire of God begins to make us uncomfortable. The light of His holiness begins to scorch the dross and the chaff within us. We experience turmoil as we become painfully aware of our sins, shortcomings, and unworthiness to be in His beautiful, holy presence. We become painfully aware that we have become idolaters, nurturing false passions of our soul and flesh, and that our idols have kept us trapped in worldliness.

Our turmoil grows deeper and stronger until it becomes a battle over our very souls. We long for Him and we remember the seal of the Holy Spirit, like the engagement ring pledged as a promise of a coming wedding day (see Eph. 4:30). Yet at the same time we are overwhelmed with our failings, angers, jealousies, and lusts. Within, we cry out, *How could He possibly love me or want me as I am?*

Oh, but our heavenly Lover already sees and knows everything. Fully aware of our every fault, He nevertheless calls us to Himself. Unfortunately, our sense of unworthiness causes us to resist Him and hold back from running into His arms with abandonment.

Eventually, we discover that there is only one thing to do. In the moment of our greatest soul agony, when we feel ourselves to be the most useless and unworthy in His eyes, we must run to Him and cry out, "Help me, my Lord and my God!" But there in His wonderful, gracious embrace, He will cover all our weaknesses, needs, and soul sickness.

Rushing toward Him, the wind of our desperation fuels the flame of His passion, which burns away our dross and chaff with consuming love. In this moment we begin to understand why He has allowed all the mistakes, sins, failures, and disappointments.

These lines from Frances Thompson's famous poem "The Hound of Heaven" echo the voice of God, revealing a great mystery of His wonderful ways:

> All which I took from thee I did but take,
> Not for thy harms,
> But just that thou might'st seek it in My arms.
> All which thy child's mistake
> Fancies as lost, I have stored for thee at home:
> Rise, clasp My hand, and come!

Why do we wait so long? We yearn for the fire of our Lover, but we're afraid to run into His arms, knowing He is a "living flame of love," as John of the Cross called Him. We are afraid of the process it takes to fully embrace Him and be caught up in Him forever.

So we hang onto our worldly passions, interests, positions, power, possessions, people—all in an attempt to anchor ourselves here on earth, where we feel a little more secure. We worry, *What will He ask of me? What will He force me to give up?* We attempt to bargain our way out of our perceived losses. *What will He let me keep?* Sometimes we fall into condemnation because we know we should not consider earthly "treasures" to be more valuable than God Himself.

Instead of being consumed by the blissful joy of godly passion and the ecstasy of spiritual freedom, we are consumed by guilt. Even our hesitancy reinforces our false belief that we don't "qualify" for His love. Now hopelessness and new turmoil begin to pull us down.

Sooner or later, we look up. Who is this Man standing before us? It's Jesus, the living, loving Son of God! God Himself in the flesh captures us with the intense look of love in His eyes. His heart calls us tenderly, *Just let go of your struggle. This minute. Let it go…and come to Me!*

What am I waiting for? we ask. Letting go of all fear and resistance, we run headlong into His arms. Instantly, the Holy Spirit breathes upon the embers of our smoldering passion, setting our hearts ablaze with love for Him.

At last—the Fire Bride of God!

Where she once feared the fire, to her own delighted amazement she now cries out for more. *More fire!* The intensity of heat that tried her heart has transformed it into precious, purified gold. She is complete in Him and her heart will never again be polluted by other, lesser loves. Her heart is no longer hers; it now belongs to Him.

Worth Everything

To finish my story, the doctors finally discovered that I had severe pneumonia and eventually were able to bring it under control. I went home to convalesce, and in time I was well again.

In the midst of all the upheaval of that terrible time, what I had needed the most I had received directly from God Himself—healing for my soul. Now I could see God's hand in all that we had endured.

Some weeks later, I had a dream. In it, an angel came to me and hit me on the head. When he struck me, my skull opened and the light of God radiated inside me. It was 4:00 a.m., and I sat bolt upright in bed, charged with a supernatural energy from this encounter with God. In this moment of illumination, I saw clearly that God is utterly faithful to be with us at all times and through all things. Even when we allow other loves and circumstances to blind us to Him, He is still there, longing to love and be loved.

Something else broke my heart. He is truly the only heavenly Lover, the sole One who has the right to our hearts. He created our hearts, and no other being in this universe will be as faithful as He is. His love is all-encompassing. How can we ignore it for another moment?

Healing for Our Souls

Most of us think "salvation" is only about getting saved from hell so we can go to heaven. But salvation is about so much more than that. Jesus opened the way for us to come into the very presence of God so that our souls, which were wounded in the Fall, might be healed and restored to wholeness. We can never be whole without God. Until we rejoin ourselves to Him, we will always have a soul wound in the place where He should be.

If we do not overcome our fear of His fire and return to His side to be made whole, we will forever be filled with that deep, empty longing for something to fill that wound. We will never fill it with what the world has to offer, no matter how much we try. The only solution is to abandon ourselves to Him so that He can rejoin Himself to us by the power of His Holy Spirit in us.

Companions for the Journey

As I have learned the way to the secret place with God, I am thankful that I've found spiritual companions to show me the way, spiritually minded men and women who have gone through the fire themselves and have come out purified and filled with a desire to share the grace they have received, wanting to share it with others by means of their writings.

What I have learned about entering the secret place with God is by no means the final word on the subject. In the next chapters, we will gain more insights regarding deep and fulfilling intimacy with God from some great women of the Christian faith, including Madame Jeanne Guyon, St. Teresa of Avila, Susanna Wesley, Fanny Crosby, Basilea Schlink, Gwen Shaw, and Elizabeth Alves.

From these women, each of whom has passed through the fire, we can receive a wealth of rich insight and heavenly blessing. However, before we begin I want to offer two words of direction.

First, their lives are to be used only as way markers. They can help you see where you might be on your own journey. The principles they learned and taught do not lay out a "step-by-step" list of dos and don'ts for entering into God's presence. They do not present a "canned" or legalistic approach to spiritual growth.

Second, let these stories help sharpen your spiritual focus so that all your attention is directed toward God and God alone. Be aware of the subtle temptation to take your eyes off Him and look at your struggles, or to forget His infinite ability by focusing on your own limited abilities. It's all about Him, not you.

All About Him

The life we are called to live, hidden and kept in the deep love of God, is not about us at all. It is about learning that we can trust Him utterly and abandon ourselves to Him completely. We can place all that concerns us into His care and learn to follow Him wherever He sees fit to lead us. He will take care of our every need, show us how to live in His kingdom, and use us however He desires to do so.

Are you ready to begin this journey? Daunting as it may sound, I urge you not to be afraid. Don't hesitate. God is your matchless Bridegroom who wants to join Himself to you in spirit. He has chosen you just as much as He has chosen me or any of the women profiled in this book. He longs to give us His Spirit, His beauty, and His grace, to infuse us with His very own eternal nature.

> Father, thank You that Your salvation is full and complete for both now and eternity. Through the wisdom of those who have walked this way before us and through your Holy Spirit present deep within, heal my wounds. Fill the emptiness deep inside my soul that drives me to seek comfort and satisfaction in everything except You. Open my eyes, Lord, as you opened the eyes of these great women of the faith who have gone before us. Let me see You and You alone. In Jesus' name I pray, amen.

Part Two

Pilgrims
of the Secret Place

Chapter 3

Jeanne Guyon (1648–1717)

CALLED DEEPER STILL

Does God have "favorites"? Sometimes we think so, but the truth is that God's call to spiritual intimacy comes to many—and only a few respond. Why is this? Is it because we instinctively know there is a cost to be paid if we want to enter into deeper mysteries of God?

One person who was willing to pay the price of spiritual intimacy with God was Madame Jeanne Guyon, a French woman born into a wealthy Roman Catholic family in the 1600s. As a result of her amazing experiences in prayer, she wrote several books, which have become known as some the greatest writings in all of Christian history, by now translated into many languages around the world.

Her writings have given me both courage and comfort, because I can identify with her struggles, which led her into extraordinary experiences in God. She asked the questions I have asked: *Why did God allow that to happen in my life? Why am I so restless, and longing for more of God?*

Madame Guyon intrigues me not because she offers spiritual formulas (which she does not), but because she gives us a glimpse of the deeper work God does inside us when we become fully yielded to Him. In this journey to the secret place, Jeanne Guyon is almost a one-of-a-kind guide. Although she was an everyday woman of her time, she entered into the depths of God, and then enabled others to find their way in the Spirit as well.

Her wisdom provides us with a truly unique spiritual perspective.

Her words and experiences lift us up to a higher spiritual realm. They allow us to soar like birds riding the winds of an upward-sweeping breeze, to a higher place in spirit. Her insights enable us to assess the places in our spiritual journey that can wound us badly and throw so many of us off course spiritually. Once we adopt her wise viewpoint for ourselves, we can begin to see in a new light the outlines of our path with our great heavenly Lover.

This is not just high-sounding spiritual talk. The wisdom I have gained from Madame Guyon's life has helped me to understand why difficult things have happened in my life and in the lives of my children. Her godly wisdom has helped guide their lives and has matured me into a more godly mother. To me that kind of spiritual growth is more precious than gold.

Amazingly, it was never Madame Guyon's intent to write a book of any kind. In the Catholic faith there are men and women known as spiritual directors, people who are responsible for the spiritual growth of anyone who is serious about faith and who wants their guidance. Jeanne would go to her spiritual directors and pose all her questions. The main reason we have her writings is because her spiritual directors commanded her to write about her spiritual experiences and insights as a matter of obedience. Then, ironic as it may seem, what she had written raised suspicion in Church officials and she was jailed as a possible heretic.

Madame Guyon's most profound insights came to us from a cold, dirty stone-walled prison cell where she wrote in defense of the one belief upon which her faith rested—that entering in unity with God happens only as we abandon ourselves totally to Him.

As she put it, "you [must become] fully convinced that it is on the nothing in man that God establishes His greatest works....He destroys that He might build. For when He is about to rear His sacred temple in us, He first totally razes that vain and pompous edifice that human art and power had erected. And from its horrible ruins, a new structure is formed, by His power only."[1]

This was the heart of Madame Guyon, filled with a faith that was rich, strong, alive, and unbeatable, no matter what rose up against her. The true story of her life is better than any fictional tale.

Beginnings

Jeanne Guyon was born prematurely on April 18, 1648, in the eighth month of her mother's pregnancy. Infant mortality rates were high in those days, and the baby girl was suspended between life and death for some time. Little Jeanne's health remained touch and go until she was almost three years old. Unfortunately, frail health would plague her the rest of her life.

Jeanne's father was wealthy and influential, and could have paid for childcare help in their home. But her mother was something of an enigma and opted to send her tiny, sick baby to a convent where Ursuline nuns would care for her for several months. Perhaps her mother had lived too long under the emotional fallout of so many infant deaths. When little Jeanne was returned to her parents, her mother's heart had cooled toward her sickly daughter and had embraced Jeanne's older brother instead. Jeanne became a neglected child. In her memoirs, she recalls that her mother spent little time with her and seemed to count her of little value. She was left entirely to the care of the household servants.

On the other hand, Jeanne's father loved her dearly. When he saw his wife neglecting their daughter, he arranged to send her to another convent where she might receive better care. So from the age of four until she was seven, she lived at a convent of Benedictine sisters.

Jeanne's life with the sisters left a lasting imprint. Living there in the convent and attending church services every day, Jeanne grew to love hearing about God, being in church, and being dressed in religious garb. Convent life planted seeds deeply in Jeanne's heart. From an early age, she became hungry for God.

In fact, she became unusually spiritually sensitive. As a little child, one night she dreamed of hell and cried out, "Oh my God, if you will have mercy on me and spare me yet a little longer I will never more offend you."[2]

Jeanne returned home briefly, but it seemed that her heart would never find a home in any earthly place. Her mother's rejection caused her to ignore Jeanne when she was ill, which was much of the time. Once she almost died of a sudden hemorrhage.

Soon, Jeanne's father sent her to another convent run by Benedictines.

Then she was moved to yet another convent, and allowed only brief visits home. When she was almost ten years of age, her father brought her home again until a nun of the order of St. Dominica, a close family friend, persuaded him to permit Jeanne to live with her at her convent. But her care was not good. In time, her father discovered that his daughter had become emaciated, and he brought her home.

At age eleven, Jeanne was sent again to the Ursulines, this time under the care of a half sister who also lived with the nuns. This young woman was very nurturing, and Jeanne's spirit flourished under her care. Jeanne grew in her love and devotion to God by leaps and bounds. Later, she once again returned home.

(Now all this shuttling in and out of convents and sending children away sounds terrible to us today. But keep in mind that it was a common practice in those days for people of means to allow their children to be brought up by monks or nuns.)

For Jeanne there was lasting benefit, because away from her mother, immersed in the holy atmosphere of these cloisters, Jeanne felt her first touches from God. What was this deep stirring she felt inside, this sense of someone calling her? Having no instruction about a personal relationship with God through Christ, Jeanne could only feel her way through institutional Christianity. She went regularly to confession, as was the Catholic custom, and she loved prayer. Even as a child she experienced a desire to suffer martyrdom; she and the other girls living at the convent would act out scenes in which they would take turns playing the role of martyr.

Though Jeanne would never go to a hostile foreign mission field or suffer physical martyrdom, she was in fact destined to suffer, not only from her unexplained illnesses, but from a kind of living death at the hands of those in authority over her.

Soul in Turmoil

When Jeanne returned home for the last time, nothing had changed in her mother's heart; if anything, it became even harder toward the little girl. She devoted most of her attentions to Jeanne's brother, whom she allowed to be absolutely brutal toward Jeanne at times. One time he threw her from the top of a coach, badly bruising her. He often beat her.

If Jeanne had something he wanted, it was taken from her and given to him. In their mother's eyes, he could do no wrong and Jeanne could do no right. As for Jeanne's care, it was mostly left to a servant girl who was allowed to beat the girl and treat her with total contempt. In fact, all the servants, if they wanted to be in good standing with her mother, would report every little "infraction."

To help Jeanne stand up under such unrelenting oppression, at that time all she had to hold onto spiritually were the written prayers in her Catholic prayer book. No one had told her that you could talk to God in your own words. Nevertheless, in moments of despair Jeanne began to cling to God, though He seemed distant.

Suddenly, at about thirteen years of age, Jeanne transformed physically. She was quite tall for her age and blossomed into a very pretty young woman. Suddenly, too, her mother seemed to like her more. She fussed and primped with Jeanne's hair and clothes, took her to parties and social events, and even took her traveling abroad. It became quite apparent that she was very proud of Jeanne's physical beauty.

All of this attention produced in Jeanne pride and vanity. In a way, who could blame her, after having been rejected for so long? However, there remained in her heart a strange tug—a sense that someone was calling to her. At one time a cousin who was on his way to a mission in China came to visit. Something in this young man—perhaps a certain spiritual fire or a single-hearted purity—spoke deeply to Jeanne, reawakening her earlier desire for God.

She passed the next years of her life, from twelve to fifteen, feeling torn inside. On the surface she dressed in fine clothes, but underneath her spirit was drawn away from the fine things of the world toward an upward calling. By reading spiritual works, such as the writings of St. Frances DeSales, Jeanne's soul deepened. Eventually, she began to spend more time with her prayer book; she was still trying to connect with that distant, elusive voice that seemed to call out to her.

The streets were full of beggars, destitute widows, and orphans; Jeanne gave all she had to the poor. Gathering a small group of poor people together, she taught the catechism. When her parents were not at home, for her mother would have loudly disapproved, she invited the poor in to eat with her, serving them with great respect.

Alone

During this time, Jeanne discovered the writings of a woman known as Madame de Chantel. Never before had she heard anyone speak of the things this woman of faith talked about—especially something she called "mental prayer," praying to God freely from the heart. According to Madame de Chantel, it was the beginning of the way into the secret place of union with God.

Something in Jeanne's young heart leaped.

However, when Jeanne asked her confessor to teach her this kind of prayer, he refused. Pray without a prayer book? He was aghast. How ridiculous! Unspiritual! Perhaps even dangerous! She should stick to the known paths. What did it matter, he said flatly, if written prayers were boring and lifeless to her? Who did she think she was to even consider other methods of prayer?

But Jeanne's heart was burning. She continued to fight in bouts with pride and vanity, and each round drove her all the more toward the desire for spiritual freedom. What if it were really possible to know God personally and experience Him intimately, as Madame de Chantel suggested?

She begged a community of nuns to take her in, but, knowing that her father would disapprove, they refused her. So, with no one to guide her, no one she could trust to lead her on her spiritual quest, Jeanne forged ahead on her own.

Teach me how to know You, Lord! her heart cried.

She had no way of knowing where that prayer would lead.

At this same time, Jeanne's family traveled to Paris. At first, her heart was nearly overwhelmed by the whirl of social engagements, beautiful clothes, jewelry, and perfumes. Handsome suitors flocked to her door. The romantic novels Jeanne occasionally read only added to her increasing vanity. Several advantageous offers of marriage came, but they were rejected by her father.

Eventually, one wealthy and influential suitor did get through to Jeanne's father. One day a servant approached Jeanne with a document to sign. "Sign quickly, please! It's for your father." Taking up a quill, Jeanne inked her name...not realizing that with each letter she scratched onto the paper she was signing herself away on formal "articles of marriage." She was just fifteen years old.

Two days before she was to be married, Jeanne saw her suitor for the first time. Her already turbulent young spirit sank into deep depression. Of her wedding day she would later write, "No sooner was I at the house of my new spouse than I perceived it would be for me a house of mourning."[3]

Immediately, it was also apparent that Jeanne's new mother-in-law despised her. She wrote:

> At my father's house we were obliged to behave in a genteel way and to speak with propriety. All that I said was applauded. Here, they never listened to me except to contradict and find fault. If I spoke well, they said it was to give them a lesson. If any questions were started at my father's, he encouraged me to speak freely. Here, if I spoke my sentiments they said it was to enter into a dispute. They put me to silence in an abrupt and shameful manner and scolded me from morning until night.... My mother-in-law conceived such a desire to oppose me in everything. And in order to vex me, she made me perform the most humiliating offices. Her disposition was so extraordinary....I was made the victim of her humors. All her occupation was to thwart me.[4]

Not only did this bitter old woman despise Jeanne, she turned the heart of her son, Jeanne's new husband, against her also: "[My mother-in-law] inspired the like sentiments in her son. And so they would make people who were my inferiors take place above me."[5]

Sadly, Jeanne found no support or comfort from her own family. She wrote, "My mother, who had a high sense of honor, could not endure that. When she heard [about my dishonor] from others—for I told her nothing—she chided me, thinking I did it because I didn't know how to keep my rank and had no spirit. And so I dared not tell her how it was, but I was almost ready to die with the agonies of grief and continual vexation.

"What made it worse," Jeanne continued, "was that my mother related to my mother-in-law the pains I had caused her from infancy. They then reproached me saying I was a challenging and an evil spirit. My husband made me stay all day long in my mother-in-law's room without any liberty of retiring into my own apartment. She spoke disadvantageously of me to everyone, to lessen the affection and esteem that some had entertained for me.

"She galled me with the grossest affronts before the finest company. [In this way] she found the secret of extinguishing my vivacity, and rendering me stupid. Some of my former acquaintances hardly knew me. Those who had not seen me before said, 'Is this the person famed for such abundance of wit? She can't say two words. She is a fine picture!'"[6]

Poor Jeanne, just sixteen years old, was driven to despair. Her spirit was dying, and in agony she wrote, "I had no one to confide in who might share my affliction and assist me to bear it….I resolved to have no confidant. It was not from any natural cruelty that my husband treated me [badly]. He loved me passionately, but was ardent and hasty, and my mother-in-law continually irritated him about me."[7]

In this horrible crucible of affliction, she began to cry out to God—not in the standard formal prayers that she had been taught by the Roman Catholic Church, but from the depths of her being.

"It was in a condition so deplorable, oh my God, that I began to perceive the need I had of Your assistance. This situation was perilous to me. I met with none but admirers abroad, those who flattered me to my hurt. It was to be feared, lest at such a tender age, amid all the strange domestic crosses I had to bear, I might be drawn away. But You, by Your goodness and love, gave it quite another turn.

"By these re-doubled strokes you did draw me to Yourself and by Your crosses effected what Your caresses could not effect. Not only this, You made use of my natural pride to keep me within the limits of my duty."[8]

Finding the Door

More time would pass before Jeanne made the discovery that turned all her sufferings into spiritual gold. At age sixteen, she had her first child, a son, and at nineteen, her second son was born. Both pregnancies wore her down physically, while her family continued to grind away at her spirit. Her only moments of solace were those times when she was alone crying out to God to help her.

Shortly after the birth of her second child, she met a man from the

Order of St. Francis. He had lived in solitude for five years, caught up in the love of God, and had just emerged from this long retreat with a kind of glow about him that was unearthly. Jeanne's father, knowing her devotion to God, arranged for her to meet with him.

There in the serene peace of a monastery, away from the glare and abuse of her mother-in-law and husband, Jeanne found it difficult to contain herself. Question after question poured out from her hungry heart. The kindly brother listened with patience, not so much to her, but as though he were listening to another voice. When she finished, he lifted his face to hers and stared into her eyes.

"You must accustom yourself, Madame, to seek God in your heart, and you will there find Him. For"—and he quoted the words of Jesus Christ—"'The kingdom of God cometh not with observation....the kingdom of God is within you'" (Luke 17:20–21, KJV).[9]

A door to a whole new world was opened to Jeanne. The light of revelation flooded in, and she became illuminated with understanding. She realized that God was not only "out there" somewhere; the God who transcends time and space dwelled in a secret place within her. What was even more stunning was the other truth that flooded her soul at the same time. She realized, *If God is in me, then nothing can separate us. Nothing can come between God's love and me.*

Suddenly, nothing was easier for her than prayer. Hours flew by like moments—and the joy and intensity of her devotion increased. As she put it, "The fervency of my love allowed me no intermission."[10]

Now, she was able to bear the ill treatment of her husband and mother-in-law, no matter how insulting or rigorous, silently and without inner tumult. She was swept away from the cares of the world around her, having found that place inside where she could go and meet with God. Within her own soul at all times, she could retreat to a secret and holy place where she could spend time with Him.

In time, Jeanne became so attuned to God's presence that she scarcely knew what she was eating. Occasionally she missed what people were saying to her, and she went for long periods without speaking. You might think such great devotion to God would earn her the admiration of her family and of the religious community, but nothing was further from the truth.

More Opposition

Jeanne's husband became jealous of her devotion to God. Her confessor, who had previously called Jeanne a "saint," began to publicly speak against her. She had privately confided in him about her experience, and he betrayed her by spreading the word that she was under a delusion. This whole idea of meeting with God—sheer insanity!

When Jeanne's family learned about her new devotion, they led the charge. She was persecuted from all sides and forbidden to pray. They went so far as to check on her every thirty minutes to interrupt her if she was in prayer. At one point, her husband refused to let her go outdoors, because he wanted to keep her where someone could watch and control her every waking moment.

But Jeanne's understanding of prayer was far deeper than they understood. It transcended words. She now understood that true prayer is resting in the real presence of God. This revelation was so deeply embedded in her spirit that she could not stop praying. To be conscious was to be in God's living presence, with a deep abiding awareness of His strength, peace, and comfort. As a result, simply the look on her face radiated the presence of God, which infuriated her family all the more.

Just when Jeanne thought she had come through the worst of the fire, she experienced new suffering in ways she never could have imagined. Shortly after the birth of Jeanne's third child, a daughter, a terrifying plague of smallpox ripped through France. Her little girl and oldest son became feverish. Though Jeanne's husband wanted to take her and their younger son away to protect them, her mother-in-law refused to allow it.

To contract smallpox was to receive a virtual death sentence, and now Jeanne found herself and all three of her children stuck in this fatal trap. Fear for herself and for her children warred against her soul, threatening to tear her away from her internal place of peace with God.

Jeanne found herself in the battle of her life. When she turned her eyes and her spirit inward, there she found her heavenly King ruling all things in serene order. Nothing was beyond His control. But when she turned her attention outward to her flushed and fevered children calling piteously for water and for comfort, her mother's heart was ripped in two.

At this moment Jeanne knew that God was calling her, once and for all, to abandon the whole world and enter into the depths of love with Him alone.

Only by an act of sheer will did Jeanne make her choice. She would take her fear of loss and death to the cross and allow this part of herself to die. She knew that only in this way could she experience the peace that comes when there is nothing left to stand between God and herself.

Jeanne wrote later about how she sacrificed herself to divine providence. Almost at once, Jeanne felt the symptoms of smallpox coming on. When she told her husband, he brushed it off as "just your imagination." But within hours, Jeanne was doubled over with intense stomach pain, a splitting headache, and a high fever. Still her family refused to believe she was ill. Her lungs became inflamed, and she was left gasping for breath and denied proper treatment because her mother-in-law refused to send for a doctor.

Divine providence alone came to her aid. A doctor who had treated her in the past felt moved for no apparent reason to pay a call and see if Jeanne was well. She wrote, "Never was a man more surprised when he saw the condition I was in. The smallpox, which could not come out, had fallen on my nose with such force that it was quite black. He thought it was gangrened and was going to fall off. My eyes were like two coals...."[11]

The surgeon was appalled. At once, he railed at the mother-in-law for her gross negligence, only to hear her insist that he leave Jeanne alone and untreated. But while they argued, Jeanne felt only tremendous peace deep within.

"I was not alarmed....For I longed to make a sacrifice of all things and was pleased that God would avenge Himself on that face which had [in the past] betrayed me into so much faithlessness."[12]

When the doctor returned, against the mother-in-law's objections, he bled Jeanne at once. (Bleeding was the means of treating most major illnesses in those times.) Jeanne wrote, "Though the smallpox came out immediately, I am more inclined to show how advantageous it is to resign oneself to God without reserve. For though in appearance He leaves us for a time, it is only to prove and exercise our faith. He never fails us when our need of Him is the more pressing."[13]

This was not the end of her terrible ordeal. "The blackness and swelling of my nose went away, and I believe had they continued to bleed me, I would have felt better, but for want of that I grew worse again. The malady fell into my eyes and inflamed them with such severe pain that I thought I should lose them both. I had violent pains for three weeks. I could not shut my eyes; they were so full of the smallpox, nor open them by reason of the pain. My throat, palate, and gums were likewise so filled with the pox that I could not swallow broth or take nourishment without suffering extremely. My whole body looked leprous. All who saw me said that they had never seen such a shocking spectacle.

"But," she continued, "as to my soul, it was kept in a contentment that cannot be expressed. The hopes of its liberty, by the loss of that beauty, which had so frequently brought me under bondage, rendered me so satisfied and so united to God, that I would not have changed my condition for that of the most happy prince in the world."[14]

The unshakable peace of her abandonment to God would sustain Jeanne through a painful loss. For though her daughter and older son survived, her younger son succumbed to the ravages of the disease.

Following her illness, Jeanne's face and body were hideously scarred. Her husband, horrified that his wife had lost her physical beauty, forced her to use an ointment "to recover [her] complexion and to fill up the hollows of the smallpox." She writes, "I had seen wonderful effects from it upon others, and therefore at first had a mind to try them. But jealous of God's work, I would not allow it. There was a voice in my heart that said, 'If I would have had you fair, I would have left you as you were.'"[15]

Jeanne was moving deeper into her ability to trust divine providence alone. And her next move was, in a way, a declaration that she would, from now on, follow God alone. She wrote that, because of her devotion to God, and against her husband's wishes, "I was obliged to lay aside every remedy, and to go into the air which made the pitting worse, to expose myself in the street when the redness of the smallpox was at its worse, in order to make my humiliation triumph where I had exalted my pride."[16]

Jeanne was moving into depths of God that few people enter, though the way lies open to us all.

Total Abandonment to God

About a year later, Jeanne's daughter died of another illness. In short order, she bore two more children. Not long afterward, Jeanne's husband became very ill, and it soon became apparent he was dying. Despite all the abuses he had heaped on her for years and years, as he lay on his deathbed she went to him and asked, "If there is anything I have ever done to hurt or to wound you—will you forgive me?"

Some hardness in her husband's heart must have broken, because he could only stare at her in disbelief. "No," he said. "You did me no wrong. I did not deserve you."[17]

You may well think that after her husband's death, life got better for Jeanne. Instead, it got worse. For years, she continued to try to find a confessor who could understand and support her. Instead, she was assigned to spiritual leaders who disliked or distrusted her, men who were caught up in the political jockeying that often went on between the religious orders of the day. Some were even jealous of her, because wherever she went, word of her holiness and great devotion spread. People were drawn to her and tried to seek her out, though all she wanted was to live a life withdrawn from the world so she could remain caught up in the constant love of God.

It was through a "providential" meeting that Jeanne met the one man in all of France who seemed to understand her. A Barnabite friar, François LaCombe, not only believed in Jeanne's spiritual wisdom, but also encouraged her to write a small book, which was published in 1685 under the title *A Short and Easy Method of Prayer*. This small work would ignite the hearts of devout men and women throughout Europe and become her most important writing, a true spiritual classic.

And it would also bring about persecution that lasted virtually for the rest of Jeanne's life. In fact, Lacombe—the one true friend she found in her lifetime—was imprisoned by the church for promoting her "heresy." He died two years after her book was published.

In 1688, at forty years of age, Jeanne also was imprisoned. It was there she was forced by spiritual directors to write more. As she wrote, she knew that every word and every phrase would be dissected by heresy hunters in the church and quite likely used against her. It was only by the intervention of Louis XIV's second wife, Madame Maintenon, that her life was spared and she was released.

Finally, Jeanne was allowed to live out the final years of her life in the solitude and peace with God she had craved throughout her entire life. On June 9, 1717, Jeanne Guyon found her way from the shackles of her earthly existence into the loving arms of her beloved heavenly Bridegroom. At long last, she was totally abandoned to the love of God.

Jeanne Guyon's Legacy

To this day, Madame Jeanne Guyon's writings are considered to be among the most powerful and pure Christian writings penned by any woman in history. Great Christian leaders such as John Wesley, Count Zinzendorf, Hudson Taylor, Jessie Penn-Lewis, and Watchman Nee considered this unassuming French woman as one of their true spiritual guides.

Through her life of utter devotion, countless Christians have been taught how to find their own way into the secret place where God abides—within.

Although Madame Guyon did not have the benefit of understanding spiritual warfare or intercession and may have therefore suffered some things unnecessarily, it is clear that the difficulties she suffered were allowed by God to train her in deeper faith. Although she may have overemphasized suffering and embraced martyrdom in an unbalanced way, especially in her younger days, given the culture and times in which she lived, we can easily overlook these imbalances for the gold that is in her writings.

Lessons Learned Through Suffering

Many of us today are looking for spiritual experiences. We run here and there, from one revival to another, seeking spiritual gifts and anointing. But very early in her walk with the Lord, Jeanne Guyon realized that "spiritual experience" can get in the way. It can delay the work of the Holy Spirit in us, which is designed to bring us into what she called "true union" with Him. Writing about our need to seek nothing other than union with God, she says, "[The prayer that brings union with God]…is far above…transports or visions, for visions are in the inferior powers of the soul and cannot produce true union. The soul must not dwell or rely upon them or be impeded by them. They are but favors and gifts, the Giver alone must be our object and aim."[18]

In other words, she warns against overemphasis on visions, because they can be deceiving and can cause pride and vanity to arise. Instead of attending to and loving, extolling, and praising God, we can dwell on our gifts and visions, which can lead us astray.

Madame Guyon also warns against overemphasizing "spiritual feelings" or "ecstasies." She wrote, "Ecstasies arise from a perceptible delight. They may be termed a kind of spiritual sensuality, wherein the soul, by letting it go too far by reason of the sweetness it finds in them, falls imperceptibly into decay."[19]

She even goes on to warn us about "personal words" from God, which so many Christians seek today. "And as to distinct interior words," she warns, "they too are subject to illusion. The enemy can form and counterfeit them. But the immediate Word of God has neither tone nor articulation. It is mute, silent, and unutterable."[20]

Many of her most brilliant insights came to her in her times of loss and desperate weakness. We have already seen how she learned to press into God as a young woman with everything against her. Later in life when she was ill and could no longer visit the poor she loved so dearly, she insisted that it was for love that God allowed even that which is most dear to your soul—your calling, gifting, or anointing—to fall away so that you might be drawn closer to Him alone.

Most importantly, Madame Guyon's life teaches us the wonderful truth about how we too can experience true intimacy with God. She wrote, "It is Jesus Christ Himself, the real and essential Word, who is in the center of the soul that is disposed for receiving Him. Never one moment ceases from His living fruitful, and divine operation."[21]

Her focus was on so loving the Lord and being so captivated by Him that she learned to bear all things with grace and humility. Because the character of Christ shone so strongly inside her, the enemy could never gain a foothold within.

May we who struggle to find God in our everyday lives learn the secret Madame Guyon knew so well. She said that "in all things, and everywhere, she found her proper center, because everywhere she found God."[22]

The hidden treasures Madame Guyon discovered were not found by her alone. She traveled a well-worn path tread upon by many others over the centuries. She was one of many women of the secret place whose lives were completely devoted and fully consecrated to knowing God.

> Lord of my life, let me hear Your call. Separate me from the clamor of other voices and draw me to Yourself. I pray for the grace of having Your divine perspective, so that I can stay by Your side as I walk this journey of faith. Help me understand how You want to use my personal sufferings and grief for the sake of Your kingdom. Preserve me from distractions and worldly viewpoints. I want to grow closer to You every day. Always Yours, amen.

Chapter 4

🌿

Teresa of Avila (1515–1582)

POSSESSED BY GOD'S LOVE

On March 28, 1515, a light flickered in a dark chapter in Spanish history. A tiny girl was born in the small provincial Castilian town of Avila (City of Knights) in southern Spain. She was given the name Teresa de Cepeda y Ahumada.[1]

It was the height of the Spanish Inquisition, in a time in which thousands of Jews were being slaughtered under the reign of Queen Isabella and King Ferdinand. It was also a time of glaring contrasts, for in the midst of such darkness it was also a season of great adventure for Spain. During this century of gold, the Spanish Armada, the conquistadors, and Christopher Columbus were discovering vast stretches of the great unknown.

Teresa of Avila was born for such a time. She became a beacon of light in an uncertain age, a messenger of the secret place of God's presence who modeled Christ as a place of safety, comfort, and certain refuge. Throughout her life, her soul would often be caught away to be with God, where she would be filled with visions of the Lover of her soul. She called Jesus "His Majesty." As she became well-known, her fellow countrymen called her "Teresa of Jesus" and a "Doctor of the Church." First and foremost, she simply loved God.

Childhood Years

Even as a young child, Teresa fiercely and passionately loved the Lord. She was the third child of her mother, the first daughter. Her father had three children by his first marriage and then nine by his second wife. So

Teresa grew up in a large family and most of her siblings were boys.[2] Her father was Don Alonso Sanchez de Cepeda, the wealthy son of a Jewish merchant from Toledo.[3] Nevertheless, he read to his family every night about the great Christian martyrs.

Even as Teresa played childhood games with her little friends, her love for Jesus was never far from her mind. A favorite game was called "monks and nuns." At age seven, she convinced her brother Rodrigo to leave home with her in search of martyrdom at the hands of the Moors. (They were discovered just outside the city gates by their uncle and returned to their parents.)

Teresa was adventuresome, but while other children ran and played, Teresa sought for ways to be alone with her Lord. She prayed often and turned her bedroom at home into a sanctuary where she hung a picture of Christ speaking with the Samaritan woman at the well. Teresa pleaded over and over again in prayer, "Lord, give me of that water that I may not thirst."[4]

Her mother, Doria Beatriz de Ahumada, was not yet twenty years old when Teresa was born. Beatriz spent much of her life ill, lying in bed reading romance novels about a dark, handsome knight. Though her husband did not approve, Beatriz often read these romantic books to her children. By the time of Beatriz's death when Teresa was a young teen, it was clear these melodramas had greatly stimulated her lively imagination.

Consumed with vanity, Teresa flirted with young men and delighted in flattery, jewelry, parties, and clothing. All these things took the place of God in her life.

Life-Changing Experiences

One day, something shocking put an end to everything worldly in Teresa's life—she fell to the floor as if dead. Many believed that she lapsed into a coma, although little proof has been offered. Doctors found no pulse, and all attempts to revive her failed.

Thinking she was dead, the doctors left and a priest anointed her body with holy oil; prayers for the dead were recited and nuns set her body aside to stiffen before burial. The family made funeral preparations and a grave was prepared.

Four days later, her father and her brother witnessed a supernatural fire as it hit her body. Her eyelids began blinking, her arms moved, blood rushed to her face, and she rose from the bed inexplicably. While everyone had been thinking that Teresa was dead, she was having a heavenly vision, seeing her family and communities of nuns.

By the time Teresa turned sixteen, she had been involved in a relationship with a young man of whom her father did not approve. As a result, her father sent Teresa off to live in a strict Spanish convent school where her social life was drastically curtailed. When Teresa entered Avila's Convent of the Incarnation, she began to see that her previous assumptions about life were now behind her, and from that moment she wanted nothing to do with the world.

She was still unwell and in pain, and she convalesced at the convent for several years, continuing to slip in and out of consciousness at times. Sometimes, it appeared as if no life inhabited her body for weeks and she lay on her bed like a beautiful corpse. Yet, each time, Teresa would recover her senses.

Some time later, another dramatic event took place. Teresa had a spiritual encounter with God so intense that she eventually questioned her own sanity. She saw the risen Jesus, not through physical eyes but as in a vision through her heart. She was questioned by the nuns regarding her experience:

"How do you know it was Jesus?"

At the point of tears, she replied, "Because He told me so, over and over again."[5]

Though she had walked through a dark night of the soul with great physical pain and affliction, from this time on it seemed as though the tangible presence of Jesus was with her.

Another even more intense encounter awaited Teresa years later. In her autobiography, Teresa wrote of a shining angel plunging a flaming golden arrow into her heart. He thrust the fiery dart into her heart several times, leaving her with an intense love for God. She says, "When he drew it out I thought he was carrying off with him the deepest part of me; and he left me all on fire with a great love of God."[6] She described the angel as small and very beautiful. Reflecting upon this encounter, she considered that this angel from the Lord was

so illuminated that he had to be one of the very highest of the angels—
the cherubim.[7]

After Teresa's death, her heart was investigated, and it appeared to
have been pierced through the center as if by a dart. As late as 1872,
three physicians who were professors of surgery examined her heart.
They reported that they found the heart still incorrupt (untouched by
decomposition) almost three hundred years later. The heart was punc-
tured on both sides, leaving a perforation through two of its chambers,
verifying what Teresa called the "transverberation" of her heart.[8]

Teresa's superiors were skeptical of her visitations, some accusing
her of being influenced by satanic powers. Nevertheless, Teresa soon
gained a large following as stories of her many encounters spread.
At times while meditating on the Lord, she would be raptured into
His presence. She would go into ecstasy, seeing the Lord Jesus while
receiving the Eucharist. Many writers say that Teresa of Avila had more
documented trances and visions of heaven and the Lord Jesus than any
other person in all of church history. She was a "Christian mystic" in
the truest sense.

Teresa's Life of Prayer

In her early forties, Teresa's inner life acquired an entirely fresh dimension. She spoke about her life in God in an analogy, describing it as
"a new book—I mean of a new life in prayer which God has given to
me."[9] She also described her life of prayer as a garden already planted,
but one in which the plants will die unless they are tended and watered
carefully. She said that such nurturing can be accomplished four ways:
(1) the laborious work of carefully drawing water from the well, (2) the
slightly easier method of using a waterwheel and buckets, (3) by means
of a stream running through the garden, saturating the ground from
beneath, and (4) the best method of all, the rain, the natural source
of water, which entails no work at all on the part of the gardener but
which comes from heaven above.[10]

Teresa used these descriptive terms to paint a vivid picture of the
stages of cultivating a life of prayer. The beginner toils, fetching water
from the well. The effort is entirely his, as he attempts to fill his bucket
with water with which to revive the flowers of the garden. If he persists,

his love for the flowers will exceed the strain of work. The privilege of seeing the arid land blossom will produce humility and endurance that will cause his soul to prosper richly.

In the second stage of prayer, the gardener uses a waterwheel and buckets. He can draw more water for the garden than before with much less effort, but long hours are still required. This kind of prayer can be a time of trial, with weeding and pruning being done within the soul. Here the believer learns the Prayer of Quiet and the beginning of pure contemplation. Effort is still necessary, but the place of striving eases and receptivity is better understood.

The third stage of prayer is when the Lord is more active, providing water by a spring or stream running through the garden. There is now no question of turning back, the delight is too sweet; it is a "glorious folly, a heavenly madness in which true wisdom is acquired."[11] Teresa said this was when Mary and Martha, contemplation and action, are in perfect harmony, though not yet entirely absorbed into God. The soul is free from worries and becomes content. God is now the gardener and the supply of water is abundant.

The last stage of the call to the secret place is where the garden is watered by rain and the gardener has nothing to do but to watch the flowers grow. This is what Madame Jeanne Guyon and many others called the Prayer of Union. The rain brings this union about from heaven itself. After this type of prayer, Teresa found herself in a state of overwhelming tenderness, bathed in tears of joy. At this stage, you know God and you experience great and sweet delight.

Love was what it was all about to Teresa; her life of prayer was the story of an intimate friendship with God. Teresa of Avila and others who have known the secret place have cherished the inner courts of the Lord. They followed in the paths of other forerunners who had gone before them, and their authentic inward journey led to empowered outward works.

Her Call to Reform and Renewal

While at Avila's Convent of the Incarnation, Teresa began noticing worldly habits among the nuns there—gossip, slander, and vanity. Many of the women were more concerned about physical matters than spiritual ones. The sisters occasionally indulged in irreverence and disorder, which the house's lax rules allowed. Teresa felt that few of them understood her visions or wanted to achieve a high level of intimacy with God. These concerns formed the basis for her lifelong effort to reform the Carmelite Order. With little support from her peers and no guidance from others, Teresa began searching for a way to be of greater practical use to God. And out of her hidden life in God she found what she needed to cause vital changes.

When Teresa requested that the Catholic Church permit her to live in poverty and serve the poor, a fierce controversy arose. At the time, women were considered so "radically inferior" to men, that the thought of a lone woman roaming the countryside having spiritual encounters roused the objections of more than a few religious authorities. In fact, Teresa herself held reservations about women, and was once quoted as saying, "I would not want you to be womanish in anything, nor would I want you to be like women, but like strong men. For if you do what is in your power, the Lord will make you so strong that you will astonish men." Teresa continued, "I am not at all like women...for I have a robust spirit."[12]

In her book *Teresa of Avila,* Carmelite nun Tessa Bielecki suggests that such statements from Teresa served two purposes: (1) to present her opinion on feminine weakness, and (2) to downplay her own femininity so as to avoid attention from the Inquisition and its scrutiny of women in the church.[13]

In 1562, when Teresa reached the age of forty-seven, she founded a new convent. There she spent many years teaching young women about God and her "reformed way of life."[14] She wrote two works, *The Way of Perfection* and *Meditations on the Song of Songs.* Later in April 1567, the Father General of the Carmelite Order gave Teresa permission to found more new convents abroad. In August of the same year, she took to the road and met a man called John of the Cross while founding Medina del Campo. Teresa eventually cofounded three convents together with John of the Cross, whom she considered her spiritual advisor. Teresa planted convents at Pastrana and Toledo in 1569, Salamanca in 1570, Alba de Tormes in 1571, and in several other locations over the years.

After Teresa established Alba of Tormes, religious authorities suddenly pulled her away from her tasks abroad and placed Teresa back at the Convent of the Incarnation, the place where she began her life as a nun. Despite her objections, she received the title of "prioress" for one term in the convent. Though she had spent many years there previously, Teresa noticed a severe lack of enthusiasm for her return. She was disliked and unwelcome. To combat the division and rebellion, she invited her good friend John of the Cross to take the position of chaplain, figuring that spiritual guides and friends are needed by all.

Friends and Guides to Teresa

Thanks to the combined efforts of Teresa and John of the Cross, the convent soon returned to order and harmony. Teresa felt God Himself had helped them through John, in effect disguising Himself as a man as He also had done with Moses' burning bush. John of the Cross became the first Carmelite friar, a mystical poet, and a Doctor of the Church.

When Teresa's term as prioress was completed, together she and John of the Cross launched out again and founded another convent, this time at Segovia. Two were better than one, and over the years their teamwork yielded excellent results.

In April 1575, Teresa met the man who would become her closest friend and advisor, Jeronimo Gracian. She called Gracian "my helper" and prayed that he would assist her in the Carmelite reform. Teresa once wrote, "I have been suffering from these Fathers of the Cloth for more than seventeen years with not a soul to help me, and it was too much for my poor strength—I did not know how to bear it any longer."[15]

Later that year, persecution as a result of her reform efforts escalated to new heights. A vengeful princess who had twice been expelled from one of Teresa's convents for outrageous behavior denounced her to the Inquisition. Betrayal followed denunciation as the Father General of the Carmelites, a man named Rubeo, originally a great encourager of Teresa's work, switched sides and began to disapprove publicly of her ministry. All Teresa's relationships, especially those with men, came under fire. Ambiguous rumors about sexuality slandered her chaste love for Gracian, and villains working for the Inquisition kidnapped

John of the Cross and imprisoned him for nine months. The leaders of the Inquisition eventually ordered Teresa to relocate to a convent of her choosing in Castile. She lost much approval and popularity, as her life's work, her message, and the reformation efforts became vulnerable. Nevertheless, her spirit continued to burn for God.

The Interior Castle

In 1577, between June 2 and November 29, Teresa wrote her most famous work on prayer, called *The Interior Castle,* known in Spanish as *Las Moradas* (The Mansions). This now-classic book is the most profound of her mystical works; it is based on the analogy of the journey and transformation of a silkworm into a beautiful butterfly. *Las Moradas* outlines a perfect balance between the inner and the outer works of the Holy Spirit in the believer's life.

The Interior Castle was written following an extremely vivid vision, which portrayed the soul of man as on a progressive journey through a castle with many rooms. John 14:2a tells us that, "My father's house has many rooms." So it is in the life of each disciple. We are temples of the living God, and He has taken up royal residence within us. In allegorical language, Teresa wrote about seven rooms that an ardent believer passes through on the journey to perfect union with God. She said, "The figure is used to describe the whole course of the mystical life—the soul's progress from the first mansion to the seventh and its transformation from an imperfect and sinful creature into the Bride of the Spiritual Marriage."[16]

The first mansion or room typifies the earliest and most basic stages of the Christian walk. Those at this stage know God but still retain much of the world's influence. Numerous temptations pull at the soul, which is unable to appreciate the beauty of the castle or to find any peace with it. To progress onto the second room, one must begin to learn the lessons of humility.

To enter the second mansion requires a person to understand the need to respond to God's call, desiring to leave the world behind and gradually coming nearer to the place where His Majesty (God) dwells. His beckoning call can be heard more often, more endearingly, more convictingly, and more clearly than ever before. The seeker must begin to understand that the One whose voice is calling from the deep is supposed to be his or her best friend forever, from that time forward.

In the third mansion of the Interior Castle, the seeker has developed a measure of discipline and virtue in life. But when reason steps in to replace love and virtuous living and God's grace, lessons of mercy are in order. Nothing can be received from Him without His great love, grace, and mercy.

The fourth room is captivating, for it is here that the mystical dimension or Spirit of revelation is released. The voice of the soul becomes diminished, and the waters of life rise higher. Here the seeker enters deeper into the Prayer of Quiet and finds consolation from God Himself. This sense of intimacy with the beloved Bridegroom entices the Bride to proceed forward into the fifth room, where the metaphor of the silkworm is introduced. Here the imagery of metamorphosis and the power of transformation help us to embrace the lessons of death to self and life unto God. Seekers now become spiritual lovers, and betrothal is now the goal.

The sixth mansion is one of growing intimacy with the Lover of one's soul, in addition to increasing levels of tribulation, trials, and times of testing. But also in this chamber a flood of heavenly favors from God is bestowed upon His Beloved, which intensifies the holy desire for oneness with the Lord. The one who has pursued God so passionately becomes clothed in the garments of His presence.

The seventh and final room in Teresa's extraordinary Interior Castle is that of Spiritual Marriage itself, where complete transformation, perfect peace, and dwelling in the King's wonderful presence are realized. Here Teresa wrote, "That union is like two wax candles that are joined so that the light now given off is but one. Or it is as if a tiny streamlet enters the sea from which it will find no way of separating itself (nor want to) from the sea of God's immense great love."[17]

No one who makes the inward journey to the place of intimate communion with the Lord will ever be the same again. That innermost chamber of our hearts where one meets Him face-to-face is not only a sanctuary of sweet fellowship, a blissful fulfillment of holy desire, but also a place of glorious transformation. Like St. Teresa's silkworm, those who enter that realm as humble, earthbound souls, emerge as beautiful butterflies, with their souls ready to take wing and soar.

Teresa's Legacy

We each leave a shadow in this life that will fall upon others. That is what happens when people walk in the light of God's love; the shadow of His presence is cast upon others from our lives. Teresa's legacy was that the secret place became her dwelling place, despite poor health that only became increasingly fragile as she grew older. (Her eventual death surprised very few people.)

An acting Provincial called Antonio of Jesus sent her on an unexpected journey to Alba de Tormes. He was jealous, cold, and insensitive to Teresa's ill health and physical needs. She humbly obeyed his orders, contrary to the advice of friends. Hunger and terrible pain marked her journey. On October 4, 1582, after finally reaching Alba de Tormes, the ailing Teresa of Jesus died from exhaustion and near starvation. With a heart of obedience, humility, and the completed work of His Majesty, she was ushered into sweet comfort and eternal heavenly bliss.

Perhaps the best way to sum up the life of Teresa is in her own words written toward the end of her life. Listen to her through them, for they describe this mystical poet's great trust.

> Let nothing trouble you,
> Let nothing scare you,
> All is fleeing,
> God alone is unchanging,
> Patience,
> Everything obtains.
> Who possesses God nothing wants.
> God alone suffices.[18]

Chapter 5

⚜

Fanny Crosby (1820-1915)

SONGS FROM
THE SECRET PLACE

Fanny Crosby was the queen of gospel music during the late nineteenth and early twentieth century, capturing a vision of God's secret place in thousands of hymns, which continue to be sung by God's people today. Her hymns still ignite spiritual passion from east and west, and when they were first published, hymns such as "Pass Me Not, O Gentle Savior" and "Saved By Grace" were sung by believers in Arab nations, Germany, and even by Queen Victoria of England and the Prince and Princess of Wales.

Noted hymn writer and evangelical singer George Stebbins said of Fanny, "There is no character in the history of the American Sunday school and evangelistic hymns so outstanding as that of Fanny Crosby, and it is quite as true that more of her hymns than of any other writer of the nineteenth century have found an abiding place in the hearts of Christians the world over. So evident is this that there is a fragrance about her very name that no other has.

"There was probably no other writer in her day who appealed more to the valid experience of the Christian life or who expressed more sympathetically the deep longings of the human heart than Fanny Crosby."[1]

In her prime, Fanny Crosby was considered of equal stature with colleagues D. L. Moody and Ira Sankey. She was renowned as a preacher and lecturer, and spent much of her life involved in home missions. People would line up for blocks to hear her speak.

356

She didn't start writing until she was in her forties; nevertheless, she wrote about nine thousand hymns. Her style was revolutionary for her day. Instead of mimicking the traditional, old-fashioned hymn language, she expressed thoughts and prayers in common words that touched the heart of worship in believers. Her obvious passion for God drew the lost into His kingdom.

Fanny also composed more than a thousand poems, and she played the harp and organ in concert. So many accomplishments seem incredible for any one person, but all the more when you realize that this woman was blind from infancy.

A Flowing River of Spiritual Expression

How was such fiery passion kindled in Fanny Crosby? How did she discover this river of spiritual expression and experience it in person? Let's journey together through the milestones of Fanny Crosby's life in search of some of the keys God used to unlock the secret place within her heart.

Fanny was born into a rural family that was fiercely proud of its history and heritage. Their lineage could be traced back to William Brewster, who sailed on the Mayflower in 1620 and was a founding father of Plymouth Plantation. Fanny's grandfather, Sylvanus, a hardworking farmer, fought in the War of 1812. Mercy, his oldest daughter, married a man named John Crosby, who was nearly as old as Sylvanus and probably a distant cousin. John and Mercy lived with her parents to help on the farm. Mercy was twenty years old when she delivered Frances Jane (Fanny) Crosby into the world on March 24, 1820.

Fanny's childhood home was in Gayville, located in the town of Southeast, in rural Putnam County, New York. There, eleven families made up the Crosby clan, and all who lived in the Southeast community wore Puritan-style clothing. Women's dresses were black with full skirts and white collars and cuffs. The community held strict Calvinistic beliefs, which included the sovereignty of God's grace, divine predestination, eternal security of the believer, total depravity of mankind, and the supreme authority of the Word of God. Children learned long passages of Scripture, received just enough education to read and write, and did farm work alongside their parents.

Damaged Vision

Fanny was about a month old when her parents noticed something was wrong with her eyes. Medical help was difficult to find in their little community, so when the family found a man who claimed to be a physician, they entrusted Fanny to his care. He placed hot poultices on the baby's inflamed eyes and told the parents the poultices would draw the infection out. The infection did leave, but Fanny's eyes were left with ugly white scars, and her vision was damaged. As a result she had little more than some light perception.

A second tragedy happened to the Crosby family that same year. In November 1820, Fanny's father, John, died from exposure after working in the fields in cold, rainy weather. To supplement the family's income, twenty-one-year-old Mercy had to take work as a maidservant for a wealthy family nearby. Mercy's grandmother Eunice cared for Fanny.

Grandmother Eunice took a great interest in her granddaughter, and the two became very close during the first five years of Fanny's life. With the passage of time, it became painfully apparent Fanny would not regain her sight, and Eunice was determined to give Fanny every advantage in training she could think of. She could not bear to see Fanny going through life being treated as a helpless invalid, utterly dependent on others.

Fanny's education began as she sat with her family in the evenings listening as a family member read by the fireplace such works as *The Iliad, The Odyssey, Paradise Lost, The Tales of Robin Hood,* and the Bible. Eunice became her granddaughter's eyes, describing her surroundings to her in careful detail. Because Fanny could at times distinguish certain hues, Eunice was able to help bring definition to colors.

She taught Fanny in a very holistic manner. If she used the word "bristle," for example, she would place in Fanny's hands an object with bristles, to correspond to the meaning of the word. When she taught Fanny about birds, she would include the song of a particular bird, its size, shape, coloring, and the shape of its wings. She taught Fanny botany and every subject she knew. Grandmother and granddaughter would take walks together, and Eunice would describe the different types of trees and flowers. Fanny was taught by smell and touch; the leaves she knew by "handling and remembering."[2]

After thoroughly teaching her granddaughter, Eunice would test her. She would gather a pile of leaves, and one by one place them in Fanny's hands. Then she would ask, "Now, what tree is this one from?"[3] Fanny absorbed everything and developed an incredible memory and an amazing talent to communicate through description.

Her grandmother taught her about God as well. Eunice had the rare gift of seeing God in all of creation; to her, creation was a mirror that reflected spiritual truth. In all their walks together in the woods and through the fields, Eunice illuminated the idea that she and Fanny were not alone, but God was walking with them. She taught Fanny that every bird, tree, and flower had been designed by God to serve His plans and purposes. Eunice taught Fanny about the loving nature of a wonderful God.

Fanny's mother, Mercy, continued laboring outside the home to earn money to support Fanny. Unfortunately, she would return home at night too tired to spend much time with her much-beloved daughter. When Mercy became weighed down with weariness and worry about her daughter's future, Eunice would offer strength and support. She would come close, place her hand on Mercy's shoulder, and recite a part of a favorite hymn, or she'd quote a favorite old adage of Puritan leader Cotton Mather: "What can't be cured can be endured."

Grandmother Eunice Plants Seeds of Faith

Grandmother Eunice loved gathering children together to read the Bible, explaining its stories in language that they could understand. "The stories of the Holy Book came from her lips and entered my heart and took deep root there," said Fanny later.[4] Eunice often reminded the children about "a kind heavenly Father who sent His only son, Jesus Christ, into this world to be the Savior and friend of all mankind."[5]

Eunice was a "firm believer in prayer," and understood it was the key to a successful Christian life. She considered prayer a "close communication with her loving Savior."[6] Everything she believed about God and the importance and place of prayer was freely poured into Fanny. Grandmother taught little Fanny how to call on God for every need, and how to trust in His goodness, certain authority, and power to accomplish every good work and to care for every need.

This is how Fanny learned to trust Jesus Christ, how to rest and rejoice in Him. This wise grandmother's classroom imparted to Fanny a deep faith and an ability to bear her sufferings and difficulties with great grace and joy, knowing that God was always walking with her, leading and guiding and loving her.

The little Southeast community church lacked an organ, and the congregation did not sing hymns that would be familiar in most of today's church services. Like the early Puritans, they did not believe in hymns of human composition. They used the "music" of the Psalms, which they felt had been dictated from God to David, and they chanted them without any musical accompaniment. The only person in the church with a copy of the hymn was a deacon who stood at the podium or desk. He would recite a line of the psalm and then the congregation would repeat it after him until they had recited the entire psalm.

This form of worship created a hunger in Fanny's heart for greater expression. To her it was lifeless. Fanny loved singing and fed her soul listening to the music of nature. She wanted to experience all that life had to offer and did not consider herself to be different from other children, except when someone would make a comment to that effect. She was a happy and contented child. Eunice and Mercy would let Fanny play outside at night with the other children of the town within the vicinity of their house. For blind Fanny, playing at night was not anything unusual.

When Fanny was five years old, Mercy took her to the Columbia University School of Medicine, in New York City, to be examined by Dr. Valentine Mott, considered one of the top surgeons in the United States. He confirmed Mercy's worst fears, that the "doctor" who had treated Fanny's eyes had done irreparable damage. Mercy comforted her daughter by assuring her that God had a special plan and purpose for her life. On the way home, Fanny had an experience with God.

"As I sat there on the deck amid the glories of the departing day, the low murmur of the waves soothed my soul into a delightful peace. Their music was translated into tones that were like a human voice...."[7] The experience touched Fanny deeply.

Mercy landed a new housekeeping job that required mother and daughter to move six miles away from their present home. Everything changed for Fanny, because her mother was much more apt to apply the rod freely for correction, in contrast to Grandmother's gentler approach. Nevertheless, Mercy truly loved her daughter and cared for her needs as well as she could. Fanny learned to climb trees "like a squirrel," rode horseback, and climbed stone walls.

Eunice visited often and continued teaching Fanny many things. As a blind person, Fanny seemed to be able to do almost anything a sighted person could. Still, she went through times of discouragement. She would ask God "whether, in all His great world, he had not some little place for me."

In response, Fanny heard Him reply, "Do not be discouraged, little girl. You shall someday be happy and useful, even in your blindness."[8]

Fanny's First Poem

Fanny composed her first work when she was eight years old; it reads as follows:

> Oh, what a happy child I am,
> Although I cannot see!
> I am resolved that in this world
> Contented I will be!
> How many blessings I enjoy
> That other people don't!
> So weep or sigh because I'm blind,
> I cannot—nor I won't.

A year later, Mercy acquired another new position, and she moved with Fanny to Ridgefield, Connecticut, where the little girl was destined to receive another installment in her training. Mrs. Hawley, the landlady who cared for Fanny while Mercy was at work, made it a goal for Fanny to memorize the entire Bible.

Fanny learned a few chapters each week. She mastered Genesis, Exodus, Leviticus, Numbers, and the four Gospels by the end of the year. Within two years, she had also memorized many of the Psalms, all of Proverbs, Ruth, and the Song of Solomon. She carried on this task throughout the rest of her life. Gradually, she eliminated the need for someone to read the Bible to her; she had absorbed every word of it into her mind and heart.

Mrs. Hawley also included selections from secular works for Fanny to memorize, including various poems of the day. Fanny was introduced to the hymns of Charles Wesley and Isaac Watts when she would occasionally visit a Methodist church, and she loved their majestic sound.

As Fanny reached adolescence, she became increasingly troubled about her handicap. She began competing with her friends, trying to prove what a blind person could do. She also spent many hours thinking, poring over the Scriptures. She felt more and more alone. Finally one night, she was able to talk to her grandmother about this ache in her heart. They prayed together, and Fanny remembered the night. It "was beautiful. I crept toward the window, and through the branches of a giant oak that stood just outside, the soft moonlight fell upon my head like the benediction of an angel, while I knelt there and repeated over and over these simple words: 'Dear Lord, please show me how I can learn like other children.'"[9] She felt an immediate release from the anxiety that had weighed her down. It was "changed to the sweet consciousness that my prayer would be answered in due time."[10]

"By the Grace of God, I Will"

On a summer evening in 1831, Fanny and her grandmother would be together one last time. Eunice had become very ill and knew she was about to die. She told Fanny, "Grandma's going home." In her soft, frail voice she asked, "Tell me, my darling, will you meet Grandma in our Father's house on high?"

Fanny responded, "By the grace of God, I will." Eunice drew Fanny to herself one last time, and they prayed their last prayer together. Eunice Crosby died a short time later, at the age of 53.[11]

Those early years laid the foundation stones of preparation in Fanny's life. She discovered a wonderful singing talent, learned to play the guitar, became an accomplished horsewoman, and developed a reputation as a storyteller. But where she really shone was in her poetry, which enabled her to burst into fulfillment of God's purpose for her life.

At age fourteen, a wonderful door of opportunity opened. Fanny enrolled in the New York Institution for the Blind, where she would spend the next twenty years of her life. There she was educated in English grammar, science, music, history, philosophy, astronomy, and political economy; and she learned Braille, although she struggled with it. (Her fingertips had become callused from playing guitar, which made it difficult to feel the raised letters.) She memorized the complete text of Brown's Grammar.

Fanny's enthusiasm for poetry continued to grow, but her teachers at the Institution felt she was letting this ability "puff up her head." One of her instructors reprimanded her, telling her "not to think too much about rhymes and the praises that come from them." At first she was hurt, but then, "through tears, she composed herself, threw her arms around his neck, and kissed his forehead. 'You have talked to me as my father would have if he were living. And I thank you for it.'"[12]

She continued to grow in her education and various talents and skills, and at the age of twenty was considered the institution's most promising student. She showed such promise in her poetic talent that she was given a poetic composition teacher named Hamilton Murray. Mr. Murray played an invaluable role in her training. He gave her long poems to memorize and taught her the use of rhyme, rhythm, and meter, as well as encouraged her to imitate well-known poets.

Fanny absorbed the rudiments and refinements of poetry, and learned to compose quickly. This thorough training was the foundation stone that would later enable her to compose as many as twelve poems a day. She became known as "the blind poetess."

Visitors to the institute would be shown the works of its brightest students. US President John Tyler, New York Governor William Henry Seward, and Count Bertrand, Napoleon's field marshal, were just a few who visited. During her time with the school, first as student, then later as instructor, Fanny contributed to various New York poetry columns and published four books of poetry. She knew her recognition as "the blind poetess" was gaining much-needed attention for the institute and for the needs of the blind, and she was delighted to serve in this way, harboring no particular aspirations of attaining a greater personal platform.

Called to the Secret Place

In 1848, cholera broke out and Fanny contracted the disease. She recovered, but her close brush with death made her think about dying. Would she be ready to meet God? She had believed in God and His goodness but had never experienced conversion. During this time of seeking and soul-searching, Fanny dreamed she visited a dying man. The man asked her if she would meet him in heaven after their deaths. She responded in the dream that by God's help, she would—the same response she had given her grandmother. The dream ended as the man said, "Remember, you promised a dying man!"

The experience drew Fanny to a deeper place of seeking God. She attended revival meetings and went to the altar twice, feeling nothing had changed. However, the third time she went to the altar, something happened.

Bonnie C. Harvey, author of the book *Fanny Crosby: Woman of Faith,* describes what occurred: "During the fifth verse of 'Alas and Did My Savior Bleed?' Fanny prayed, 'Here Lord, I give myself away. 'Tis all that I can do.' Suddenly Fanny felt 'my very soul was flooded with celestial light.' She jumped to her feet, shouting, 'Hallelujah! Hallelujah!' She said, 'For the first time I realized that I had been trying to hold the world in one hand and the Lord in the other.'"[13]

Fanny's life was dramatically changed. She called it her "November experience." From that point on, her life was totally dedicated to God. A desire to do His will alone consumed her, and all other desires fell away. It was out of this experience that many of her later hymns were born. One unpublished poem, called "Valley of Silence," explains more than any other of Fanny's writings her mystical experience of November 20, 1850. She wrote this poem two months before she died:

> I walk down the Valley of Silence,
> Down the dim, voiceless valley alone,
> And I hear not the fall of a footstep
> Around me, save God's and my own;
> And the hush of my heart is as holy
> As hours when angels have flown.
> Long ago I was weary of voices
> Whose music my heart could not win,
> Long ago I was weary of noises
> That fretted my soul with their din;
> Long ago I was weary with places,

When I met but the human and sin.
Do you ask what I found in this Valley?
'Tis my trysting place with the Divine,
For I fell at the feet of the Holy,
And above me a voice said, "Be Mine."
And there rose from the depth of my spirit,
The echo, "My heart shall be Thine."
Do you ask how I live in this Valley?
I weep and I dream and I pray;
But my tears are so sweet as the dewdrops
That fall from the roses in May,
And my prayer, like a perfume from censers,
Ascendeth to God night and day.

The sweetness and nearness of God is so evident in this poem. Fanny surely knew the call to the secret place. She moved forward with her life, married, and had a child (who, sadly, died in infancy). She met presidents and befriended influential people. God blessed Fanny by linking her with songwriters who could open doors to share her hymns with the masses of Christians who needed to have their faith bolstered.

Living during the time when the national Sunday school movement was sweeping the nation, when mission societies were proliferating, and when a revival called the Second Great Awakening was shaking America, Fanny found plenty of opportunities to put her well-honed talent to work. Her years of preparation through hardship and poverty had refined her heart into gold that was now ready to be poured out into the world.

Gold Poured Out to the World

How did she find the secret place in God? From which treasures of her life experiences can we glean and learn? Let's now examine some of these treasures, take them into our own hearts, and deeply cherish them.

For a child to have a mentor is truly God's gift, and Fanny had a wonderful mentor in her grandmother Eunice. Eunice taught her to believe in the goodness and faithfulness of God. Believing is the antidote to bitterness, resentment, and fear. Fanny literally was led by the hand

and walked through pastures, woods, and valleys as she was taught of God's faithfulness in creation. Grandmother Eunice taught young Fanny to look for and find God in every place and every situation. He is always there, but we have to be taught to expect to find Him.

The Bible tells us to renew our minds by meditating on the Scripture. Fanny certainly did. In order to find God's secret place, we must discover markers to point the way, and reading and meditating on God's Word permits our Father to speak to us about what's important to Him. He longs to share His secrets. The power, illumination, and transformation that come to us through God's Word are beyond description.

Fanny associated with the poor in spirit, slum dwellers, alcoholics, and prisoners. She gave herself to a life of simplicity, giving away money and aid to those in need. She knew God's heart for the poor and needy, and in embracing them she embraced Him. One of the keys to the secret place is cultivating a tender heart for the alien, the orphan, and the widow.

Fanny did not equate giftedness with godliness, and she was never "holier than thou." She freely gave away the gift that God deposited within her. She wrote under at least 204 pen names, and she wrote verses for friends who published them with their own melodies. No one actually knows just how many hymns and poems she wrote. It did not matter to her who got the credit, as long as God could be glorified.

Fanny understood the power of distraction and would purposely take time alone with God in the long night watches. Every day, she found a place to be alone with Him, even when it meant sleepless nights. He was her rest and peace.

Fanny learned how to apply herself, employing all her energies to realize the full maturity and effectiveness of her gifting. She harnessed the strength of her mind to the Spirit of God, thus enabling her mind to become an effective tool. She brought her mental ability into the secret place with her.

By learning to embrace criticism from others, Fanny remained humble all her life. She established a lifestyle of selflessness, not giving room in her heart to pride. She learned to receive from God and others, whether in gentleness or in conflict, and she knew how to ask God to make her heart right within her.

The grace of God is boundless, and His Truth is unending. We are on a journey in which we never "arrive" until the day we enter heaven's gates. Fanny Crosby is there now, beholding His face. God's gift through her is still giving life and hope to countless people, continuing to light the way to that secret place in God. In Fanny's own words:

> Savior, more than life to me,
> I am clinging, clinging close to Thee;
> Let Thy precious blood applied
> Keep me ever near Thy side.
> Every day, every hour,
> Let me feel Thy cleansing power;
> May Thy tender love to me
> Bind me closer, closer, Lord to Thee.

Chapter 6

Susanna Wesley (1669–1742)

THE MOTHER OF REVIVAL

When more than two thousand Puritan pastors were threatened to stop practicing their faith by English Royalist officials under King Charles II, Dr. Samuel Annesley flatly refused. The consequences of opposing the king of England were harsh. Samuel was evicted from his clerical position and harassed. Still, he never wavered from his courageous convictions. Born into this tumultuous time was Samuel's impressionable youngest daughter, Susanna.

England had become embattled in a religious civil war. Royalists had fought for King Charles I and the Church of England against the Parliamentarians who sided with the Puritans, a religious sect that had separated from the Church of England. The Parliamentarians emerged as the initial victors, but a few years later, the Royalist army with King Charles II regained power. Consequently, in 1662 legislation was passed forcing all ministers to conform to the practices and beliefs of the Church of England. This legislation was called the Act of Uniformity. When two thousand Puritan pastors refused to conform, the Great Ejection followed.

After ten years, King Charles II recanted somewhat and decided to permit a certain amount of religious freedom. Samuel then started a new ministry, reaching out to the poor, the fatherless, and the widows in London. Growing up in the midst of these events, Susanna's heart was imprinted with the basic principles of Christianity.

A Mother of Superior Understanding

Susanna Annesley was born in London on January 20, 1669, the twenty-fifth child of Dr. and Mrs. Annesley. (Of that number, records show only seven surviving to maturity.) The Annesleys were deeply devout Puritans, wholeheartedly committed to raising their children to fear the Lord. Susanna's mother was deeply loved and honored by her husband. She appears to have been a woman of superior understanding and earnest, consistent piety, devoted to promoting the religious welfare of all her children.

Samuel found great fulfillment in educating people in the ways of the Lord. He could not remember a time when he did not know Him. At five years of age, he began reading twenty chapters of the Bible every day. After graduating from Oxford University in 1644, he had become the pastor of a church in the county of Kent, where the people expressed their gratitude for his ministry. Later, he moved the family to London.

Susanna grew into a very accomplished young lady. She pursued the study of many subjects, including other religious beliefs and the political views of the day. Her parents provided her with a thorough knowledge of the Bible and a well-rounded education, although it was uncommon for girls to be formally educated in those days. Susanna excelled. She studied logic, metaphysics, philosophy, and theology. She also became proficient in French and in English grammar. Digging deeply into the religious controversy that had engulfed England, Susanna entered into debates alongside her father and his guests as they discussed these difficult matters. Before she was thirteen years old, Susanna already had studied the entire controversy between the Church of England and the Dissenters, and she had gained the respect of her elders for her opinions and insights.

As it turned out, having been raised in a family that was considered to be radical in its beliefs and uncompromising in its principles gave Susanna a solid foundation that would serve her well in the years to come.

Susanna met her future husband, whose name was also Samuel, in her parent's home. He was often a guest of her father and participated in the discussions in which Susanna took part. Samuel Wesley also came from a long family line of nonconformists, and his father was a minister who had been affected by the Great Ejection of 1662.

Samuel Wesley's father had held meetings in secret and had been imprisoned four times. He had died at the age of forty-two, when Samuel was quite young, and his son had been sent to various academies in London. During these years, he became convinced that he should join the established Church of England, so he had turned away from his Puritan roots.

At the time he made this decision, he and Susanna were probably discussing these matters together. Separately but simultaneously, they both made the same decision to join the Church of England, and in late 1688 or early 1689, they were married.

Love and Commitment

Samuel and Susanna had very different temperaments. Samuel was outgoing and jovial. Unfortunately, he was also a poor money manager, which created great difficulty for the couple throughout their life together. Susanna was introverted and quiet; she gave little attention to humor. She was very methodical in her approach to life, and though she was very passionate, she kept her emotions in check. Despite their strong personalities and great differences, Susanna and Samuel loved each other very much. Samuel lavished praise and respect upon Susanna. In the years of their marriage, their love and commitment for each other was greatly tested.

Two years after their marriage, in 1690, their first son, Samuel, was born. Then came Susanna in 1691. Emilia followed in 1692. Susanna's body became afflicted with rheumatism and other ailments because of the physical strain of her pregnancies being so close together. In 1694, little Susanna died, which must have been terribly painful for Susanna and Samuel. Twin boys were born at the end of 1694, named Annesley and Jedediah, but both died after only one month. In 1695, Sukey was born. Her given name was Susanna, after her deceased sister. Child number seven came along in 1696, named Mary, and then Hetty came in 1697.

At this time, the growing family received a new ministerial assignment. It promised to bring an increase in salary, and the rectory was supposed to be larger and more suitable for their large family. Actually, it turned out to be a hardship. The house and outbuildings were in great need of repair, Samuel's debts multiplied, and children were being added to their family at the rate of at least one per year. This period of time brought them to the brink of marital crisis.

A second set of twins was born in 1701, a boy and a girl. The infants must have died shortly after their birth, because they never were named. After baby Anne was born late in 1702, their financial difficulty increased even more, causing a marital crisis that climaxed with Samuel leaving Susanna and the children for a period of time. As Samuel was on his way to London, he learned that their house had caught fire. He returned home immediately, and the realization that he nearly lost his entire family brought him to his senses. He remained at home, repaired the house, and resumed his clerical duties. He and Susanna made a fresh start, forgiving each other and putting the whole difficult time behind them.

John Wesley came along in 1703, followed by his brother Charles in 1705. Both John and Charles entered the world in a very fragile state, but as time passed their health improved.

The Wesley family endured many hateful acts at the hands of the people from the surrounding area. Much of the general population did not want to have anything to do with God or the Church, and many people vented their feelings by rampaging with impunity. The Wesleys were threatened, their fields were set ablaze, their cattle were attacked, and the children were often put to bed at night to the sound of gunfire in the streets. The children were afraid and rarely went outside. Another one of the children died.

Adding to the family's difficulty, a creditor had Samuel imprisoned for a debt of thirty pounds, which forced Susanna and the children to live on the earnings from their tiny dairy and the scant amount of money she had. Through these terribly sorrowful and difficult times, Samuel was impressed by his wife's resilient and steadfast spirit.

God Spared Their Son

A terrible fire occurred in the dead of winter in February 1709, probably set by mean-spirited local townspeople. Not only did it ravage their possessions, but it also almost took little John Wesley's life. He was saved by a neighbor who rescued him from the second story. Susanna lost all her books, her teaching papers, and her family treasures. Nevertheless, she was grateful to God for sparing her son's life.

After the fire, Samuel and Susanna, along with two-year-old Charles, went to live with one of their few friends. Their nineteenth and final child, Kezia, was born at this time. The rest of the children were sent to live in various homes until Susanna and Samuel could reestablish their household. Susanna learned the difficult lesson of trusting God completely in the face of disaster and years of real physical and emotional need. She did not surrender to despair but found strength in her sense of abandonment to God's care. Knowing that she was the Lord's, she believed that He could do with her life as He pleased.

Samuel completed repairs on their home, this time with fire-resistant bricks, and the Wesley family was reunited. Still, the neighboring people clung to their harsh judgments against them and continued to wish them harm.

Although 1712 began in hardship, Samuel Wesley felt it necessary to attend a religious convocation in London. Besides bringing even more financial stress upon the family with his travel and lodging expenses and having to pay a curate to care for his parish, it also meant he would be absent from his family for months on end.

While he was away, five of the children came down with smallpox. In addition, the temporary curate began working to undermine Samuel's position, purposely preaching about the evils of indebtedness, knowing full well that it was an unresolved issue in Samuel Wesley's life. Susanna was in a difficult place. The church lacked genuine spiritual guidance, her husband was being openly disrespected, and she disagreed with this man's policy of having only one church service on Sunday.

With her children's welfare in mind, Susanna decided to hold meetings in their kitchen on Sunday evenings. She included not only her children but the servants also. They sang psalms and read prayers. She preached a sermon taken from Samuel's library. Word spread into the community concerning these meetings, and soon there were thirty to forty people in attendance. She searched for the most impressive sermons she could find and read them to her gathering of hungry hearts.

Soon, the attendance grew to standing room only—about two hundred people.

Susanna also began meeting individually with her children to determine the condition of their souls and their commitment to God.

Susanna informed Samuel about the meetings in a letter, and Samuel responded, expressing many concerns. He was unsure they should continue. Susanna wrote back in a very straightforward manner, going head-to-head with each one of his arguments with clarity and humility. Then Samuel gave his approval, and the meetings continued, enabling both the family and community to experience the grace of God together.

Stop the Meetings

Susanna's success unleashed the fury anger and jealousy of the curate, Mr. Inman. He wrote a letter to Samuel, accusing Susanna of holding illegal religious meetings. Afraid her gatherings would bring disapproval from the church and ruin his future ministerial career, Samuel changed his stance and asked Susanna to stop the meetings. Susanna's reply to this latest challenge is worthy of quoting, at least in part:

> I shall not inquire how it was possible that you should be prevailed on by the senseless clamors of two or three of the worst of your parish, to condemn what you so lately approved....It is plain in fact that this one thing has brought more people to church that ever anything did in so short a time. We used not to have above twenty to twenty-five at evening service, whereas we have now between two and three hundred; which are more than ever came before to hear Inman in the morning....Now, I beseech you, weigh all these things in an impartial balance: on the one side, the honor of almighty God, the doing much good to many souls, and the friendship of the best among whom we live; on the other, the senseless objections of a few scandalous persons...and when you have duly considered all things, let me have your positive determination....If you do, after all, think fit to dissolve this assembly, do not tell me that you desire me to do it, for that will not satisfy my conscience; but send me your positive command, in such full and express terms as may

absolve me from all guilt and punishment, for neglecting this opportunity of doing good, when you and I shall appear before the great and awful tribunal of our Lord Jesus Christ.[1]

Fire was burning in her soul, but wisdom kept her on sound footing. There is no record of Samuel writing back to command that Susanna stop the meetings. They continued until he returned home.

Samuel reaped great benefit from his wife's efforts. His children were being spiritually nurtured. His parish was growing considerably in attendance and in the grace of God. Neighbors who before had fired their guns off in front of his home and who probably had been responsible for setting his home on fire were now supporting them for the first time. The most important benefit of all was that the form and structure of Susanna's meetings would eventually make up the basis for the entire Methodist movement. God lit a fire in Susanna's soul that would eventually ignite many souls around the world.

All this was accomplished by one woman's commitment to nurturing in her children a love for God. She achieved a delicate balance of walking within the boundaries of the cultural understanding about women's roles while daring to step out and do something radical. While honoring her husband and submitting herself to him, she was confident enough to do what had never been done before, braving great criticism.

An Innovator and Educator

Susanna was also an energetic innovator in education. She believed that all children, girls as well as boys, should receive a good education that included religious training, and she was convinced that the only way she could be sure it would happen was to do it herself. She developed extensive teaching manuals, including three theological manuals, the first of which discussed the order and design of creation and how it testified to God's existence. The second manual dealt with the great doctrines of the Christian faith using the Apostles' Creed, and the third expounded upon the Ten Commandments, teaching the major tenets of divine moral law. She also wrote many theologically instructive letters to her children.

Susanna ordered her children's daily schedule strictly. She believed that bringing a child's will into respectful subjection to their parents and to God was the key to nurturing their spirits. Her lessons were consistently undergirded by her love and devotion, and the Wesley children excelled under her loving instruction.

Susanna's writings concerned salvation and every theological concern. She wrote concerning the sin of the will, the sin of the imagination, the sin of the memory, the sin of the passions of the soul, summing it up by writing that "sin is the greatest contradiction imaginable to his most holy nature."[2]

About God, she wrote of His "infinite purity, absolutely separated from all moral imperfection."[3] "He is goodness, and his most holy will cannot swerve or decline from what is so. He always wills what is absolutely best; nor can he possibly be deceived or deceive anyone."[4] "But the infinite goodness of God, who delights that his mercy should triumph over justice, though he provided no remedy for the fallen angels, yet man being a more simple kind of creature, who perhaps did not sin so maliciously against so much knowledge as those apostate spirits did, he would not subject the whole race of mankind to be ruined and destroyed by the fraud and subtlety of Satan; but he gave us help by one who was mighty, that is able and willing to save to the uttermost all such as shall come to God through him."[5]

Through her children, especially John and Charles and their Methodist movement, Susanna touched the entire world. Her message of devotion to God and hunger to see lost souls come to God was much needed in the society of eighteenth-century England, where true religious conviction had become a rare commodity. Reason was exalted above the Bible, and Christianity was reduced to a code of ethics. Nearly lost was the understanding that sin must be forgiven and cleansed by a miracle-working God who had become man and died on a cross.

Passing Down the Seed of Spiritual Desire

In 1728, Charles experienced an awakening in the Spirit while he and John were attending Oxford University. He began praying and ministering to the sick and needy, and eventually formed what was called the Holy Club, later known as the Methodist Society. John joined the group and became a leader within this new movement.

John and Susanna exchanged many letters discussing doctrinal issues.

She helped him formulate the foundation stones for the Methodism. Convinced that the gospel message could transform society, John built on what he had experienced under his mother's tutelage, advocating a methodical expression of devotion and frequent meetings with other believers. Eventually, he also promoted lay preaching and teaching, which are still part of the Methodist church today.

On May 21, 1738, Charles attended a meeting with the Moravian Society, a fiery evangelistic group that preached justification by faith alone. This meeting was a life-changing experience.[6] During this meeting, God touched Charles and he received an assurance of his salvation.

Three days later, in what has become known as his Aldersgate Street experience, John had a similar encounter with the same Moravian Society. He wrote his now-famous words: "I felt my heart strangely warmed. I felt I did trust in Christ, Christ alone for salvation; and an assurance was given me that he had taken away my sins, even mine, and saved me from the law of sin and death."[7]

John had been ordained as a minister in the Church of England but was expelled because of his "fanatic" ideas. So, he took to the streets and open fields, preaching wherever people would listen. As a result, many people came to Christ. He opened a free medical dispensary in 1746 and spent much of his time visiting the sick, ministering to the poor, and preaching to masses of people. "The world is my parish" expressed John's heart well.

By the end of his life, Charles became known as one of the greatest hymn writers in the world, writing the words to over six thousand hymns. Most of his clearly articulated, theologically sound hymns continue to be sung today. The Methodist revival, led by John and Charles Wesley, transformed church life in both Britain and the American colonies, and gave rise to much-needed social reform. By the grace of God, Susanna's influence for the kingdom of God reached the ends of the earth.

Susanna faithfully loved God and served Him every way she knew how. She saw the vital importance of developing a thoroughly biblical foundation for one's life, and she believed that everyone needed to search the heart regularly and confess sins to God. She was a person "in process," just as we all are, who did not receive a revelation of the assurance of her salvation until later in life, but that did not stop her from pursuing her secret place in God.

After Samuel's death in 1735, Susanna was compelled to live with her adult children in turn. She had made her peace with her many losses and privations, and she made herself a welcome addition to their households. When she herself was at death's doorstep, she asked her children to sing a psalm of praise to God at her funeral.

The following words were inscribed on the tombstone of this great lover of God:

> Here lies the body of Mrs. Susanna Wesley,
> the youngest and last surviving daughter
> of Dr. Samuel Annesley.
> In sure and steadfast hope to rise
> And claim her mansion in the skies,
> A Christian here her flesh laid down,
> The cross exchanging for a crown.
> True daughter of affliction, she,
> Inured to pain and misery,
> Mourn'd a long night of griefs and fears,
> A legal night of seventy years:
> The Father then reveal'd his son,
> Him in the broken bread made known;
> She knew and felt her sins forgiven,
> And found the earnest of heaven.
> Meet for the fellowship above,
> She heard the call, "Arise, my love."
> "I come," her dying looks replied,
> And lamblike, as her Lord, she died.[8]

Years later, her tombstone was changed to reflect her faithfulness to her husband and respect for her sons, John and Charles.

> Here lies the body of
> MRS. SUSANNA WESLEY,
> Widow of the Rev. Samuel Wesley, M.A.
> (late Rector of Epworth, in Lincolnshire,)

who died July 23, 1742,
aged 73 years.
She was the youngest daughter of the
Rev. Samuel Annesley, D.D.
Ejected by the Act of Uniformity
From the Rectory of St. Giles's,
Cripplegate, August 24, 1662.
She was the mother of nineteen children,
Of whom the most eminent were the
REV. JOHN WESLEY AND CHARLES WESLEY;
The former of whom was under God the
Founder of the Societies of the People
Called Methodists.[9]

Surely, her secret place with God had been her most treasured place. She wrote:

My joys all center in him, and it is he himself that I desire; it is his favor, it is his acceptance, the communications of his grace, that I earnestly wish for more than anything in the world; and I have no relish or delight in anything when under apprehensions of his displeasure. I rejoice in my relationship to him, that he is my Father, my Lord, my God. I rejoice that he has power over me, and I desire to live in subjection to him; that he condescends to punish me when I transgress his laws, as a father chastens the son whom he loves. I thank him that he has brought me thus far; and I will beware of despairing of his mercy for the time which is yet to come, but will give God the glory of his free grace.[10]

Make this prayer of Susanna Wesley's your own:

Help me, O Lord, to make true use of all disappointments and calamities in this life, in such a way that they may unite my heart more closely with you. Cause them to separate my affections from worldly things and inspire my soul with more vigor in the pursuit of true happiness. Until this temper of mind be attained, I can never enjoy any settled peace, much less a calm serenity. You only, O God, can satisfy my immortal soul and bestow those spiritual pleasures that alone are proper to its nature. Grant me grace to stay and center my soul in you; to confine its desire, hopes, and expectations of happiness to you alone; calmly to attend to the seasons of your providence and to have a firm, habitual resignation to your will. Enable me to love you, my God, with all my heart, with all my mind, with all my strength; so to love you as to desire you; so to desire you as to be uneasy without you, without your favor, without some such resemblance to you as my nature in this imperfect state can bear. Amen.[11]

Chapter 7

🌿

Basilea Schlink (1904–2001):

GOD SENT
ME TO THE CROSS

At the same time that Basilea Schlink was setting out to discover the world as a young woman, Hitler's influence was beginning to emerge within Germany. She began her studies in social welfare in 1923, while Hitler was attempting his first revolution, which severely shook the economy, causing inflation and bread rationing. Even as her nation was shaken to the core by political upheaval, Basilea's heart experienced its own kind of unrest, as she came to grips with interior issues of true humility and repentance from sin, pride, and ambition.

She stated, "In my childhood and early youth it was always the same. When my sinful nature sought satisfaction, God sent me a cross so that a part of me had to die."[1]

Born in Darmstadt, Germany, on October 21, 1904, Basilea's heart from an early age was turned toward the Lord. Although she was high-spirited and enjoyed as many activities as other girls of her age, the call of God echoed deep in her soul. At the age of twenty, Basilea's prayer was, "Preserve this inner life, but take away my self-esteem. All that I have comes from You and all the good in me can only be attributed to You, Lord Jesus. That I know very well."[2]

As a young woman, Basilea longed for someone to lead her to God. Finding no one, she worked hard to improve herself. Living without the transforming power of God soon brought her to the end of her striving. She realized she needed a revelation of God in her heart. In August 1922, God answered her plea and she beheld Jesus inwardly as the

380

crucified Lord. She knew that she had come into the saving knowledge of Jesus Christ

Revelation of the Father's love began to flow into her. The mystery of the grace of God unfolded in her heart, and her self-effort fell away as she yearned to discover how to pray and grow in God's love. Jesus Himself led her and taught her. When she became aware that a particular activity that brought her pleasure actually grieved the Holy Spirit, she let go of that thing out of love for Him.

Treasures of the Heart

God deposited many treasures into Basilea's heart as she matured into adulthood. She learned that God would reveal Himself to her to the extent that she would allow His Word to convict her heart. God spoke to her of the need to come to the end of self and to walk in repentance so that the death that sin produces would be broken off and new life would result. She experienced greater dimensions of His love, and her heart became increasingly sensitive to the things that God values.

The purifying process continued in Basilea as the Lord brought His light to the motives of her heart. Why did she want to help people? Was she giving them God's love—or *her* love? She was learning how important it is to love people with divine love, because human love is impure and limited. Divine love is constant and sure; it does not waiver with the ebb and flow of human emotions and circumstances. Basilea learned how to give Him the highest place not because of any desire to minister to others, but because of love for Him alone.

Like Peeling an Onion

During her university years, as she completed her studies and then turned to teaching, she experienced mountain peaks and valleys with the Lord. At times she felt very alone. It seemed that God was silently asking her, *Am I enough for you even when it feels like I'm dead, even when I do not give you inner consolation or loving proofs of My presence?*[3]

As Basilea allowed the Lord's piercing question go deep into her spirit, she was convicted of her sin and she asked for His forgiveness. He transformed her heart to experience true thankfulness, and gratitude for His goodness and faithfulness spilled over from her soul.

Like peeling the skin of an onion, He was dealing with issues of her heart, layer by layer, exposing darkness she didn't even know was there. His great love and compassion were exposing darkness of the soul and bringing her to the light. She was learning that in the valleys, in dark and lonely places, was where His glorious light could shine the very brightest.

In 1930 Basilea attended the university in Berlin to work on her Ph.D. in psychology. She lived part of this time with her friend Erika, and she began to feel that God planned for the two of them to found and build up a ministry. During this time also, Basilea felt convicted to live a celibate life.

In 1933, at the height of Nazi National Socialism, Basilea's Jewish professors were forced to relinquish their positions. From 1933 to 1935, this young student held the position of national president of the Women's Division of the German Student Christian Movement. As part of the government-resisting Confessing Church, Basilea was used to influence the Christian student group to reject a paragraph stating that only German (Aryan) girls would be permitted to attend the meetings. The fact that Hebrew Christian students would continue to be accepted within these circles meant that their entire organization could be dissolved. Basilea was beginning to step out in courageous faith to stand up for the Jewish people under the Nazis.

Frontline Courage

Trials, poverty, and hardships followed in the years from 1936 to 1938. Basilea and Erika moved to Darmstadt, where they felt they were to begin a Bible training course for women who were to become pastors' wives or go into ministry themselves. With no way of earning a living, the two young women trusted God for every need. They lived in real poverty, and dug into God for their continual sustenance and spiritual development. By the end of the second year, a handful of women had completed their course.

By the fall of 1938, with no money and no women registering for their course, it seemed the dream had died. But at the last moment, a couple of local pastors pulled together some financial aid to help fund youth work. Basilea started a girls' youth ministry, which quickly grew to a hundred members under Erika's leadership. Basilea was by then in her mid-thirties, still without a clear ministry.

In 1939, the Missionary Society for Moslems asked Basilea to take over its traveling lectureship. So, during the desperate, difficult years of war throughout Europe, Basilea traveled in crowded trains, enduring blackouts, severe coal shortages, and bombing raids. In the frigid winter of 1940–1941, she traveled for four weeks across Prussia, where the temperatures often sank below zero. Wherever she went, she found that God was her faithful and constant companion, her security, and her peace.

Sometimes informers were present in her meetings, but she continued to feel compelled to speak of God's plan of salvation for the Jews, and of His special covenant with them. Twice she was reported by these informants and interrogated for hours by the secret police. Still, God kept her safe and she was not arrested. Her Bible studies were allowed to continue even though both the Old and New Testaments were taught, which was forbidden under Hitler.

As Basilea traveled from place to place, she spoke on the power of Jesus' blood, His victory over the enemy, and His triumphant return. She covered Jesus' second coming, God's plan of salvation for Israel and the city of God, heaven and hell, the blessings of suffering, and how to overcome.

For years, she prayed, "Grant me love, love which is not irritable or resentful, which bears all things, hopes all things, believes all things, endures all things."[4] In part through her experiences during World War II, God taught her the way of humility. She learned to cease from self-justification and to endure with patience and forbearance. God's perfect love became her life's message.

Revival

On September 11, 1944, an air raid targeted Darmstadt. Buildings were toppled everywhere. Yet this black cloud contained a silver lining. It so sobered the girls with whom Erika and Basilea had been working that revival was unleashed. These young women were seized with the intense need for personal repentance. And as they spent extra time in prayer, the Lord dealt with the two leaders concerning the sins of their nation.

During the war years, Basilea and Erika had spent time in prayer over personal issues, but they realized they had not cried out for national sins, nor had they repented for the prisoners of war and for the millions of Jews who had been slaughtered. They had thought they were devoting their lives to God, but had they seen their lives in light of the sin of their nation? Great conviction fell upon the ashes of Darmstadt, and from that, great revival.

The stage was being set for the foundation of one of Basilea's dreams—the Evangelical Sisterhood of Mary.

The Evangelical Sisterhood of Mary

On March 30, 1947, the dream became a reality. The Sisterhood was established, founded by Basilea Schlink and Paul Riedinger, a Methodist church leader. It had Lutheran roots, but eventually it became interdenominational. In the early days, they weathered criticism, lacks, and sickness, but they grew steadily to become a community of women living in an attitude of contrition and fellowship in bridal love for Jesus. The Sisters of Mary would stand in the gap for their nation, identifying Germany's sins as their own and crying out for mercy and forgiveness.

Often, Basilea retreated into seclusion with God. She spent weeks rarely seeing or talking to anyone. During such times she experienced the sweet presence of God and the sense of eternity resting in her room. In times of seclusion, she received revelations from God concerning His nature or the Scripture. Many times He would direct her into serious assignments that would take much prayer to be accomplished.

The Sufferings of Jesus

Basilea gained understanding into the sufferings of Jesus, and she learned that loneliness is one of the ways He suffered while here on earth. The Lord would come to her in those times and share burdens of His heart with her. He spoke to her of His pain that the body of Christ was not unified. This sent her on many missions to build up and repair the breach, in an attitude of humility and repentance, asking for forgiveness. She was often met with divisive words, but sometimes true reconciliation took place. She was a true forerunner, one who not only understood the power and importance of what we call "identificational repentance," but who actually practiced it.

In May 1949, Mother Basilea (as she was called) felt inspired to build a chapel for Jesus, where He would be adored. The Sisters of Mary also needed a house where new sisters could join the ministry. When they started these projects, they had only thirty German marks. It seemed that the Lord was serving as their banker. Both buildings were completed in a timely fashion; the chapel was built from bricks salvaged from the ruins of the city. This home for the Evangelical Sisterhood of Mary became known as Kanaan.

During one of her times of seclusion, Mother Basilea received a commission from God to speak to the Pope. She was to go and discuss God's desire for all His body to become one. Specifically, she would discuss the breach between Protestants and Roman Catholics.

Before she could go, she knew that much work would need to be completed. She knew that the enemy's attacks always correspond to the spiritual significance of the commission. She had learned to identify with the words of Paul: "Now I rejoice in my sufferings on your behalf. And with my own body I supplement whatever is lacking [on our part] of Christ's afflictions, on behalf of His body, which is the church" (Col. 1:24, AMP). Mother Basilea learned to suffer for the unity of love. The inner conflicts she endured were an essential part of preparing for this assignment, so she repented of faultfinding and personal opinions and submitted her mind anew to the lordship of Jesus.

Through prayer, she was able to attain a private audience with Pope Pius XII. Her assignment was fulfilled. She could not determine his response, but she had faithfully answered God's call to be a voice echoing the ache in God's heart. The pope responded to her, "Is that really the Savior's wish?"[5]

Mother Basilea knew that the seeds we are asked to sow take time to germinate and we cannot guarantee when the fruit will become evident. We sowers must be patient and always carry an eternal perspective, with plenty of faith that *God's seeds always grow.*

After her trip to Rome, the Evangelical Sisterhood of Mary opened up branches in England, Greece, and Italy. The work crossed denominational borders into the Anglican, Greek Orthodox, and Roman

Catholic churches. Eventually, branches included more than two hundred women from twenty countries, along with fourteen men in the Canaan Franciscan Brothers.

God's Heart for Israel

In other times of seclusion beginning in 1954, God spoke to Mother Basilea about His heart for Israel, His specially chosen people. A cry for God's people arose from her heart toward the throne of mercy: "Awaken souls amongst Your chosen people Israel to love You like a bride so that one day they may be with You in the City of God."[6]

With this call came the realization that Germany, Basilea's homeland, had committed horrible atrocities against the Jewish people and by doing so, they had heaped terrible guilt upon themselves. As she entered into specific times of prayer and fasting concerning this overpowering weight of sin, the light of God broke through. No longer did the sisters avoid houses they knew belonged to Jewish families because of guilt or shame. With God's renewed love in their hearts, they visited these families, asking for forgiveness on behalf of their nation. Repentance began to do the work of reconciliation.

When the sisters desired to visit Israel, an invitation was required in order to issue visas because of their German citizenship. The door was opened; an invitation came to the doorstep. They obtained the necessary visas and walked through the land of Israel, asking God's forgiveness for Germany's sin. Their labors toward reconciliation resulted in sending two sisters to live there in 1957. Mother Basilea went on to write a book calling Christians to an awareness of its sins against the Jews.

Later, an additional branch of the Sisters of Mary was established in Jerusalem, called Beth Abraham. These events brought invitations from Jewish communities within the United States and Canada for Mother Basilea to speak in their synagogues. Rabbis and students attended her meetings.

The Valley of the Shadow of Death

In 1959, Mother Basilea was suffering from a serious heart condition. Inwardly, she felt she was being led through the valley of the shadow of death. After releasing her will into God's will for her life, she received an assurance from God that she would recover. The Lord granted health to her, and she became stronger than before. Soon after this trial, she wrote the book *Repentance—The Joy-Filled Life* (Bethany House, 1984). She understood that "a person lacking contrition lacks everything. If he has contrition and repentance, he has everything he needs, for repentance draws down God's grace."[7]

In 1959 came another call from God concerning the land of Israel. Mother Basilea was to spend time in the Holy Land seeking out the places where Jesus had lived and suffered in order to pray for an awakening of God's purposes for those places. As she traveled through the land, she felt the grief of Jesus Christ, because His people remained so unmoved toward the places where He had lived His earthly life and so little was being done to keep those sights holy.

She spent time in prayer in Gethsemane at Lithostrotos, where Christ was crowned with thorns, and at the Kidron Valley, where He was led away as a prisoner. Here she experienced a living encounter with God and wrote many songs, devotional readings, and texts. She compiled these writings into books for pilgrims visiting these sites. Booklets and leaflets were created from her book and distributed by the thousands at the holy sites, as well as given away at various hotels. After this, the Sisters of Mary began hosting spiritual pilgrimages of the Holy Land.

A few years later, the Sisters were permitted to place plaques at the holy sites. Each one was inscribed with devotional thoughts to help visitors open their hearts to God in these places.

Memorials to God's Glory

After the enthusiastic success of the memorial plaques in Israel, Mother Basilea and her sisters began praying about a new project in their home country of Germany. The Sisters of Mary sought permission to erect plaques at various scenic points to bring glory to God. After the plaques were erected, stories were told of many individuals who were kept from committing suicide because of their presence. Eventually, this project became an international effort, with plaques being placed at points of majestic beauty in many nations.

Mother Basilea accomplished many things during her lifetime, much more than can be accounted for here. Throughout her life, her primary goal was to love Jesus and to call others to love Him as our wonderful Bridegroom should be loved. Her many written works resulted from this devotion in her heart for Him. The effects of her love and devotion continue to bless those in many nations.

Mother Basilea went to be with the Lord on March 21, 2001, but her work and vision for the Evangelical Sisterhood of Mary continues. This community is dedicated to Christian radio ministry and to Christian literature. The Sisterhood publishes tracts in ninety languages, which are distributed on five continents. Radio and television programs are broadcast in twenty-three languages. But more important than the programs and other efforts is the fire of His love and the call to the secret place.

That privileged cry continues to echo across generations and ages of time. Let's turn now to hear its message to our own generation through the lives of those who have cultivated blessed friendship in the secret place.

> Our Savior, You are the only one worth living for! Like Mother Basilea, I offer myself to You entirely and freely, trusting that You will form Your desires in my heart and use me in whatever ways You choose. Teach me Your eternal perspective and show me how to carry Your love wherever You may send me. Very few of us are called as part of a band of women like the Sisterhood, but we are all called as part of Your body, the Church, to spread the fragrance of Your gracious presence everywhere, driving out darkness with Your radiant light. Always in Jesus' name, amen.

Part Three

Friends of the
Secret Place

Chapter 8

🌿

Gwen Shaw (1924–2013)

A PASSION FOR NATIONS

Gwen Shaw ministered in more than one hundred nations and was the founder of the End-Time Handmaidens, an organization that has lit the pathway to the secret place for nearly a generation. She was truly born to serve the Lord, and it was an honor and a joy to be her friend.

Loving and serving her Lord was her destiny. Gwendolyn Ruth had parents who dedicated her to the Lord from the womb. Gwen's mother came from a godly family of sincere Mennonites who had served the Lord for many generations. Her God-fearing forefathers had paid a terrible price for their testimony.

Years earlier, these new believers had been banished from their beautiful homes in the Emmental Valley of the Swiss Alps because of their conviction that salvation was by grace alone. The teachings of Martin Luther had swept across Europe and many of the faithful had died as martyrs, being burned at the stake or speared through. Young men were sold as galley slaves, and old fathers were left to die in dark dungeons. Gwen's ancestors had been forced to leave their homes and live a life of wandering for decades until Russia opened its doors. There they found religious freedom.[1]

During the first bitter Russian winter in their new homeland, they existed by digging holes in the ground and living under the earth. Gradually, they began to raise crops and prosper until they finally owned their own homes. Towns and villages of German-speaking people, all of them seeking religious freedom, arrived in Russia.[2]

When all seemed to be going well, the Lord visited His people and warned them through the gift of prophecy that great persecution was coming to Russia. This persecution would be greater than any they had ever known in the past, and for those who stayed, there would be no survivors. God told them to leave Russia and go to a new homeland. Some heeded the word of the Lord, while others mocked it and stayed behind where, sadly, they suffered and died.

This is how Gwen came to be born in Canada. As a young man, her maternal grandfather, Peter Miller (Mueller) and others traveled to Canada in obedience to the word of the Lord. These hardworking farmers grew hearty wheat from the grain that they had brought with them from Russia.[3] They founded churches and raised families. Gwen grew up attending the Emmanuel Mennonite Church, which had been founded by her grandfather in Saskatchewan, the middle prairie province of Canada. Here her parents dedicated their three children—Gwen, Earl, and Jamie—to the Lord. The entire family faithfully attended the church built on the land dedicated by Grandfather Miller.

In her middle teens, Gwen grew bored with rural prairie life and escaped with a friend to the big city. While she was away, her family was dramatically touched by the Pentecostal movement sweeping through the community. Meanwhile, Gwen was part of a more liberal congregation where sin was seldom mentioned and people felt free to live any way they wanted.

After a few months of rebellion and desperate prayers by her family, Gwen came back to the Lord and was gloriously filled with the Holy Spirit. She went off to the Assembly of God (Pentecostal Assembly of Canada) Bible School in Ontario to be trained for the Lord's work.

While she was there, revival fire fell among the students; visions, spiritual gifts, intercession, and deep conviction of the Lord's presence flowed freely during those special days. In the midst of this outpouring, God called Gwen to China. However, somewhat ignorantly, Gwen had married a young man who was not as fervent about God's purposes. Gwen prayed and prayed. Eventually, the Lord moved on his heart, and in obedience they went off as faith missionaries to China.

Launching Out Into the Deep

In December 1947, they landed in Shanghai. Gwen had just turned twenty-three. Having responded in obedience to the call of God upon her life, she received a passionate burden from the Lord for the Chinese people.

Sometimes that burden was greater than at other times. As the years went by and China fell into the hands of Communism, the doors for the gospel in Mainland China slammed shut. Even so, Gwen continued to serve the Lord among the Chinese people in Taiwan and Hong Kong, not missing a step in fulfilling that call of God. Never for a moment did she think of turning back from that call.

Gwen loved the Chinese, and she considered them her people. She shared, "I belonged to them, and their need was my need; their pain, my pain."[4] In fact, Gwen had been God's spokeswoman, used to warn and foretell the closing of the nation of China to missionary work long before it ever fell to the Communists.[5] The prophetic utterance doubtless fueled the flame of passion within her heart, and the Canadian volunteer reached out to China with a deep sense of urgency.

After ten years of marriage on the mission field, three sons arrived: David, Danny, and Tommy. As a mother of young children, Gwen's life was now occupied with family affairs. She admitted later that it was hard to be a mother of three lively boys and still keep her missionary vision alive. But with the help of an *amah* (housemaid and nanny), the boys' early years were spent growing up on the mission field in Hong Kong.

One day in 1963, after sixteen years of missionary service, God met her with a new and wonderful anointing. Fresh desire arose in her heart. Gwen hungered for more of God, and she longed for her life to make a difference. Dedicating her life afresh to God, Gwen determined that from that point on it would be 100 percent, complete, unconditional, and total surrender to His will—whatever the cost. And God took her up on the vow she had made to Him.

Fresh Anointing—Renewed Vision

With God's renewal of His calling in Gwen's life, Gwen followed, adding to her mission field the nations of the world. She never imagined all that God had planned for her. "I simply put my hand in His and began to follow Him step-by-step, day-by-day, and nation by nation."[6] She also never anticipated the great cost of her obedience—difficulties that would fix her eyes completely on Jesus, the Lover of her soul.

With this new "double-portion" anointing came a tremendous burden for souls and an overwhelming vision for the nations. Her fresh call took her to various parts of China, Mongolia, Taiwan, the Philippines, and on to Indonesia, where she saw the Lord do great miracles of deliverance and salvation. She would minister among the Presbyterians in one location, the Pentecostal Assemblies in another, and with Catholic nuns and Orthodox priests. She came alongside the Methodists, Baptists, Missionary Alliance, Salvation Army—whoever was hungry for more of God. Wherever the Spirit said, "Come," Sister Gwen went.

During the children's summer vacation, Gwen often would take one of them with her when she went to minister. Nine-year-old David, the oldest, played the trumpet and always knew how to get a crowd. He would borrow someone's bicycle, ride out to the marketplace, and play his trumpet while passing out tracts and flyers about the meetings. Turning toward the gathering, he would encourage them to come and hear his mother preach. They had great times together.

The Terrible Price

On other occasions when the children were in school, Gwen went out alone. Long before this time, she and her husband had grown apart in vision and calling, and this had resulted in a painful separation of ways. The Lord used this pain redemptively as a part of a breaking process in which He took Gwen into a deeper place where He alone became her husband, shelter, and refuge.

At times Gwen's loneliness became so acute that it pierced into her heart like a knife. Only God knew her tears, pain, loneliness, and longing—the price she paid to fulfill her vow to God.

At one point, she started to make excuses to try to escape God's call, and she nearly lost all three of her boys. Danny almost drowned in the South China Sea; David slipped right in front of a fast oncoming car; and Tommy was miraculously rescued out of a sewage-filled river. Still, the Lord promised His fatherly protection if she would only keep following Him.

Gwen knew that God was speaking loud and clear, warning her of how costly it could be to put anything before Him—even her children. The price might be more costly than the one she was already paying. So again, she counted the cost and said yes to her Lord. That's when she received her next assignment—India.

India, "My Great Love"

India became Gwen's great love. She often would say, "China was my first love, and India was my great love."[7] She couldn't find words to describe what it meant to feel God's heartbeat of love for a nation. She would have gladly laid down her whole life for the Lord in India. In fact, that became her desire.

In this season of her life, she experienced great joy in service to God. She traveled to many parts of northern India, erected a tent, and openly preached the gospel of the Lord Jesus Christ. She was a woman on the front lines. What joy to see people respond to the mercy of God! How exciting to lead many Hindus and Muslims to Jesus!

Gwen translated her tract called *Who Is Jesus?* into the Bengali language and used it as she ministered from Punjab to Calcutta, New Delhi to Allahabad, and from coast to coast.[8] Her father and brother joined her in those harvest fields of souls under the big tent. Gwen played an accordion and brother Earl joined her in singing songs of Zion. Revival was in the air.

After India, Gwen moved on to Russia, and once again God's heart of passion for the lost beat inside her as if it were her own. Miraculously, she was the first woman to preach in the Baptist Church in Moscow. Like the apostolic ambassadors of old, Gwen would pray, fast, and agonize for the nations. When no door was open to her, God would be the door. When no finances existed, He would be her provider.

Jesus became the doorkeeper of the nations, opening entry to Finland, Bali, Denmark, Norway, Sweden, England, Germany, Africa, Pakistan, the United States, and Canada. If she could pronounce it, Jesus took this little Canadian lady there. He introduced her to kings and princesses, paupers and lepers, and she shared with all the timeless story of God's great grace and wonderful love.

Argentina, the Founding
of the End-Time Handmaidens

If God's love is in your heart, then your heart will expand to be like His. This is just what happened in Sister Gwen. How much can one heart contain? Remember, "For God so loved the world…" (John 3:16).

Her next call came and she went to Argentina, where once again she felt the heartbeat of God, now for the Spanish-speaking people of that great land. Throughout Argentina, she saw the mighty hand of God working with mighty displays of supernatural power following her preaching of His Word.

Then one night in Buenos Aires, something happened that was destined to change many lives. Gwen had just ministered in a large Assembly of God church where God had poured out His Spirit. Miracles of healing had taken place, and people had seen angels. God's tangible presence had manifested among them. No one wanted to leave the meetings as the God of the secret place was being revealed so openly.

Gwen went back tired and exhausted to her lonely hotel room that night, and lay there on her bed. Looking up to heaven, she asked God questions. "God, how can you use me? Why do you use me? I am nothing. I make mistakes. I am far from perfect. Yet I have seen your glory like a trail of fire following me everywhere. How? Why?"

Amazingly, she heard His answer: "It is because you are willing to do anything I ask you to do!"

With the curiosity of a child, Gwen inquired, "Is that all, Lord? Then You could use anyone, any woman who like myself would be totally surrendered to You!"

"Yes, My child, I could," He answered.

Strengthened in faith, Gwen responded, "Then, Lord, raise up ten thousand women—women just like myself who will pay any price, make any sacrifice, and be totally obedient to Your will."[9] The year was 1966.

The End of the Road

Four years later, after she had ministered in many other nations all over the world, Gwen found herself in Chicago, seemingly at the end of the road. Her children were in Hong Kong. Her marriage was over. Her heart was broken, and she was sure that she could never serve God again. Her emotions overwhelmed her as the enemy whispered that no one would accept a woman whose marriage had fallen apart.

Gwen underwent a twenty-one-day fast and waited upon the Lord. "I did the only thing I knew to do. I went back to the drawing board, back to the Cross."[11] He spoke to her again. Night after night the Lord came to her releasing His plans, visiting her by His angels, answering her questions.

To confirm these encounters, the Lord of Hosts sent a prophet to tell her that she must begin to call out the End-Time Handmaidens. God told her that there was an army of women out there in the background, standing "idle in the marketplace, whom no one had hired." They were waiting to hear the call to go out and serve the Lord in the harvest fields of the world.

Perhaps no one knew those harvest fields better than Sister Gwen. Already, she had been to many of the nations of the world. Although she had been thinking, *It's all over*, God was revealing that it was not.

The Beginning of a New Calling

With fresh resolve and faith, in obedience Gwen began to give the call to women everywhere to join her in sharing her burden for souls. A new and living company of women was born—one full of consecration, holiness, and the Word of the Lord. The End-Time Handmaidens rose up from many nations as the Holy Spirit prepared women's hearts around the world in the same way He had prepared hers. God's chosen daughters would fast and pray, in brokenness wondering if God even knew their names. Then, from the stillness in His wonderful presence, He would call their names. A growing number of End-Time Handmaidens were commissioned into the harvest, radiating the glow of holiness from the secret place.

The Lord did not forget his handmaiden Gwen. He sent to her a "Simon" to help her carry the cross and lighten the load. At a time of fellowship in Santa Barbara, California, Gwen met Lieutenant Colonel James von Doornum Shaw, a retired Baptist US Air Force pilot.

When she saw him, the Holy Spirit told her to go and lay hands upon this stranger and prophesy to him. Reluctantly, she obeyed and declared to this Baptist man that God was bringing him into a new consecration and that times of satisfaction and joy from the Holy Spirit were waiting for him like none he had never known. She declared that as he had flown in the natural, so would he fly in the spiritual realm. Gwen spoke the word "completeness" over this man.

Jim Shaw went on a fast to seek the face of the Lord, and a new heart for missions bubbled up in him. Little did Gwen realize that she would end up marrying this wonderful man who had flown numerous aircraft for well over thirty years and that together they would fly to many nations, serving the Lord. The End-Time Handmaidens would also become complete by adding the male component, End-Time Servants, as well, and that they would serve the Master together for another thirty years.

Looking Back

Gwen first gave her heart to the Lord when she was seventeen years old, and since then she has served Him with all her heart. In her words:

> If I could live my life over again, I would give it all to God again. God has given me supernatural strength to fulfill a supernatural calling. But, as hard as I work and as fast as I run, I can't keep up with Him. I have now been to over one hundred nations and still they keep calling. Day after day they're calling, calling, calling. This call to the nations is there, ringing in my ears, burning in my heart. I want to go, but I'm getting older now. I can't preach four and five times a day as I used to in Indonesia. I can understand the heart's cry of Moses when he said, "I am not able to bear all this people alone, because it is too heavy for me." (Num. 11:14, KJV)
>
> Yes, it is getting too heavy for me. This terrible burden for Cambodia, North Korea, Tibet, Zambia, Pakistan, Albania, Chile, Iceland, and all the nations where I have not yet told the old, old story of Jesus and His love—besides the nations where I want to return again! Moses wept. I weep too!
>
> Then I hear God say to me what He said to Moses, "I will take of the spirit which is upon thee, and will put it upon them;

and they shall bear the burden of the people with thee, that thou bear it not thyself alone." (Num. 11:17b, KJV)[11]

Sharing Her Burden

When God calls people in the same way He called Gwen Shaw, He sovereignly and supernaturally places a burden on their hearts. If they are willing to accept it, they must recognize that it will not be easy. Following the call will cost everything. Like the tribe of Levi, which had no earthly inheritance, the Lord must be their inheritance.

Total, unconditional surrender to the glorious Father of the Lord Jesus Christ can be expressed by praying the following prayer, composed by Gwen Shaw:

> Lord, I give myself to You. I give my life to You. I feel Your call. I believe I was sent to do the will of my Father. I will take orders from You.
>
> I will submit to You. I will let You break my will. I will not seek for comfort nor high position, nor do what I want to do. I love You, Jesus; I thank You for calling me, and I am grateful that you want me, and that You can use me.
>
> All I can say is, "Send the fire and burn up the sacrifice. Fill me with Thy Holy Spirit and give me a double portion of Thine anointing."[12]

Chapter 9

⚜

Elizabeth Alves

THE GRANDMA OF
THE PRAYER SHIELD

I never wanted a ministry. All I ever wanted was to know Christ!" These words epitomize the heart and motive of another intimate friend of the secret place, Elizabeth (Beth) Alves.

When you're sitting in a meeting listening to Beth speak, you might easily feel as though you have been ushered into her living room. Her mothering grace is calm and unassuming. Here is a woman who has traveled to over thirty nations, faithfully bringing the life of Christ to others, rich or poor. Beth Alves exudes the love of God, and she knows that all her accomplishments are not really hers, but His.

Beth and her late husband, Floyd, began the early years of their marriage in the Lutheran church. In Beth's words, they were Lutherans first and Christians second. But God didn't let it stay that way.

Power From on High

Beth remembers the pivotal time within her family that was key to their spiritual awakening. Her daughter had been diagnosed with an inoperable brain tumor. As Beth watched her become increasingly debilitated, she prayed night and day. Walking the floors, she pleaded, "Jesus, if you're the same yesterday, today, and forever; and if I called you and you would walk this floor, then you would heal my daughter." Eventually, however, Beth's daughter no longer could talk or swallow. She no longer recognized her father—her favorite person. The only person she did know was Beth.

One day Beth came into her daughter's room in the hospital and busied herself because she was so depressed. As she started to clean the bedside table drawer, she pulled out a Gideon Bible and opened it, longing for something special to read. Growing up in the church, she had learned many wonderful Bible stories, but she didn't really know what else was in the Bible. She thought that was what the preacher was paid for—to study the Bible and preach from it. Beth had been praying to the Lord, but she didn't know much about Him.

Opening up the Bible, she uttered a prayer of desperation asking for something special from Him. As she turned the pages, she came across Mark 16 and read, "He that believes and is baptized shall be saved, and he that believes not will be damned. And these signs shall follow those who believe, in My name they'll cast out demons..."

Oh, Beth thought, *it's not Halloween. I certainly don't need that!* "In My name they'll speak with new tongues." She looked at her daughter and thought, *I can't go to another country and learn a new tongue right now. I've got to take care of her here and now.* "They will pick up serpents." *Now, God...you know that I'm afraid of snakes. I'd never do that!*

"And if they drink any deadly thing, they will recover." Finally, Beth's eyes fell on a part of the passage that would change her life forever. Slowly, absorbing every word, she read, "They will lay hands on the sick, and they will recover" (Mark 16:18, NKJV).

Aha! That was exactly what she needed! Beth laid the open Bible across her daughter's feet, as if she were showing God what He had written. Carefully, tentatively placing her hands on the dying child's feet, Beth looked up to heaven and declared aloud: "God...I'm doing it. It doesn't say pray. Here it says to lay hands on them."

Feeling a little more hopeful, she closed the Bible and finished cleaning out the drawer. The next morning, her daughter went in for another test, a pneumoencephalogram. Beth had no guarantee her daughter would come out alive.

The doctors came out of the test with tears running down their faces. Panic filled Beth's heart; she was afraid she had lost her daughter. They brought Beth's daughter to her room still under the anesthetic. Sitting next to her emaciated daughter, Beth's hot tears rolled freely down her face and soaked her dress.

Suddenly she heard, "Hey Mom, where's Daddy? I'm hungry—let's eat." Beth's daughter was sitting up in bed—completely healed!

"What Would You Have Me to Do?"

This amazing experience sent Beth on a search for more of God. She cried out to Him continually for His help, desperately wanting to know Him better.

Then on Good Friday of 1970, her prayers were dramatically answered. Beth was getting dressed to go somewhere when she looked up and saw the form of Jesus. Beth fell to the floor and cried out, "My Lord Jesus Christ, what would you have me to do?"

A blanket of divine peace filled the room, and she heard the words, "Stand up, for thou art worthy through My Son, Jesus." His eyes were pools of liquid living love. Much more happened on that wonderful day, and that powerful visitation changed her life forever.

Learning to Walk the Walk

After the experience of meeting the resurrected Savior, she couldn't speak at all for three days, but neither did she want to talk. Tears of joy and wonder just flowed down her cheeks. When she did speak, she found that she could speak in tongues, but she didn't know what it was. Then the Lord sent her to a man whom she had never heard of before, a Lutheran minister who lived five hours away. This pastor explained what had happened to her.

When she was finally able to explain to her husband what had happened, he became very concerned. He, together with their local Lutheran pastor, agreed that it was good for Beth to be seeing this other Lutheran pastor. After all, he was Lutheran, so he must be all right.

Beth and her husband went to see the local Lutheran pastor and also a psychologist. Beth's husband, their pastor, and the psychologist decided that Beth had experienced a pseudo-religious experience before having a mental breakdown.

Afterward, Beth spent five days with her newly found pastor friend and his wife. They pored over Scripture around the clock, and she wrote down as much as possible. She had an insatiable hunger for the things of God. As she was leaving, her new pastor friend told her, "Beth, you must go home, and you must pray often in the Spirit. They think you're crazy. I've had five calls from them, but you must pray to build yourself up in the Holy Spirit. That will be your keeping power. But whatever you do, don't do it in front of them or anybody else, because they won't understand. There is something that you must always remember, Beth; go home and walk the walk before you talk the talk. People will follow after your walk, but you'll lose them with your talk."

When Beth got home she discovered that her husband had taken her name off the charge accounts and the bank account. In those days, if the husband didn't want to be held responsible for his wife's debts, he had to write a letter and have it publicly published—which he did. In addition, Floyd started working nights so he could watch her all day long. Beth, on the other hand, was like a champagne bottle that somebody had shaken and put the cap back on. She was bubbling over with joy, but now she dared not express it. Beth determined she would follow the wise advice of her new friend and "walk the walk."

Secret Joy

The psychologist explained to her husband that after a pseudoreligious experience, people begin to feel dirty and are driven to get clean all the time. So, everyone watched Beth for this cue. Meanwhile, in an effort to not pray in front of anyone, Beth began to retreat to the bathroom and take four to six showers a day, so that she could pray in tongues in the shower. She was so full of joy that she was about to explode. However, this new behavior sent all the wrong messages to her husband.

The local Lutheran church relieved Beth of all her responsibilities, now viewing her as a threat. She lost her church friends, and she and her husband lost their mutual friends. She felt totally and completely alone. Their communication as a couple disintegrated. Floyd was running away from God as hard as she was running toward Him. He and his mother even attempted to have the children taken away from her so that they could have her committed to an institution and give her shock treatments, thinking this was the only way to erase her religious fantasy from her mind.

In the Lion's Den

In the midst of this turmoil, the Lord led Beth to a woman who became her mentor. "What should I do?" Beth asked, fearing for her future in the face of the threat of being committed to an institution. Her mentor said, "Just remember this, Beth: Daniel trusted God in the lion's den, and God shut the lion's mouths. If he tries to take you to a mental institution, I'll pray that God shuts its mouth."

Her husband put her in the car, drove about six blocks, and came back home. "I can't do it," he said.

Beth and her husband lived the next two and a half years in great difficulty. Eventually, her husband too received the baptism of the Holy Spirit—by reading his Bible. After he had heard Beth talk and pray, he had gone to the Bible to check it out...and he read himself right into Jesus.

Pathway to the Secret Place

On the day that God visited Beth, He baptized her with love for her husband. No matter how difficult her husband made life for her, she just loved him that much more. She would get hurt but not angry. She had no one to talk to but her spiritual mentor.

She began to feel that her experience with God had brought a seed of pride into her life because she thought she knew everything, while in reality she knew nothing. Completely alone, except for her children and her spiritual mentor, God was using these difficult times to burn out the dross in her heart. These were her beginnings with God, glorious and yet so difficult. The pathway to abiding in the secret place was a rocky, bumpy, painful road.

Rabbi—Teacher

"Lord, please help me; I don't have time to pray." The Lord was Beth's teacher in such practical ways. She had four daughters of her own and had adopted another. She also cared for three more whose mother had died, and two other girls whose mother was in a mental hospital. In addition, Beth was working full time. She asked God, "When am I going to pray for those you've given me charge over?"

The Lord told her to make a list of everything she did every day. She listed washing dishes every morning, ironing, hanging out the clothes to dry on the clothesline, and making the bed. She took the list of household chores and assigned a name from her prayer list to each chore. Whenever she would work on a particular chore she would pray for the person listed beside that chore.

At that time her husband wasn't walking with the Lord, and Beth admits that she assigned his name beside the chore of cleaning the toilet. But then the Lord dealt with her attitude; He told her, "Beth, you came to the right place, because all those prayers belong in the pity pot." So she shunned self-pity and began to bless her husband, her enemies, and those who hurt her. Eventually the toilet became her "bless-me pot."

A Gift of Intercession

Once when Beth was about to hang the clean laundry on the clothesline, a neighbor dropped by. While they drank some iced tea and talked, she kept thinking about how she needed to go and hang out those clothes. *But how rude that would seem,* she thought.

Suddenly, she jumped up so fast that the basket of clothes went flying across the floor. "You have to excuse me. I've got a project to do. Just wait here. I'll be back."

Beth went to hang out the clothes, and as she did she started to weep, and then wail. She became so troubled that she had to cling to the clothesline pole to hold herself up. The person she had assigned to this chore was her daughter who was in junior high school. So she found herself praying in the Spirit for this daughter, not knowing specifically what was happening. She glanced at the clock as she came back into the house.

Beth's daughter came home from school later that afternoon. As they were washing dishes together after dinner, Beth asked her daughter what happened to her at 2:15 p.m. Looking startled, her daughter began to cry and said that some kids had talked her into running away from school with them. At 2:15 she had gone to her locker to put her things away and get what she needed to leave with them. However, she found that she couldn't move. All she could do was stand there and cry. She had closed her locker and returned to her class.

Beth was left with the joyful knowledge that God had used her prayers that day to make a crucial difference in her daughter's life. Had she not obeyed the inner prompting that was easier to capture because of spending time with Him, she might have missed her God-given assignment.

Grandma of the Prayer Shield

"Lord, teach me to pray," became Beth's desperate cry in those early days. God faithfully answered her prayer. Over the years, the Lord has unfolded to Beth simple yet profound truths about prayer and intercession that she continues to impart to others. Thousands from many nations have been released into ministry as they have learned principles of prayer and prophecy. With gentleness, humor, and simplicity, she captures the hearts of her listeners, encouraging them that they too can hear the voice of the Lord.

In 1971, Beth sensed the Lord impressing upon her the importance of praying for spiritual leaders worldwide. Her vision was based on Isaiah 62:6–7, which reads:

> On your walls, O Jerusalem, I have appointed watchmen; all day and all night they will never keep silent. You who remind the Lord, take no rest for yourselves; and give Him no rest until He establishes and makes Jerusalem a praise in the earth. (NASB)

The following year, Beth and Floyd founded Intercessors International. This gave Beth a forum for sharing her rich insights about loving intercessory prayer as a tool and shield or cover. Besides teaching Beth to pray, the Lord has given her much wisdom, along with extremely practical applications.

She started to be called the "Grandma of the Prayer Shield" when she received great understanding about the need for our leaders to be covered in prayer. These leaders include ministers, missionaries, and business and spiritual leaders around the world. She teaches on many different types of intercessors and, with her great insight, is able to extend grace to others to flow in their own individually tailored intercessory gifts.

Godly Mentoring

Beth highly values the importance of godly mentoring. While her children were still young and at home, she turned down a significant opportunity from the Lord to start a prayer ministry. She felt it necessary to stay home with her children, so she passed that opportunity onto another person, believing that if the call truly was from God, it would still be there when her children were grown. It was.

According to Beth, oftentimes you lay the groundwork and others get the credit, but that's a sign of a good mentor. You don't mentor to *be* somebody; you mentor because God gives you that privilege and that opportunity. A mentor is somebody God trusts. The word mentor means "teacher, guide, coach, trainer, and instructor." Nowhere does it say "possessor." Mentors must never, ever dominate or control. Being a mentor is like taking care of a baby whose bottle keeps falling out of his mouth. The baby may burp all over you and make a mess of things, but if you're his caretaker, you'll make certain that he is fed.

You can't mentor somebody in a class because mentoring requires a heart-to-heart connection. Such connections are necessary to bring out the best in a person, identify his or her giftings, understand weaknesses, and help that individual turn those weaknesses into strengths. "Love bears all things," Paul wrote to the Corinthians. And *bear* means "to carry or sustain." Love also "believes all things," which indicates total faith and trust.

A Servant's Heart

Sometimes we forget the simple things. We forget that Jesus spent His life here on earth teaching us how to serve. He was the greatest servant who ever lived.

We look for an explosion of power, signs, and wonders, and what does God do? In Beth's case, He sent her to be a servant and to keep the house of an evangelist. She had always employed people to clean her house, and then God sent her to clean someone else's. As she did so, she would cry and complain to God, "God, I've got a call on my life, and here I am scrubbing and dusting. How can I do my calling by cleaning these pots all day?"

The Lord answered her saying, "You came to the right place." And He mentioned the "pity pot" again. Conviction hit her heart, and she repented.

One day, the evangelist's wife asked Beth to pray with her, and God spoke through her in a profound way as they prayed together. Later the evangelist was called away to teach on prayer but he couldn't go. So he sent Beth in his place, and that's how she started in the work of the ministry.

Subsequently, Beth poured out her life to help teach and mentor others, traveling extensively, teaching and ministering in seminars and conferences worldwide. Her great proficiency and accuracy in delivering prophetic messages has earned her great credibility among world leaders.

Beth has authored a number of books, including *Becoming a Prayer Warrior, The Mighty Warrior (A Guide to Effective Prayer),* and booklets in the Praying with Purpose series. She also coauthored *Intercessors: Discover Your Prayer Power.*

Beth became a core faculty member of the Wagner Leadership Institute and Harvest Evangelism's City Reacher's School. She has served as part of the Spiritual Warfare Network and on the board of directors of Aglow International. She has also been a part-time faculty member at Christ for the Nations Institute in Dallas, Texas.

Beth would not want this chapter to end focusing on her merits. Therefore, it would be appropriate to end with one of her prayers, the cry of her heart.

> Father, let Your will be done, Your kingdom come. There is so much information, Father. But we don't want information; we want that which will bring life to Your people, in the name of Jesus, and we give You the praise, honor, and glory in Jesus' name, amen.

Chapter 10

SHELTER FOR THE SWALLOW

Of all the men and women in the Bible who came to know God intimately, David seems to have been the premier one who understood what it meant to enter the secret place of the Holy Spirit. In Psalm 84, David paints a sensitive and inviting word picture for us:

> How lovely are Your dwelling places, O Lord of hosts! My soul (my life, my inner self) longs for and greatly desires the courts of the Lord; my heart and my flesh sing for joy to the living God. The bird has found a house, and the swallow a nest for herself, where she may lay her young—even Your altars, O Lord of hosts, my King and my God. Blessed and greatly favored are those who dwell in Your house and Your presence; they will be singing Your praises all the day long.
>
> Blessed and greatly favored is the man whose strength is in You, in whose heart are the highways to Zion. Passing through the Valley of Weeping (Baca), they make it a place of springs; the early rain also covers it with blessings. They go from strength to strength [increasing in victorious power]; each of them appears before God in Zion.
>
> O Lord God of hosts, hear my prayer; listen, O God of Jacob! See our shield, O God, and look at the face of Your anointed [the king as Your representative].
>
> For a day in Your courts is better than a thousand [anywhere else]; I would rather stand [as a doorkeeper] at the threshold of the house of my God than to live [at ease] in the tents of wickedness.
>
> For the Lord God is a sun and shield; the Lord bestows grace

and favor and honor; no good thing will He withhold from those who walk uprightly. O Lord of hosts, how blessed and greatly favored is the man who trusts in You [believing in You, relying on You, and committing himself to You with confident hope and expectation]. (Ps. 84, AMP)

Often, the Lord has drawn my attention to verse 3: "The bird has found a house, and the swallow a nest for herself, where she may lay her young—even Your altars, O Lord of hosts, my King and my God."

I treasure this psalm, as did my mother and grandmother before me, especially this one line. It has become part of my family heritage. I gained further insights from it through a personal experience:

My girls were taking riding lessons at our neighbor's place. As the horses were being brought in, groomed, and saddled up, I was enjoying myself by watching everyone and all the animals. I happened to look up and see a barn swallow's nest built against the rafters of the barn. *What a delightful find!* I thought to myself.

My excitement was genuine, because my mother had been an avid bird watcher and had taught me to highly value these beautiful creatures for their unique qualities. Personally, I think that barn swallows are some of the most beautiful birds in God's creation, with their iridescent bluish-black bodies contrasted with rich shades of deep orange on their faces, throats, and breasts. These little creatures perform like flying acrobats as they swoop and dive after insects in the early evening light.

As I stood there admiring these fascinating birds, the Lord reminded me of the words of Psalm 84. I found myself thinking, *What an accurate picture David painted of their nature and their nests.*

When a swallow builds its nest, it will first find a barn or other structure with a supply of mud close by. It will carry mud and twigs in its little beak, making trip after trip, carefully constructing a sturdy nest on joist, strut, or rafter beam of the barn. The outside of the mud-dauber-type structure dries and hardens, becoming very solid and secure. Yet the inside of the nest is lined with downy feathers and is soft, warm, and inviting. Instinctively, swallows know how to do this, and it serves them well.

The thought struck me: *Swallows build their nests the way they do because, instinctively, they know that the safest place to build is up against the wall.* Now we humans use the expression "up against the wall" to describe feeling trapped or being out of options, when we have no place to run and no way out.

We don't have the same instincts as swallows and other animals. God's Holy Spirit leaves us to make our own choices, having shown us in His Word the narrow road to follow. Sadly, we misjudge and miscalculate. Our mistakes and failures leave scars of fear and anxiety, which cause us to think that running away is the only way to stay safe. Oh, that we would learn from the graceful swallow the wisdom of God, allowing our Divine Shepherd's leading and guiding to become such a deep part of us that we can mirror the powerful instincts He has built into His creation. May He weave into the fabric of our lives this truth: the place of abiding is found where difficulty crosses our will and our fear. That is actually the safest place.

To quote an old and wise saying, "Going to the cross is going to the point where my will crosses God's will." How desperately we need to abide in God by "nesting" close to the cross.

When We Are Weak...

Throughout this book, we've been looking at the lessons we can learn from some of history's great Christian women, women who knew how to enter the secret place of the Most High. Certainly, their lives were not easy. These women were not natural-born saints. Every one of them went through trials, persecutions, and testings, just as we do. Now that we can look back on their victorious lives, we have a tendency to see the fact that they walked mightily with God and passed every test, and think, *There must have been something different about her. Somehow it must have been easier for that individual to choose God than it is for me.*

I don't believe that for one minute.

Each one of us must go to the cross. There are no exceptions. The cross is the place where our will and God's will cross each other. The cross is always the place where God's will stands before me—and I am afraid of the pain. I want to run from it as fast as I can.

We do not realize that God will meet us right there—where we are spiritually weakest. If we let Him meet us there, He will give us His grace and strength in place of our weakness.

The truth is, God has designed a cross perfectly for each one of us. He knows the details of our lives, and He knows exactly how to direct us into situations where our natural strength will be tested. He knows how to apply pressure so that every natural desire—those forces in us that make us want to cling to anything but Him—can be exposed as idolatry.

Spiritual storms, winds, and billows will blow into our lives, pulling us this way and that. We will become like swallows tossed around on gale winds, and we'll feel torn about which way we want to go. We will plead with Him—or rail at Him—to make the storm winds stop. Nevertheless, the testing gets tougher.

Sometimes, in the face of winds and danger, we know there is a place of safety in God, but still we don't fly to that safe place in Him. Instead, we fly away, resisting the wisdom that tells us to fly to Him. Why do we all seem to do this? I believe that it's because we all know in our spirits what flying toward Him will mean. We know it will require first going to the cross.

Peace, safety, comfort, rest are found in God, but testing and discomfort are also woven into His design. Therefore, we should turn around and start running toward what is uncomfortable, because that is exactly where we are going to find Him. *We will find our rest only after we choose to nest on a crossbeam.*

David knew this. In Psalm 84, he tells us to fly to that place in God—the secret place, often the place of our greatest testing, known only to God and us. Contrary to our natural feelings and fears, contrary to what the world tells us about seeking comfort and ease, we are to make our nest right there. By abiding in this place, we build a strong history with God. Every trial and storm He brings us through becomes a part of the nest. Day by day, He lines our nest with His faithfulness, His goodness, His mercy, His comfort. We rest secure in His strong tower, built to last.

I believe that if you and I resist the temptation to run away, and instead fly to the cross God has prepared for us, then we will find all the provision and safety we need and long for. Where we are weakest, He will be strong. He will take care of us.

David said, "The bird has found a house, and the swallow a nest for herself, where she may lay her young—even Your altars, O Lord of hosts, my King and my God." We can rest our "young" in the shelter of His wonderful presence also. Our young may be our children, our dreams, our goals, our ministries, our gifts, or anything we cherish. The shelter of the secret place is not for us alone; it's also a place for those concerns in our lives that matter most to us.

Where Is Your Nest?

A few days after discovering the swallows' nest, I was outside our office, trimming one of the trees. As I brought my blade up underneath some branches, I found another bird's nest.

This nest was nothing like the sturdy swallows' nest in the barn. It was lying sort of haphazardly on a couple of dead, weak branches. The nest itself was really small, and very flimsy. It was made of some dried grasses and not much else.

Immediately I thought, *This is the way most of us build nests. We pick the weakest site—trusting in fickle people who change, or in possessions that break, or in jobs and positions that can be taken from us. We look for our greatest security where there really is no security.*

Not only that, but we build out of the flimsiest materials. We base our sense of well-being on how we feel, on current opinions, and on what this or that trendy expert on a daytime talk show advises—fluff that the world has to offer.

On our own, apart from the Lord, we don't know how to build a nest that's secure. We don't know where our hiding place is. Too often we wait until difficulty comes, and then we frantically try to throw together a nest—a piece of homespun philosophy here, what Oprah said there—anything to grasp at security. All we can manage to build looks like the flimsy little nest I discovered on the two dead branches outside our office.

Some of us convince ourselves that we're doing okay all on our own. What we've latched onto seems good, but there is a big problem: the nests of security we build out of what the world has to offer are not anchored. They offer no real security, only the illusion of it. When the wind comes, that flimsy little nest will fall apart. Security of our own making grants us no real abiding place.

I am not pointing any fingers here, because we're all guilty. We all start out wanting to find our security in things, people, and positions of power or honor. As Christians we look for security in our churches, our Christian friends, or in our identity as a Bible study leader or whatever. Many of us women find our security in our identity as a wife or mother.

What we need is a place for our spirit that is solid and secure. God's Word is filled with assurances that He wants to be a shelter for us in times of trouble. He wants to be our rock (see Ps. 92), our fortress (see Ps. 18), and our strong tower (see Prov. 18). These are all good images of places to which we can flee when danger has come upon us and we need a temporary hiding place. Yet these are not intended as places to live for a long time.

What's so wonderful about David's imagery in Psalm 84 is that a nest is more than an emergency shelter. A nest is where you can live always. Here you can abide in peace whether everything around you is being shaken or everything around you is calm.

Where is your nest? What do you trust in for your security, peace, and strength? If you know the Lord as your God and Savior, let me ask you: Has He become for you a nest for your spirit, a secure shelter?

Softly and Tenderly

As children in Sunday school, we used to sing a hymn, "Softly and Tenderly Jesus is Calling." He called the apostle John in the book of the Revelation to "come up here." He called the shepherd king David's longing heart into His presence. Throughout the ages and centuries He has called, and one by one they have come, counting in their number Jeanne Guyon, Teresa of Avila, Fanny Crosby, Susanna Wesley, Gwen Shaw, and Beth Alves. With longing hearts and passionate desire, all were drawn to His secret place.

If you quiet yourself and listen, you will hear Him calling you too. David and so many others found their rest at the altars of the Lord. And now it's your turn. Softly, tenderly, quietly He's calling you from the depths of His wonderful presence. How will you respond? Will you join Him in the secret place?

Dear Heavenly Father, I come to you in the name of Jesus, Your Son. I am longing to enter a deeper place of fellowship with you, but I'm not quite sure I know how to get there. Help me find my secret place to meet with You. Help me open up the room in my heart that is meant for only You and me together, forever! Let me hear the song You are singing over the mountains, trying to reach my heart. Give me the song to sing that will so bless Your heart, and bring You great joy. Lord, come, and take all the bits and pieces of my life and my heart, and make them into a beautiful symphony of love of devotion to You! I love You! In Jesus' name, amen.

ACKNOWLEDGMENTS

We want to thank all the prayer warriors, pastors and various leaders, staff and interns, researchers, writing assistants, editors, strategic planners, art cover designers, endorsers, publicists, and all the other people who have helped us formulate into words what the Holy Spirit has done in our lives. We acknowledge you. We thank you. We could not have penned and perfected these messages without your help. We do it better together.

The Women on the Frontlines series of books took years to complete. Why? Because these books are not just topical teaching books, but rather they concern the journey of life. Each book highlights the lives of different women from different periods of time and different ethnic backgrounds, with a diversity of giftings and callings. But all of them held one thing in common—Jesus was and is the love of their souls.

We want to acknowledge God the Father, God the Son, and God the Holy Spirit. These books are about Your marvelous hand at work in taking ordinary people and propelling them forward to do extraordinary things.

These books are not written only for those of a certain gender or age or ethnic background. They are about an equal-opportunity God who can take any ordinary life and create a godly lineage and legacy out of it.

Thank You, Lord. May Your shadow continue to be cast!

A Call to the Secret Place NOTES

Chapter 3: Jeanne Guyon

1. *Jeanne Guyon: An Autobiography* (Pittsburgh, PA: Whitaker House, 1997), 7.
2. Ibid., 12.
3. Ibid., 32.
4. Ibid., 32–33.
5. Ibid., 33.
6. Ibid., 34.
7. Ibid.
8. Ibid., 45.
9. Ibid., 47.
10. Ibid., 71–72.
11. Ibid., 72.
12. Ibid., 72–73.
13. Ibid., 74.
14. Ibid.
15. Ibid.
16. Ibid.
17. Ibid.
18. *Autobiography of Madame Guyon* (Chicago: Moody Press, n.d.), Chapter 9.
19. *Jeanne Guyon: An Autobiography* 74.
20. Ibid.
21. Ibid.
22. Ibid.

Chapter 4: Teresa of Avilas

1. (This chapter was written with the help of James and Justin Goll.)
2. Bob and Penny Lord, *Saints and Other Powerful Women of the Church* (Baton Rouge, LA: Journeys of Faith, 1989), 161.
3. Tessa Bielecki, *Teresa of Avila: An Introduction to Her Life and Writings* (Kent, England: Burns & Oates, 1994), 17.
4. Lord, 162.
5. Ibid., 178.
6. Bielecki, 20.
7. Lord, 178.
8. Ibid., 179.
9. Shirley du Boulay, *Teresa of Avila: Her Story* (Ann Arbor, MI: Charis/Servant, 1991), 38.
10. Ibid.
11. Ibid., 39.
12. Bieleki, paraphrases from writings on pages 66–69.
13. du Boulay, 82.
14. Bieleki, 43.
15. Jim W. Goll, *Wasted on Jesus* (Shippensburg, PA: Destiny Image, 2001), 58.
16. Ibid., 68.

17. Lord, 209.
18. Teresa of Avila (Kieran Cavanaugh, O.C.D. and Otilio Rodriguez, O.C.D., trans.), *The Collected Works of St. Teresa of Avila,* Vol. 3 (Washington, DC: ICS Publications, 1985), n.p.

Chapter 5: Fanny Crosby

1. Bonnie C. Harvey, *Fanny Crosby,* Woman of Faith series (Minneapolis MN: Bethany House, 1999), 11.
2. Ibid., 20.
3. Ibid.
4. Ibid., 21–22.
5. Ibid., 22.
6. Ibid., 26.
7. Ibid., 28.
8. Ibid., 32.
9. Ibid., 32.
10. Ibid., 33.
11. Ibid., 39.
12. Ibid., 54.
13. Ibid., 55.

Chapter 6: Susanna Wesley

1. Kathy McReynolds, *Susanna Wesley,* Woman of Faith series (Minneapolis MN: Bethany House, 1998), 68–70.
2. Ibid., 94.
3. Ibid., 94.
4. Ibid., 95.
5. Ibid., 95–96.
6. Bruce L. Shelley, *Church History in Plain Language* (Waco, TX: Word Books, 1982), 354.
7. Ibid., 106.
8. Ibid., 119.
9. Ibid., 120.
10. Ibid., 155–156.
11. Ibid., 157–158.

Chapter 7: Basilea Schlink

1. Basilea Schlink, *I Found the Key to the Heart of God: My Personal Story* (Minneapolis, MN: Bethany House, 1975), 19.
2. Ibid., 33.
3. Ibid., 74.
4. Ibid., 108.
5. Ibid., 212.
6. Ibid., 217.
7. Ibid., 265.

Chapter 8: Gwen Shaw

1. Gwen R. Shaw, *Share My Burden* (Jasper, AR: Engetal Press, 1984), 3.
2. Ibid.
3. Gwen R. Shaw, *Unconditional Surrender: My Life Story* (Jasper, AR: Engetal Press, 1986), 5.

4. Shaw, *Share My Burden*, 2.

5. Shaw, *Unconditional Surrender*, 65–66.

6. Shaw, *Share My Burden*, 4.

7. Ibid., 5.

8. Shaw, *Unconditional Surrender*, 128–129.

9. Ibid., 126.

10. Shaw, *Share My Burden*, 6.

11. Ibid., 7–8.

12. Shaw, *Unconditional Surrender*, 293–294.

ABOUT THE AUTHORS

DR. JAMES W. GOLL is the founder of God Encounters Ministries, an international best-selling author, a certified Life Language Trainer, and has taught in more than fifty nations. James was married to Michal Ann for thirty-two years before her graduation to heaven in the fall of 2008. James has four adult children who are married and a growing number of grandchildren. James makes his home in Franklin, Tennessee.

MICHAL ANN GOLL was a lover of Jesus all her life, the devoted wife of James Goll for thirty-two years, and mother of four beloved children. She was the founder of Compassion Acts, a member of the Debra Company Founder's Group, and honored to be listed in the Cambridge Who's Who. She traveled the globe demonstrating that love takes action. She authored eight books and co-established the Women on the Frontlines con-

ferences. She graduated to her heavenly reward in the fall of 2008 and is greatly missed to this day by thousands of people around the world.

GodEncounters.com
PO Box 1653, Franklin, TN 37065
info@godencounters.com
615-599-5552 | 877-200-1604